Elaine Dundy has .... the
bestselling *The D*.. the
Sunday Times, Inde.. *York*
Times and *Esquire* a..

Also by Elaine Dundy

Novels
The Dud Avocado
The Old Man and Me
The Injured Party

Biographies
Finch, Bloody Finch: The Life of Peter Finch
Elvis and Gladys: Biography of Elvis and his Mother
Ferriday, Louisiana: Portrait of a Remarkable Southern Town

Short Stories
The Sound of a Marriage
Death in the Country

Plays
My Place
Death in the Country

Life Itself!

ELAINE DUNDY

Virago

A *Virago* Book

Published by Virago Press 2002

First published by Virago Press 2001

Copyright © Elaine Dundy 2001

A CIP catalogue record for this book
is available from the British Library.

ISBN 1 86049 558 3

Typeset in Goudy by M Rules
Printed and bound in Great Britain
by Clays Ltd, St Ives plc

Virago Press
An imprint of
Time Warner Books UK
Brettenham House
Lancaster Place
London WC2E 7EN

www.virago.co.uk

Contents

Preface

I was much helped in these memoirs by Gore Vidal and Francis Wyndham, who indeed have been beacons of light to me all the years I have known them. They read this book in manuscript and listened to my problems. They were important in encouraging me and catching some of the howlers that landed, willy-nilly, therein.

I would like to thank Susan Stafford Doniger and Vikki Jacobs, to whom I read chapters in zygote form. Time after time it was only through their breathing presence in the room that I discovered what I was trying to say. My thanks also to Ellis Amburn, Jim Rooks, Ramon Arango, Roy Turner, Rhoda Huffey and Louisa Callery for reading the manuscript and for their suggestions.

I am much indebted to my cousin Audrey Marcus, who shared valuable information with me about our family tree and our forebears. She is the daughter of my mother's sister Anne. We have been in touch throughout this project and remain so. I also want to thank my cousin Margot Tulin, daughter of my mother's sister Helen, who was also of help to me, as was my cousin Joan Slifka, daughter of my mother's youngest sister Mildred. My special thanks to my niece Wendy Clarke.

I have not followed up on the life of my younger sister, Betty, to whom I am especially grateful for her memorabilia of our childhood and all our subsequent conversations. Although she has been a force in my life and I love her, I feel she has her own story to tell in her own way.

My special thanks go to my knowledgeable and prescient literary agent, Andrew Hewson, and to my fine editor, Lennie Goodings, as well as two other Virago editors, the painstaking Elise Dillsworth and the invaluable Andrew Wille.

PART ONE

WAITING TO
BE DISCOVERED

1

Childhood

In the beginning, almost as far back as I can remember, every night I said my prayers in bed to my mother or my governess, whichever was at hand, as well as to God. I can still reel off by rote these prayers, which now seem to unroll before my eyes as if in Gothic script on finest vellum. They contained the ever-expanding list of people I was petitioning God to bless.

'God Bless Mother, and Daddy,' I began, and went on with, 'God bless Shirley and Betty (my sisters), Mademoiselle (my French governess), Anna (Betty's German Fräulein).' Then came the three Marys: 'And Mary the cook (Polish; dank black hair), Mary the waitress (Irish; fiery red hair), Mary the cleaner (nationality unknown; hair hidden under a bandanna).' Then: 'Jerry (our, chauffeur; Irish; whom I loved unconditionally).' There were also a chambermaid and a laundress too vaguely noted to be entered in my supplications. On I trudged, with: 'Grandma, Grandpa, all my aunts, all my uncles and all my cousins.' Then came a continually changing rota of best friends to be blessed – or allowed to slip into oblivion – after which, thinking the job well done, I asked Him to bless me too.

That pretty well pins down the economic background of my first eight years. We lived in a sunny many-roomed apartment in New York at 88 Central Park West overlooking Central Park at 69th Street. We – father Samuel Brimberg, mother Florence, daughters Shirley, Elaine and Betty, in order of appearance – were part of the Jewish new rich who in the twenties had staked out the concrete towers of Central Park West. In this respect we were very much like the rest of our cliff-dwelling neighbors. My sisters and I all went to the Ethical Culture School, two blocks down from us on Central Park, and were togged by Tots Toggery, Fifth Avenue's most expensive children's store.

We went with our governesses and nannies and played in Central Park. We roller-skated and rolled hoops, and we skipped rope and bounced balls to a combination of numbers and nonsense rhymes. Everything we did we then did backwards. We skipped rope backwards, we roller-skated backwards, we hopscotched backwards, we played jacks backwards, picking up the jacks in reverse order in one of the 'fancies' we called 'backies'.

We got ourselves and our clothes covered with chalk from drawing hopscotch games on the sidewalks. We fed peanuts to the pigeons, who pecked them out of our hands, and we went to the Sheep's Meadow to listen to the sheep baahing, gingerly stroking their noses while we fed them bits of bread. We went through an echoing Central Park tunnel, which always smelled of urine, to the merry-go-round. And once I caught the gold ring and had so many free rides that when I got off I was sick and dizzy and threw up.

In the spring we looked for four-leaf clovers in the grass and wove the clover blossoms into wreaths and bracelets and necklaces. We would take them home and be saddened when two hours later they wilted and died.

My memories of the twenties are scented with the clouds of Shalimar and L'Heure Bleu that I sprayed on myself from crystal cut-glass atomizers when dressing up in my mother's beautiful Paris evening gowns, all embroidered beads and floating chiffon and so skillfully sewn, with little weights hidden in the skirts to make them hang just so that they even clung gracefully to my seven-year-old frame.

One day stands out as the very distillation of twenties bliss. It was the day before my seventh birthday and we were at our summer home in Deal, New Jersey. I was lucky to be born in August, when all the children were on vacation and, like their elders, were in a permanent state of hectic partying. My parents' friends, Cliff and Arlene Hollander, whom I adored, were our house guests, gaily joining my parents in rounds of such sports as horseback riding and playing tennis on our court.

Significantly, in the twenties a new kind of heroine had emerged on stage, in the movies and in literature. The sweet but put-upon 'ingénue' was no longer a leading character of the drama; her place was now usurped by the peppy jazz baby, a winning combination of rebel, tomboy, hoyden, flirt and siren, in other words the 'It' girl personified by the stunning Clara Bow. For me, Arlene was a real-life Clara Bow. With bobbed red hair and cupid's bow mouth, playful as a kitten and palpably in love, in her just-married happiness she bubbled over. Her stockbroker husband Cliff was a handsome Harold Lloyd type with the same tortoiseshell glasses that Lloyd had popularized. For my birthday they brought me a tin filled with a sort of caramel coffee candy from Holland that I had never eaten before. Candy from Holland from the Hollanders struck me as significantly 'right'. I loved the little square pieces wrapped in white paper with a little round black seal proclaiming its name: *Hopjes*. The unwrapping of candy, like the opening of the shell of a pistachio nut, always increased my enjoyment of the meat therein by making me work for it.

For lunch that day, aside from the Hollanders, we had another guest, a tall, stately young girl, Rita, who was about ten. When the corn-on-the-cob was passed around, instead of taking one off the platter she paused, looked at the corn, then at the table settings, and finally at my mother. She said in a daintily decorous voice, 'Haven't you forgotten something, Mrs Brimberg?' 'Have I? What?' asked my mother with concern. 'The corn-on-the-cob holders,' Rita gently informed her. Heavens! Mother had not forgotten them. She didn't have them. Had never even heard of them before.

After Rita left we all played croquet on the lawn, imitating Rita's etiquettey tones, laughing and calling to one another, 'Haven't you forgotten something?' at each missed shot.

Nevertheless, soon after that lunch, at mealtimes the serving plat-
ters of the hot sweet corn-on-the-cob appeared with beautifully carved
little silver prongs stuck into both ends of the corn ears with sharp
blades.

In the beginning my life seemed to be divided equally between the
things I got right and the things I got wrong.

I recall the exact moments in childhood when I crossed the line
between knowing and not knowing, when I saw myself doing something I had not been able to do before but would always be able to do
from then on. For instance, I remember the very first words I correctly
identified. I was in a room with some cousins and aunts and everyone
was talking and I suddenly caught hold of, as if plucked from the air,
the words 'Elaine', 'ice cream', 'telephone', and 'radio'. And I knew
what they meant and I knew I was right.

When I was six my governess would talk to me in French, which I
understood, but I always replied in English. Then one day in a hotel on
Lack Placid she asked me where my red sweater was. I'd left it in the
dining room downstairs and I answered without thinking, '*Toute en
bas.*' And I knew how to speak in French from then on. So I got that
right.

As a child I was in the grip of certain obsessions to which I joyfully
surrendered with a particular sense of their rightness. I awoke every
morning anticipating the part of the day in school when I would enter
the Kingdom of Acrobats, the gym, wherein my body would daily perform those graceful acrobatics that were to me both thrilling
challenges and deep sources of comfort.

I looked forward to weekends because then I could practice for
hours in our large living room. I got to know its oriental carpet intimately from the closeness of our association. Daily I memorized the
carpet's intricate patterns as its rough dry smell lingered in my nose
from standing on my head or doing a cricket walk or chest roll on it.
In my self-propelling mania, in my need to keep turning myself upside-
down, it was my friend, my helper, my support.

It was there, with blind ecstasy, that my body described rhythmic
circle after circle in a series of linked cartwheels. Then I would turn

cartwheels again but this time one-handed to make it more difficult. In rhythmic circles I would do handsprings and backbends, landing on my feet in one fluid motion.

I have read somewhere that circles are signs of 'God's perfection', but as a child I only knew that these circles were signs of my own perfection. I was born on a Tuesday and took very seriously the nursery rhyme that told us that Tuesday's child was full of grace. I was determined to live up to it. In performing these acrobatics, form was everything. I knew that practice made perfect and I practiced until the desired grace I was striving for in these rhythmic rings became second nature. Toes must be pointed, legs straight, back arched or curved, arms supple. I slicked down my hair with water and pulled it back in a duck tail. Nothing must mar the streamline of my silhouette.

At the beginning of our summer vacations, heralded by the arrival of dust sheets shrouding our furniture, I would start dreaming of summer houses where I would exchange my carpet for sweet-smelling, sloping lawns that I rolled down like an ocean wave rolling into the blazing ring of the sun.

Swimming was another thing I got right. I remember the first time I knew I could swim. One day when I was five the instructor stood away from me, up to his shoulders in the water, and extending his arms said, 'Swim to me.' And I did. I was buoyant in the water. It was done. And never would it be undone.

Diving off a ten-foot board was the ultimate sensation. I felt not passively but actively airborne. With a back dive, or a jack-knife, or a one-and-a-half but most of all with a swan dive I was not falling, I was flying; with perfect control I was defying gravity.

In the beginning there was also a catalogue of things I got right by actually doing them wrong. At four years old I astonished my parents by my ability to read. I did this by noticing the specific patterns that letters made on the labels of victrola records, accurately selecting those I most wanted to hear by 'reading' the names of the songs and the singers on the labels.

Right off I got arithmetic wrong. Specifically I was wrong about addition and multiplication. Having mastered the concept of one and one making two, it followed logically for me that two and two made three, and three and three four, and so on, to infinity. Similarly with multiplication: if one times one was one, two times two was two and so on. What were my first-grade schoolmates complaining of, I wondered? For a short time, arithmetic was easy.

From early girlhood I was toilet-trained. Moving your bowels was called in those days 'doing your duty'. Right after breakfast I was installed in my parents' bathroom and my older sister in ours and duty must be done before school. With so much importance placed on my bowel movements I became fascinated, and would study my feces in the toilet bowl. Sometimes they looked like chocolate – were they good to eat? The idea that I could eat something that I alone could make pleased me. One day I tried. It tasted indescribably foul. It was sticky and clinging and hard to wash off my hands and my mouth. Although I still wondered that something I was congratulated on producing was in fact so nasty, the discovery caused me no trauma, nor was it a pivotal event in my life. It was just another thing I got wrong.

Well, I got life all wrong. I understood that the progression of life went as follows: when you grow up, you marry, have children and die. However I took exception to the grimness of this path laid out before me, and I was determined to stop the whole process by simply not growing up, not marrying and not having children. Then I would not die. I was confident I could accomplish this simply by refusing to accept numerical changes to my age after my twelfth birthday. I had two strong models. The first was Peter Pan, who stayed young forever and had a lot to say about this ideal state of affairs. The other was Alice, who although she didn't talk about it was always there before me seven years old, as in the Tenniel drawings. True, she grew taller and smaller depending on what she drank or which side of the mushroom she ate, but she never grew older.

When by any laws of rationality I would have been expected to drop this notion, something in me was still sure I could stop aging and avoid dying. Up to the very last moment I believed this could be avoided. It couldn't. The reckoning took place at a summer camp in Maine where I cried all night before my thirteenth birthday. I had failed to stay twelve forever and now saw only death ahead.

All my life I've been in conflict with the received wisdom of what

I should be doing at what age. I've never really been the right age for what I've been doing. At fifteen I was too young to be going to nightclubs yet I went to them all the time. Undoubtedly I am too old for the lightning speed with which I throw myself at every new enthusiasm. I suppose I am too old to delight in the schoolgirl crushes I still get. I have not so much been marching to a different drum as listening to a different timepiece.

It was August 2, 1929, and we were back in Deal, New Jersey. Early that morning the chauffeur was driving my sister Shirley, our governess and me down Ocean Avenue, a wide road paved with shiny rose-colored bricks. We were going to the beach for a morning swim before my eighth birthday party. I was happy and excited even though the sun was in and out. When I saw Ann, who was my best friend that summer, standing in the dunes across the road I begged my governess to let us stop the car.

She gave me permission because it was a special day. I had been sitting on one of the jump seats and I banged on the glass for the chauffeur to pull up, and when he did so I skipped right out of the car. Instead of waiting for my governess to take me across the road I sprinted across on my own.

The sun had gone in again. The sky was overcast. Now the other side of the road seemed far away. I was wearing my white summer sandals, which didn't have rubber soles, and the shiny brick road felt slippery under my feet. I slowed down to a walk. The road seemed to rise in the middle and I had to get over the hump to reach the other side. The road was empty when I started across it, but as I reached the middle I saw a car coming towards me. Then it was almost on top of me. I stepped forward and put out my hands to stop it. But the car kept coming. It braked too late and caught me, flinging me down hard on my left side. The impact opened a deep gash on my forehead and dislocated my jaw, and my arms and legs were badly scraped and bleeding. It was curious that although I saw that I had been badly hurt, I was not in pain. With perfect awareness I watched as someone picked me up and put me on the couch in the living room of the friends of our parents who lived nearby.

Nor in the hospital did I feel any pain. What I did react to was my mother's wild, disordered appearance at my hospital bed. She was still in her nightgown and negligee, her stockings half on, her hair uncombed. She was a frightening sight and she carried on in a way that made me frightened too. For the first time that morning I began to cry. Up to that point I had been gloriously brave, basking in the admiration of the doctor and the nurses, holding them spellbound with my account of the event and ending with a jaunty 'So I tried to stop the car and the car stopped me.' Now I was made to feel the enormity of what had happened and the trouble I'd caused. I had expected my mother to hug me with joy and relief, and here she was, just upset. The doctor had already dressed my wounds and sewn up the gash on my forehead, and he assured my mother that I was all right, ready to go home after he had given me the first in a series of tetanus shots to guard against infection.

Eventually they took me back and put me to bed. They gave the birthday party anyway. Shirley hid from Daddy when he came home because she knew he would blame her for not stopping me from crossing the road. I do not remember my father hugging me with love or relief either. It had, after all, been my fault. Still, I was in good spirits another day when the doctor came to take the stitches out of my head. He gave me a mirror so that I could watch him carefully cut the big black stitches made of horse hair.

In spite of the unfortunate timing of the accident on my birthday, I do not believe this would have so entirely changed my character had it not been for what happened in its wake. I turned out to be that one-in-ten person who was allergic to tetanus shots. I developed a severe case of what was then called 'serum sickness' and lay seriously ill with a high fever for weeks.

I was moved to a room away from the rest of the family, where I would be free from disturbance, and in the long convalescence, I developed a taste for solitude and a taste for reading. It was at this point that I met Garbo. She wouldn't talk to other people. She wanted to be alone. But as my imaginary companion she would talk to me.

Years later, at the Museum of Motion Picture Arts and Sciences Library in Los Angeles, I sat down at a microfilm machine and looked long at the August 1929 *Photoplay* cover of Garbo and recalled how I used to draw her, endlessly trying to capture her beauty, sometimes just to keep her there with me. Pensive and unselfconscious, her face insisted that each feature be adored separately. The serene brow, the high arched eyebrows under which the eyelids so faultlessly duplicated the curve above them – it was as if they were deliberately molded by a master sculptor. Together they formed an exquisite setting for the large deep-set eyes.

'The Garbo hair cut', said *Photoplay*, 'needs no introduction. It has spread like wildfire through every city and town.' In fact she wore her hair straight back, swooping smoothly like a dark wing covering no part of her beautiful face and fully exposing her perfect winged ears.

I gave in to the impulse that made me whisper, 'I love you,' to the image on the machine, knowing I had whispered this to her before.

In that summer of 1929, as I recovered I was allowed to go down to the beach. It was cold now, and I wore a sweater. Instead of swimming I walked away from all the people to where it got lonely. I strolled along the ocean's foaming edge, barefoot, letting waves of aloneness crash over me like ocean breakers. It felt like drowning, walking on the beach. Then, one afternoon, my imaginary Garbo came and walked beside me, and she walked with me on the beach for the rest of the summer. It made me so happy, knowing that she wouldn't talk to anyone else and wanted to be alone but that she would talk to me and be my friend. It made me feel grand. No other word for it. Being with her was just grand – that wonderful word we used, like the early Hemingway heroes and heroines, to express supreme and surpassing pleasure.

The main thing about our friendship was that it felt like she had *discovered* me. It is, I see, to *Photoplay* that I owe a lifetime of confidence that I, like all the *Photoplay* movie stars, will be discovered. When good fortune favors me I still feel that it's because I've been discovered.

2

Family

My sisters and I grew up in the great American tradition that decrees wealth, luxury and opportunity be counter-balanced by fear, unhappiness and repression. I was in turns agonized and ecstatic.

One evening in 1929 – about three months after my car accident – I was playing with a model theatre in the living room when Daddy came home and sat down in his armchair. He was carrying, as always, his newspapers, but he let them fall to the floor. Suddenly he began crying with loud racking sobs. He looked so sad that I knew I must cheer him up. I ran towards him and jumped onto his lap, but he pushed me away. I stumbled to my feet and tried to sit on his lap again. This time he put me down and held me and began slapping my face. I tried to wiggle free but he pulled me back and kept hitting me, and all the time he was shouting. My toy theatre got in his way and he destroyed it; the room was in an uproar. Shirley had begun to scream too and he was slapping her as well.

Somehow we escaped to the nursery. We decided to run away. We took pillow cases and stuffed them with things we would need, and when we thought everyone was asleep we headed for the front door.

We had gotten as far as the vestibule and were waiting for the elevator when he yanked us back and began to hit us again.

And my mother – where was she when this was happening to us? Why didn't she stop him? What had we done that she wouldn't protect us that evening in October that we were to learn soon afterwards was the day the stock market crashed?

It was all about money, of course. The mighty fortress that was our wealth had crumbled as if made of cardboard. Bridges had been flung across its moat, hooking into the no-longer solid concrete walls, and over them charged the invading armies, those ugly realities, wreaking havoc on every member of the household.

The family withdrew to the sticks: Great Neck, Long Island. But only three years later, having left the rag trade Daddy made a comeback as president of Universal Steel Equipment. We returned to New York City, and this time we lived on Park Avenue.

It seemed to me that only after the Crash did we become a dysfunctional family – a phrase that covers rather than exposes what was going on, just as describing my father in the current term as a rageaholic covers but does not expose him.

I loved school, but coming home every afternoon was like returning to a prison where my father was the warden, we sisters the inmates and my mother the snitch. It seemed to me that, in order to stay on my father's right side, she would wring out of me confessions of wrongdoing – I was far from a model child – and then feed the information to him, whereupon I would either be yelled at or slapped.

Daddy was a hard-working businessman. Every night, at the dinner table, fueled by a couple of Scotches before and beer throughout the meal, he would go over his day and everything that had annoyed him during it, working himself into a towering rage that fed upon itself with increasing force as he vented his resentments against his business associates. Later on would come his complaints about us.

What started with grumblings and complaints gained force as he veered into sarcasm and sneers and rose to rantings and ravings and shouts. Throughout the meal the maid came into the dining room, served us, went out and in again several times, but never for a moment did this cause my father to break his stride. In the first stage his anger seemed to loosen his face as if to clear the way for the frenzy that would fill it. Then, thrusting his head forward, his expression hardened with purpose as his escalating rage seemed to bring him nearer his goal of justified mayhem. The eyes that stared out at us were not those of an animal but of a merciless human being. What I felt was not the fear caused by seeing a person spin out of control as a result of some physical ailment. My father was mercilessly in control and therefore far more frightening.

Nightly I sat through these dinners vigilant in dread, knowing that any one of us could cause the fury to turn on her, repeating to myself over and over again, 'Don't scream, dream,' as I peopled my dreams in Elsewhere. His constant warning – 'Don't provoke me' – neatly let him off the hook. It was all our fault.

I ate very little during those meals, while Daddy, having exhausted his business recriminations, would bring it all back home by shoving his plate away and saying, 'I'm being poisoned.'

Every night, all through my teens, I nurtured fantasies of killing him and thus releasing us all from his bondage. Actually putting real poison in his food was the plan I favored.

I have an early memory of my mother, in her dressing gown on her silken chaise longue, drawing Shirley and me to her and saying, 'Shall I divorce Daddy?' and us begging, 'Oh yes. Oh please, please, please.' But nothing came of it.

Still earlier is my memory of my mother's birthday the year of the Crash. I had gone shopping with my governess at a Fifth Avenue shoe store to buy her a present of bedroom slippers. I was shown some beautiful gold kid mules with gold kid rosettes and knew at once that I must buy them for her. Her auburn hair was no longer carefully groomed and frown lines had appeared between her eyes, and she had taken to wearing the same blue suit day after day. I desperately needed back the mother of the safe, rich, carefree days when, as I insisted to myself, all was love and harmony. I was sure my gift of the golden slippers would restore her to me as she was then.

My governess objected; they were far too expensive. So we also selected some less expensive ones of blue brocade to take with us so that Mother could choose between them. The outcome was that Mother, seeing how much the gold slippers meant to me, kept them. And this is curious: not only did she keep them, but she wore them for years and years.

Mother presented a puzzle to me, because there was so much to love about her. To begin with, she was so pretty. She came from a happy family, one that was coming up in the world. There were four girls, of which my mother, Florence, was the eldest. Her father doted on his children and they in turn adored him. For Mother's sixteenth birthday, in 1912, he gave her an early model Ford car and she took her friends riding every Sunday.

My grandfather, Heyman Rosenberg, HR as he was known, arrived in America a poor immigrant from Latvia and became just the sort of success story the country loves best. A turn-of-the-century inventor, he invented a self-tapping screw known by his company's name, the Parker Kalon screw.

It was awesome growing up with a genius in my backyard. Geniuses come in all sizes, all shapes, all backgrounds and in all areas. Grandpa's character was as unlike that of the Einstein-type genius – sockless-and-tennis shoed, straggling hair and baggy trousers – as it was of the Tennessee Williams type of genius – unhappy, neurasthenic, haunted by demons.

When I conjure up a picture of Grandpa I see a short, rosy-complexioned man, ramrod straight, with even features and a brief bristly mustache. He was always correctly dressed – not a dandy, closer to dapper. I never saw him in casual clothes. In my mind he is never alone but surrounded by his ever-burgeoning family. Always he carries about him an air of benevolent dignity. If I had to sum him up in a word it would be 'amiable'.

The last half of the nineteenth century had produced a new breed of man: the industrial inventor whose far-seeing vision of the applications of his innovations turns him into a millionaire entrepreneur and a source of unlimited power. In short, a man who like Ford or Edison had the vision to make vast personal profits and at the same time benefit mankind and change life forever.

HR owed his success to more than amiability, yet I believe the genial genes he seemed to possess in abundance played a significant part in his achievements. His quiet confidence also contributed. When HR was praised for his inventions, one of which was literally revolutionary in its field, his answer was always the same: 'A practical invention by a practical man.' Still I wonder if his inventions might not have come to fruition so easily had not his easy-going manner with his workers made them eager to work in the pleasant, relaxed atmosphere of his plant.

He was born March 15, 1874 in Latvia, then annexed to Russia, in the village of Dunaberg near the German border. His father, Morris, was a coppersmith, and it was in his shop that from an early age my grandfather came in direct contact with expert coppersmiths whom he watched constructing large copper vats for breweries. By the age of ten he was traveling with his father, helping him make copper installations in breweries and factories. His exceptional ability to work with every kind of metal fabrication was rapidly recognized.

By 1891, when he was seventeen, he was well enough established as a sheet metal worker to marry my grandmother, Jennie Rousseman, a beautiful but poor young girl of fifteen who made paper flowers and sold them on the streets. It was a love match, though at first the rabbi refused to marry them because Jennie had an older unmarried sister. Under pressure he soon acquiesced.

In 1893 my grandfather became part of the great wave of Eastern European immigrants who arrived in America to escape poverty and pogroms. His story continued in Curry's Sheet Metal Works in Lower Manhattan in 1894. He could hardly speak English when he got the job, so Curry had to point at various items and ask Grandpa if he could make them. Quickly, however, Curry realized that this young immigrant was someone unique, someone he could send out to fix the worst smoking chimneys and leaking boilers, someone who saved Curry money with various inventions, such as a form of copper tubing that was made better, cheaper and faster than any other.

Within a year Grandpa was able to bring my grandmother Jennie over to join him, making his ambition keener. On May 1, 1896 she gave birth to my mother, Florence. No one was more aware of his own worth than Grandpa. The changes in his private life requiring changes in his income and status, he told Curry he was leaving to start his own business. Curry countered by making him his partner. It had taken just three years for HR to become a full partner in a growing concern.

In 1900 HR went on to form a partnership with a Dr Parker. The Parker Sheet Metal Works specialized in warm-air heating and ventilation systems, and they prospered, with 500 men working all over New York. The New York Public Library was one of the first buildings to use HR's air duct systems, followed by the Metropolitan Museum of Art, the Flat Iron Building, the Woolworth Building and many of New York's public schools. In 1912 the company was also installing air-cooling systems that reduced temperature to ten below zero using ammonia chemicals, the same used now for air-conditioning.

The Parker Sheet Metal Works was doing fine except for a serious problem that arose with increasing frequency. HR's employers complained that the screws used in the nuts and bolts – the only ones on the market – kept coming loose and falling out. Good workmen never quarrel with their tools, it is said, but HR did. And with his native know-how and can-do, helped along by what Henry James has called the 'stiff American breeze of example and opportunity', he discarded the quarrelsome old tools and set about inventing new ones that were to be spectacularly able to do his bidding.

Screws had not kept up with the new inventions. As late as the mid-nineteenth century they were still made without sharp points at the end. Surprisingly, there had been no advance in their design since the Middle Ages. Why, thought HR, could two metal strips not be joined together like nails joining pieces of wood? He began experimenting and finally invented a metal screw with hardened threads capable of cutting their own way through sheet metal, thereby fastening two strips together while being driven. By 1913 he had placed on the market a 'Type A Case-Hardened Process', which immediately became the standard component throughout the sheet metal industry. A job that previously required two men now, with this revolutionary screw, needed only one.

HR also invented and installed the machinery for the mechanical assembly line necessary for producing his screws. 'What used to take two months, we did in a week,' says HR. 'We changed the whole way of making screws. We could make one hundred and fifty in a minute. I made up my mind that everyone in the trade would want to use everything we made.'

His Parker Kalon self-threading (alternatively called 'self-tapping') screws became known around the world. The name was derived from Parker, Grandpa's partner and backer, and 'Kalon', which was the key word; the Greek for quality. Said HR: 'We were always known and admired for our original way of doing things.'

In May 1930 Grandpa was made a member of the renowned Franklin Institute in Philadelphia, then the leading scientific society in the United States. In accepting this honor he shared the podium with other distinguished men of science, including the chief engineer of the Panama Canal.

For every invention of Edison and Ford, Grandpa's screws would fasten them together; the same with airplanes, radios, toasters, television sets, refrigerators, air-conditioners. 'There isn't anything that's coming up in the future,' he once said, 'that isn't using our screws.'

Lucky HR. His work was his play, always urging him on to concoct games with his peers to prove a point. It was as if in this way he kept everything fresh, fun, and challenging. For him the inventor's life was a singularly happy one in that so many of his efforts were replete with the kind of fulfillment every artist most desires: instant recognition.

Perhaps recognition would never be so instant or so gratifying as the telegram he received on May 22, 1927, after Charles Lindbergh's *Spirit of St Louis* had landed in Paris the day before: 'Parker Kalon drive screws were used on Captain Lindbergh's engine in his historic flight and are used on all other Wright Whirlwind engines. (Signed) Wright Aeronautical Corporation.' In 1942 another cable must have gratified him too: '10 North American B-25s flew 2,000 miles across the Pacific from Australia to the Philippines and blasted Japanese invaders night of April 13. Docks were wrecked ships were sunk airfields and grounded craft destroyed. Flight Leader General Royce and Lt. Col. Davies were cited quote for heroism and extraordinary achievement unquote. Your workmanship helped get them there and bring them back. We recognize that fact and know you join us in pride in their accomplishment. (Signed) Lovett Assistant Secretary of War for Air, dated April 16, 1942.'

But it was in 1938 that Grandpa's most showy feat took place. He actually saved the Statue of Liberty's life. It was his Parker Kalon screws – all 64,000 of them – that alone came to her rescue. But for Grandpa, America's most instantly recognizable, most highly visible, most deeply symbolic landmark would have crumbled, had Grandpa's wonderfully clever Parker Kalon screws not fit into every nook and cranny of her body in the renovation from top to toe of Liberty's aging Grecian drapes.

In the early years of the century Mother, having graduated from a teachers' college connected with Hunter College, had started her own nursery school, one of the first of its kind. In 1918 she left it to marry Daddy, at thirty-five already a millionaire who drove a dashing Stutz Bearcat. She was cultured and cultivated, with a lovely speaking voice, and she was an avid reader of French literature, which she read in the original, slicing the pages of the books with her paper knife. She loved opera and later in life would attend dress rehearsals at the Metropolitan Opera House of productions that she would later see again on opening night.

She was an expert needlewoman, who developed her tapestry work to the point of artistry. She loved clothes and perfume, and her fascination with jewelry was almost child-like. She was infatuated by it, bewitched by it, and adored the rituals of owning it: purchasing, insuring, putting it in a vault, taking it out. She kept a drawer full in her bedroom bureau, and I played with it as a child. As the years went by she built a collection of costume jewelry mixed with real stones, pieces remarkable for their boldness and originality. For her the answer was ever in the baroque.

Mother was unfailingly courteous and considerate of the people in her employment. In fact, she was kind and generous to everyone. Even if she was not demonstrative, I knew that she loved me. But I couldn't trust her – she was his accomplice.

There were two particular incidents with my father that are significant because I was no longer a child when they happened. I was seventeen years old, a senior in high school, when one evening at dinner Daddy made one of his sneering sarcastic remarks to me. This time I answered back and the whole thing escalated into a major confrontation. 'You'd like to kill me, wouldn't you?' I said, grabbing a knife. 'Just try,' I said. 'Come on, try,' I'm going to do it, I thought. I'm going to do it and it will be self-defense. He started to come towards me. My anger melted into fear and ran down my legs like ice water. I dropped the knife and began to run, tearing down fourteen flights of stairs in our Park Avenue apartment building with him following me some of the way until I no longer heard his footsteps. I walked the streets for hours.

When I returned, around midnight, my mother was waiting up for me. I said, 'I'm going to tell my teachers about this.' And she said (and I have never forgotten her words), 'Oh, please don't, Elaine. It would embarrass me so.' I didn't.

So three years later, when I was twenty and a junior in college, the same damn scene happened again, this time in Scarsdale, most respectable of all the respectable suburbs in Westchester. We had taken a house there that summer and were a mere week away from Shirley's wedding to Bert Clarke, an attractive man in every way and also Jewish. But I had noticed the storm brewing. In some Freudian way, certain landmarks in Shirley's progress to adulthood and autonomy, such as her purchase of a car and, now, getting married, played hell with Daddy's psyche. Again at the dinner table, I watched his fury mounting. I saw him looking around for a target and knew it would be me. He accused me of showing more courtesy to the servant waiting on us than I did to him. Whatever my reply, it enraged him. He started to come at me. I ran out of the house and into the street, Daddy followed and Mother after him. Shirley jumped into her car, caught up with me, and flung open the door. I climbed in just as Daddy arrived. He was shouting at us, at which point an irate neighbor ran down his pathway telling us if we didn't leave immediately he would send for the police.

There were such oddities in my upbringing. My father never called me by my name. I was 'you' when he was talking to me and 'she' when he was talking about me in my presence to a third person. Sitting down and talking things over quietly and calmly was never an option.

But nothing was ever said by anyone to him about his eruptions. They were never referred to.

Both my mother and father were active in Jewish charities as befitted their economic and social position in New York Jewish society. My father, as well as contributing money to these causes, was a masterful fundraiser, and he occupied key positions in many philanthropic organizations. He was a founder of the Albert Einstein College of Medicine of Yeshiva University, a director of the Hebrew Home for the Aged, a trustee of the Jewish Culture Foundation of New York University, and a benefactor of Brandeis, the Jewish Guild for the Blind and the Federation of Jewish Philanthropies.

His was also an immigrant's success story of which, given our antagonistic relationship, I was only sketchily aware. From the Brimberg Society Papers and my father's obituary in the *New York Times* on June 12, 1963 I have assembled the following facts:

Samuel Nathaniel Brimberg was born in 1884 in Warsaw. He came first to Canada with his parents, three brothers and three sisters. When they moved to New York in 1901 my father, aged seventeen, became their principal source of support. His first job was selling gaslight fixtures. In 1912 he founded a clothing manufacturing company in New York. During the First World War his company made blankets for the army, and afterwards he established Samuel N. Brimberg Inc., a manufacturer of ladies' and misses' suits and coats. He was appointed a director of the National Wholesale Women's Wear Association and of the Merchants Ladies Garment Association. He was a member of the American Arbitration Association. In 1934 he bought the major interest in Universal Steel Equipment Corporation, a manufacturer of metal and steel products, and was its president until he retired in 1958 at seventy-three. During the Second World War Universal received numerous citations from the US government for its contributions for the war effort. From the early 1920s until 1953 he was also a director of my grandfather's Parker Kalon Corporation.

Here is Sam Brimberg, successful businessman, active philanthropist and popular raconteur of locker room jokes at his golf club, but a tyrant in his home and a damaging, destructive father.

*

Some emotions never grow up; it always seems to be the same day with them. Many years later, aged sixty-five and in a blue funk, I had just hung up on my mother after telling her to leave me alone. She was old now, and for all the years since my father's death had been truly generous and supportive of me. Yet I was never able to spend an extended period of time with her; I would shorten my visits in order to escape before my feelings overtook me and I was back at that family dinner table where we forever sat together.

In a letter I apologized for my rudeness and then for the first time I confronted the issue straight on. I wrote that when I had these depressions I blamed them on the deep unhappiness I experienced throughout my growing up as a result of my real terror of Daddy and my not being able to stand up to him. 'It is then,' I continued, 'that the blame spills over on you because you allowed that frightening situation to continue . . . I know that you must have had many reasons for allowing everything to go on that went on, but I hope you will understand that when you rang me just now and kept asking me if everything was all right, I simply could not control myself any longer . . . I hope you will forgive my outburst, understand it, and wish me well.' I signed it 'Yours for a happier future'.

     She replied.

I do understand only too well that you are suffering. And I
want you to understand that anything I can do to make you
happy just ask. But for your deep hurt I am helpless.
    Only when Sam told me about *his* father did I understand
his childhood and have any sympathy for him. As a young boy
he was sent away to a distant town to a strange relative who
knew nothing of his parents and whom he was to ask to give
him a job. In fact his father just threw him out of his home to
look for a job elsewhere. He found one in a shop that sold fab-
rics and he made himself so useful he stayed on for a while
until his father called him back home to leave for Canada with
the family which he did.
    In New York the family had relatives who found work for
Sam. His father spent his days praying in the synagogue and
the sons worked.

I assure you Sam's early life with his family consisted only in working hard at whatever he could to support them and saving money so he could go on to other work. He did this by opening a savings account in a nearby bank. One evening Sam's passbook fell out of his pocket and his father found it and realized his son was not turning in all his money to him. Again he threw him out of the house. Sam would laugh when he told me these stories but I assure you they left a bitter mark.

Nevertheless his parents lived to have a nice home and to have every wish or desire answered. Mainly through his contribution they had a home in Brooklyn, money to distribute to the poor and the synagogue.

Life went on pleasantly at the beginning when we were first married but became very difficult when things went wrong, and they did – business, the Crash, etc. I suddenly realized I could not cope. I spoke to my mother about leaving Sam. She told me to be patient, that Sam was having problems in business, that he was kind when things went well. I realized I had no place to go and that I would make the best of a bad situation. So there were good times and bad times.

You say you were never able to stand up to Sam, well I too never stood up to him, except I understood him only too well and I tried never to antagonize him, even at first not having the doctor come to the house when he didn't want me to when he was dying. However finally I did have the doctor . . .

I hope you can read this letter, the writing is so bad. I tried to type it but I have forgotten how.

I will send the letter hoping you will understand and that you will know that I will help you just tell me how.

PS Have not reread this too difficult for my eyes.

Mother was ninety-one years old at the time.

When we lived in Great Neck after the Crash I remember Daddy leaving the house every morning for months, going to the city looking for a business he could set up or join, and coming back every night empty-handed. And then one evening he showed us a new invention: a tube of toothpaste designed so that the flat top of its cap was broad enough to stand the tube on its end. It saved space that way, he said, it's for people now living crowded together in smaller areas. He asked me if I thought he should invest in it. I don't know what I said, but I thought it was a dumb idea. But in another instant it hit me, his blood talking to mine, and I understood that he was desperate. And I felt such a rush of pity for the man and the starkness of his situation that it knocked the breath out of me. It was unbearable. It was easier hating him.

3

The Brimberg Girls Go to Lincoln

Still, my schooldays were not of unleavened gloom.

We left Great Neck in the school year of 1935–36 and moved back to New York, living at 1185 Park Avenue. My sisters and I, famous as 'the Brimberg Girls', rode on the regular Fifth Avenue bus to and from the famous progressive school, Lincoln. Although it was situated on the cutting edge of Harlem, at 123rd Street and Morningside Drive, and we had to walk several blocks to get there, we did so in perfect safety. Such things were possible in the thirties.

Shirley was sixteen, I was fourteen and Betty was eleven. By descending together, several weeks after the term started, we caught the attention of a school whose students had attended it for years. We, from the sticks, were perceived as exotic. They were used to the pupils who came from China, and Switzerland – such places where Americans were doing good solid progressive work, but to come from nearby but so-different Great Neck? I think we were a first. We were good-looking, energetic, playful, a fresh breeze. We created a stir that would not have been possible had we arrived singly. I was lucky in my sisters. They saved my life. Though we all held our own views, had different interests and goals, I felt we were bonded by a mutual love, loyalty and support of each other. For myself, I simply could not afford to indulge in the banality of sibling rivalry. There was too much at stake.

Turning the pages of my Lincoln yearbooks from '36 to '39 and reading what my schoolmates wrote forms a picture of how we were regarded as a single entity. Dotted throughout the albums are comments such as: 'To one of those great Brimbergs', 'Hello you brat. Live up to your namesake', 'I'll sign anything for a Brimberg'. Far from feeling overshadowed or lacking a separate identity, I was perfectly happy to share the spotlight with my sisters. I took great pride in them and constantly referred to them in conversation: 'Shirley told me this' or 'Betty thinks that'.

The day before we started school Shirley gave me some advice: 'First impressions are very important, so look your best the first couple of weeks. After that you can relax because they'll always remember how you looked when they first saw you.'

That night I washed my hair and put it up in pin curls and next morning combed it out in one of the new styles then favored by singers in swing bands, which at the time I aspired to be: curly bangs, sides up and held in place with little combs, coiffure ending in a collar-length pageboy. I wore my new moss green knit dress, which subtly outlined my figure, and off we went.

What I took to be admiration causing my classmates to look at me and look again turned out to be something different. Finally one of them came right out and asked me if I knew I still had the price tag on my belt. I said, no, it wasn't a price tag, it was my locker key tab, in case I forgot my locker number. I mark this as the first time I became conscious of there being something askew, something amiss, in the way I assembled myself to greet the world. So it would be for the rest of my life. On various important occasions I seemed destined to appear with an unzipped skirt, or a falling down hem, or rolled-up sleeves held in place with safety pins. I have never seen a button on the floor without checking to see if it was mine.

In the beginning Lincoln was just another school. Though I had done well scholastically at Great Neck Junior High, I had no great love of school nor any wish to involve myself in its activities. Why bother when my one goal in life – besides that of being the star attraction of a big band – was to wear red lipstick and a red dress and be seen with a handsome and popular boy who was passionately and publicly in love with me?

Yet my first act at Lincoln indicated how much I did need to involve myself in school. I started a sorority, of the social kind they had at Great Neck High (although I had never been a member there). I invited a handful of my classmates, some four or five girls that I liked best, to join, and explained that its aim would be to cement our friendship with each other and to have fun.

The girls were agreeable and in prearranged bizarre costumes we arrived at school on a Thursday morning. We lasted all of two classes. At the end of the second I was sent to the principal, a mild-mannered gentleman called Dr Clark. What, he mildly wanted to know, was the reason for the strange costumes that I and several of my classmates were wearing? I explained that we were a sorority.

'We don't have these things at Lincoln,' he replied, not at all mildly. 'We don't form cliques so that others feel excluded.' And he gave me a look that was both sad and puzzled at the extent of my snobbery. At first it surprised me and then it made me go all hot.

What he didn't know was that I had not gotten into the sorority in Great Neck because, I was told, I was Jewish. It was as if there was a placard where they met saying: No Jews allowed. I had found social anti-semitism coming up often in Great Neck, as when a friend told me that I had not been invited to two birthday parties because I was Jewish. These shafts were two among others that had caused me much hurt and anger in the past. And now I sat in Dr Clark's office realizing that my whole point in forming a sorority was to create one as snobbish and exclusionary as those in Great Neck. Except that I would be in it.

It was my first lesson that 'progressive' did not necessarily mean 'permissive'.

It was no accident that when Lincoln opened its doors in 1920 so many other institutions in the new spirit of the twenties were undergoing reassessment. Propelled by its crusading spirit and held together by its strong intellectual sinews at the time I entered it, Lincoln had become prominent for its innovative approaches to learning.

The key word of the thirties was 'progress'. We believed in progress. We were sure it would work. Labeling anything, any movement, school or person 'progressive' automatically gave anything it referred to a splendid luster.

Of the experimental schools at the time, the eyes of progressive education were upon Lincoln. Student teachers from all over filed through our classes, 'observing' us. We saw ourselves as elite guinea pigs and we loved it. From time to time we would be given 'personality tests' designed to discover with multiple-choice questions just what sort of individuals we were. I saw these tests as a challenge to my creativity, designing my answers to present myself in one as a Social Butterfly, in another a Greasy Grind, then a Hot-Eyed Rebel. I posed in one as having a social conscience and caring for the world, in another as selfish and caring only for myself. Once I was an introvert, next an extrovert. There were, after all, so many people inside me. We were told that students of Dartington Hall, a progressive school in England, were also taking these tests and I used to wonder if some girl over there, the same age as me, was lying her head off too.

The Rockefellers were among patrons who donated huge sums of money and their children to the school. Adventurous oil-rich multimillionaires sent their children and grandchildren there. It was favored by members of the intelligentsia with names such as Van Doren and Fadiman, and by famous figures of Roosevelt's Brain Trust such as Tugwell, Hapgood and Davis. Professors from Columbia sent their children there, as did American diplomats abroad and League of Nations officials.

Lincoln encouraged independence of thought and action, and showed us how to find information when we needed it, so I was learning how to learn and organize, how to think. My English teacher, Miss Daringer, in her blue rayon dress with an ivory lace collar, her black hair in a prim bun and her schoolmarm pince-nez with its black ribbon, was strict on spelling, stricter on grammar. She urged us to disagree with the received critical assessments down the ages of any book we were studying. Never mind what 'they' said. What did we think?

And why? The 'why', of course, was the important thing. You couldn't just say, 'I think it stinks', and sit down. We were taught to question everything, to make up our own minds and back it up with reasons. Needless to say this was in direct opposition to my life at home. Lincoln provided an atmosphere where I could learn to express myself in safety.

But the most precious gift this school bestowed upon me was what I call the light-hearted Lincoln approach to the world of the solemn, the pompous and the sacerdotal. It was there that I learned the joy of laughing, of laughing a lot, and often over nothing very much. It was where I felt free to wallow in the divine silliness of adolescence.

If I could choose a day at Lincoln to relive, it would be a rainy day. Bad weather storming around outside while we were cozy and dry within seemed to give us more energy. In rainy weather I noticed that we talked more and talked louder, the decibels rising to a pitch of excitement. The rain pelting on the windowpanes seemed to gather us together, make us want to work together. A rainy day at Lincoln was the reality that shut out my life at home.

On one such day Mr Bingham, our science teacher, informed me that I had not presented my topic to the class although the term was nearly over. (We had 'projects' that we all worked on together and 'topics' that we did on our own.) Could I have it ready for Friday? Oh sure, I replied. I looked at the list of topics and saw that arson had not been chosen. I flew to the library, raced through a couple of books that had chapters on arson, took some notes, ran my eyes down some newspaper clippings on the subject, and finally I was all set. Confidently I faced the class.

I read out my notes and concluded triumphantly that 'arson can always be detected because it burns at such a low temperature'.

This information, I was gratified to note, had stunned my audience to silence.

Finally somebody piped up: 'Do you know what arson *is*?'

It turned out that I didn't. I'd thought it was the name of some kind of difficult-to-detect explosive, something along the lines of dynamite but more of a fluid. Most embarrassing. But instead of retreating in confusion, my Lincoln thinking urged me to stick up for myself.

While admitting my error, I said in extenuation, 'When you have got it firmly lodged in your head that arson is a *chemical*, a batch of newspaper clippings with headlines such as: "Ten Die in Warehouse Blaze – Arson Suspected" is not going to dislodge it.'

The students began laughing. Nice laughter. And instead of feeling disgraced and discredited, I felt happy to be the source of their enjoyment.

I was an erratic student. In my last two years in high school I was dreaming in class, only coming to with the sound of the chairs scraping as my classmates left. Only then would I realize I'd been dreaming of being in the Stork Club with Orson Welles or another of my idols. My other partners included a colorful mix of favorite movie stars, singers, musicians and public figures. I would be photographed with my hair a dark cloud, my complexion dead white with Max Factor pancake, my lipstick a deep purple.

Among my idols was Noël Coward. Noël and I went way back to my early childhood. He was, at first, only a voice on the victrola but, as no child has difficulty recognizing star quality when exposed to it, I was passionate about his records, playing them over and over again, learning all the words some of which I can recite today. I loved not just 'Mad Dogs and Englishmen', but ones about decadent creatures such as 'Dance Little Lady, Dance' ('so obsessed with second best . . .) and 'Parisien Pierrot', and soppy ones like 'Someday I'll Find You'.

In 1937 he played on Broadway in *Tonight at 8.30* with Gertrude Lawrence in three separate bills of three one-acters. They were the toast of the town. I attended matinees of all three by myself. After one I decided to go to the stage door and get Noël's autograph when he came out. He appeared wearing a polo coat with Gertrude Lawrence on his arm and a small crowd surrounding him. He autographed their programs. Then he saw me and nodded questioningly. I had been frozen to the spot. My feet moved a few steps closer to him, but I was unable to raise my arm. He took my theatre program from me, signed it, handed it back and favored me with a brilliant smile, exactly like the one he wore on stage.

I yearned to know my idols, to worship them, and, above all, to encourage and advise them. It did not seem strange to me that I, a young and inexperienced girl, should be doing this. Rather, I felt my youth to be a positive factor in presenting my heroes with fresh and original points of view.

It was, therefore, soon after the death of the King, his father, in January 20, 1936, that I wrote my first fan letter to Buckingham Palace. Addressed to King Edward VIII, it expressed my sorrow at the loss of his father and my happiness that he was now king. I urged him to come back to America again; we admired him so much that it would cement Anglo-American relations. I got a reply, a beautiful engraved black-bordered card telling me that Edward Albert Christian George Andrew Patrick David, King of England and the Commonwealth, Emperor of India etc., etc., thanked me for my condolences and good wishes. From that time on I often wrote letters to celebrities. A surprising number of them replied.

What I was really having in these affairs was a relationship with myself. And what became clear to me in my journey into self-discovery was that stirrings of sex-and-love and love-of-sex had begun to play a big part in my life.

When I was ten years old I had been sitting on a rock in Central Park with my schoolmate Shirley Bradshaw when she told me that at night she did something that made her feel absolutely lovely. 'If you rub your hands up there between your legs and think sexy thoughts your whole body suddenly gets the most wonderful tingly feeling.' 'And then what?' I asked. 'And then it's over,' she said.

I tried and it worked. What a grip my imagination had over my body. I had discovered the power of the mind over matter. It would not enable me to levitate, or walk on coals, or lie down on a bed of nails, but all my life I would look for other ways to harness it.

At first my sexual imagery was hazy and generalized, but in my teens it had matured into very specific images of particular people. In my highly sensitized state it sometimes took no more than a phrase to set me off. My Lincoln classmate, Terry, son of the playwright Maxwell Anderson, took me on a visit to his home in Rockland County across the Hudson. As we entered the living room the playwright was talking to Burgess – Buzz – Meredith, a leading man and major heart-throb, about a proposed road tour beginning in Syracuse. 'Ah, Syracuse,' said

the silvery-voiced Buzz ruminatively. 'I used to lay with a girl in
Syracuse.' And then they saw us and introductions were made and the
subject changed.

But I had thrilled immediately to Buzz's words: *to lay with* . . . What
a beautiful sound, what erotic imagery. How much better to use than
fucking or *getting fucked*. Lay, and laid, or, getting laid, was so horizon-
tal, so langorous and lazing, two bodies stretching naked on a white
bed and afterwards relaxed to the point of sighing. The long windows
opening out to the sea, the sea breezes caressing our nakedness . . .

The thought *I wonder what it would be like getting laid?* was smolder-
ing into *I want to get laid*.

Just before our Christmas vacation in my second year of Lincoln,
when I was fifteen, I was walking down the hall to the school library
when I passed a group of senior boys who were talking with another
boy I had never seen before. As I walked by, he and I just looked at
each other.

I walked past him into the library. I checked out the book I wanted.
I sat down and opened it and waited. I'd barely turned the first page
when he came in and sat next to me.

His name was Gil and he was a former student at Lincoln. He was
tall, lanky and loose-limbed, like a basketball player. He was a preppie
from a prestigious prep school, but two things set him apart from that
lofty breed. His hair flopped all over the place, which gave him a
humorous, informal air, and he had a special way of looking at the
world with wonderment and pleasure. When he asked me for a date, I
accepted.

Gil took me to a nightclub, my first. At Nick's the music was a soaring upbeat Dixieland mixed in with blues, and the main attraction was
a large dignified black drummer, Zutty Singleton, who had a powerful
effect on me. From there we went on to another jazz club, and then
another. I noticed the friendly looks of recognition bestowed on Gil by
the members of the band wherever we went.

On subsequent dates Gil and I plunged into the wonderful world of
New York nightclubs. Nowhere in the whole round world would you
have found such a profusion of clubs with such high-caliber

entertainers than in Greenwich Village, 52nd Street and Harlem in the thirties and forties.

I think it was at the Uptown House in Harlem that I first saw Billie Holiday. As always backed by superb musicians, she stood in the spotlight, a beautiful woman in an evening gown, a still, ceremonious figure. She wore a corsage of orchids that never moved because she never moved. Listening to her fueled and thrilled me. I loved the raw bluesy way she took us on a sexual journey, with its yearning, questing desires, its blissful fulfilling satisfactions, and the mortifications and rejections that follow fast upon it. She wore her blues with pride, made them sound so good. She drew me in, she made me understand. After seeing her once I then tried to see her wherever she played at Café, Society Downtown or at the Downbeat and other clubs on 52nd Street.

It was a strange romance I had with Gil. I went out with him during his school holiday breaks for two years. It was mostly me listening while he talked with encyclopedic knowledge of jazz and blues. We almost never corresponded, but we were perfectly happy and comfortable together in our shared passion for the black music of the day. We wrapped ourselves into the music and then around each other in his car.

Gil had been the most special of all the boys I knew. But later almost any attractive young man, some five or six in fact, had an easier time with me if he took me to a nightclub, black music serving as foreplay.

Afterward, in their cars, parked around the corner of our apartment building on 93rd Street and Park Avenue, we would neck, working up to French kissing. And we would pet, hands exploring under clothes. And we would almost. We would be heading for it, towards the frontier, but always we stopped short at the border. We saw the sign that said City Limits and heeded the warning, and both together we would draw away. We would smoke a last cigarette and the teasing, flirting, dizzy sweetness of the unresolved evening would come to its close.

I suppose I could categorize myself during that period as belonging to my age group's ever-growing company of hot virgins.

*

Beginning with Frank Capra's *It Happened One Night*, the great screwball comedies of the thirties and forties served as successful antidotes to the Great Depression. I was a fan of all the Preston Sturges comedies, also of *My Man Godfrey*, *Bringing Up Baby*, *His Girl Friday*, *The Awful Truth* and many more. They were successful in promising young girls growing up in that era a thrill-packed present with a splendid future of wedded bliss to Cary Grant, William Powell, Joel McCrea, Henry Fonda, Jimmy Stewart or Melvyn Douglas, with the added bonus of growing up to look and act like the heroines played by Katharine Hepburn, Carole Lombard, Myrna Loy, Jean Arthur, Claudette Colbert and Rosalind Russell – also wearing their sensational clothes.

The screwball woman was captivating, charming, light-hearted. She was capable of holding down a job and at the same time having deep feelings. She was also impulsive, capable of doing the first thing that came into her head, no matter what. She was well-written too, well conceived. The development of her character was skillful; I memorized her dialogue.

I will never forget my utter relief when I first came upon these characters. I knew at once I would have to be like them because I could not be like anyone else. For me they sanctioned the outrageous urges I could not suppress. The close friendship I was to enjoy in the future with Gore Vidal was partly based on our sharing the same screwball heritage, which decreed that men be witty, dashing, debonair, sophisticated, suave and charming (and when those words disappeared, the people they described did too, and so did part of my life). It also decreed that whatever these men did, they did so superbly but effortlessly.

At the Saturday afternoon movies in every city, town and hamlet in America, children and adolescents sat entranced through these comedies, osmozing the pure Hollywood concept of how ladies and gentleman were expected to behave. We were all left with a passionate desire to emulate them.

Screwball behavior was what I understood to be the proper reaction towards the events in my life, and I welcomed it in other people. In the sixties, when Ava Gardner turned up at our flat in the rain needing to borrow money for a taxi, holding a piece of broken umbrella in each hand and explaining that she had broken it over the head of her lover, Walter Chiari, this was to me, purely and simply, acceptable screwball behavior.

In my last year at Lincoln many of us had started to drink. I loved drinking. It let me express myself gloriously and to the fullest extent, freeing me to chase after my inalienable rights of life, liberty and the pursuit of happiness.

The summer of 1939 Gil and I would once or twice a week go with friends to nightclubs in Greenwich Village and listen to such blues performers as Josh White and Leadbelly or hear Jimmy Daniels sing 'Venez y Chez Moi' at his *boîte* and I would drink gin and tonics and smoke cigarettes and beat time with my swizzle stick and feel one step closer to the deliverance that a college would give me. I had become a merry madcap, much admired because I would say and do things that everyone else would if only they had the nerve. A drink or two was all I needed. I did not get so much drunk as exhilarated. It also had not escaped me that, with the situation at home as it was, I would have trouble relating to men. I thought this a good way to resolve it.

I felt it essential to let my rather original conduct come out in plain air so I could look at it. I felt like a bird imprisoned in a cage that had to be let out at night in order to maintain its health and sanity.

One night in the Village, after we'd left a club and said goodnight to our friends, Gil and I got in a taxi that had its sun roof open. It was a balmy night pierced with bright stars and, looking up at them, I was seized with a sudden inspiration. I stood on the seat and lifted myself onto the sun roof, then stripped to the waist and rode home up Park Avenue with the wind in my hair, on my face and my shoulders and my naked body. Just before we arrived at 1185, I pulled my clothes back on and slipped down into the taxi. I felt bright and right, in touch with the infinite, peaceful and – exonerated.

'You're something rare,' said Gil in approval. 'You're a *nice* hot babe.'

I was to repeat this experience several times that summer,

sometimes with other men. And what I still find extraordinary is that no one else seemed to remark upon it: not the passing cars, nor the taxi driver, nor my date. Perhaps they were as wrapped up in the cinematic screwball world as I was.

4

Shirley, My Sister

'To be popular in your class at Lincoln,' Shirley is reminiscing to an interviewer in the eighties, 'you didn't have to be rich or good-looking or have famous parents – though there were a lot of students who had all three – but you had to *do* something you would be known for. We had a class poet, a class chess player, a class actor, a class chemical engineer, and so on. But there was one thing we didn't have. So that's what I decided to be . . .'

I am watching this tape at the Wisconsin Heritage Society in Madison, Wisconsin, where Shirley's film collection is housed. In 1993 I see her filmed interviews for the first time.

Shirley Clarke (her ex-husband's surname) – ground-breaking film-maker at sixtysomething – appears on the screen wearing a large brimmed felt hat at a rakish angle. Her hair peeps out from under it in a pixie cut. Her trademark Felix the Cat button is on her lapel, and her various emblematic chains of jewelry are around her neck. It all fits together. Even her features corroborate her freewheeling style. She has obviously taken her own advice: 'If you're not a character when you're over sixty – you're nothing.'

Clearly comfortable in front of a camera, she looks back on her life and gives each transforming event its full dramatic significance: 'My parents spent a fortune on tutors in order to get me promoted from one grade to the next,' she begins, describing her stress-filled early years in school. She remembers running out of reading classes as a child when it came her turn to read. Later, she says, she learned to fake it. Finally, at the age of ten, when she badly wanted to find out something that required her to read a certain book, she began laboriously to teach herself how to read. She was dyslexic, a concept neither understood nor even known by the majority of educators until the sixties. It affected her progress in all her studies.

But, unexpectedly on the TV screen Shirley lights up as she recalls, 'I was happy to go every year to summer camp till I was sixteen because I was away from home for two months. As a highly motivated kid I decided I wanted to be captain of the Green Team. I got my sisters to get out the vote. I said, Elaine, you can be song leader and Betty, you can be head of baseball if you get out the vote. I got elected because we had a little childhood Mafia going. We were very, very close as kids . . .'

It was at Camp Fernwood, in Maine, that I watched Shirley transform herself from an unprepossessing adolescent into a decidedly prepossessing one. In her campaign for captain I watched her leap over the competition with the agility of a mountain goat and observed her become an expert politician, quickly sizing up situations and acting upon them. Her looks underwent alteration. She produced a radiant smile, which sparkled everywhere. Her features sharpened, her jaw line became clearly defined, her hair shone.

This camp, where wealthy Jewish parents from as far away as Los Angeles and Dallas – no commercial planes in those days – sent their young daughters every summer, was run like a boot camp, with a laundry service, a candy store and delicious meals thrown in to lessen the shock of its Spartan existence. The campers were driven by bugle calls blasting out reveille, flag-raising, chow, taps and whatever other blasts were necessary to announce a change of activity. We had every minute of the day mapped out for us, from tumbling out of our bungalows in the morning for flag-raising to falling back into our cots at night after the flag was lowered and day was done and God was nigh. In a setting of pine-scented beauty, young girls, many of whom had never made a bed before – much less one with hospital corners – were introduced to crass reality. Every morning after breakfast we scrubbed and swept and cleaned our bunks, made our beds and took turns at latrine detail. There were afternoon naps for the younger campers. And for everyone there was swimming and singing and, above all, team sports of every description.

Fernwood's main goal, besides honing our athletic skills, was to develop our leadership qualities or, failing that, our followership qualities. Shirley and Betty were both natural leaders. I was not. But I was not a follower either. I preferred activities that I did alone, such as swimming, diving, high jumping and modeling clay busts of other campers in the sculpture bunk.

The program was filled with physical challenges. There were overnight camping trips where you lay sleepless under the stars, ceaselessly tormented by mosquitoes. There were five-day canoe trips, during which you and your packroll remained rain-sodden for the entire trip. There were mountains to be climbed. The big one was the Presidential Range in New Hampshire, where, in the midst of a gale, you took your life in your hands crawling along Knife's Edge, the passage that connected Mount Madison to Mount Washington.

The atmosphere was charged with competition and contests held campwise and, locally, within the bunks, which also competed with each other for the weekly neatness prize. Certainly the oddest contest was my bunk's beauty contest, where we voted, segment by segment, for who had the best hair, eyes, nose, lips, figure, legs. One year I won legs. Green posture bands were awarded weekly to those of us who sat up particularly straight. The best all-around campers at the end of the season were awarded a Green F, which was good, or a White F, which was even better. Shirley got a Green F, Betty a White F. I got nothing. You don't forget these things.

Newly arrived at Lincoln and determined to make a splash in her class, Shirley arrived at the viable theory that in order to gain recognition she must do something no one else was doing.

'I became a dancer,' she explains to the interviewer, 'because my grade didn't have a dancer.'

It happened in her first year at school, when her class went to the Metropolitan Opera. She was drawn to the ballet corps because 'they seemed to have a nice time dancing.' They went backstage and her feeling was reinforced when she saw a group of them talking and laughing together. On the way home Shirley said to her friend Ann McAvoy: 'I'm going to be a dancer.' Ann said, 'Of course you are.' Soon after she enrolled in the Fokine School of Ballet and, though she would not become a ballet dancer, it was immediately apparent that dancing was something she could excel in. It gave her the confidence to announce to her Lincoln classmates: 'I'm a dancer.' And they said, 'Of course you are.' With that and the knowledge that she could do something, she started to do well scholastically. It was as if at last she was able to open the door of learning and dance through it.

Switching to modern dance, she found a career and a vocation that anchored her and made her brave. I see her now in my imagination as if silhouetted on a hilltop scanning the horizon for signs of the avant garde. In my own daydreams I would be drinking champagne with Orson Welles, whom I had seen as Brutus in the Mercury's famous production of *Julius Caesar*. When my class went backstage to meet him, I instantly fell in love.

Shirley argued with Daddy, pitted herself against him, knowing full well the denunciations and derisive mockeries she was subjecting herself to. It made dinner a different kind of hell, but she stood her ground. Nevertheless, I know his constant disapproval took its toll on her. She was wounded by him in a way that would last for the rest of her life and lead her to seek more and more dangerous ways of rebelling against him. When some project of hers met with adversity, I saw how deeply it distressed her. It was frightening – I felt I was watching her fall down an elevator shaft too fast to grab her. Then, after a while, she would rise with grim determination and I would be uneasy that this time she was going to do something really defiant like run off with the famous dancer from India with whom she had become romantically involved. I was relieved when that blew over. During her film career this same spirit of rebellion made her dig in against certain censorship problems when compromise would have been wiser.

She actually invited Daddy, *insisted* that he come with us to watch her performing in dance troupes in places such as Bennington College during the summer. Hoping, I guess, to educate and enlighten him, or maybe just to rub his nose in it. Whatever her reasons, it was a folly I would never have committed.

Friends of my parents, the Nemerovs, had a son, Howard, who would become a poet, and a daughter, Diane (aka Diane Arbus, the photographer). Young Howard Nemerov was ardent in his love for classical music and one day at our house he found an album of a symphony he liked. He played it on our victrola, standing next to it and vigorously conducting the invisible orchestra. And there was Daddy behind him imitating Howard's gestures, hoping to make us snigger. I vowed I would never give him a chance to do that to me.

So I presented myself to my parents as having no plans, goals or aspirations as a way of avoiding confrontation. Daddy even found that reprehensible, though. 'All she wants is to have fun,' he would say disgruntledly. Good, I thought, that is exactly what I want him to think. Sometimes, if pressed, I would say I planned to be a painter. I painted quite well, enjoyed it and above all as an occupation it was the least likely to be censored. Mainly I was sitting on the side lines, but sitting in judgment, you may be sure, piling up the evidence against my father.

Shirley soon began to look like a dancer in the image of modern dance's charismatic leader Martha Graham. She pulled her long dark hair back from her forehead and held it in place with a hairband. Her very features took on a high-cheekboned modern dance cast. Like the other acolytes she sat in a certain way, held her head in a certain way, moved in a certain way. She would, for instance, swoop down on some book she wanted to show you and without one unnecessary step or gesture move with it to your side. In motion she seemed to cleave through the air. She was well aware of it.

I loved Shirley's friends, particularly Ann McAvoy, who became a distinguished doctor. (Years later Shirley would say to her, 'I know you became a doctor because we didn't have one in our class' and Ann would say, 'You're right.') Another was Liz Reitell, a long tall girl with a wicked wit who was to be the mistress of Dylan Thomas when in New York on his last go-round. These two were always around our apartment. I loved the way they talked about their new grownup world with the wit and audacity and lustrous sophistication that only sixteen- and seventeen-year-old girls are blessed with.

In 1940, the abstract painter Harry Holtzman, one of my sister's many friends in the art world, brought to New York as wartime exile the great Dutch painter Piet Mondrian. More than anything, Harry told Shirley, the sixty-eight-year-old genius wished to learn to jitterbug. She said that her sister, Elaine, was the best jitterbug dancer she knew. And thus it was that I found myself one evening at a Madison Square Garden dance gala jitterbugging with Mondrian while chewing gum – another American custom of which he was enamored.

By the time each of us had graduated Lincoln, certain things were apparent.

Shirley was going to pursue her career as a modern dancer. In every aspect of the arts as well as in her life she was to pin her colors to the avant garde, speed after it, and, in catching up, become one of its leaders. As she put it later: 'When dance got big I was in dance. When independent films got big I made them. When video started there I was, right in there from the beginning.'

It was, in my opinion, characteristic of my sister Betty's young idealism that her favorite project at Lincoln was creating a utopian city. Presenting the model to her teacher, the latter pointed out that the apartment buildings looked exactly like our dwelling, 1185 Park Avenue, complete with courtyard and fountain, signifying – to me anyway – Betty's affection for her hearth and home. She would major in economics at Vassar and become actively involved in education, politics and the social and economic problems of the disenfranchised. Upon graduation she went to Washington to work for one of the prominent progressives of that time, Congressman Claude Pepper.

While I, for a rather a long time would sit in nightclubs listening to black jazz and blues. Or dance to Benny Goodman at the Waldorf, Tommy Dorsey at the Commodore or Glenn Miller at Glen Island Casino. And I would sample all the available cocktails while I waited to be discovered.

Although Shirley and I entered the dinner table arena at the same time and shared a common perception of those years, Betty, besides being three years younger than me, would not be ready to eat with the grownups until she was five or six, which made for an almost generational gap between us. Several years ago she told me that as a child she made a conscious decision to be the 'good' daughter, as she perceived us to be the naughty ones. That may be the case, but she was also genuinely good by nature. Nor do I remember her as either an instigator or recipient of the dinner table scenes.

If there were shared give and takes between Shirley and me, I did most of the taking. Did I think for a fleeting moment that I should be a writer? Shirley knew just the right editor on the *New Yorker* to advise me. My classmate, Joan Caulfield, was making a lot of money modeling; maybe I should try being a model? Shirley supplied the right photographer for my portfolio . . .

Shirley, as I have indicated, was expert at networking. She had a pragmatic side that knew just how to capture those big performing arts grants that she and her associates so desperately needed for the experimental film projects they were involved in. In the sixties, the captain of the Green Team and the designated dancer of the Lincoln class of '38 had become the leading woman filmmaker of the American underground cinema.

5

A Card Trick and a Parable

The closer I got to high school graduation the more anxious I became about my future. I had wanted to go to one of the big Eastern women's colleges but didn't get into any of them. I did, however, get into Mills College in Oakland, California. The nightmarish memory of running down fourteen flights of stairs to escape my father a month before made me eager to accept Mills, which was about as far away from home as I could go without getting my feet wet.

Thinking of my future I saw that Shirley, by becoming the dancer in her class, had emerged as a significant figure. I, as a screwball, had no resonance whatsoever.

One day a few weeks before I was about to leave for California, I woke up and decided I would go to see my grandfather. I walked into the Beresford Apartments on Central Park West and asked the elevator man to take me to the top.

It was here, in his penthouse, that HR had finally attained his dearest social aspiration. He had wanted to be rich so he could live on the top floor of an apartment house, and now he was rich he was living on the top floor of what was considered the grandest, highest and most imposing edifice on Central Park West.

The apartment itself was, in its way, not all that different from ours or those of other families we knew who shared our background and self-made wealth. It was filled with tapestries, paneling, oriental carpets and antique furniture – or good copies of them. HR collected clocks, as might be expected of a man so enamored of precision. At the entrance there was a turtle clock; when filled with water, its magnetized turtle told time. As a child I kept taking the turtle out of the water and putting it back in again to watch it head straight for the right time on its sundial design.

HR led me to his den and flipped on the light switch and, as always, I had the impression that it caused the room to be assembled. The room was suffused with an eerie green light emanating from some unknown source. It gave me the feeling of being hundreds of leagues under the sea at the same time as being high up in the Alps.

Going up in the elevator I'd rehearsed my plan. I'd explain to Grandpa that I didn't know what to do with my life. Maybe I could work for him, help him invent something. Save me, was what I wanted to convey: Discover me!

I never had the chance. What I got instead was a card trick and a parable. I sat down on the sofa, and HR gave me a Coke from the bar and sat next to me. There was a pack of cards on the coffee table in front of us. 'I'm going to show you a card trick,' he said. *Card tricks! Oh no!* He must think I'm still a child. I feigned interest.

With the palm of his hand he pressed down on the pack and then twisted it so that the deck split fanwise into several parts. He chose the pile that had made the widest split and, holding out the bottom card so he could only see its back, asked me to remember it but not tell him out loud. It was, let us say, the Queen of Hearts. He asked me to shuffle the pack as many times as I wanted and to put the deck back on the table. I did. Again he pressed then twisted the pack and turned up the bottom card of the widest split. It was the Queen of Hearts. He went through the routine again: shuffle, press, twist. Up came the Queen of Hearts again. In spite of myself, I was fascinated.

He said, 'You can do it too. Come on. I'll show you.' He moved the pack in front of me and told me to press down as he had and come up with a card, being sure to use the same pressure that I had before. After several tries I succeeded. The card came up again. And again.

I loved it. Whenever I worked it right, it gave me a feeling of power. Imagine: you have formed a special relationship with a playing card. You can call it up at will, any day, any hour, any minute.

Then came the parable. I learned later it was Grandpa's favorite story, the one his workers loved to hear him tell. Nothing placed his origins so firmly in the latter half of the nineteenth century in a small agricultural Eastern European country as did this, the tale of the Rich Farmer and the Poor Farmer.

A Poor Farmer went over to see his neighbor, the Rich Farmer, to ask his advice. His farm was doing very badly. How could he save it from ruin, he wanted to know. The Rich Farmer gave him a sealed silver box. 'Take this box,' he said. 'It is a magic box. Do not open it but three times a day for three months walk around your farm holding it, and at the end of the three months come to see me again.'

At the end of the three months the Poor Farmer went back to Rich Farmer, who asked him how his farm was doing. 'Better,' said the Poor Farmer. 'Much better. Now what shall I do?' 'Take the magic box with you again,' instructed the Rich Farmer, 'and again walk around your farm with it three times a day for three months and at the end of that time come back to see me.'

Again at the end of three months the Poor Farmer came back as he had pledged 'And how is your farm doing now?' asked the Rich Farmer. 'It is doing wonderfully!' cried the Poor Farmer excitedly, shaking his head in amazement. 'This magic box you gave me is truly remarkable. What is in it?' he asked eagerly.

'Nothing is in it,' replied the Rich Farmer. And then he added, 'Always remember, in farming or in business, or in anything you do in life, you must work but you must always carry your magic box.'

I finished my Coke. We went into the dining room and joined my grandmother. She was short and stout with fair skin and blue eyes set far apart, and her gray hair was arranged in stiff waves. She had a large corseted Victorian bosom on which a square diamond-chipped pin was always perched. She had small feet encased in high-heeled pumps. My cousin Audrey thinks that she did not read English. My cousin Margot is sure that she did not, that she could not even read a menu and that Grandpa always read it out to her in a restaurant. She had, nevertheless, an encyclopedic knowledge of each and every one of Grandpa's inventions and protectively and firmly supervised his health regime. 'I believe in all things domestic he acceded totally to Grandma's wishes,' says Audrey. My mother had found her 'bossy' when growing up, while I found her pronouncements on what was good for you and what was bad somewhat Olympian. 'You dassen't do that,' she would say, using this nineteenth-century form of 'dare'.

Over the years I would remember that afternoon with Grandpa. Each time it came back to me I would ascribe more profundity to it. What was I seeking to unearth? I came upon the answer not as a novelist but as a biographer: the belief in magic is inherent in us all.

When Audrey was a youngster she asked Grandpa if he believed in God. 'No,' he said, quickly adding, 'but don't tell your grandmother.'

I think it interesting that Grandpa, who did not believe in God, had absolute faith in himself and the universal laws of science, while I, who did believe in God, had little faith in myself then and was scarcely aware that scientific laws existed. My grandfather had shown me a card trick that was magic but not a trick. With a deck of cards he demonstrated how magic results can be self-created by following the laws of science. With his parable he demonstrated how magic results come with the application of work.

In retrospect my grandfather had given me exactly what I'd wanted from him: a blueprint for success.

While Grandpa was perfecting one of his numerous invention variations of the screwnail, I was perfecting my invention of the screwball. I had no doubt which of our inventions was more likely to benefit mankind, but it struck me then that along with the well-known American tradition of shirtsleeves to shirtsleeves in three generations, there was another one, not so well known, of shirtsleeves to frivolity in three generations. In choosing frivolity I was simply following my family's basic tradition of self-invention.

6

Colleges

The first thing I discovered in my freshman year at Mills was that America consisted of two separate nations. There was the country of New York, whose arms extended in summer to include Westchester, Long Island, Fire Island, the New Jersey coast and the Hudson Valley (with Provincetown and Martha's Vineyard as honorary members). And there was another country: the rest of America.

Something else I noticed that year: Western and Midwestern faces were different from those of New Yorkers. It seemed to me that the very weave of their skin was different. I decided this was because they took things easier, so the muscles under their skin were more relaxed, which made their features more rounded and their brows clearer than those of taut-skinned sharp-featured New Yorkers, whose muscles were ever on the alert.

I had a good time at Mills. I knew it was only for a year. My parents made it clear it was too far away from New York and they weren't going to keep shelling out the high cost of transportation. There were very few commercial flights at the time and train travel was very expensive and took days. 'We can't afford it' – was the post-Crash phrase much in use by my parents from the beginning of my school-days on. After the Crash my parents never went back to the golden excesses of the twenties. My father stood careful watch over our expenditures so that he would never be caught like he had been in '29. I went to Mills to make the good grades that would enable me to transfer to a good Eastern college.

I passed the year pleasantly, basking in the mild California climate, soothed by the easygoing company of my new friends, and the months away from home had a good effect on me. Cleared my mind. Focused my concentration. Unfurrowed my brow. My grades were excellent. I had decided to major in art history. I liked it and I was good at it. Thanks to Lincoln I knew how to use a library: how to research a term paper, write a thesis or bone up for a quiz. I read all texts with scrupulous care. Another arson fiasco must be avoided at all costs.

One further discovery out West was a fruit I had never heard of, much less eaten: the avocado. I loved its taste and was delighted to add it to the list of things I liked to eat. My relationship with it was strange, and lay dormant for years. When it resurfaced, I discovered I had imbued this fruit with all sorts of emotional and symbolic meanings that climaxed one evening, seventeen years later, when I lived in London and was writing a novel.

My closest friend, Barbie Pabst, was to go East to be 'finished'. The only college that would take her and her beloved horse Shugie was Sweet Briar in Virginia. Wouldn't it be great, she said, if we went there together? Though I was confident my grades were good enough for me to get into an Ivy League college, it couldn't hurt to cover my bets and also apply to one that a good friend would be attending.

My first choice colleges regretfully turned me down, but Sweet Briar accepted me. Then at the last minute, with war clouds looming, Barbie and her boyfriend Billy decided to get married. And I, without rhyme or reason, landed in the South.

My first days at Sweet Briar in Lynchburg, Virginia, were delightful. The green campus nestled in the foothills of the Blue Mountain range, majestically rising in the distance. The girls – those Southern Belles! – were so friendly, hospitable and helpful and had such charming ways.

Late one morning I was sitting on the verandah outside the college inn, enjoying great gulps of a good strong Southern Coke in a Dixie cup and chewing on the ice shavings when some girls came up and introduced themselves and sat down at my table. And then a girl I shall call Lou Ellen stopped by, and we looked at each other and the other girls looked at us and we could not believe it.

'You two look so alike you could be twins,' someone said. It was extraordinary. We both wore our curly dark hair in the same short cut, our features and the shape of our faces seemed similar, and we were the same height and weight. As she looked me up and down with approval, Lou Ellen's first words to me were: 'Well, we could both double our wardrobes by exchanging clothes.'

How entertaining she was; what good stories she told, enlivened by her mischievous wit. In her company I had the sensation of viewing myself from the outside and being very pleased with what I saw. For several weeks we were inseparable. I began speaking in her native Texas twang to be even more like her.

For the first few weeks all new girls were grounded but after that we were allowed to date off campus. A big college weekend was coming up at the nearby University of Virginia and Lou Ellen was going along with her boyfriend, a member of one of the most notorious fraternities. It was the most wealthy, the most stylish, the most athletic, and the most hell-raising. It sounded great. She had suggested her friend could fix me up with a blind date and we talked about what fun it would be to double date.

One afternoon she asked me to come to her room before dinner. I was looking forward to what I assumed would be a discussion of what clothes to take and where to stay in Charlottesville, all the more because in my social studies class that morning I'd had a rather disturbing experience. Some aspect of her subject led Professor Frazier suddenly to say, 'All Catholics raise their hands.' A show of hands. 'All Protestants raise their hands.' A show of hands. As I had not raised my hand, she turned to me and said, 'Of course, you're Jewish.' To my ears it sounded as if she was exposing a thief who had sneaked into her class. There was a sort of rustle in the classroom and everyone seemed to be staring at me. I felt my face burning.

When I came into Lou Ellen's room that evening she told me, 'I can't get you a blind date, Elaine, because you're Jewish.' She uttered it as if I'd tried to put something over on her.

I felt sick at the familiarity of it. In the thirties the rise of Hitler had let loose in America as virulent a tidal wave of anti-Semitism as ever had swept the nation. Having experienced it in my years in Great Neck with its sharp line of social exclusions, I was no stranger to its undertow. But this was different: this was my twin.

As Lou Ellen turned her back to look in the mirror she cocked her head in a dismissive motion as if to say to me: You have betrayed me, but I can shrug it off. At the same time her eyes, meeting mine in the mirror, were small and hard and mean.

'That's the way it is,' she said angrily. 'There's a rule at the fraternity house that they can't have Jewish girls as dates.'

That weekend, when everyone else was off having fun, I refused to mope around Sweet Briar. One of the few Jewish girls got me a blind date to ZBT, the Jewish fraternity. A dance at their fraternity house was invaded by members of the very same fraternity that Lou Ellen's boyfriend belonged to. This made an interesting sociological point for future historians to ponder – and, while at it, they can consider why I let myself be carried off by one of its charismatic young fellows. We went on a hayride and he literally fell off the wagon and had to go to the infirmary for his wounds to be bound up. So I continued the round of festivities with a third date, who returned me safely back to Sweet Briar. To change dates once was considered rather dashing; to change dates twice was to get yourself talked about. I liked that. It showed that I had left my mark on my first weekend away.

I was to learn that anti-Semitism was legitimized by house rules in fraternities all over the country. One weekend, visiting a fraternity at Cornell in the enlightened East, it was revealed to me that they couldn't *stop* you from dating a Jewish girl but that if you brought her to their dance they would fine you fifty dollars. I'd come with a price.

Over the next months I deeply felt my loss of Lou Ellen. My favorite friend had turned into a hostile stranger. I'd had a twin, and now I had none. I was heartsick, hurt beyond words.

It made me wonder how anti-Semitic the student body really was. Indirectly the answer soon came. I was in one of the common rooms glancing through a Richmond newspaper. Its society section always gave weddings a big play, and marriage ceremonies were reported in full, from the details of the bride's gown to those of the last little flower girl's.

That day a full account was given to an obviously Jewish wedding, solid with Jewish names, and as I was reading it my instinct told me to fold the newspaper under my arm and walk out. Instead something stronger, more like curiosity, made me put it back on the table, still open at the society page, and wait to see what would happen.

I watched a senior, a court jester type, pick up the paper and begin to read. I saw her start to laugh. She called over to a group of her friends, 'Hey, come here and listen to this!' She read the piece aloud in her sneering version of a Jewish accent, her scorn apparent in her every inflection. And I listened to the other girls hooting with laughter.

Soon after, in a discussion with a classmate, I opined that surely a colored lady was entitled to just as much respect as a white lady, only to have her inform me patiently that there was no such thing as a 'nigra lady. There is only a nigra woman.' So it was true what they said about Dixie and about Sweet Briar in the forties.

My shit list was growing apace and I had only been there for two months.

I suppose I should have looked upon all this as a challenge; I should either have faced them down with stinging rebukes or plunged into lots of extra-curricular activities to show my true worth and that, in spite of my unfortunate handicap, I was really a good person, a white Jew as the expression went. But I did not. Instead I joined nothing, and the time this saved I devoted to honing my skills as an outsider. By refusing to conform I also saved myself from that smoothing down of personality that is the inevitable result of turning yourself inside-out to please others. I sharpened my edges and kept them spiky.

As the war advanced, many of the girls departed to get married, which left vacant many student government positions. I was suggested for several. I enjoyed rejecting their suggestions. I allowed the literary magazine to publish a couple of my short stories, all the time noting how vastly inferior the magazine was to the corresponding one at

Bennington. And I played one of the trolls in the college production of *Peer Gynt* because I liked the play and I liked watching Mary James, a superb actress, in the title role.

In fact I was not entirely alone and friendless for three years of monolithic misery. I had good friends, all of whom had certain things in common: they were extremely bright, got good marks, were individualists, actually liked learning and talking about their subjects – and were low on school spirit. My two closest friends were seniors who graduated the year after I arrived but not before they had insisted that I sign up the following year for a new course called Seventeenth-Century Metaphysical Poets. Not only were some of the greatest poets in the English language studied on the course, but Dr Short, the new professor who was teaching it, had previously taught at Yale. So I signed up not because I knew or wanted to know anything about religious poetry but because I wanted to know what they were being taught at Yale.

Dr Short was a small, crippled man who walked awkwardly on crutches. His intellectual vigor was second to none. The class was small and we sat around a table; everyone there was a senior and an English major except me. For the first assignment I chose to write about the Metaphysical poet Henry Vaughan. I wasn't looking forward to it – religious poetry or for that matter prose was not my forte. I had not counted on the high emotional content of his work. When in 'The Search' I came across:

> The skin and shell of things
> > Though fair
> > Are not
> Thy wish or prayer,
> > But got
> By mere despair
> > of wings

it was as though I had been looking for those words all my life. It was not so much that I believed in a deity but that I believed Vaughan in *his* belief, so strongly held that it also deepened the texture of my life.

When I was a child I used to open the children's encyclopedia to the full-page picture of Joan of Arc at the stake, all set to go up in flames. I would spend hours gazing at her, wondering if I too would have the courage to die for my religion. I knew all about the Inquisition and that Jews never converted, so I knew I must be prepared for this contingent and hoped I would be as brave as she.

Years later, after sharing Vaughan's spellbinding belief in his God (and Richard Crashaw's and George Herbert's and John Donne's, et al.), I found myself believing even more passionately in the God of David's psalms, a personal God who, as William James put it, is on your side and whom you can appeal to in every crisis.

Monday morning Dr Short gave us our papers back. He had given me an A. No one else in the class – all those English major seniors – got higher than a C and there were some outright Ds. Leaving the class I bounded down the stairs two at a time, hugging my paper to me.

The less I wished to please the student body, the more I wished to please the faculty. The more I listened to the lectures, the more I absorbed the subjects from the professors' perspectives. The more I gave them back what they were teaching, the better I performed. It was strangely like what I was to feel in the future, when, as an actress, I would put myself in the hands of a director I trusted, who would then pull a performance out of me that I could not have done on my own.

This method of learning, I realized, was the necessary other side of the coin to the Lincoln method, where you were encouraged to put forth your own opinions.

Most of all, I was discovering that I could study hard and work well in spite of unhappiness, or maybe because of it. I graduated with honors. My mood at graduation is best expressed in a letter I wrote to my 'folks' – meaning my mother as my father and I never corresponded – explaining my reasons for not staying for the commencement ceremonies. 'This is to me no Big Moment. I don't consider that I've done anything but stay put in this hole for three years.' I caught the next train to Washington, getting the hell out of Lynchburg fast.

7

Wartime Washington

September of 1943: only three months after I'd graduated from college and my mood in this short time had swung 180 degrees, from screwball heroine, to outsider, to honours student, to top secret work at the Army Signal Corps.

I was to work at Arlington Hall in Arlington, Virginia, a suburb of Washington. The place had been a boarding school before the Army Signal Corps commandeered and converted it for the duration. On its campus the army had built various prefabs such as barracks and offices that were needed to accommodate a military base; they looked as if they had popped up overnight during a heavy rainfall. To me they were beautiful.

On my first day in the auditorium where we had convened for briefing, there were besides the new employees – those girls freshly graduated from college, of which I was one – a sea of soldiers, of varying ranks, and a smattering of civilians. We were told in very general terms that we would be working on codes and various other methods of communications. The work we would be doing, it was emphasized, was top secret. I had gathered this already from the smooth recruiting officer who came to Sweet Briar looking for smart girls with good grades in the senior class and who – after a security check – had signed me up. So I didn't listen very closely. In fact I was too busy looking at the young T-5 (T for technical) sergeants who were soon to be made lieutenants. Word had gotten around that these were very special soldiers skimmed off the top of Ivy League colleges and that they needed to have IQs of at least 135 even to be considered, so I did snap to when I heard that these young men would be working very closely with us young women on projects for which we would be trained.

I looked around and was happy. I would be doing war work and getting paid eighty-eight dollars every two weeks for it. My mind and muscles relaxed and it was as if this freed all my senses. I was wide awake, my spirits soared. I'd just turned twenty-one.

Soon after I realized I was also filled with a down-to-earth craving, which came over me whenever I met or even just viewed the aforementioned young men in the workplace, in the canteen, in the Arlington village restaurant, the Grill, or at the bus stop waiting for the bus to take us to Washington. Put frankly, my guts were saying: *What a place to lose your virginity!* To which my mind responded: *And what a time to do it!*

In the second year of the war it could already be seen that morality had shifted, had transformed itself into something quite different than before.

You could say that the majority of us at that army post were in our early twenties, when testosterone and hormones are supposed to be running wild, but there was more to it. We were all together in unexpected and special circumstances, and it was as though our wartime acts of love were seen as unselfishly friendly actions. I think it was because we all shared in common at least one death or disablement of someone we knew, which gave us simultaneously a feeling of mortality and immortality. It made us see how important we all were to each other. And under these circumstances our coming together was sinless, blameless, even faultless.

I must find my seducer: the perfect man with whom to lose my virginity.

My search turned out to be no small undertaking. It was a while before I found what I was looking for. Meanwhile, there were all the other firsts for me to enjoy.

Like my job. Right away I got what I considered preferential treatment. No lowly government clerk I. Since I had been an art major I was put to work painting posters and handbills in bold colors to capture the employees' attention to various events, changes of schedules, housing listings and updates on workplace locations.

Soon I was taken out of that department by Frank Lewis, the top brass civilian, a wiry, sharp-featured mathematical genius. He was the head of the Japanese section – my section – and was one of the two major heroes on the base, the other being Major Edwin Reischauer, arguably the most distinguished Japanese scholar of the day. Together they had cracked the Japanese naval code. Mr Lewis was conducting a series of classes for the trainees as well as the high brass, and he put me to work making charts to clarify his lectures. I would drop in on them every chance I got in order to thrill again to the story of how they had succeeded.

These days would later be written up in Second World War history books as the time of the great cryptographers. We knew it then; we were there.

When Mr Lewis's lectures came to an end so did my job of making charts. I became a worker among workers, a cryptographer among cryptographers. As cryptographers, what we did seemed not unlike a complicated mixture of crossword puzzles and bingo and it was impossible to explain. In an enormous room the newly graduated college girls worked at sliding Japanese naval code messages in a certain way so that the whiz lieutenants reading them could find out what Japanese ship was about to turn up where. Obviously time was of the essence, and the base worked round the clock in three shifts.

Later given a choice of going on swing shift or graveyard, I chose the latter as it interfered less with my social life. Sliding Japanese messages in the dead of night at an army base in Virginia was exactly what I wished to be doing. So was taking coffee breaks in the cubicle of a shy Irish-American lieutenant from Buffalo who translated diplomatic messages (we had managed to steal the dip. codebook); he had a crush on me.

Hard as I try, there is no way I can inflate my importance in the big picture. I was neither Rosie the Riveter nor an officer in the WAACS.

But neither was I taking Seconal to sleep off boring chunks of Sunday afternoons, as I used to do at Sweet Briar. I was not indispensable. If I left the army post, it wouldn't collapse, though I liked to think it might take a while to replace me.

I spent the rest of the war years working at Arlington Hall. I loved everything about it, even the identification badges we had to show to get through the gate. Far from seeing it as a restriction that transformed you, as a friend of mine complained, 'from a person to a sheep', (this was back in the days when no ordinary person ever wore identification badges), I saw it as a badge of freedom.

One of the earliest letters I wrote home, postmarked October 21, 1943, reflects my euphoria. 'Life here continues to be blissful with one wonderful thing after another happening,' I began, my high spirits breaking through the bleakness of the blank image that I was always striving to present to my parents. I signed off with 'It's now 7.00 p.m. and I am expecting company at 8.00 p.m. My first soirée – isn't that exciting?' Up in the clouds, I wrote this letter down in an Arlington basement bedsit on 130 North Oakland Drive, where I was living at the time.

I forget how I heard about the basement apartment, but the minute I set eyes on it I knew I wanted to live there. It was a large room decorated in warm colors. It had a divan that opened into a bed at night. It had a wardrobe, bookshelves and chairs, and a good-sized table to dine on (which I never did because I always ate out), and a nice coffee table. It was also conveniently near Arlington Hall and the Grill and the bus stop into Washington.

I read poetry. My head filled with rhythms and rhymes. In my crystalline awareness I would often go and lie down under one of the giant oaks in the vast tranquillity of the nearby Arlington Cemetery, where I would watch the squirrels flying from branch to branch in the trees. I felt so serene. I felt so well. My soul grew happy in that cemetery. I wanted to stay all day.

Gradually I became conscious that my bedsit had one huge generic problem. It started with my record player. Every time I turned it on I received a pulverizing shock. A friend told me to take my feet off the floor, so I tucked them under me on a chair and turned on the record player. No shock. He said the dampness of the linoleum floor was acting as a conductor.

I began to notice other things. One day I saw the tops of my unworn shoes had green stuff on them. It was mold. Then my bed sheets were damp. Mrs Atkins, whom I rented the basement from, gave me some sort of dehumidizing contraption and for a day or two I was able to think it dried the air. It didn't. The dampness stayed; in fact it grew. I shook talcum powder over my damp sheets and woke up in the morning all powdery. My clothes felt damp; so did my books and everything else.

The damp basement climate began to smell, and an unearthly odor of ammonia and sulphur – rather like that of hell – greeted me every time I came into that room. It got up my nose and stayed there. Today I could still identify it blindfold.

It had taken me a long time to become aware of it because I wasn't there for any amount of time. I ate breakfast at a local coffee shop, lunch at the canteen on the base, and in the evening I was always out on dates in Washington – dining, dancing, drinking in jam-packed cocktail lounges like the Statler, among the uniformed throngs of all nations. When I had people over, we all smoked constantly, which must have disguised the smell and maybe even dried the place out for the evening.

When I went to the cemetery I realized there was another reason I felt so well there – I was drying out.

It was on the buses going into Washington in the evening that I became acquainted with the Bus Stop Aesthetes, as I called them. The first time I noticed these young lieutenants I was sitting behind them on the bus eavesdropping as they chatted happily amongst themselves on elevated topics, sprinkling their conversation with French phrases. One of them suddenly switched to a less grand subject and said with a cosmopolitan sigh: 'Poor old Ed. C'est toujours la même histoire.' 'Oh?' said another. 'What's the matter with Ed?' 'Well at least he got rid of that girl.' 'Did he?' 'Yes. Had to, you know.' They were adorable; so young, so fresh-faced, so fearlessly affected. Everything they approved of they proclaimed chi-chi or chon-chon.

By the third bus trip we had all become friends. I even got to meet 'poor old Ed', their ringleader, still chubby with puppy fat. He'd been going to Harvard Law School and was richer than the others, more secure, more worldly and equally – if not more – affected. He had a collection of rare books and spoke beautiful French.

Around this time, when I had spent a year underground, I was suddenly given the chance to rent a white clapboard house on North Taylor Street. I snapped it up. It had enough rooms for me to ask an ever-changing cast of girls to go in with me; sometimes we slept as many as five. We all got along. So now instead of living underground – the natural habitat of moles and mold – I began living above ground – the natural habitat of *Homo sapiens*.

With my change of altitude my stay in Washington altered. Psychologically I was no longer plagued with bouts of loneliness I'd only half admitted to myself in my subterranean lair. I had to cook, sort of. I learned the comfort of staying in and talking with my flatmates well into the night and then not having everyone go home but staying on and sleeping there. I felt calmer, and a great deal healthier. I didn't know it, but I was subliminally preparing myself for the Big Chance.

I would quite often see them walking around the base after lunch, but always, it seemed to me, from a distance, as if they were intentionally distancing themselves from everyone but each other. He was tall, lean, elongated, his brow intellectually high, his pale brown hair thinning. Several years older than the average young man about the base, Paul Talchett, a Princeton graduate, was a superb linguist who had already become a well-known translator of Japanese poetry. His bearing was graceful rather than epicene. I was intrigued rather than electrified. The girl he was always with fascinated me equally. When I first asked someone who she was I was told – not as gossip, just as fact – that her name was Liz and she was his mistress. Not girlfriend, but mistress. This sophisticated accolade was bestowed upon her because he already had a wife somewhere back East.

That glamorized him for me on the spot. That and the fact that Liz, in her casual clothes and loafers with her steady blue-eyed gaze, looked so level-headed. She looked so much more like a college grad taking a degree in sociology than a mistress. Most of all I admired her calm open manner in the face of public scrutiny.

Then at one of those Saturday night parties people were always giving in Arlington I saw him up close and alone. Perhaps we were dancing or just talking. He'd heard I liked blues and jazz and that I had a good collection of records. I was surprised that he was even interested in black music. It revealed an unexpected side to his character. I said yes, I'd loved that kind of music all my life. He offered to show me some of the black nightclubs for which Washington was famous.

He began taking me to these clubs where, like my friend Gil in my Lincoln days, Paul too was always warmly greeted. But he went one better. Sometimes, during an evening, he would be invited by the musicians to sit in on piano. His long delicate fingers played a fantastic boogie woogie.

Late one night, while watching him perform at one of these piano sessions, my skin began tingling and a ferocious yearning took possession of me. A light above the piano in the darkened room did its old chiaroscuro trick of illuminating his attenuated features and turning his pale brown hair into a golden aureole above his lofty brow. His expression was detached yet fully submerged in the music, and his hands flew over the keys, confident, expert. I felt them on me.

When he came back to the table I reached up and pulled him down and hugged him. He put his arms around me and we began kissing. 'I'm a virgin,' I said between kisses, 'and I don't want to be. So, what do you think?'

He smiled and said, 'When?' and I let out a sigh of relief. It was going to happen. At last.

We drew apart and began to plan my coming out. We decided on Saturday afternoon of the next week because, it turned out, we had both been invited to the same party that night. Of course we would arrive separately and leave separately and then each get to his apartment separately. We never appeared on the base together, keeping the fact that we were seeing each other secret from everyone.

To ready myself for the event I called up my sister Shirley, living in Baltimore, where her husband was stationed in the Coast Guard. I told her about it. 'Suppose I get cold feet at the last moment?' I asked. She said there came a time in every girl's life when she had to jump in, no matter how cold the water. She added I must not feel I had to fall in love with him because we'd gone to bed. Out of the question, I assured her.

She found a doctor in Washington to fit me for a diaphragm, which I bought along with gel at a drugstore. I went to Elizabeth Arden and got my legs waxed, and the evening of the date I bathed in bath oil. I scrubbed myself clean and stainless and put on fresh underwear. The dress I chose was easy to get out of.

His apartment was curiously empty of Paul, the man. Except for a piano and bookshelves filled with Japanese literature, it could have been a hotel suite.

We had champagne. He took off my dress and it did not catch on anything. I watched him take off his clothes. I had never seen a man completely naked before. Something in me stirred. We lay naked in bed and began our activity. What happened to me was precisely what was supposed to – bone, blood and all. It was painless and even slightly pleasant, and I felt triumphant rather than ecstatic. I went to the dresser and looked in the mirror to see if my face had changed. It hadn't. I caught him looking at me in the glass, reading my thoughts, and I was embarrassed. Interesting: it was the one and only time that day that I was embarrassed.

We did it again and again over a period of time, and I got the hang of it.

It was all sinless, blameless, and faultless. Well, not quite. One day he broke a date with me, and the violence of my reaction astounded me. My carefully thought-out, cool, contemporary attitude towards our affair vanished into thin air. I was as jealous as if I were madly in love with him. My frenzied response was to go out with another man, Ed Brown – as in 'poor old Ed' – and go to bed with him that night.

Next morning, after I left, I telephoned Paul from a phone booth. I was furious. 'You know what you've done to me?' I accused him. 'I went to bed with Ed Brown last night. You've made a whore out of me!'

His tone was mild but serious. 'How *exactly* do you feel?'

'I . . . feel,' and then I stopped for a long moment. 'I feel rather *worldly*,' I said to my surprise.

'Good for you,' he said. I hung up the phone and opened the telephone booth and stepped into the crisp, clear, autumn day. I had entered the booth a girl. I emerged from it *une femme du monde*.

8

Stage Fever

Although for months we at Arlington Hall, like the rest of Washington, had been hearing false reports of the Allied victory over Germany, finally, on May 7, 1945, the good news was confirmed.

That evening, with a group of my friends, we joined the crowds that had been collecting in Lafayette Park across the street from the White House and began shouting for the president. At last, from somewhere above our heads, Harry Truman appeared before us.

This middle-sized, middle-aged president of twenty-five days, wearing a double-breasted suit and owlish eyeglasses, cut an unimpressive, even comical figure. Gesticulating awkwardly with both hands, as if to scatter us like chickens in his yard, he said something like, 'Go home. It's over. Go home. Get to work tomorrow.' As an early live appearance before the Great American Public, his performance was brief but unpolished. Later on, his celebrated remarks would still be brief but highly polished. For me and my friends, however, the European war was not over until the next day, when we heard Churchill on the radio confirming the event in surging, balanced, syntactically perfect sentences.

But three months later, on VJ Day, August 14, President Truman rose to the occasion. When the crowd in Lafayette Park formed a conga line and streamed across the street and shouted, 'We want Harry!' he responded by coming out on the front lawn and reaching through the iron fence to shake hands with those he could touch. Then, from a hastily assembled sound system on the portico, he made a speech – so poignant in hindsight – that was to express the spirit of optimism and high endeavour that prevailed during that short-lived period and that would set it aside forever from future years.

'This is a great day,' said Truman. 'This is the day we have been looking forward to since December 7, 1941. This is the day when fascism and police government ceases in the world. This is the day for democracies. This is the day when we can start on our real task of implementation of free government in the world.'

With peace, the exodus from Arlington Hall Signal Corps began.

Like many others who worked in Washington for the duration, war had brought me security, while peace brought me anxiety. My state of mind could be summed up in two words: *Now what?*

Unsuccessfully I tried several peacetime jobs including ones at Travelers Aid and the post-war Office of War Information. I would hang in for a couple of months and then quit.

For months after I left Arlington Hall the problem of *Now what?* went unsolved. I could not hold on to a decision for even so short a time as overnight. I would go to bed all set to put a new plan into action the next day and, upon waking up, discard it. Yet in spite of all my chopping and changing, at no matter what time of day, morning, noon or night, I remained steadfast in my resolve that whatever career I chose would be pursued in Washington. I would not go home. Relations at home were very much the same: strained.

At a date that should be etched in my mind in blood but isn't, sometime at the end of '45, Terry Anderson, my Lincoln schoolmate to whom I had always been attracted, got his discharge from the army and came back into my life. Ever since we left Lincoln, whenever I was not involved with someone else he would resurface in my thoughts

and I would miss him and wonder where he was and what he was
doing. When he was at college at Amherst and I was at Sweet Briar I
wrote him long letters and his replies were the ones I most looked forward to receiving during my incarceration.

Terry had the sort of charm that I had noticed often turns up in
young offspring of famous artistic and intellectual parents. It may have
been because of the sympathetic attention I had observed the famous
friends of their famous parents bestowing upon these youngsters, or
perhaps watching high bohemia's congenial and graceful company
manners made the children absorb these manners. For whatever reasons, no matter how screwed up some of these children became later,
I noticed they were always socially at ease.

His looks grew on you. At first glance he was an inconspicuous
young man in glasses. Only when you looked closer did you see they
were hiding beautiful green eyes. He had a short round nose and a soft
full mouth made for kissing. In his quiet, dry way he had been a def-
inite presence throughout our school years. He had been class
president twice, but more importantly to me from the stories and
poems he wrote and his English papers it seemed a foregone conclusion that he too – like his father Maxwell Anderson – would become
a writer.

Several years before, Terry had taken me once again to the
Anderson house in Rockland County. That day neighbors Kurt Weill
and his wife Lenya dropped in. So did Henry Varnum Poore, the
painter and architect, and Milton Caniff, creator of the popular *Terry
and the Pirates* comics. They were so nice, so interesting, and I loved
every minute of it. That evening I had also fallen under the spell of
Terry's large, shambling, welcoming father whom I learned to call
Max. He discussed every subject with a kind of omniscience counter-
balanced by his sharp wit. There was not a pompous bone in his body.
Most marvelously, he always solicited your opinions.

Afterwards, when Terry told me his father had said of me, 'She's just
the kind of girl I like: spirited', I treasured the remark, not only because
it came from the illustrious playwright but from *a father who actually
approved of me*.

*

The first time Terry and I saw each other after the war was the first time we ended up in bed. I wasn't prepared for what happened. It was as if a tidal wave had pulled me down to places I'd never been – delicious, dangerous, fiery places, down where the music played. It was as if I had never lain with a man before. I had to revise my realities. Sex wasn't just a new dance step; it was dynamite. I would never have picked Terry out of a lineup as the most likely candidate to effect this change in me. It did a lot to explain my obstinate obsession with him.

One weekend, in January of 1946, Terry and I were with Max in New York while he was attending casting calls for his new play *Truckline Café*. He was worried. He had deep misgivings about the actress they'd cast as one of the leads. She was not a bad actress, but she was not right. She *looked* all wrong. He turned to me. 'She should look like *you*,' he said seriously. 'Would you come and read for the part?'

Those last eight words were to shape and mold my life for the next ten years. At last it had happened: I had been discovered – and by one of Broadway's leading playwrights. Beginning with the first issue of *Photoplay* I'd ever read as a child, I'd waited for this to happen. When I tried out for a lead in the senior class play at Lincoln and didn't get the part I was so devastated I decided never to try out again but to wait until someone would recognize at a glance my enormous potential and immediately give me a leading part in a play or a movie. And now, with my dream on the brink of fulfillment, a terrible pusillanimity held me back. Stand on an empty stage in a cavernous playhouse and read in front of all those important theatrical people? I had stage fright just thinking about it. I thanked Max and laughingly declined the offer, pleading lack of experience and silently hating myself for my cowardice.

Nevertheless, in that moment of declining, I knew I was going to be an actress and promptly devoted my energies to finding an acting company or acting school in Washington.

Four months later I had found what I was looking for: the Jarvis Theatre School, run by an Englishman of the same name. There I studied, at first only at night as I still had a job. I had gone back to Arlington Hall, this time working on amassing political data from

translated newspaper clippings of a small European country. Not exciting, but it put off the dreaded day when I would have to tell my
parents I was at acting school and ride out their disapproval.

That September my sister Betty married Boris Lorwin, a recently dis-
charged naval officer. Built along the lines of a friendly bear, he was a
sympathetic type, ebullient yet highly sensitive to the needs of others.
He was related through both his maternal and paternal lines to distinguished Jewish families who were prominent intellectuals in academic
circles and in progressive movements, as well as the arts and literature.
His father had been attached to the League of Nations. I was made
happy by the marriage of Betty and Boris, not only because they were
in love but because I saw it as an event that would get me off the hook.
With two of their daughters safely and respectably married, my parents
would, I figured, let me be the one that got away. After all, two out of
three was a good average in those days when children were beginning
to break away from family supervision. I was right – though not entirely.
When I did finally write them after Betty and Boris's wedding, telling
them I was taking acting lessons and asking for money to pay for them
in order to be a full-time pupil, I received to my great relief a letter from
my father (the only one I ever remember getting), saying he would pay.
From then until June of '47 I attended the Jarvis Theatre School.

Sometime in the late summer Terry came to Washington looking
for a job so I asked my well-connected brother-in-law for his help.
Boris introduced Terry to arguably the best drama critic in the capital,
Tom Donelly of the Washington *Daily News*. Tom offered to take
Terry on as a trainee to show him the ropes and let him review the odd
play as it came up. Later on, when the odd play had come up and Terry
had reviewed it, I was elated to think that I was the one who had mas-
terminded the whole thing.

I had been in correspondence with Max, who always extended an
invitation himself whenever Terry asked me up for a weekend. In one
such letter, in June of 1946, he added that I seemed to be in touch with
what was going on with people under thirty who read books in a way
that he was no longer doing himself. That was *echt* Max: saying just
the thing you wanted to hear. Besides, he continued, I always wrote
him the best bread and butter letters at a time when both were scarce.

I had written Max about Terry's review when it was published in the newspaper and Max wrote back humorously, 'Of course [Terry] may feel that his style doesn't rise to the occasion but I'd like to see the review if you happen to be going by a news-stand and buying a copy of the *News* that you don't want to save intact.' I detected a note of sadness under the humor that Terry had not sent it to his father.

In October, Max's new play, *Joan of Lorraine*, starring Ingrid Bergman, arrived in Washington, where its out-of-town opening was soon to take place. The first weekend Max came down to oversee it, we spent some time with him and Ingrid Bergman and Sam Wanamaker and other luminaries attached to the play; heady stuff for me. Afterward Max told us that Ingrid's husband, Dr Lindstrom, was driving them nuts over her contract. They called him 'the man with the mortuary mind', because he was always impeding the signing of it with questions such as 'What if Max has a heart attack?' Or 'What if Harold Friedman [Max's play agent] goes blind?' Or 'What if Sam Wanamaker falls off the set and dislocates his back?' This was the kind of theatre gossip I adored. It made me feel such an insider.

The next weekend Terry and I went to stay again at what I'd come to think of as Paradise-on-the-Hudson where the hills were alive with well-known artists, actors and writers. Again I had a wonderful time. Max was the father I'd never had, living in surroundings that never were mine.

Max was back in Washington a week later for the inevitable reworkings and fine tunings of his play. One night he asked Terry and me to come to his hotel suite for drinks early as he would have to leave to watch the run-through of the play. When we arrived he said he had a proposal to put to us. It seemed obvious to him that we were in love, were happy with each other and were good for each other. Why didn't we get married here in Washington? He would give us the wedding and arrange it all. We were to think it over and let him know.

Then his theatrical colleagues dropped by to pick him up and they all went off to the theatre.

This, I thought, is too good to be true. And I was right.

The mistake Max and I both made was to think that the three of us were in accord with his idea, when in reality only two of us were. The one who wasn't was Terry.

And he told me so. He said bluntly that he wasn't going to marry me. 'It wouldn't work,' he said. 'I couldn't make you happy because you're too ambitious for me.' Because I wanted to be an actress? I asked. That wasn't what he meant; I was too ambitious for *him*. 'You'd try to make something of me. And I don't want that!' he said with growing anger. I said nothing. I was numb.

I woke up the next morning angry. What he'd said about my ambition for him was true, but why was I supposed to feel guilty for trying to help Terry become a writer? The talent was there. Wouldn't anyone genuinely fond of him do the same? But good wives were not supposed to be naggers and pushers, we all knew that. I would be one of those terrible, emasculating wives who drive men mad. I felt caught out, exposed as if – Lady Macbeth-ishly – I was urging him to commit a crime. By the end of the day I had reasoned myself around into thinking it was all my fault. When I didn't hear from him I began to feel the cold finality of his rejection.

And then there was Max. I felt bad about him, as if I'd let him down. It had come through so clearly, that evening of his proposal, his love for Terry. And because of it he'd wanted me to be his daughter-in-law! A father actually wanted me for a daughter-in-law. I would have to tell him myself that the wedding was off. I picked up the phone and called him.

As per our arrangement, at eleven o'clock the next morning I joined Max in his hotel suite. It was an uncomfortable meeting to begin with but along the way it took a turn so unexpected as to verge on the bizarre.

I sat on the sofa and Max sat on an armchair opposite with a space between us. I said that the wedding was off because Terry felt he couldn't make me happy because I was too ambitious for him. Max looked puzzled and said nothing. Probably he thought I was complaining about Terry, which I was, but it was just the opposite of what I meant to convey. I wanted the mood to be tender, to console Max, so I began assuring him that Terry was not to blame, that I should have sensed Terry's resistance and put the brakes on Max's generous wedding plans. I should have known Terry wasn't ready, that I'd been trying to force his hand, adding further spiritless self-condemning bullshit that – as I listened to myself – I couldn't believe I was saying.

I couldn't look Max in the face, so I stared at the carpet. All of a sudden there came crashing into my mind a flashback of our previous meeting. What I was recalling, in living color and vivid detail, was that here, in this very same room, two days ago, after Max had made his proposal and gone off to the theatre, Terry and I had stayed on, finished our drinks and in a rush of lust made love on that carpet. On that very same space of carpet that lay between Max and me.

The recollection utterly derailed me, and if Max said anything I didn't hear it. I raised my eyes to get back on track and there he was as expected, seated on his chair, wearing comfortable clothes as usual. Everything about him was as usual except that he had, under his trousers, a very noticeable erection. Had my thoughts jumped, I wondered? An errant thought flitted through my mind: Why don't I fling myself upon him and have another roll on that consecrated ground? But this seemed a little extreme to me – as it would no doubt have been to him. He was probably just as surprised at this manifestation as I was. Though I didn't refer to it, I took it very personally; considered it an endorsement of my allure. And after we somehow said our goodbyes and I was out of the room I have to say it made me feel better about myself than I'd felt when I'd come in.

Curiously my affair with Terry limped on for a while. Then, at some point, Max wrote to ask me if I had Terry's address as he had lost touch with him. At that point so had I.

Years later I would occasionally hear news of Terry and his wife Lulu from Betty and Boris and subsequently from a classmate at Lincoln. At some point Terry went to Columbia to finish college and did brilliantly, a straight A student. Then, perhaps still shunning ambition, he worked at a number of jobs: as a bit player, as a stage manager, as a teacher in a grade school, a real estate agent and, for some time, as a postman.

Being asked to read for *Truckline Café* by its playwright might seem like a fairly flimsy excuse to drop everything at the age of twenty-four and embark on an acting career with no previous experience or encouragement. It was not only my impetuosity at work but my intuition that gave me the green light. Intuitively I knew that acting, and all that came with it, was for me. Intuition, I have always believed, is really reasoning speeded up.

Just as I could pinpoint the moment when a *Photoplay* cover and the movies gave me the friend I needed in Garbo, I can also locate the time when I became forever stagestruck. Mother loved theatre and would take me to matinees, her choices based solely on the plays she wanted to see herself. When I was nine or ten we saw the Rodgers and Hart musical *Girl Crazy*, with Ethel Merman in her Broadway debut stopping the show with 'I Got Rhythm'. That was fine enough, but it was nothing to the moment when, the very afternoon I saw it, the leading man playing opposite Ginger Rogers said, 'I love you, Ginger – I mean – I love you – ' he hastily corrected, 'Jane' (or whatever was the name was of the character she was playing). A titter flew over the audience, and I happily joined in. I, too, had caught the slip and knew that the actor really was in love with Ginger herself. In that moment make-believe and reality merged. Everything was possible.

Beginning with classes in Washington, for years acting did everything I wanted it to do for me, including, thank God, ultimately giving me up. It was my vocation, my psychoanalysis, my group therapy, my circle of friends, my makeover, my goal, my place to exchange my old, injured, irrational self for new ones, that worked better. It was my solace and my excitement. After my break-up with Terry, it gave me the chance to mend my broken heart. I was back at school. After the war everyone was back at school.

Mr Jarvis, as I have said, was an Englishman. Only later would I find that in this he was not the exception but the rule. The waves of theatrical Brits invading the New World have never stopped from the moment the Crown colonists set foot on American soil.

The English accent plays well in all manner of artistic endeavor in the States, but especially in theatre, with its promise of enlightenment, elegance, grace, polish, and distinction. The English temperament and attitude, are, on both sides of the stage, ideally suited to theatre.

English theatre folk are people with just the right combination of cool, unflappable confidence spiced with their own brand of picturesque eccentricities to prepare a satisfying meal for hungry audiences in every corner of that damp sceptered isle. Even before the curtain goes up, English audiences are already profoundly thankful to have a place to come into out of the cold and the damp. As bad as the climate is outdoors, so much better is the climate inside a cosy playhouse where all hell can break loose.

Mr Jarvis was the embodiment of theatrical English virtues: happy, hopeful, eccentric and efficient. There were about fifteen of us in class. We did monologues and scenes with the other students, and he critiqued them afterwards. We put on plays for invited audiences — friends and relatives — who all thought we were marvelous.

One day, after doing a scene, Mr Jarvis looked at me thoughtfully. The pause was long and it made me nervous. Something was making him frown.

'Your name doesn't suit you,' he finally said. 'You should change it.' 'To what?' I asked. He said he'd think about it and let me know tomorrow. The next day he said Elaine Dundy. Instantly I knew it was right. Lighthearted, playful yet forceful, serious — I read all sorts of adjectives into it. The important thing was that it seemed to reflect the person I saw in the mirror.

Now that I had a new name (spelled with a 'y' to differentiate it from Dundee marmalade), who were my new relatives? I wondered. The only ones I found were an Italian family of boxers, wrestlers, trainers and managers of the same name. The most famous was Angelo Dundee, who was to manage Muhammad Ali.

The critic, Tom Donelly, and I had become fast friends. We enjoyed each other's company, loved talking endlessly about movies and plays and actors. With him I first experienced the joys of seeing a first-rate play with a first-rate critic in a first-rate seat on the aisle.

Anyone who has ever been stagestruck can identify with the camaraderie, vainglory and nurturing of everyone else's stagestruck vainglories that come with the territory. Our group madness was such that if someone did a scene from a Broadway play, we told them they were better than the actor whose role they were playing. What's more, we believed it. We thought we were all better than anyone on Broadway.

I myself was ignited by a fire that propelled me, not many months after starting with Jarvis, to produce, direct, star in (and do the posters for) *The Weak Spot*, written by one of my favorite playwrights, George Kelly.

There was a theatre on the grounds of Arlington Hall, left over from when it had been a school. As it was located away from the restricted area I managed to talk the military brass into giving it to me for a week. I called my company the Stage Guild. What Stage? What Guild? It consisted of a couple of friends who shifted the scenery and one other actor beside me. Tom Donelly came to see it, wrote it up for his newspaper and called me, deadpan, the 'future Tallulah Bankhead'. A prophecy that went unfulfilled.

I had always loved the plays of George Kelly. As Mary McCarthy put it, he was a unique case of a writer who was a box-office success, an esoteric excitement and a name almost unknown by the serious intellectual public, who were only then slowly discovering that he was just about the oddest playwright in America. His real heroes, as she goes on to say, are glasses of water, telephones, pocketbooks and after-dinner cups of coffee. I myself love the way he has characters incorporate the last thing that someone has said to them and deliver it completely refurbished and renovated to the next character that came on stage.

In mid-October of 1947, having seen his plays *Reflected Glory* with Tallulah Bankhead and *The Fatal Weakness* with Ina Claire and read all his others, I wrote him a fan letter. On November 10 he responded, writing that I was very generous in my estimate of his plays and that he was delighted that I found them interesting and amusing. And he closed with the suggestion that 'when you hear of me doing something, or trying to [on Broadway], please drop me a note and we can have a chat anyway, even if there is nothing of interest to you in the play'. It is one of the letters I have saved to this day.

We were a happy crew of acting students in our *folie de grandeur*. Too green to know any upstaging tricks, we instinctively chose – as the most natural way of representing the life lived in a play – to interact. In short, we worked together. To my surprise, the joys of being an actress included not only the stardom I was seeking but the company I was keeping.

As our term came to an end in '47, some of us wanted to go to summer stock as apprentices. Since we had become such good friends we decided we would apply to the various summer stock companies as a group, asking them to take us all together. Naturally we started at the top and applied to Ogunquit, the famous company in Maine, ruled with an iron hand by Maude Hartwig. A group letter impressed her so much with our spirit of solidarity that she promptly accepted us all.

The weather in our corner of Maine that summer was glorious. Each new day presented a freshly laundered blue sky. Facing inland, the air was sun-sweet and fern-smelling; facing out at the navy blue Atlantic Ocean it smelled raw, salty and ice-cold. The Ogunquit Playhouse was beautiful to look at and well equipped to work in, and so was the little theatre in the open, where we apprentices put on plays.

Ogunquit was a prestigious gig. It put on hit plays fresh from Broadway like *State of the Union* and *Joan of Lorraine*, without Ingrid of course, but with well-known actors.

As apprentices we were gofers for everything that needed on-the-spot going for, like coffee, snacks, cigarettes, newspapers, lost straw hats and misplaced playscripts. We cued in actors in scenes that gave them trouble. We painted scenery, sewed costumes. In the front of the house we were ushers and box office assistants.

I had a brief affair with a hot-shot up-and-coming director-in-residence. He made a big play for me, and I succumbed. I was flattered, excited; I felt I was on my way to the big time. But I backed off when I saw he was not interested in forwarding my career and only wanted me for sex and my opinion of his work. The last thing he wanted was to discover me as an actress or to give me a boost with his influential theatre friends. As this became plainer, I began to complain. And he was *hurt*. Is that why you're with me? he asked. I said yes. He went on about not really having any influence with his influential friends, and then I broke it off with him.

One other thing I remember: George Abbott, probably the most successful musical comedy director on Broadway for many decades, had been to Ogunquit that summer and was impressed with our fellow Jarvis actress Julie. He kept calling her back up to the final audition of his new Broadway musical, yet she didn't get a part. She felt terrible, and so did we. We went to Mr Abbott, saying, 'You've had a lot of experience in this, what is the best thing we can do to cheer her up?'

His answer was chilling, though he did not deliver it in that way. He just gave it to us straight: 'There are no consolation prizes in theatre.' I never forgot it.

9

1185 Redux

After that summer in Ogunquit I left Washington and moved back to New York. I was too ambitious even to contemplate regional theatre.

Of course I would have to stay at 1185 Park while I got organized, but only temporarily. Then I'd find my own living quarters, as I had for four years in Washington. I'd figured that my father, having accepted my acting career, would accept that too. As to living at home in the interim, I had years ago become adept at staying out of his way.

On the whole I led a fragmented life, as one whose current address was only temporary, a mere stop gap. I kept a strict social distance from my parents' home. I never gave parties; I never brought anyone home.

In mid-November Tom Donelly called. A new play by Tennessee Williams had opened in New Haven for the first of its out-of-town try-outs (the only previous one on Broadway had been *The Glass Menagerie*). What Tom had gleaned from the theatrical grapevine made him decide to go up to Boston and see it for himself. He invited me along.

The play was *A Streetcar Named Desire*. The best-known names associated with the production were those of the new playwright

Tennessee Williams and the director Elia Kazan, together for the first time. Its interest centered mainly on what the pairing of these two talents would produce. As for the cast, there were no stars. The actors, such as Jessica Tandy, Kim Hunter and Karl Malden, were, at that time, esteemed but not household names. Of them all, Marlon Brando was the least known. Any reputation he had was mainly based on him being difficult. The play was too new for critical opinion to have gotten its teeth into it. All I knew was that it was set in New Orleans and was 'a powerful family drama'.

Unfettered by fanfare, unhampered by preconceived notions, that night in Boston I was free to experience the full impact of the play as its perfect production unfolded itself into a masterpiece before my eyes.

On the stage there was, for me, no playwright. There were no actors, but real people, who moved not at a director's command but of their own volition. Its atmosphere, which a critic would later describe as 'tenderness and brutality woven into a single strand of panic and doom', overflowed the stage and engulfed me. At the same time that I was following the action, I was exploring my own life and its tremors. In the perfection of its creation I fused with Blanche Du Bois; all her infirmities and debilities became my own. I was going through the same desperate actions as she was, and as each escape hatch was blocked for her, it was blocked for me. There is hardly a sentence Blanche utters that does not contain, along with a yearning for life as it should be, the frightened awareness of life as it is, lifting the play from a mere recitation of the pitiful adventures of its heroine to a universal level. I was in a cold sweat at its end.

Immediately after seeing *Streetcar*, still under its inspiration, I turned up at an audition at the Cherry Lane Theatre in Greenwich Village. I read for a part, and got it then and there. It was my first acting job in New York.

The play was Garcia Lorca's *Yerma*, and the title role was played by Bea Arthur, who, even in those days, was a striking presence, possessed of a voice that resonated like a bowling ball rolling down the alley, climaxing with great crashes of emotion as the pins were sent flying. I played Maria, Yerma's young friend, and appeared in a scene holding a small heap of blankets representing my baby, which Yerma tried to snatch away from me, so badly did she want her own child, for she was barren. The production also had songs, a fertility dance and a tragic ending.

Bea's pre-curtain prep for the tragic, barren Yerma consisted of sitting in her dressing room singing selections from Pearl Bailey's repertoire in a thrilling blues voice that easily penetrated the walls and filled the empty theatre . When the play started she would truck on down backstage, wait for her cue and make her entrance.

It was Bea who suggested I look into the Dramatic Workshop Repertory Theatre. Actors with experience could apply and if they passed the audition would be accepted. It was, she said, sort of like being a graduate student or a semi-pro. You were eligible for roles alongside Equity actors in tryouts of new Workshop plays and you had big parts in student productions. It was an excellent showcase. It would be a good move for me.

Early in the new year of '48 I handed in my photos and a substantial list of unsubstantiated credits. I auditioned and I got in. Looking around me I was thrilled by what I saw and the prospect of being part of it.

The Dramatic Workshop was a great big thriving adjunct of the New School of Social Research, with lots of staff and management. And lots of teachers. And lots of first-rate European directors, and lots of students, and lots of classes. It had a playwrights' unit and a directors' unit. We were to become familiar with classics of different countries as well as those of American and English playwrights.

It was run by Erwin Piscator, an illustrious man of the theatre; a refugee from Nazi Germany, who was responsible for its spirit, soul and European flavor. Silver-haired, dapper, a polo coat thrown casually over his shoulders and a Cadillac in attendance for his arrivals and departures, he was very much the impresario, grand in manner and flamboyant of speech. Good, bad or indifferent, no acting student ever left the school without being able to do a creditable imitation of his Mittel European accent.

The Workshop operated two theatres: a large one with an apron stage, downtown on Houston Street in the Bowery, and a neat little theatre uptown, in the Broadway theatre district.

Most importantly, the school was accredited by the GI Bill of Rights, which meant that veterans of the Second World War who wanted to be actors, playwrights and directors could attend for free. This meant it now had a large number of students drawn from the lower-income brackets, who brought a much needed infusion of 'proletarian' blood to the profession, which had hitherto been the province of the middle class. Some of these students from impoverished backgrounds would purchase a vastly larger block of fame than fifteen minutes. They would in fact change the dynamics of both stage and film.

At the beginning of the term, students of the Dramatic Workshop gathered for the school's official opening assembly, held in the Houston Street Theatre. I arrived via the Third Avenue El. The Bowery was a part of New York I had never seen before, and for the first time I saw Bowery bums asleep on the El stairways, under the El and in doorways. Whether sleeping or inertly propped up against a wall, next to them there was always a torn brown paper bag that contained empty bottles. I was surprised to see how small and pathetic and vulnerable they looked. They were not the red-faced dangerous bullies of my imagination but small men, aged children, too frail to cope with life without solace.

When I arrived and went up the flight of stairs to the auditorium it was already filled with students. The atmosphere was breezy and noisy. Yells broke out here and there, along with yelps of laughter. Everyone took a good look at everyone else and talked to their neighbors. No one seemed to pay much attention to what we were being told by the speakers on the platform. In the sea of faces I noted one whose looks were so outstanding that when the meeting was over and we all filed out doing our getting-to-know-you shuffle I found myself searching for him. I passed through a door leading to the street and there he was, already surrounded by a group.

A rosy complexion set off a tousled head of lustrous black curls and sparkling blue eyes. His whole flawless being was animated, impish and irresistible. He was talking. I listened. And could not believe my ears. His looks set him up on Parnassus, but his voice landed him back in the Bronx. From out of the rose-petal mouth and the perfect pearly teeth came that special harsh noise that the Bronx calls speech. It is not exactly shouting, but it is penetrating enough to pierce through the city noises that drill into New York's nerves all day long.

He was Bernie Schwartz, who would become the famous Hollywood star Tony Curtis. 'I have trouble with my S's,' he was saying. 'I'm told I *aspirate my S's*,' he added, sending his S's aspirating down the street. We all laughed. He laughed. He was a natural.

Besides Tony Curtis there were two other naturals among the students when I was at the Workshop. They were Rod Steiger and Harry Belafonte.

My first memory of Rod Steiger is of us sitting in the auditorium of the Houston Street Theatre watching rehearsals. We were both in *Princess Turandot*. I played the villainous Zerlina and he was one of the *commedia dell'arte* clowns. As he sat in front of me talking to a friend, I heard him say: 'So he turns to me and says, "Who the hell are you?" and I say "Who the hell are *you*? *That's* who the hell I am."' Whimsical, I thought. And later I heard him admonishing a pal with: 'Don't dig me with that downbeat conversation.'

Then I watched him on stage. The *commedia dell'arte* clowns had been told to invent their own comic turns, and Rod decided to come on with a vacuum cleaner as a prop. When he plugged it in, though, it fused all the lights, plunging stage and auditorium into darkness, resulting in chaos and consternation. Everyone was stumbling around in the dark, things reaching near-panic before a flashlight was produced and the lights went back on. Everyone was pissed off at Rod, but he was unrepentant. In fact, he was delighted. 'Look at the chance we got to watch people caught off guard. That's what acting's all about, isn't it?'

Harry Belafonte and I did a staged reading together. It was one of the plays on the black and white theme that were beginning to be written at the time. He was the young black man and I the young white girl and we were passionately in love. I remember only the experience of Harry and that he wore a Harris tweed overcoat. We sat next to each other and I kept losing my place because I kept staring at his incredible beauty, at the harmony of his features.

Harry was very popular among the students. If there ever was a

Serene Highness, it was Belafonte. He had that indefinable something. Even before his calypso songs became the rage, he was everyone's favorite. Everyone's eyes lit up, everyone smiled when they saw him; everyone was always looking up to him, wanting to work with him, seeking his advice. All the girls dreamed romantically of him.

One of the most talented directors at the Workshop was Alexis Solomos, an attractive young Greek director with a confident man-of-the world air and determined elfin features. Attached to the school by one of those bountiful theatre grants that abounded after the war, he was directing a new play chosen from the playwrights' unit. He cast me as a sophisticated wife on the verge of divorce, then one day after rehearsal took me aside and said I was not right for the part. I stormed out. Late that evening, furious and having gotten his address, I went there to have it out with him. He'd wanted an extrovert for the role, he said, which he'd thought I was, but then saw that my true nature was that of an introvert, which worked against the part. I said I was an ambivert; sometimes I was an introvert and sometimes an extrovert and he should have told me what he wanted. Would he give me another chance? He agreed.

One thing led to another and we ended up in bed. And our affair began. One day, while walking in Central Park, I decided it was over. I liked him a lot – he was very talented – but I didn't love him, so I broke it off. We parted friends. At the end of the term he went back to Greece and I was not to see him till fourteen years later.

I spent about a year at the Workshop and its summer theatre in Falmouth. I played a number of good parts: Emily in *Our Town*, Viola in *Twelfth Night*, the Red Queen in *Alice* and Lavinia in *Androcles and the Lion* were the ones I enjoyed the most. All were stable productions with rotating casts.

At the beginning of 1949 I left the Dramatic Workshop and was doing the rounds, looking for paying jobs as an actress. I showed up for open casting calls, and sat in reception rooms of casting offices filled with pretty young actresses. Everyone seemed to be just as good-looking and talented as I was, if not more so. I noted how bravely they went in to see the casting director and how quickly they came out. Not right for the part, went the curt dismissal. Nor was I.

I did a play at Lucille Lortel's White Barn, which, except for me, had an English cast and for which I don't remember being paid. I also did some radio work, which paid, but not much. Neither did the television commercials I appeared in. I worked as a super in several operas at the City Center, which paid even less. I played the maid Don Giovanni sings '*Deh, vieni alla finestra*' to. In *Der Rosenkavalier* I played the barber's assistant in the first act and later the pageboy who lights up all the candelabra in the Baron Ochs scene. I got crabs from the knee britches of the costume I had to wear.

In other words I was going nowhere fast. And living, or rather staying, at 1185 was getting me down. I'd been there for almost two years hoping after hope I'd somehow land paying acting jobs that would enable me to move out. I now saw it wasn't going to happen that way.

One day I told my mother I had begun to look for a place to live.

'I'll ask Daddy about it,' she said.

'No,' I shouted 'You will *tell* him about it!'

A couple of days later she came to my room to say she had spoken with Daddy, who said if I lived in New York I must live at home.

I found myself sinking into that old familiar terrain of terror. I was still afraid of this short, bald yet not physically powerful man who had terrorized a houseful of women with his towering rages.

I could feel the bile rising in my throat. I swallowed hard and spoke over it. 'How can he stop me?' We both knew the answer: by stopping my allowance. I said that I was determined to be an actress, which meant staying in New York, but she had to know I couldn't keep living in this atmosphere; for God's sake I was well into my twenties. 'Why are you letting him do this?' I said. '*What is the matter with you?*'

She was silent. Then she said, 'Shall I divorce him?'

I exploded. 'Oh no! You don't mean that any more than you did when I was a kid. I don't care what the hell you do. It's too late now.' And I walked out of my room and left her there.

Then like all good Americans I began thinking of Paris.

Someone had told me that Mary James, the actress who had played *Peer Gynt* at Sweet Briar, was in Paris, where she was one of the founders of The American Club Theatre. I wrote and said I was thinking of coming over and asked her about the opportunities for an American actress finding work.

While waiting for her reply a wave of sanity swept over me. Should my father object to Paris, I saw that I didn't need his money. I could borrow enough to get there and stick around till I could support myself. I found out that jobs were certainly available in Paris for an American girl who'd done war work in Washington. It was the center of all European aid and relief agencies where my very correct governess French would be a plus for liaison posts.

In the midst of following up job leads came the letter from Mary James. A born enthusiast, she replied positively. Yes, there were lots of opportunities for American actors in Paris – any number of American film companies were using their frozen assets to produce movies in co-operation with European companies. There was also radio work. The American Club Theatre was run by the famous Czech actor George Voskovic and his then wife Anne Gillette, and was receiving excellent reviews and good audiences for the plays they produced. A large American population occupying Paris was waiting to be tapped. So come on over, the water's fine, she concluded.

I showed the letter to Mother, who passed it to my father and relayed back to me his consent to my going to Paris. I went to Rockefeller Center and got my first passport. A monthly allowance would be worked out, subject to my expenses, plus I had my insurance policies that had come due. American Express travelers' checks had been bought, and a letter of introduction to a Paris branch of an American bank was among my papers. A Cabin Class ticket had been purchased for a November sailing on the *Ile de France*, and a reservation had been made for me at the Oxford and Cambridge Hotel in Paris. My new steamer trunk had arrived and was ready to be packed.

The scene of my final encounter with my father was played out in our living room, a morgue of antique furniture, oriental carpets and tapestries. We sat there, my mother and father and I, in the same corner where, as children, we would sit by the radio to listen to Jack Benny. On the corner table was a large baroque lamp in the shape of a huge marble turtle on which sat the god Poseidon, holding aloft a torch

from which an electric light bulb shed its light in a milky glass orna-
ment shaped like a flame.

There was really no need for the meeting; all had been settled. But
my father had to have his innings, had to lay down the law over and
over to me. That was his form. I arranged my features in what I determined to be both pleasant and cooperative. I said nothing, but nodded
my head at intervals to indicate I would be following his instructions.

Several times he repeated his warning that in the future I could
only live away from home if I lived outside of New York. In New York
I was to live with my parents. I repeated the word Paris in my head to
block him out. And then suddenly I heard something I had not heard
before. The reason that he insisted I live at home when in New York
was that if his friends at the country club found out that I was not
living at home they would think that he and I didn't get along
together.

What a confession! How ruthless the lengths to sacrifice my freedom at the altar of his respectability. The session was winding to a
close.

I wondered if I should get up and leave or wait for him to leave first.
The dilemma was solved. The telephone rang in another room and the
maid came in and said it was for me. I excused myself and left.

At long last the time came to leave. I remember it as a solitary act. No
family goodbyes. I closed the front door and looked at it hard for a
moment and my spirits rose. As the taxi left Park Avenue and headed
for the Battery, where the *Ile de France* was waiting for me, I glanced at
the red-brick gothic facade of 1185 Park Avenue. I leaned back in the
cab and promised myself I would never set foot in it again.

10

Paris

Like the break that divides Act I from Act II in the theatre, crossing the ocean was the break that divided Part I of my life from Part II.

After a week and a half in Paris, with that surge of verve that always hits me when I change towns, I also changed hotels. The one I'd been booked into was on the Right Bank, therefore the wrong one. Crossing the Seine to the Left Bank I found the Hotel Lutece, on Rue Jules Chaplain close to the Boulevard Montparnasse, so I was now living among the artists. My room was a pleasant one, hung with maroon velvet everywhere, looking like a bed-sit rather than a bedroom. It cost two dollars a day and I figured on spending another three each day on food. Which came to five dollars a day or 140 dollars a month, as I carefully spelled out to my parents.

Throughout my letters home I treated my parents to itemized expenses translated into dollars. I had become a fanatic account-keeper, describing every cent of my expenditure, making sure they were aware of my economies. My father was footing my bills by shelling out a not very large but adequate monthly income, which would be sent to a Paris branch of a New York bank. Anything extra

I would have to ask him for. I didn't want to. Putting the best construction on both our motives, he may have been sincere in doing
what he thought was best for me by not giving me too much money,
just as nit-picking my expenses was my way of showing him I was
capable of running my life. Then too, practicing frugality was my way
of preparing myself for the hoped-for day when I would be living solely
on my earnings as an actress.

Soon caught up in the beauty of Paris, I walked and walked everywhere. One day I started strolling down the Champs Elysées. I was
dismayed at the way it looked. Grim. Dark. Uninteresting. Few shops
and cafés. Fewer people. The ravages of war, I philosophized, are deep
and not soon mended. It was only a few years since Paris had been liberated from the Nazi Occupation. I thought of the films made during
the Occupation, and how, as silent proof of the Spartan conditions
under which the actors worked in unheated studios, you saw on the
screen their frozen breath, coming out of their mouths like puffs of
smoke as they whispered endearments to each other in intimate love
scenes. Abruptly my philosophical thoughts were interrupted by a
street sign indicating I was not on the Champs Elysées. I was on something called the Avenue d'Iena. So I retraced my footsteps back to
Étoile, took the correct turning and all at once I found myself gazing
down that enchanted boulevard in the blue, blue evening. Here was
all the gaiety, glory and sparkle I knew was going to be life if I could
just grasp it. I began floating down those Elysian Fields three inches off
the ground as easily as a Cocteau character floats through Hell. Luxury
and order seemed to be shining from every street lamp along the
Boulevard, shining from every window of its toy-shops and dress-shops,
its cafés and cinemas and theatres; from its bonbonneries and par-
fumeries and nighteries. Talk about seeing Eternity in a Grain of Sand
and Heaven in a Wild Flower, I really think I was having some sort of
mystic revelation. (I would not write these words until years later
when they seemed to pour out of me as if in a single exclamation.)

On my walks I began to feel surrounded by that famous Parisian
stare, a particular way both men and women had of looking at you –
not carnally exactly, more like *intensely*, as if memorizing you for some
question they would be asked on an upcoming exam. It made you feel

you were worth studying, and this became reflected in the way I wore my clothes.

Parisian haute couture was beyond my means and the clothes in the strange French department stores were simply awful. But my own clothes, those I had worn in New York, looked new to me because no one in Paris had seen them before. In fact they looked even better than new because of the Parisian stare. Post-war American fashions had hit a high point. How becoming, how reasonably priced, how easy to wear were young women's clothes from stores such as Bergdorf's, Bendel's, Bonwits and Lord and Taylor. To my glee I had arrived at Parisian chic by being clad from inside out in nothing but American clothes. Even my French friends admired them.

In my letters home I relived the early days of the Nylon Revolution. America worshipped all things nylon, beginning with the stockings. David Brinkley in *Washington Goes to War* tells of a general's wife who 'nursed just five nylon stockings, two and a half pairs, through the entire war'. 'Do you know,' she said to him, 'in army circles on VJ Day there was more talk about nylons than anything else.' Smooth, sheer, flesh-colored, unrippable, unsnaggable, they promised to be everlasting. But this wouldn't do profitwise, and over the years they would be manufactured to be almost as fragile as the silk stockings of yore.

This magic material washed easily, dried instantly, didn't need ironing. Well, it looked better if you did, but you could get away without. Slowly we discovered that nylon was non-porous, and at the end of the day your shirts and blouses felt as if you were wearing rubber. Sticky, they made you perspire, made the material stick to your body. The smell was a weird mixture of your own perspiration and the nylon's chemical scent. If you smoked – and everyone did – little holes suddenly appeared in shirts and skirts and nightgowns, caused by even the tiniest fleck of a cigarette ash. It was highly flammable, but otherwise tough and enduring.

Living in Montparnasse, I discovered two famous cafés: the Dome and the Select. It was in them that I encountered the amazing young men on the GI Bill of Rights, who came there at *l'heure bleu* of the evening – actually at *l'heure* anything round the clock. They were attending the Sorbonne's famous Cours de Civilisation – when they could spare the time.

I say the young men were amazing because they'd fought a long hard war and never talked about it. They were just giddy at being alive. That year they were being budding artists, poets, writers and scholars, chasing after every kind of artistic pursuit, glorying in it and being very funny about it.

Generally the group would be sitting at a table headed by C.F. MacIntyre, a scrawny aging poet and translator of well-respected reputation. Mac, as we called him, was a ribald man with a foul mouth and a certain amount of charisma, who wore an old blue sweat shirt and a beret, and drove a little red MG. Whenever the group saw it parked in front of either café, that was where they went. The group instinctively deferred to him and soaked up his snarling opinions.

I also got to know the Fulbrights, whom I described thus in a letter: 'Senator Fulbright has thought up a kind of glorified GI Bill for particularly gifted students – arts, theatre, international relations, the works.' Here again I was compulsively driven to add, 'And the government pays for their transportation both ways plus $150 month – not bad, eh?'

Also in those early days I went to Maxim's (thumbs down – too expensive, too showy). And 'I have been taken to many nightclubs, all of which impressed me very favorably, all very nice-looking and good American bands.' And so I should have been 'impressed'. These clubs not only featured jazz greats such as Sidney Bechet but also sensational French singers such as Juliette Greco and Leo Ferry. A popular cabaret in St Germain featured the gay black American actor and singer Gordon Heath with his white partner, Lee Payant, folk singers in French and English. They came to Paris – as had the black jazz artists – for some of that *liberté, egalité* and *fraternité* they never got in America.

In that period I also found time to start taking a course at the Alliance Française to brush up my French, but I left after a couple of weeks. Didn't need it. I was doing fine.

Betty and Boris were at that time on their year-long *Wanderjahr* in Europe. They arrived in Paris and rented a little house always filled with young men that Boris had gone to school with in Switzerland.

Boris knew the city like the back of his hand and was extremely helpful.

I saw Jean-Louis Barrault's fascinating controversial *Hamlet* at the Marigny. The elfin mime went nuts well before most Hamlets, with lots of crazed body language both during and after the ghost scene, unsettling the audience with early proof of the Prince of Denmark's instability. I also saw the French version of my beloved *Streetcar*. The French critics loathed it. One of them pronounced it squalid, foul and fetid, and remarked how grateful he was to enter into the fresh night air upon leaving the theatre. I went to see it and was *outraged*. How dare they do this to my *Streetcar*? I got off an angry letter to the *New York Times* to set the record straight. As I remember I described the horrendous production with French star Arletty playing Blanche as a tough, shrill virago, more Madame than Miss. I described a scrim on the back wall of the set that lit up from time to time to show us sweating black voodoo dancers beating jungle drums and writhing orgiastically in case you missed the point that something pretty wild and sexy was going on.

I was thrilled when the then staid, austere organ printed my letter in its theatre section. It was my first appearance in print in a newspaper – or anywhere in public for that matter – and I felt I had started at the top.

One day I got arrested. Or, as I put it in a letter in the Franglais I was beginning to write and talk, 'J'avais été arrêtée dans le métro parce que I was traveling first class on a second-class ticket. But when I showed up at the Police Station they thought I spoke French so well that instead of fining me 350 francs they let me go.'

This letter also said: 'I have met an awfully nice girl from California, Judy Sheftel.' One day early in December, I was sitting at the Select at around noon and as it was my first meal of the day I was having breakfast. At the next table was a young American girl, attractive, smiling, auburn hair, faint freckles, hazel eyes. I was reading an American magazine so she knew my nationality. We struck up a conversation and she told me her name was Judy Sheftel and she was with Nate Polewetsky, a young man with a stoic heroic stance and a growly voice, as befitted an American journalist working for the AP wire service who had just been kicked out of Prague by the communist takeover in Czechoslovakia.

Judy was about nineteen. I revealed that I was an actress and she told me she was in Paris to chaperone her brother Paul, aged fifteen, while he pursued his musical studies.

I found Judy's personality interesting – now dreamily idealistic, now bright, focused and committed to . . . what? She was seriously looking for a career, I saw that. What increased my interest in her was not only her conversational style – free-flowing, free-associating, subterranean subtexts rising to the surface – but its content. Her views on the overflowing Parisian cornucopia of works of art, past and present, were informed, sound, enthusiastic. And I also heard the note, the tune of something in her voice that said she utterly cared about such things. It was something we shared. The arts took up a great deal of emotional space in our lives. We held violent opinions about what we loved and hated in what we read, saw and heard.

So it was very wonderful when we discovered we were both staying at the Lutece. By the time we had finished eating and talking and made plans to meet again I realized I'd made a new friend. This instant friendship came as a relief as well as an enjoyment, a source of comfort. The feeling was light-hearted, like those periods of carefree gaiety my sisters and I shared as children. Judy (known as Judy Feiffer after her marriage to cartoonist Jules Feiffer) went on to work as a film producer in Los Angeles and in publishing in New York, and has written several novels. Although circumstances took us in different directions, we became friends for life.

One afternoon Judy and I were sitting in Bob Breer's room at the Grande Chaumière, a popular student-filled *pension* in Montparnasse. Bob was a young painter and we were admiring his work when the door opened and a spectacular-looking young girl whom I'd never seen before came in. She was a South Sea Island beauty, a *café au lait* Gauguin maid, breathtakingly luscious. Tessa Prendegast was in fact Jamaican, the stepdaughter of Noel Nethersole, a former minister of finance and deputy prime minister in Jamaica.

Tessa had a soft low voice and a soft gurgling laugh. She had long brown hair, a sweet heart-shaped face and soft brown eyes; one had a slight cast that somehow made them more fascinating. Her breasts were large, her waist tiny, her hips curvy, her legs long and slender. She was dressed casually in a skirt and sweater, and she was carrying a red ball of Edam cheese, a present she'd just brought back from Amsterdam for a mutual friend. The juxtaposition of the Gauguin maid in a sweater and skirt was striking, but the Dutch cheese in her hands, instead of a tropical fruit or flower, rendered the image unforgettable.

Tessa and Judy and Bob never became other than casual acquaintances of each other, but Tessa and I would also become lifelong friends. And soon, for a while, Bob and I would become lovers.

As time went on Tessa would discard the skirt and sweater in favor of outfits more original and striking, more often than not in various shades of her favorite color, green. One evening we were sitting at a bar while waiting for a table in a restaurant and her time was spent with warding off male comers. 'Well, Tessa,' I snapped, no doubt annoyed that it wasn't happening to me, 'if you do get yourself up like this, of course they think you're signaling to them.' 'Look,' she said, 'they're going to stare at me anyway, so I've decided to give them something to stare at.'

One day Tessa came to me seeking advice. Should she or shouldn't go to bed with her boyfriend? She knew I had affairs and was therefore the voice of experience. We had a long, long talk sifting the evidence while she speculated on all the consequences of this daring act. In the end it came down to whether she wanted to. She said yes. I said then do it. I wonder if I gave her the same advice my sister Shirley had given me: get a diaphragm and don't think you have to marry him. I hope I did.

Later I was to be around for Tessa's emotionally packed involvement with Ken Adam, the great film and opera art director; the infamous Stephen Ward of the Profumo scandal, whom she had sense enough to leave before the liaison became dangerous; the *dolce vita* Italian aristocrat Prince Vittorio Massimo; and – the longest and most serious relationship – Gareth Browne, son of Lord Oranmore and Browne and the former Oona Guinness.

*

In letters home I gave detailed accounts of my brilliant career. Faithfully I recorded each part I got on stage, each audition I went to, each film I was in, my work on radio and in dubbing. With dubbing I had found a way to make some money. A number of French films were being dubbed in English and it paid better than all other acting jobs I'd found. To my surprise I loved it, and looked upon it as a new skill.

In retrospect I look at my list of jobs with a certain dismay. A high point: playing the role of Maria, Julie's best friend for the America Center Stage production of *Liliom*. It was well reviewed in the Paris *Herald Tribune* and some of the more intellectual French newspapers, and got a total rave review in a New York Hungarian newspaper that Ferenc Molnar himself sent to the director Herbert Machiz. I was flabbergasted by the review, and that Molnar was still alive. Another high point for me: dubbing the leading lady played by a beautiful French actress Madelene Robinson in a film called *Dr Louise*. As she was in almost every frame I worked ten days, making 6,500 francs a day – a fortune. Then there was an acting role in a double version film of *The Wallflower* starring Joan Greenwood and the French comedian Bourvil. It was a small part but everyone concerned was 'very excited because I photograph so well and the director who calls me "la petite biche" (which means the little doe and not what I thought at first) is VERY interested in me as a new personality'.

My brilliant career was anything but brilliant, but curiously I didn't see it that way. As I was listing my credits in these letters to show my parents how well I was doing, I must have been optimistic. I think I had the proper psychological profile for an actress, possessing pluck, persistence, a perhaps unrealistic assessment of my talent and a keen belief that I could be a star if only I got the right part. Above all I had the ability to kid myself that I was getting somewhere. I did a lot of radio work in Paris as Europe was filled to bursting with American army bases and United Nations relief personnel, and this was a bolster to my ego, giving me the impression that I could keep above water until the big break came. Then there was the fun of being an actress, which really meant something that year in Paris. Eyes lit up if you identified yourself as such at cocktail parties.

One letter home very definitely needs the chemical powder to bring up the invisible ink. *Dr Louise* is followed by *Liliom* plus a certain amount of radio work, but there is something else, a change in the weather. The February thaw: 'And spring has come to Paris. All the sidewalk cafés are open and everything is going so well I'm happy, happy as a lark.' I signed the letter with my special musical-staff-and-notes signature, adding a doodle of a flower and a blithe 'Bye, bye'. No one can be entirely happy in Paris without being in love: Bob Breer and I had become lovers. That it turned out not to be the real thing for either of us hardly hurt. In Paris you got over liaisons in record time.

While working as an interne at *Jardin des Modes* Judy took me to a Schiaparelli sale and pointed to a silk dress and said, 'Buy it.' So I did. I put it on and knew instantly it was for me. It was worth writing home about, and even worth sketching in the letter – twice in fact, with and without its small jacket. 'Whole dress is orange background with brown stripes, one shoulder bare. I look like a tiger. Heavens. Stops people cold. Wore it to a party given by a contessa and knocked 'em dead. Only trouble – I can't walk in it.'

Not long after I bought the dress I was walking down the Boulevard Raspail with the photographer Ricco Zermano. We passed a hairdresser's shop and he suddenly stopped in front of it and said, 'I'm tired of hearing you say that you're going to change the color of your hair. Let's go in here and do it.' In we went. I wanted to be blonde but the hairdresser had an idea of his own, taking my thick mass of dark curls and turning them into a mass of beautiful autumn leaves. Highlights of golden blonde and different shades of brown were mixed together and shaped by a glorious cut giving my curls a wonderful sculptured look. I was thrilled, and so was Ricco, who pointed out that there was a photographer next door. 'Get your picture taken right now, so you can show it to other hairdressers when you need to.' I did, and the shop put my photo in the window.

In the middle of July I was sitting with friends at Fouquets, a landmark café on the Champs Elysées. I was pleased with myself: I was wearing my Schiaparelli original. And my new Parisian coiffeur was an original. And I, myself, was an original.

Before I'd left my hotel that day I'd taken a long look in the mirror.

I'd finally got it right. This was the way I was supposed to look. The changes I'd made on my outside, the new hair color and my new dress, were changing me on my inside, giving me an entirely new cosmopolitan sense of self. For a moment I had a mad desire to rush back to the Schiaparelli sale and buy up the remainder of the dresses but my Spartan mode forbade it. I wore the dress whenever I could. Sometimes it felt as if it was on me whether I wore it or not.

At Fouquets I felt a sudden urge. There was something I must do. I left my friends and, walking slowly, I began to cross the wide expanse of the Champs Elysées' traffic-filled boulevard. I was remembering myself on my eighth birthday trying to cross another wide street in New Jersey and being hit by a car, so it was important that I walked slowly, slowly into the middle of the traffic (the dress did not permit long strides anyway). The traffic coming towards me slowed down. It stopped! Safely I walked at my own pace from one side of the boulevard to the other.

PART TWO

BEING DISCOVERED

11

A Cable From London

At the beginning of July I flew to London for the first time. I had been trying to get there but whenever I was ready, job possibilities or the sidewalk cafés in the sun or the possibility of being in love would stop me. Although London was only an hour away, I couldn't leave Paris. It is not easily parted from.

In July, however, theatrical and film activity had slowed to a standstill. Soon Paris would be empty: *la grande fermeture*. Some American actresses in Paris who had gone to various British drama schools such as RADA and the Old Vic had established ties in London and flew back and forth all the time, so I joined one on a five-day trip. I saw three plays, including T.S. Eliot's *The Cocktail Party* with Rex Harrison, which caused me to fly into a rage. I couldn't understand what the fuss was about. I concluded the critics had been cowered by the Eliot name.

During that trip I saw something else that did impress me though: Wendy Hiller on the same bus I was taking into the West End, just matter-of-factly sitting there. As a schoolgirl I had worshipped this star in such films as Shaw's *Pygmalion* and *Major Barbara*. Later I went gaga over her again in *I Know Where I'm Going*. And there she was, two rows in front of me, just across the aisle, a worker among workers, an artist among artists. It is impossible to describe the appeal this sight held for me and what it said (and still says to me) about English actors and their down-to-earth approach to their profession. No wonder they not only last forever but work happily ever after.

I went to London in August, planning to stay a week, and had such a good time and met so many wonderful people that I stayed for three and a half weeks. I also did some job-hunting and was actually encouraged! I faced the inevitable: there was certainly more work in a country where everyone speaks English than in France. I thought about moving over there for a while.

Many good times and wonderful encounters stemmed from meeting up again with Hazel Vincent Wallace and Peter Martyn, two English actors whom I had befriended when we appeared together in the English play in the White Barn in New York. It was a great reunion. Peter was an ex-boyfriend, attractive and charming and with a decidedly upper-class air about him. In New York he used to regale me with what turned out to be U and Non-U class distinctions, revealed by giveaway code words that separated the gentry from the 'not quite'. NQOC he called it – Not Quite Our Class. The first name Norman was NQOC, as was calling table napkins 'serviettes'. He'd acted a bit on Broadway but returned to England having decided his future lay there. Tragically, his future would be short. Making a name for himself not as an actor but as one of the more glamorous up-and-coming TV news broadcasters, he died of cancer within three years.

Hazel Vincent Wallace was a clear-eyed, level-headed, well-organized Brit. She was a good actress, but her real value lay in being a dedicated theatre person. Together with another actor, Oscar Quitak, they ran an excellent repertory theatre in Leatherhead and were founders of a significant theatrical club called the Buckstone.

This basement club, located in Suffolk Street, opposite the stage door of the Haymarket Theatre in the heart of the theatre district, had only been going for a year but it was already a great success. There was no sign outside so you could easily pass by and miss the most popular after-hours theatrical club in London. Not grand like the Ivy or the Caprice, where you were on show, it was a working actors' meeting place where you could unbend. Many well-known or, more excitingly, about to be well-known theatre people, such as young Richard Burton and young Peter Finch, hung out there. Run by a cheerful plump actor named Gerry Campion, its members ate cheaply but well enough and drank equally cheaply a lethal cider of high alcoholic content that tasted like steel shavings and exploded into the nervous system like dynamite. It also functioned as a pipeline through which flowed the freshest, straightest and latest theatrical news. As it stayed open late, by closing time things were apt to get a bit rowdy. I can still hear Gerry's voice ringing out nightly, 'No Dougie! You *cannot* have another brandy.' Through Hazel, Peter and I became members and went there often.

I found myself back-and-forthing from Paris to London, and by September I'd half moved in with Hazel in her flat in Dorset Square (half my clothes in Paris, half in London). I did lots of radio audition-ing, triumphantly landing a part in Stephen Vincent Benet's poem, *John Brown's Body* on BBC Radio.

I first set eyes on him in the Buckstone.

He was holding court in a booth. That alone made it an incredible sight. Dozens of people kept squeezing in, some climbing in, some climbing out, some hanging over its edge. Peter Martyn with whom I was lunching, said, 'That's Ken Tynan. I think you should meet him. I don't know if it'll do you any good but it may. Let's go over.' And, steering me skillfully through the wall of human flesh three deep around the booth, he introduced me to the young lion, mentioning that I was an American actress. 'Sit down,' said Ken by way of acknowledging the introduction. Someone obligingly gave up his small portion of space and I squeezed in while Peter joined the stand-ing room. I found myself looking at a thin young man holding a cigarette between his third and fourth fingers and stammering out bon mots to his mesmerized audience.

He wore a double-breasted camel's hair jacket, plum-colored trousers, yellow socks and black shoes and a Mickey Mouse wrist-watch. His long legs projected sideways from the booth, and his stammer was so violent it distorted his features so I could get no clear impression of them. After five minutes of reflected glory Peter and I were off.

'Who is he?' I asked. Peter explained that Ken, not long down from Oxford, where he had already made a name for himself as a wonderboy as critic, director and actor, had just published a book of theatrical criticisms called *He That Play the King*. It was causing a sensation. Peter hadn't read it but apparently the young critic was outrageously rude, tearing into everyone and everything in the English theatre. Well, I thought, that's one book I won't have to read. Small literary magazines in New York were full of aspiring drama critics clamoring for attention by vilifying the 'commercial' (hold nose) theatre. They were one of my pet peeves. They didn't have to write well, just offensively. Lumping Ken in with them, I dismissed him from my mind, until someone happened to bring his name up again.

On November 29 I did my role at the BBC in *John Brown's Body*. I was Lucy Weatherby, a Southern Belle from hell, egging on her beaux to fight and die for the cause and not to quit until no one was left standing. Immediately afterwards, I picked up a discarded copy of *The Stage*, the actors' trade paper, and read that Peter Ustinov was looking for an American actress for his forthcoming play *The Love of Four Colonels*. I called Mr Ustinov and spoke my piece about being an American actress from Paris and he agreed to see me that afternoon. The address turned out to be his house on the King's Road. On opening his front door, he looked at me, shook his head and said, 'Oh no, you're too young. I'm looking for an American *matron*.' But he invited me in and I followed him into a large, high bohemian studio with a wood fire blazing in the fireplace. He said the house had once belonged to Ellen Terry. Then came tea and conversation. He had just finished playing in the film *Quo Vadis* in Rome and I sat enthralled while this supreme raconteur treated me to uproarious stories about the film unit, with him portraying each member of the international cast of characters with his faultless mimicry. He asked me what I'd seen in London, and I told him what I liked and didn't like. We talked some more, logs blazing, theatre opinions blazing. I left his house filled with the desire to see him again. But how? During our conversation he mentioned only one person I had ever met, Ken Tynan. He knew him and said how much he had liked his book, so I decided to read it. Immediately.

About a week later I was dining with a non-theatrical friend at the Buckstone when Ken came in. As he passed by my table I sprang to my feet and said, 'I read your book and I love it.' 'Have lunch with me tomorrow,' he replied, and I said yes. What had happened in that short space of time to turn me 180 degrees around? For one thing I had read his book. 'Who is he?' asked my friend. I said, 'Part of a plot.'

Next morning I phoned Peter Martyn to brag that I was lunching with Ken. 'Watch out when you get to the salad course,' he said. 'I once saw Ken eating with a girl and as she started her salad he was apparently seized with a fit of passion and began kissing her. Salad flew out of her mouth and all over both of them.'

I arrived at the Buckstone wearing a black sweater with a small embroidered gold emblem set off by a white Peter Pan collar. A gray skirt. Black velvet pumps. Gray fur coat. Knitted green hat stuffed in pocket of coat in case of rain. Ken was waiting for me. I talked a lot about his book. I was lavish in my praise. And this was utterly genuine. My life as far back as I remember took this direction: telling talented people specifically what I liked about their work. And because I meant it, I was, perhaps, good at it.

Orson Welles had written the preface for Ken's book, announcing that he was doing it because Ken had materialized out of a puff of Paris fog, handed him his manuscript and somehow 'bamboozled me into reading it and writing this'. The result was riveting. At one point Welles congratulated Ken for his 'capacity for violent opinion, for knowing how to cheer and not being afraid to hiss' and for being 'transparently in love with the theatre'.

I found Ken's passion for the theatre impressive, but so was his knowledge of stagecraft. What other critic discussed the lighting plot, noting that it was in blues and ambers instead of the conventional pinks and golds, showing you its effect on the mood of the play? He wrote from the inside of a theatrical experience as if he inhabited all the parts that made up the sum, simultaneously wildly funny and mind-bogglingly erudite. We talked of Danny Kaye, about whom he had written at great length, giving him the same attention he bestowed on Laurence Olivier, Ralph Richardson, John Gielgud or, for that matter, Shakespeare, Marlowe, Jonson, Webster and the rest of the Elizabethan gang.

Lunch proceeded pleasantly. We exchanged the necessary superficialities, and the salad course passed without incident. Suddenly he looked at his Mickey Mouse wristwatch and said he would have to leave immediately to see a double bill of *It's a Gift* with W.C. Fields and *A Day at the Races* with the Marx Brothers, which he was reviewing for some magazine. I felt a touch of frustration. This is it? I wondered. This is all? As I started to gather up my things and thank him for lunch, though, he invited me to come along with him.

We sat in the balcony of the Odeon in the Haymarket and smoked cigarettes and laughed all through the double feature. We agreed *It's a Gift* was a masterpiece and that W.C. Fields was a genius. Afterwards he took me to the Rockingham, a drinking club decorated with campy flocked wallpaper and pink lampshades, where we drank champagne and waited for the already renowned young stage director Peter Brook, whom Ken was to interview for a magazine. When Peter had come and gone Ken asked me what I thought of him. I said he was always being described as a sprite or elf or leprechaun, but I thought he was a *man*, a small one, yes, but human. Pronouncing these not very extraordinary words as 'brilliant', Ken took out a small black notebook from his jacket, scribbled them down and ordered another bottle of champagne.

Suddenly he was saying, 'I am the illegitimate son of the late Sir Peter Peacock. I have an annual income. I'm twenty-three and I will either die or kill myself when I reach thirty because by then I will have said everything I have to say. Will you marry me?'

The stammer had stopped. His features had come to rest and I found myself looking into the face of a beautiful young man.

Now for the moment of truth, I decided. 'I'm sorry,' I said, 'but I can't marry you. I've just met Peter Ustinov. I'm mad about him and he told me he knew you so I was going to ask you if we can't all go out together and have dinner some night, or something . . .' I trailed off. I was weighing in the balance this young man in front of me and the entrancing Peter Ustinov in his Ellen Terry house in the King's Road.

Ken didn't bat an eyelash. 'Oh, I shouldn't bother about him,' he said, waving his hand with the cigarette aloft. 'He's recently divorced but he's already been taken.'

True or not, I chose to believe Ken because I was actually thinking to myself: it's crazy but I might – I just might – marry him. The fairy-tale illegitimacy, the prediction of his demise seven years hence, the marriage proposal: all seemed to make him, then and there, just right for me. He began to look just right for me, too. Tall and thin, fair English-pink complexion, high cheekbones dramatically dominating the outline of his elongated face. His forehead was high and bony, his pale beige-blond hair curved back from his brow like a wing, and his large well-shaped mouth gave him an attractive equine look. All this, together with his Mickey Mouse wristwatch, cast a spell over me.

We had more champagne and talked some more and finally I had to be somewhere and he had to be somewhere else. But when we parted that day something between us had silently been settled.

Two days after that crucial afternoon, Ken took me with him to tea at the home of playwright Christopher Fry, who had a house in Little Venice in north London overlooking the canal. Several interesting members of the English theatre were there, as well as Harold Clurman, a formidable figure on the American theatrical scene and one of the founders of the famous Group Theatre. Our host had a colony of ants under glass; you saw them busily carrying grains of sand to build a hill and then carting them away to build another. Fry told us he had hoped he might profit by this example of diligence, but instead he passed hours in its contemplation. It reminded me of Maxwell Anderson, who had installed a telescope in his living room the last time I was there; in the evening he would stare through it, lost in the stars for hours. The whole pleasant atmosphere reminded me of my lost Paradise-on-the-Hudson. Perhaps Paradise was everywhere. You stood outside the gates with the right person and someone inside opened them up and welcomed you in.

Ken and I began to see each other every day. In my room in Hazel's flat Ken and I coupled for the first time; it was the second time really. The first time, shortly after we met, we stripped off our clothes and faced each other. My eyes registered his cock, a beautiful cock, perfectly proportionate with his tall body, and we fell into each other's arms. We tried every which way round the clock, and when it started to feel like *work* we stopped. Dammit, said Ken, after he failed yet again, I'm going to try every night for a year. We only had to wait till the next night and he stayed up and we were away.

I sought no more jobs in Paris and canceled radio engagements I had previously made. In spite of his entreaties to live with him, I wanted to stay on in Hazel's flat, though. For all my sophistication I had never actually lived with a man and I was rather reluctant to try. Besides, I loved the way he pursued me; he had such zest for the chase. I held out for two weeks, then moved into his flat at 19 Upper Berkeley Street. Now I was emphatically in London.

My first morning there I woke up to hear Ken on the phone. I could tell that he was talking to some government official because the language of his request was formal. He wished to know if an American actress would be permitted to work in England if she were married to an Englishman. I could tell by his jubilant tone as he thanked the official that the answer was yes. This was a first. A lover actually looking out for my career! I rushed out and threw my arms around him. 'What is it?' he asked. I said, 'I heard you on the phone. All this, and free theatre tickets too!' Life was perfect, perfect, perfect.

I had gained the love of an extraordinary young man. I could act in England. And, finally, I had been discovered. Not by world acclaim, as planned, but by a lover: a soon-to-be husband. It didn't mean that I stopped loving acting, but it had somehow slipped to second place.

We led a life of undomesticated bliss. The only home virtue I practiced in our flat in Upper Berkeley Street was making English tea and fried bread and bacon and eggs (when food coupons allowed) for him in the mornings. The only ones he practiced were setting traps for mice in the kitchen every night and throwing them out the window the next day.

I admired Ken's talent to the point of worship. I was further drawn to it because it took the form of drama criticism. I had grown up in New York during that thirty-year period when, theatre historians agree, Broadway was at its peak, both as an art and as show business. In the thirties Broadway, with its seventy to eighty playhouses, enjoyed world recognition as theatre at its most dynamic, original, outspoken, experimental and melodious, filled with American masterpieces and welcoming those from abroad. It was an essential part of life in New York. The need for drama critics who could meet the high standards set by the plays and players produced a group of critics of the caliber of Robert Benchley and Dorothy Parker writing in the multiplicity of newspapers and magazines. Their reviews were vehement, fiery, witty and bold, and all of them possessed a felicity of language and a sophistication of background. And here was Ken, well below their ages, well up to their standards: at twenty-three already writing brilliant articles for a half a dozen English magazines and weekly papers, among them the *Spectator*, *Sight and Sound*, *Lilliput*, *Bandwagon* and *Picture Post*.

Never before had I been so focused on another person. Never had I studied anyone so closely. Some things about him would remain mysteries. His stammer was one. I listened night and day to find out what words presented problems. They all did. Sometimes he didn't stammer on a word he'd stammered on before. Nor did there seem any reason why, in the ordinary course of conversation, he stammered sometimes but not others. He had no difficulties when he delivered a speech he'd written or someone else's he'd studied, nor were there problems when he acted. Someone told me that people stammered as a way of controlling others but did not do so when they were alone. It seemed possible. Anything did. But if he was alone, how would I know whether he stammered or not? Then I heard him singing selections of Fred Astaire songs in the bathroom. He never stammered when he sang. That is basically all I could find out. Except I discovered that a man with a stammer is not unknown to the English, and that their good manners always give the stammerer the time he needs.

On the other hand, I did find out why he held his cigarette aloft between the middle and fourth fingers. It was simply, he informed me, to avoid tobacco stains.

The way he discovered he was illegitimate, Ken told me, began one night in the late forties, when he was at Oxford. He'd gone to Stratford to see a play, and afterwards he received a call from his mother at her home in Birmingham. She told him to come as soon as possible. His father had died.

That he died did not come as a shock to Ken. His father was elderly and had been gravely ill for some time. What came as a shock occurred at Leamington Spa station as he waited for the next train to Birmingham: he saw his father's picture staring up at him from a newspaper. Moreover the caption gave the name of the deceased not as Peter Tynan, his father, but as *Sir Peter Peacock*.

Unbeknownst to Ken, his father had lived a double life. A self-made millionaire, he had created a successful chain of inexpensive clothing and dry goods establishments all over the North Midlands, called Peacock Stores. The first store was located in Warrington where he had his home and where for many years he was its mayor.

When he fell in love with Ken's mother, Rose Tynan, he was already married with children. His wife refused to divorce him and Sir Peter moved with Rose to Birmingham, which had become the center of his enterprises. There he used Rose's surname and proceeded to style himself Peter Tynan. Somehow Sir Peter, although surely a figure of some prominence in Birmingham business circles, got away with posing as his own personal secretary in his second ménage, which accounted for his regular absences when he returned weekly to Warrington and also explained why all the mail addressed to Sir Peter came to him. During the war he even had two ration cards. (This disclosure by his mother was what impressed Ken most about the deception.) His mother's proudest moment, he said, came when his father was to be knighted. It was Rose, not his real wife, whom he took to Buckingham Palace to witness the ceremony.

What I had trouble grasping at the time was that Ken would not see his illegitimacy as I saw it: a fascinating and romantic condition. To Ken it was anything but. He told me his first action on returning home the day after his father died was angrily to demand an explanation from his mother. Tearfully she told him the story. He did not think it romantic. It left him bitter. He had been denied his birthright. The patrimony that should have been his, had his parents married, was stolen by the other family. He had been lied to and he had been fooled, and worse, he had been made a fool of. He found it embarrassing to remember his former view of the elderly, distant father, whom he had privately dismissed over the years as ordinary and uninteresting, someone he considered, somewhat condescendingly, as a mere company employee of Sir Peter, someone who simply did what he was ordered to. It was disorienting for Ken to have to rethink his father into Sir Peter Peacock, the man who gave the orders. I did not fully appreciate then that the discovery that he was a bastard would have such a deep and lasting effect. In all the time I knew him he never once expressed any desire to find his half-siblings.

In 1962, when Ken began seeing Dr Senft, a psychoanalyst, he looked deeper into his illegitimacy and told me that several things were now becoming clear. He realized that he must have suspected an irregularity in his parents' relationship long before having proof of it. Memories began to surface of overheard conversations with his mother and his aunts, of discussions between his mother and father abruptly broken off upon his entry into a room, or odd telephone calls for Sir Peter. Ken also surmised that his father had not wanted him but desired his mother entirely for himself and resented having to share her attention and affection with this son of his late middle age. Ken said he was now able to feel his father's dislike of him, and how it manifested itself in acts of humiliation. He had a clear recollection of his father forcing him to kneel down and tie his shoelaces for him.

The word 'bastard' has dual meanings: one identifies a blameless child born out of wedlock; the other, as a term of abuse, is provocative. Do the conditions that surround a bastard babe turn the child into an adult scoundrel?

I saw that Ken had a talent for success, that he was intended for it, that he was truly one of Destiny's Tots. Although the spotlight seemed his natural element and he preened himself in it, I saw that it scared him too. He would stiffen, eyes alert, in readiness for the next attack. I liked the realistic way he understood and accepted that, in his ferocious pursuit of notoriety, he was making himself a target. His pose was decadent, very *fin de siècle*, Yellow Book, Oxford flamboyant. The things that drove other people crazy about him, I thought marvelous. To the charge that he was affected, he would quote Ronald Firbank, the tubercular writer, who responded to the same allegation with, 'Of course I am affected. Even my lungs are affected.' In the future for Ken this answer was to be too close to the truth.

I believed in Ken and he believed in me. That was the important thing. He raised me. I promised myself I would help him in every way I could, that I would never let him down. Self-invented, divorced from our backgrounds, we had met and commingled to create something new, something we alone owned, a world with our own myths and traditions. As he would say to me as long as we knew each other, 'We gave each other a tremendous feeling of specialness, uniqueness, even glamour. We looked on each other with the absolute certainty that nobody quite like us had ever existed.'

Even our differences seemed to complement each other; we gloried in them. He was Midlands Methodist, I New York Jewish. About my being Jewish, he gave all the right answers: ancient race, gifted, talented, geniuses, important to world progress. I was older than Ken, and it worried me, and I brought it up early, saying, with a sigh at this complication, 'It's not that I am too much older but that you're too much younger.' 'Don't you see it has taken all this time for fate to put you where I could find you?' he replied. To which I heartily concurred. Coming up against his precocity, I often felt the younger.

At the age of nine he had demanded of his mother one hundred books for Christmas and got them. He was the rarest of all creatures, the born critic. He had always written drama criticism, he told me, from early childhood on, before he had ever seen a play.

I loved the young provincial at Oxford (at that time several rungs lower down the social scale than a Yank at Oxford), shaking its dreaming spires while at the same time doing things as incalculably beyond ordinary comprehension as signing his name to all the picture frames of prints he had hung on the walls of his rooms at Magdalen 'so that no one would try to steal them'.

I saw also that it was not just me that he wanted, but marriage itself. Marriage was an estate he aspired to. Over the years I have observed that they often marry young, Destiny's Tots. In truth they need company for their journey, someone at their side to watch all the wonderful things that are happening, witness them coming into being, share the joy ride, double the pleasure. They need a close, loving spectator to appreciate how well they are playing their game. In wanting to marry me, it was as if Ken were saying, 'Come aboard my golden chariot, this is going to be quite a ride.' And what a ride it was!

Ben Jonson's *Bartholomew Fair* at the Old Vic was the first play I ever saw with Ken. In the taxi going to the theatre he said, 'You must tell me your reaction to it afterwards,' and I replied, 'No. One critic in the family is enough.' From the beginning I saw the importance of leaving that area for him to dwell in alone, except, of course, when we were equally stirred by what we were seeing. Whenever this happened we would reach for each other's hand, and wonder again at the cleverness of the Grand Design that had arranged for us to meet just at that very point in time when we were both free and unfettered.

We went to Paris for Christmas and spent our days in bed eating oranges and making love and our nights seeing plays. We decided to be married in January, in a civil ceremony at Marylebone Town Hall. Tessa would be bridesmaid and Peter Wildeblood would be best man – he had been a close friend of Ken's since Oxford, where they had been rival speakers in Union debates. He now worked as a reporter on the *Daily Mail*. Of all Ken's friends, Peter and I liked each other best.

After Ken returned from Paris to London, I stayed on for several days to tidy up the loose ends of my life before flying to London to join him.

Suddenly I changed my mind and decided not to chance a plane but to take the boat train, which landed me safely in Victoria Station. Collecting my suitcase and other gear, I stepped off the train. I was dozens of carriages down the track from the gateway and began walking, dragging my case along. I did not recognize a man some distance away coming in my direction. Why should I? There was nothing familiar about him. I kept walking and he kept walking and then he was running towards me and he was hugging me so I had to say to myself that this must be Ken. Oh my God, I thought, how unreal could this last month have been? Had I forgotten so quickly what he really looked like? Or had I only imagined what he looked like? What had I gotten myself into? Okay, I thought as his former features settled themselves over the new ones, it's okay. Just remember: you haven't gotten into anything you can't get out of. And then it was all right again. I was again the beholder; again the beholden.

We went to the theatre every night and afterwards, true to my word, instead of launching into floods of opinions I would instead ask questions about the plot of what we had just seen, especially with Shakespeare's plays. What was the historical background, and how accurate was the Bard, and how much did he invent? And what did this word mean, and that one? Being with Ken meant never having to use a dictionary.

We often frequented Le Petit Club Français (the French Club) in St James's Street, run by Olwyn Vaughan, a heroine during the war to the Free French, whom she looked after when they came over to England for Rest and Recuperation. One night, when Peter Wildeblood was dining with us there, he chose the exact date of our wedding: January 25, a day he could take off from the newspaper. When the wedding date grew nearer he insisted that a modicum of tradition be observed. Ken and I must not see each other before the wedding, therefore Ken had to get out of the flat early that day and take Tessa to lunch. Peter would take me to lunch, and we would all meet outside Marylebone Town Hall.

I had gone to Knightsbridge in search of a wedding dress. The one I found in Harvey Nichols was champagne-coloured and looked like organdy but was made of nylon. It had a strapless top and the fairly low décolletage was trimmed with champagne-coloured roses of the same material. It had a small sheer jacket that was a mere covering of my shoulders. On my head I wore a bandeau of curly feathers. The whole effect looked better than it sounds.

When all four of us met up outside the town hall I noticed that Ken wore a green carnation in his buttonhole. Perfect.

Peter, as a *Daily Mail* reporter, had alerted one of the papers' photographers, and he had written a short item about us in the Londoner's Diary. The next day I was astonished to find that all the London newspapers, morning and evening ones, carried wedding pictures of Ken and me on their front page. Sometimes it would be just me, with Ken cut out, which, of course, infuriated him, as it would have me. I was astonished to discover that the one time a woman was always of more interest than a man, in those days, was when she was a bride.

After the wedding ceremony we went to Peter's flat for further festivities and later in the afternoon Ken and Tessa and I took the train to Oxford. We stayed at the Randolph Hotel. Tessa's great friend from Jamaica, Corinne Peel, had married an Englishman and they owned a restaurant in Oxford popular with the students. Friends of Ken's too, they gave us a huge reception next day at their house.

On our wedding day I wired my parents: 'Have married Englishman. Letter follows.'

12

Life With Ken

By saying, 'I do,' I was at last not only committed to but protected by my new life. The fear of my father vanished.

Some days prior to our wedding, timed so it would arrive several days after the event, I wrote my mother about Ken, enclosing a copy of *He That Plays the King*. The only return address I gave was that of my London bank, the New York First National. I explained I was doing this as a precaution. It was perfectly all right with me, I went on, if Daddy disinherited me because Ken was not Jewish, but I would not put up with any unpleasantness from him. I knew, I said, I was happy at last.

My mother wrote me back a sweet letter saying I reminded her of the little girl 'who only wanted to be happy', and that Daddy was reconciled, and they would like to give me a wedding gift of a higher yearly income. The correspondence my mother saved during my married years shows me over and over again thanking my parents for their generosity. Ken and I were immensely grateful. It also shows how my attitude towards my father's money changed. I went from being determined to take as little as possible from him to thanking God he was rich and so what if I had to ask for it? Today, I wonder if he was not just as relieved as I was that, in a manner of speaking, I was gone for good.

Our honeymoon lasted only for the weekend, which was all the time we could spare. Ken was about to start directing an adaptation of Cocteau's *Intimate Relations* at the highly regarded Arts Club. It was to star Fay Compton, an actress of distinction, with the long and varied career of that superior breed. She had toured during the war and chosen this vehicle for her return to the West End. That Alec Clunes, an actor who also managed the Arts Club, would choose Ken, who had only directed two London productions, neither of them in the West End, shows the amount of interest everyone in the English theatre held for this tyro.

Ken loved the script and the challenge of directing this star. In anticipation in the sitting room he'd set up a miniature theatre in which he moved small cutouts of actors around for hours. I was to start rehearsals for my role in the BBC TV production of George Kaufman and Edna Ferber's *Dinner at Eight*, in which I played the maid, Dora, who was part of the below-the-stairs plot.

19 Upper Berkeley Street was in a quiet row of town houses near enough to Sherlock Holmes and Madame Tussaud's Baker Street and Professor Henry Higgins and the Barretts' Wimpole Street to make it invigoratingly historic for me to wander around its environs. We lived on the top floor and had four rooms: a bedroom, a room Ken used to work in, a sitting room and a kitchen.

There was a love between us that lived in the bedroom but a love that lived out of it too. The tenderness we felt for each other was so unexpected, so powerful, so new to me. It found expression in day-long exchanged glances, our eyes threaded together with John Donne's double eye string; in feathery kisses; in held hands. He called me Skippy because, he said, it suited me. And it did – I was feeling a dizzy, daffy skippiness all the time, a buoyancy verging on ecstasy. He wrote on the bathroom mirror with my lipstick 'I love you Skippy'. And I wrote on the mirror in the sitting room 'I love you Ken'. And then I started calling him Skippy too because it suited us both, and in that special name we called each other, we found a thousand different ways to say it.

In Upper Berkeley Street Ken worked almost daily, while I worked pretty regularly. Sometimes we would go out to lunch at a nearby Indian restaurant. I'd never eaten Indian food before, and I loved it. Though London was wholly new to me, and I was a stranger, I had the advantage of being married to an insider with gilt-edged connections and with whom further bright discoveries would be made together.

I look back in amazement at how many people, places and things Ken and I met, saw and did during the first year of our marriage. They would remain in place throughout it as well as during the dissolving of it and beyond. That first year laid the foundation of the world we would inhabit.

Under 'things' I include CRISES, which from the very beginning took place on a regular basis. And there was nothing trivial or wishy-washy about them. They were first-class and full-blown, and would take place steadily and persistently through the years.

In February, after my second day of rehearsals for *Dinner at Eight*, though I had not been parted from Ken for more than a few hours, I was missing him so badly I couldn't wait to get home. Home, home, at last I have a home. I walked in the door and went into the sitting room. Then I just stopped. Ken was sitting in front of his theatre model, immobile, his feet turned inward, his long hands drooped between his knees. It was as if he had removed himself to a place where he couldn't be reached. Fay Compton, he finally told me, had that day given Alec Clunes an ultimatum: 'Either Ken Tynan goes, or I go.' Clunes chose the actress, Ken got the boot. He had been sitting there all afternoon.

My heart went out to him but another feeling was stirring inside me: disappointment. I was not disappointed in him for getting fired but for taking it so hard. He was supposed to be above that. He was *not* supposed to be like other men; he was *not* supposed to be human. Not satisfied with a prodigy, I wanted a paragon, such was my exalted, dangerously unrealistic and unshakable view of him.

I tried to comfort him, saying an aging former star fraught with anxiety was throwing her weight around. He was well out of it, wasn't he? He didn't reply. I pressed on. Shouldn't we talk about it? He said no. Was it because he was English, I wondered, or because he was Ken?

The effect on Ken at being removed from *Intimate Relations* then and in the future was immoderate. Other events soon claimed his attention and, in rallying from that setback, he often proclaimed he would only ever direct someone who was under thirty years old. A year later the chance came along when he beautifully directed a television play of Jean-Jacques Bernard's *Martine* with the young Claire Bloom and Denholm Elliott. It won highest praise from television critics, yet he directed no more television plays.

The only other directorial assignment he undertook during our marriage was at a little theatre called the Irving where, early in the fifties, he presented a condensed Grand Guignol version of Shakespeare's *Titus Andronicus*. The Lord Chamberlain, who viewed all plays before they opened, announced that there must be two St John's ambulance men in attendance for each performance, a decision that all concerned thought absurd. It wasn't. Men fainted at every performance and had to be carried out. Women remained seated and upright till the end.

Should Ken have pursued being a director? The record says no. Without his drama criticism the world would have been a lot poorer. Judging from the record theatre survived very well without his directorial pursuits.

Meanwhile I played the little maid Dora in *Dinner at Eight*. The butler and the chauffeur get into a knife fight over her. It is one of those small parts an actress can do absolutely nothing with except look as pretty as possible, act as naive as possible and stay out of the way of the knives.

Shortly thereafter I worked with Orson Welles on Radio Luxembourg's *Harry Lime* series, named after the notorious character he created in *The Third Man*. For these segments I played any number of parts, mostly seductive co-conspirators for which I used a variety of fantasy accents. These two acting chores proscribed the perimeters of my brilliant acting career for then and, alas, forever. Always I played cameos, never leads. In the pretty and naive (i.e., dumb blonde) category, such as another wide-eyed innocent in Kaufman and Hart's *Once in a Lifetime*, I noticed that the better I did my Judy Holliday imitation, the more likely I would be to get noticed.

My acting stint with Orson Welles was short but memorable. I had worked with him several days running when one afternoon he handed me a script and said, 'Let's do this cold.' We were sharing a microphone – I was, in fact, standing on a box to be level with him – when in the middle of a scene – again I was playing several roles – I stopped and said, 'Orson, I'm following myself on.' 'This is ridiculous' he roared at the producer in the sound booth. 'What happened to the other actors?' 'Don't you remember?' said the producer, 'you fired them at lunchtime, Orson.'

Life with Ken was action-packed. As his book gained more renown, more magazines and newspapers wanted articles from him. By mid-1951 his name was established in English theatrical and literary circles and by the end of that year his fame had become international.

In that first year there were spring evenings with the trees budding and the long English twilight where we would meet all manner of well-seasoned, well-established actors, directors and playwrights for pre-theatre drinks, all in their easy, tweedy, pipe-smoking middle years. I would sit spellbound – and surprised – as they, with earnest furrowed brows, solicited opinions and advice from this youth (Ken's twenty-fourth birthday was April 2). Then, giddy with pride, I would say to myself that besides having a genius in my own backyard with my grandfather, I had a genius in my own bed.

Soon after our wedding Ken became the regular drama critic of the *Spectator*, then he also began to do work for the *Evening Standard*, owned by the redoubtable, powerful and mischievous Lord Beaverbrook. At first he contributed articles on theatrical personalities, then he filled in as its film critic while its regular one, Milton Shulman, was on holiday. In August he did more pieces, and in October he did another guest shot, this time as drama critic. Finally, in 1951, he became the *Standard*'s regular drama critic and remained there for two years.

1951 was the year of the Festival of Britain, when the nation, emerging from its war-torn hardships, displayed its not inconsiderable artistic wares to the world.

Alec Guinness's *Hamlet* was to be one of the Festival's offerings.

Guinness had already played *Hamlet* in Tyrone Guthrie's modern-dress production and now he wanted to do a Hamlet whose every aspect he would control. He made some interesting choices. For instance, he had a dream one night that the Player King was Ken, so in real life he offered him the part. Ken, in the spirit of adventure, accepted. In April rehearsals began.

As co-director, Guinness chose Frank Hauser, which was another odd choice. Hauser had previously only directed BBC radio productions. As it developed, however, Guinness became more and more dependent on him in matters of 'taste'. Watching this happen, Ken was furious. He felt Hauser was severely reining in the actor's interpretation. For instance, in the 'rogue and peasant slave' speech Alec had invented a chilling piece of stage business: at the moment Hamlet declares vengeance on Claudius, Alec unsheathed his sword and savagely thrust it *upward* as if disemboweling the usurper. It was stunning, said Ken, but Hauser thought this gesture went 'a bit too far' and it was cut.

I invited Harold Clurman, in London at the time, to go with me to the opening night. As we arrived at the theatre and took our seats, the atmosphere was alive with expectation. Finally the curtain rose.

And one of those disastrous theatrical evenings took place that are hilarious only in retrospect. Something went very wrong from the very start. It was the lighting plot, which was several cues off. This became blindingly apparent when the scene with the ghost was flooded with light and subsequent scenes were plunged into darkness. And it continued that way for a very long time, the lights brightening and darkening incomprehensibly as they skipped along their unchecked lunatic way. In Alec Guinness's *Hamlet* that night, the lighting man was the villain, not Claudius.

The acting itself also seemed several cues off. At the final curtain the gallery booed.

There was a cast party afterwards and I implored Clurman to tell me what to say. 'Head straight for the buffet,' he instructed me, 'and keep your mouth full of food.' Which is exactly what I did.

As for Alec Guinness, at the party, he comported himself with regal dignity, right down to his stocking feet, having early on discarded his shoes.

'At least they still *had* the party,' Clurman said in admiration. 'If this had been Broadway they would have canceled it.'

After Hamlet closed its short run, Ken and I went off to Madrid for another honeymoon. Neither of us had been to Spain. I saw how thoroughly Ken would prepare himself before embarking on new territory. (Days before we were married, I had come across him reading a book about Americans.) Our trip was preceded by him surrounding himself with books on Spain, studying maps of Madrid, phrasebooks, dictionaries, Baedeckers, floor plans of the rooms of the Prado, and schedules and seat prices of bullfights. There were lengthy consultations with the Thomas Cook travel agency, and Hemingway's *Death in the Afternoon* became his bible.

The seats he chose for our first bullfight were those he would always insist on: first row and in the shade. Before it began we were both nervous. Would we be horrified by the bulls charging the horses? Made queasy by all the spilled blood? Repelled by the brutal spectacle? Aghast at the bull's death? We were none of those things. We watched the first five bulls being dispatched and took them in our stride. Worse, our main reaction was precisely the one Hemingway had decreed to be the only unforgivable reaction to the bullfight: boredom. We were bored. Was there something wrong with us? Or with Hemingway?

Then came the final bull of the afternoon. The shade had lengthened across the ring so that only the last vestiges of sun gleamed on the side opposite us. That was where the bullfight took place. The torero, stocky, balding, blond and past his first youth, was called Rafael Ortega. Then it happened. Before we knew it the crowd solidified into a mass and we became one with it. The *olés* expelled from our mouths were as rhythmic and natural as breathing. It was a long fight. The sun went down, and the arc lights went on. With pass after pass Ortega trained the bull, and finally killed it with one perfect stroke, the torero and the bull charging *each other* at the same time. We learned later this was a dangerous method, rarely seen. In a flood of emotion the crowd went wild, we with it. Ortega went round and round the bullring accepting flowers, cigars, shawls, fans, cheers.

We left on a cloud. Immediately Ken took out a subscription to *El Ruedo*, the bullfight magazine, and back home he read everything he could find about the *corrida*, undaunted that most of it was in Spanish. A *feria* he liked the sound of – a week's worth of bullfighting at the end of July – was taking place in Valencia. The newest sensation, Litri, a young matador dubbed El Atomico, whose pictures and write-ups intrigued Ken, would be fighting there. Ken decided we must go. He had decided to write about bullfighting.

Among Ken's theatrical pieces for the *Evening Standard* was an interview with Charles Laughton, who seemed gladly to offer himself to the writer's gift of description: 'The chasm between Laughton's jowls is bridged by slack, surly lips, on which words sit lovingly . . . He thanks the waiter with the air of a man quietly closing a distasteful subject . . . He walks top-heavily like a salmon standing on its tail. He invests his simplest exit with an atmosphere of furtive flamboyance.'

His piece on Vivien Leigh caused a sensation. Sir Laurence and Lady Olivier had opened in their Festival of Britain offering in May with a season of George Bernard Shaw's *Caesar and Cleopatra* and Shakespeare's *Antony and Cleopatra* at the St James's Theatre. Both plays were enormously well received, except by Ken, who poured scorn upon the actress. Though he found her sufficiently adequate to fill out the 'small personality' of Shaw's Cleopatra, he thought she was woefully inadequate to the Cleopatra of Shakespeare, and he said so in many different and increasingly harsh ways. At the end he accused Olivier of subduing his performances to meet Vivien Leigh halfway, concluding, 'Antony steps down, Cleopatra pats him on the head.' An enraged Sir Laurence, we heard, threatened to punch Ken if he came across him.

Ken met Noël Coward soon after the article appeared. The Master wagged a finger at him and said, 'It sounded as if Viv had snubbed you at a cocktail party.' But half the acting profession came to whisper their agreement with Ken. Never mind that Vivien would become a far greater film actor than Larry. Never mind that when the Oliviers took these plays to Broadway her Cleopatras had improved beyond all recognition. There are no consolation prizes in the theatre. Ken wrote accurately about what he saw, and wrote it brilliantly, wittily and destructively. When people would compliment him on the 'bravery' and 'fearlessness' of his reviews he would reply that there was nothing brave about hiding behind a piece of white typing paper.

In that Festival year the English theatre gave special attention to putting its glittering galaxy of stage stars on show. In the July issue of the English *Harper's Bazaar* Ken covered the theatrical scene. Upon the twenty new productions he reviewed, which included plays of Shaw, Chekov, and Shakespeare, he pronounced a severe judgment: 'It has been in general an inglorious season, in which miscasting and wasteful casting vied for the brightest lights.'

Waters of the Moon by N.C. Hunter was the all-star production at the Haymarket, showcasing a conventional middlebrow middle-class West End production that drove Ken insane. It was a type of play he would work tirelessly all his critical life to demolish. 'The play is by now a success,' he announced bitterly, 'and I cannot hope to diminish its triumph by pointing out by how very wide a margin it fails to be worthy of its stars.' It was 'opulently shallow', 'insistently derivative', and 'left tepid even the vulgarest corners of my heart'. He derided the wasteful casting of Dame Edith Evans, Dame Sybil Thorndike and Wendy Hiller. 'As it stands *Waters of the Moon* is a plain dish of unvarnished truism, far too well acted.'

With the Olivier season he was briefer – if not more polite – to Vivien Leigh than he was in the *Evening Standard*. In the future he would go after her mercilessly every time she appeared on stage with Olivier, but upon revisiting *Antony and Cleopatra* he raved about the actor's 'blazing reserves of grace and power . . . There are touches of double-distilled tenderness and gouging fury in this performance which few men and no other actor can reach.' From then on Ken's worship of Olivier's performances on stage was unabashed and unconditional. Many people would see these public displays as embarrassing personal confessions of love. I saw them differently. From the first I saw Ken not as a man surrendering himself body and soul to his idol but as a man cannily campaigning for a big job with his idol. Ever since I'd known him he was as determined that England have a National Theatre as he was determined to be part of it. It took no feat of intelligence to figure out that if this glorious circumstance came to pass, Sir

Laurence Olivier, premier English actor *and* premier actor-manager, would be running it.

Ken also went to Stratford that summer to view 'one of the sturdiest male companies ever assembled in this country doing honour to Shakespeare's tetrology of history plays'. The big event was the young actor Richard Burton playing Prince Hal in *Henry IV*. Ken introduced him as the shrewd Welsh boy 'who shines out with true greatness . . . Burton is a still, brimming pool running disturbingly deep. At twenty-five he commands repose and can make silence garrulous.'

Ken and Richard had known each other at Oxford. After seeing a matinee of *Henry IV, Part I* we had drinks with him between shows. He asked if we'd noticed anything odd taking place during his fight scene. He'd made the mistake of having beer with his lunch and just before that scene he found he'd badly needed to pee but wasn't able to unbuckle his armor in time. So he went on stage and in the middle of the fight he looked down to see a trail of shimmering wetness in his wake on the stage floor picked up by the lights. How charming he was. How happy we all were in ourselves and each other to be laughing in the sun in the garden of a pub in Stratford with Richard after his magnificent performance. I would always remember the heavenbound moment when he became a star, and the earthbound moment when he peed on stage.

In mid-July we went to Valencia for the *feria*. I loved the article Ken wrote about it for the *Evening Standard*. It was so Ken. We had seen, what, six bullfights there? Yet he wrote confidently: 'That afternoon in the bullring, Litri fought one of the greatest bullfights in the history of the Valencian ring.' Those bullfights we saw in '51 marked the beginning not only of our running with the bulls every spring and summer for the next ten years, but also of our involvement with the celebrities and nuts who ran along with them.

There appear to me to have been more celebrities in the '50s than there are today, perhaps because they all seemed to come at me in a bunch. The line between reality and unreality was blurring. When doing his stint as the *Standard*'s film critic, Ken wrote of Humphrey Bogart in *Murder Inc.*: 'time has bestowed an agelessness on his trademarks – the lazy sewage snarl, the gnarled lisp of a voice, the face that looks like a triumph of plastic surgery.' The next night Richard Burton, up in London, introduced us to Bogey himself along with John Huston and wife Ricky, about to embark on the film *The African Queen*. Bogart seemed somewhat cool. Then Ken reviewed Alec Guinness in the Ealing comedy *The Man in the White Suit* and commented: 'He is one of the few Englishmen who can make greasepaint act; though in this case his face does not look quite so young as his hair.' Later that week we dined with a smiling Alec Guinness.

At this point Cecil Beaton came into our lives. He had been a fan of Ken's since the latter's Oxford days, and over lunch at his house one day he proposed that they do a book together. It would use Beaton's photographs and Ken's text and feature a hundred people mainly in the arts whom they both admired. It was published in 1953 and called *Persona Grata*. To this day, whenever some stage or screen personality in the book dies, Ken's words about them find their way into print again.

Cecil came to our flat early in '52 when we'd just moved from 19 Upper Berkeley Street to 29 Hyde Park Gardens. In leaving he said to me, 'I see you aren't houseproud.' I thought this was a compliment to my plain living and high thinking. Ken explained that it was an insult.

Which was the real Beaton? The one with houses in Pelham Crescent and Salisbury reminding me of the sets of stage revivals I wouldn't want to see? Or the one who raved about the artistry of the young Jerry Lewis and Dean Martin at the Palladium and tirelessly turned up at off-Broadway theatres? Or the innovator who photographed us with his brownie camera, placing us lying down on the floor of his drawing room because he'd discovered that position assured him of his subjects' relaxation?

We would soon meet Tennessee Williams; Ken for the first time, I for the second. My history with him is one of weird synchronicities. Not only did he keep turning up at extreme emotional crises in my life but unbeknownst to me I had been an uncomprehending witness to what he recalled as one of the most painful episodes in his existence.

I first met him in the summer of 1940 in Provincetown where as a teenager I was taking art lessons. His fame was yet to come and what distinguished the shortish playwright most from the other artistic types that summer was his odd name and abstracted air.

Reading his *Memoirs*, written in the seventies, a buried memory of that summer surfaced when I learned that the most overwhelmingly romantic attachment in his life was a dancer named Kip, and that the girl who took him away from Tennessee was 'Elaine Dundy's sister . . .'

That summer Shirley was also in Provincetown with a dance troupe. Another member was a young male dancer, Kip Kiernan, who was having an affair with Tennessee until he left him for my sister. Tennessee, strongly objecting, engaged her in a screaming match outside our boarding house at midnight, which very nearly got us all kicked out. It was a situation potentially of far more consequence to me at the time than a discarded lover caterwauling at his rival over a summer romance.

I remembered none of this when I met Tennessee again, now one of our greatest playwrights. Someone had invited us along on an afternoon outing with an improbable cast that included Hermione Baddeley and her lover Laurence Harvey, the Maharajah of Cooch Behar and his English girlfriend, and Tennessee and his friend Maria Britneva. Somehow we found ourselves together drinking champagne and fending off wasps while watching the one-armed Maharajah of Jaipur play polo in Cowdray Park. Afterwards there was a serious altercation in the limo carrying Tennessee and Maria between her and Laurence Harvey, which resulted in Maria and Tennessee being unceremoniously dumped on the road, the Cooch Behar contingent being very close friends of Harvey's. Fortunately we were in another limo following behind and they hailed us and we picked them up, and the affair ended happily with us full of sympathy and them full of gratitude.

From that day on Maria and Tennessee would interact unendingly in our lives, together and separately.

When Ken began work in his permanent role as the *Standard*'s drama critic, with his vastly expanded audience he made history. I was not the only one experiencing the euphoria of his performances. For what he induced in what must be called his 'audience' (rather than use a word so essentially passive as his 'readership') was the happy contagion its spectators shared with each other. It was as if they were watching him perform live. His reviews were seductive, alluring, appealing, erudite, outrageous and funny, funny, funny. The apt quotations with which he sprinkled his writing were bonuses, ones you'd never come across before so you were learning at the same time that you were laughing. These pieces changed one's very mood.

He kicked off with Orson Welles's *Othello*, which opened at the St James. I read his first sentence: 'No doubt about it, Orson Welles has the courage of his restrictions.' It continued, awful and funny in equal parts. Orson, who had congratulated Ken for his capacity for 'violent opinion', was coming in for his share of it. The actor's performance, wrote the critic was a 'huge shrug . . . His face expressed wryness and strangulation and little else.' Never able to resist the pun, even a senseless one, Ken wrote that 'Citizen Cane had become "Citizen Coon"' (his quote marks seeking to distance himself from it). The review was, in short, the kind that Charles Curran, his editor at the *Standard*, would later characterize as a 'successful operation without an anesthetic'.

Ken was not alone in his stinging assessment of Orson's performance. Some critics – as well as the entire fed-up cast – agreed with him. Rehearsals had been shambles with the great man flying in and out of the country without warning, working simultaneously on his film *Othello* in Italy. At the Buckstone, Peter Finch, Orson's Iago, would give us in detail the whole story of how the Great Man would suddenly reappear again in London to hold day-long rehearsals with no lunch break, ending it, 'Well, you're all awful.'

Some days after Ken's review appeared we went backstage to see Orson. Although his mission was benevolent I trailed along in some anxiety. Knowing how badly Welles needed money to finish his film version of *Othello*, Ken had talked the manager of London's celebrated nightclub the Café de Paris into offering Welles a gig to perform his famous magic tricks for a substantial salary. I was pretty sure that Orson would perceive the gig as *infra dig*. Orson, after listening to the proposal, rose to his full height, rolled his head on his massive shoulders to glance at me apologetically, turned to Ken and pointed to the door. He uttered one word with a bellow that shook everything in the room made of glass. 'Out!' he roared. Ken obeyed. Glancing apologetically at Orson, I trailed after him.

Of Ralph Richardson in his performance in the Stratford production of *Macbeth*, Ken wrote, 'he moved as if by numbers and such charm as he possessed was . . . an unfocused bluffness . . . [In the lines] "Why should I play the Roman fool and die on mine own sword?" Sir Ralph gripped his blade by the sharp end and with both hands practised putts with it; it was as if the Roman fool had been the local golf pro.'

Ken was writing within the great satiric English tradition. Give his words on Richardson to Dickens, to Wilde, to Wodehouse, and the reader roars with laughter and curls up in enjoyment. Sir Ralph happened to be a real person, yet Ken successfully fictionalized him into that recognizable and delightful character, the English eccentric.

In truth English stage greats of that time tended to get locked into their performing style, no matter what role they played. While English audiences were familiar and comfortable with their mannerisms, strangers, seeing them for the first time and not familiar with their body of work, were bewildered by the performances and surprised at the actors' reputations.

After remaining in their Wodehousian/Dickensian molds for a few years, though, these actors could suddenly break out to hold a mirror up to actual life, taking your breath away, as both Gielgud and Richardson did in Pinter's *No Man's Land*.

Ken must have made enemies, although I do not remember anyone walking out of a party in those days if we walked in, and we kept going regularly to the Buckstone too. Gielgud said it all in his famous remark, 'It's wonderful if it isn't you.'

Ken's rave review of *South Pacific* revealed something about Ken which separated him from his English colleagues at the time. He appreciated the American musical as no other English critic did. They seemed uncomfortable with what they perceived as its slickness and sentimentality. In truth it was showbiz which turned them off. Ken loved showbiz as a fundamental and essential part of the theatrical feast, without which he would starve. In his love for American musicals he would be at one with the British public no matter how tepid the notices were.

In pinning his colors to *South Pacific* he paid special homage to the importance of the score, to the 'peasant graces of Richard Rodgers's music' and the 'boldness of Oscar Hammerstein's lyrics'. Ken had an uncannily musical ear. Watching a new musical he could instantly pick out which songs would become standards.

It was gradually coming over me that I was doing an awful lot of drinking, or, perhaps, that we were doing an awful lot of drinking. The number of openings in West End theatres and smaller ones across London and its outlying districts made it possible for us to see a new play almost every night. During a typical evening we first had pre-theatre drinks with friends, then at the theatre during the interval we had drinks at bars placed conveniently indoors to save the audience from having to dash across the street in the rain looking for a pub. After the theatre we'd go to the Buckstone, or the French Club, or any number of clubs or restaurants, always searching for new places. We did not want to go home, eat supper and so to bed. The stimulation of a first night, its keyed-up, high-pitched festive air, combined with our being in the dark for two-and-a-half hours, made us want to be out and about. We always had wine with dinner (or, at the Buckstone, that lethal cider), a liqueur afterwards, perhaps a night cap somewhere else. People kept buying us drinks, then Ken would buy them drinks, and so it went. I would be high by the time I got to bed. The fact that nobody forced me at gunpoint to accept any drink was something that never occurred to me.

I was baffled and alarmed that marriage didn't stop me from drinking so much. Drinking through the night in Paris was fun – so many places to go till the early hours. But by the end of my stay I'd started to have peculiar time lapses that might last anywhere from ten minutes to an hour. Upon coming to I would remember nothing. Coming to sometimes I would not even be in the same nightclub or café as before. These blanks would be of different densities. Some of them would be thinly veiled brownouts and the gaps could be filled in, but there were blackouts that would remain opaque.

I never drank in the morning or at mid-day, but in the evening I never seemed to stop, winding up late at night riding the Paris merry-go-round. Didn't those before us – Hemingway and Fitzgerald, Picasso and Modigliani, and all the wild young women of their time – didn't they give us, the new post-war generation, permission to drink? In fact, insist we do?

In London I had been sure that I would stop my excessive drinking now that I had met Ken and my search was ended. I was sure that in Paris my insecurities and rootless feelings were the underlying cause for my intemperance. Now I was safely ensconced in the dearness of now, the past dim, the delicious future never more than five minutes away.

One night, at a pleasant informal party given by some of Ken's Oxford friends just after we were married, I was sitting at the dinner table one moment and the next I was standing in the kitchen in my slip and the hostess was ironing my dress. Between those moments I'd blacked out. I gathered I'd spilled wine all over my dress and she had washed out the stains. It was frightening; it was as though my life had a life of its own. I said nothing about this to Ken but knew I could no longer deny the seriousness of my predicament.

Then suddenly I left off drinking, even left off smoking. It was curious, more as if these habits had walked away from me. In November our doctor confirmed I was three months pregnant. I counted the months back. I became certain – in the way that women often are – that I'd conceived in a berth on a night train from Madrid to Barcelona. I was ecstatic, Ken delighted. He hoped it would be a girl. Either way we settled that our child would be named after the character played by Katharine Hepburn in our favorite film, *The Philadelphia Story*. We would name our future child Tracy Tynan.

All in all, though every day had seemed like my birthday, this was the high point of my year.

13

Life Still With Ken

In the course of my pregnancy I temporarily gave up acting and was no longer involved in the bonhomie of television casts so my home-making chores might have expected to take priority. That they didn't I attributed to what I saw going on around me.

In fifties England whole areas destroyed by bombs still lay in rubble for all to see, though a determined weed called London Pride pushed its way up through the devastation. It was still a country of austerity and ration cards, but more importantly it was the country whose courage and moral superiority in having stood alone against the Nazis in 1940 was acknowledged by the world. It was a place where young people, besieged for six years of war, could finally see that they had a future. You could fairly feel the rush of air as they raced forward to greet it. For its artists it was an orderly place in which it was safe to take risks. Peace and austerity had produced an ideal climate in which all the arts were thriving.

London played a pivotal role in the success of English actors at that time. Unlike Americans, whose stage and film centers were 3,000 miles apart, they were able to work simultaneously in theatre, films, television and radio in the same week or even the same day. Plentiful jobs were all based in and around the city.

Ken and the fifties were a perfect match. The explosion of post-war theatre needed a pre-eminent illuminator and memorializer, and there was Ken, able to illuminate, memorialize, celebrate and excoriate like no other critic. Like Beerbohm and Shaw before him, he was as much a star as those performing on the stage. Moreover, for the delectation of first-night audiences among whom he sat, he would appear in eye-catching outfits, such as a suit of dove gray with a velvet collar, enlivened by pastel-colored shirts in primrose, ashes of rose or apple green.

There was, of course, a price to pay for this pre-eminence. As a regular drama critic with a weekly column on one or another paper for over twelve years, the day he sat down to write his column was the day before or even the early morning of the day he had to deliver his copy. I became intimately acquainted with the method and madness of the task he set himself.

That day was always a very long one. It began around ten in the morning and sometimes lasted till three or four the next morning. In the early fifties he remained in his beige woolen bathrobe all day. By the end of the decade he had graduated to a yellow silk dressing gown with dark blue piping.

His long day's journey into night began with magazines: the *Spectator*, the *New Statesman*, *Punch*, *Picture Post*, *Time*, *Newsweek* and two or three others. He must read all from cover to cover in order to rev himself up to start – or put off starting – his work. Then he moved to his study. The day progressed; the sun went down; it was evening. The long solitary hours began. Through the night several packs of cigarettes would be smoked; his favorites were the expensive ones called Three Castles. A bottle – sometimes two – of hock would be drunk: a German Riesling or a Gewürztraminer, or an Alsatian Traminer or Sylvaner. Cans of chili, or corned beef hash, or mulligatawny soup would be eaten. I heated them up at intervals and served them on demand. When I opened the door of his study the smoke, as if from a nuclear blast, shot out to engulf me.

Around eleven I would go to bed and lie listening to the deafening silence, then, starting up very slowly a tentative rat-tat from his typewriter. Then a pause. Then more rat-tats followed by a string of rat-tat-tats that would get faster and sound surer and happier. I would relax in relief and realize I had been praying, but I would tense up again as silence closed in once more. And so it went on all night until I finally drifted off. He woke me when he was finished to give me his final copy and at that moment he always looked very strange; rather insane. In the first year I noticed two bumps like incipient horns standing out on his forehead between his eyebrows: eye strain – eventually he would have to wear glasses. He would take off his dressing gown, and in his pajamas with the wine and smoke smell clinging to them, fall into bed like a log, plunging instantly to sleep.

In the beginning, either late at night or in the early morning, I would get dressed and, with his copy in a manila envelope, take a taxi to Fleet Street to deliver it myself. Later I entrusted the envelope to the taxi driver and, along with the money for the fare and the address of the newspaper, give him a lecture on the inestimable value and importance of its contents. Being the days before Xeroxes or faxes a wave of uneasiness would hit me as I watched the cab depart: there went Ken's only correct copy. Yet, courtesy of the trusty London cabbies, it always arrived safely. It was usually his third draft, single-spaced with a few penned corrections in the margin inserted in a small, spidery but highly legible hand.

From 1952 on we would go to America at least once a year. That year, in January, when I was about five and a half months pregnant, we went to New York for the first time together. My parents put us up at the Essex House on 59th Street, on a floor high enough to see the whole vista of Manhattan from Central Park and east and west up to the Bronx. They also gave us a party at 1185 Park with my sisters and their husbands and family members and friends mainly from my Lincoln days. It was all so different from when I left. Even the apartment itself signaled the end of an era, for my parents would close it and instead spend half their time in Palm Beach, Florida, and half in Atlantic Beach, Long Island. It was a nice party. I was careful not to let it provoke unhappy memories. Looking back wasn't the way I was going to live my life, I promised myself.

That trip to New York was my first experience of being invited to parties by telegram from celebrities we'd never met. We were spinning into the celebrity circuit and Ken's comings and goings – and later mine – would be recorded faithfully and accurately by a newsletter called *Celebrity Service*, whose copies you could obtain free of charge if you were listed in it.

On January 29 Ken was introduced for the first time to the vast public of the *New York Times*. He wrote a piece on the current Broadway theatre, praising its leading playwrights for writing interesting parts for the 'young girl, who is not a plot contrivance, not simply a daughter or a son's betrothed but who exists in her own right, independently and eccentrically alive'. The lack of these parts written for young women under thirty in the English theatre was a serious failing he would endlessly rage against down his years as an English drama critic.

During our fortnight's stay, we attended the best theatrical parties, dined at the best tables in Sardi's and 21, met the choicest stars and playwrights and drama critics, saw the best plays and were fêted in penthouses by the wealthiest hosts and hostesses assiduously courting that starry world.

Back in London the new flat at 29 Hyde Park Gardens was on the top floor of a recently renovated row of Regency terraced houses off the Bayswater Road with a wide lawn in front for a baby to romp in. I was completely bewildered by the task of having to decorate it. My rooms at my parents' apartments were decorated by them, and I had never bought anything to make them my own, nor did I at college. In Washington and Paris I lived happily in furnished rooms and hotels, having accustomed myself to a nomadic existence, and Upper Berkeley Street belonged to Ken. Now I had to domesticate myself and choose carpets and curtains for four rooms. As far as buying furniture and stuff, I knew Bloomingdale's in New York but I was unaware of any comparable stores in London. My English women friends at the time – besides Tessa – were the actress Maxine Audley, newly married (again), Ellen Baker, whose husband was Stanley Baker, Sybil Burton, married to Richard, Hilary Mackendrick, married to the Ealing writer/director Alexander Mackendrick, and the actress Jill Bennett. Together they must have guided me for I found myself walking around

Peter Jones and John Lewis trying to concentrate on the problem. In those days decorating one wall with wallpaper and having the other three painted was the going thing. The furniture I would characterize as 'austerity' – that's all there was in the stores – and I wasn't into antiques, having had my fill at 1185. The nursery for the baby-to-be was papered with a pink pattern of balloons and teddy bears. We took some 19 Upper Berkeley furniture like our bed there and put it in the living room where it served as a divan in the daytime and a bed for the mother's-help-to-be at night. I thought it all looked okay. At any rate it was new. I liked Ken's small study best. Very colorful. Very personal. It was papered with bullfight photographs from *El Ruedo*, the Spanish bullfight magazine. It was his idea. All the best ideas pertaining to everything, I had decided, were Ken's ideas.

Besides his regular post as drama critic Ken worked on a great number of projects in '52. There were two books to be written, both published a year later: a slim volume on Alec Guinness, as part of a series of books on distinguished English actors, and *Persona Grata*, with Cecil Beaton. And there were always magazine articles, so on any given day he would have a backlog of work due.

All this was accomplished with our busy theatre and social life and with the ever-widening circle of celebrities who poured into our Hyde Park Gardens living room.

Moira Shearer and her husband Ludovic Kennedy came round the same evening as Graham Greene. I watched him fall in love with her delicate features, bright golden red hair and her ballerina grace. Each time I offered to refill Greene's glass he smiled at me amiably and shook his head without even checking then went back to drinking in Moira.

Sandy Wilson, a friend of Ken's at Oxford, dropped by and told us that he was writing a musical comedy spoof of the twenties. I privately thought, Poor jerk! It's already been spoofed to death. But *The Boy Friend*, a hit on both sides of the ocean, introduced Julie Andrews to America.

Sybil Burton confided in me that she and Richard longed for a baby but as she couldn't seem to get pregnant they were thinking of adopting one. When they'd chosen one from a Welsh adoption agency, Sybil promptly became pregnant. They canceled the adoption and had Kate Burton, now an actress.

Young Tony Richardson, a director fresh from Oxford, university flamboyance still in place, talked about a new theatrical venture he and George Devine were founding, the Royal Court in Sloane Square. It styled itself 'the playwrights' theatre, and beginning with John Osborne's *Look Back In Anger* down the years remained just that.

William Rees Mogg, another Oxford friend, was shy and without affectation. He would become the editor of *The Times*. Nick Ray, the film director of *Rebel Without a Cause* also visited, and after a couple of drinks broke down and began sobbing about having lost his boy. I thought his son had died until I finally realized he was talking about the death of James Dean. The astonishingly beautiful Ava Gardner came over and after a couple of drinks began talking about her 'old man' with candor. I thought she was talking about her father until I realized she meant Frank Sinatra.

Tracy was born on May 12 at the Westminster Hospital. Ken was informed between acts of a play about the atom bomb called *Uranium 235*. She took forty-eight hours to arrive. The nurses kept giving me hot baths and several times asked me to stop screaming as I was disturbing the other patients. Ken and Tessa dropped in during the proceedings. Finally my doctor, a Mr Briant Evans, who had been playing golf during the Sunday part of my ordeal, decided to induce labor. I was taken to the delivery room where a handsome anesthetist covered my face with a mask that sent me straight into a nirvana-like trance. There we held a cozy conversation. He told me his name. It was Peacock, and I said that's my husband's real name, and he said he knew it and that they were related. Or perhaps I just dreamed it. I must have been partly conscious because as the baby came out I said, 'Is it a boy or a girl?' and my doctor said, 'I can't tell yet.' Then seconds later he announced, 'It's a girl.' She lay beside me, still wet like a water baby. She smiled and I saw her dimple and the afterbirth came out in a whoosh of love.

Almost immediately, as friends and intimate acquaintances dropped in to view her, Tracy's fame spread. Everyone who wanted to meet Ken now wanted to meet her — and she wanted to see them! She was the friendliest, funniest, happiest most beautiful child in the world.

'Girls are the thing,' the editor of the *Spectator* had written me at her birth. 'Girls are the thing. They are natural-born comedians.' Her godparents were Cecil Beaton, Katharine Hepburn, Vera Russell (then Lady [Gerald] Barry) and Richard Watts Jr, the drama critic of the *New York Post*. Shortly after Tracy was born, Ken, who had never met Hepburn, dashed down to Brighton to see her in the stage production of Bernard Shaw's *The Millionairess*. Backstage he asked her to be one of Tracy's godmothers as she was the reason we had so named her. No doubt astonished by the request, she nevertheless accepted, telling Ken that she herself had named the character Tracy because of the Tracy boats she used to see in East River — the J.M. Tracy tug boats, which seemed so 'yar' to her, chugging up and down the river in all weathers. So we'd named our child after a tug boat. Richard Watts was so enchanted with Tracy that he brought streams of his friends, newspaper colleagues from all over, to meet her. She smiled on them all, and received them all with equal pleasure. They were her slaves. Mary Martin held her in her arms as a baby, and when Tracy chewed contentedly on her pearl necklace, she said, 'That's right darling, get used to the real thing.'

James Thurber came around with his wife Helen, then returned with a present for Tracy — what she called her Thurberbook. It was a small English publication, a collection of his most profoundly funny cartoons, each with that eerie down-to-earth surreal touch that was uniquely his. It was an important gift. At an early age Tracy learned to read from it. Dick Avedon was another fan. When Tracy was five, he took her to a pet shop to choose a kitten as a gift.

After a quick stumble lasting two months — an Irish girl called Mary who was much too young — we found the perfect nanny, a German au pair called Friedl. Or rather she found Tracy, giving a gasp of affection upon first seeing her and only leaving after two and a half years to get married so she could have her own Tracy. She did not go until she satisfied herself she had found a suitable replacement, Elizabeth, who then in the same way found another suitable replacement, Christina, who was a highly skilled dressmaker and clothes designer too. She may have given Tracy her absorbing interest in fashion that later led her to become a costume designer in films.

That July Ken and I went to Pamplona for the bullfights. He had been commissioned to do an article for *Harper's Bazaar* by the powerful long-entrenched American editor Carmel Snow. She'd had us to lunch at the Dorchester that spring and offered Ken carte blanche to write anything he chose for a goodly sum of money. He chose Pamplona and the famous running of the bulls. Done. Anything else he wanted in particular? Yes, he wanted a photographer. Who? Ken thought. Henri Cartier-Bresson. Done.

Ken's mother arrived to help Mary look after Tracy. I was out when she arrived but when I came in Mary followed me to the bedroom and whispered in shocked tones, 'She keeps talking about all the terrible Jews on the train coming down from Birmingham and how they kept pushing her and trying to trip her up.' This did not further endear me to Ken's mother. Shortly after our marriage we'd gone to Birmingham so I could meet her. It was like a scene in a play. 'Elaine's an actress,' Ken said. 'Oh, I was just watching an American play on television, *Counselor at Law*. You could have been in it,' she said to me. 'Of course, they were all Jews,' she added with an appropriately disagreeable anti-Semitic expression on her face. When Ken told her I was Jewish, she made no reply. Neither did I.

And so we went to Pamplona. My resistance to detailing each and every one of the ten years of our bullfight summers is somewhat the same as Mark Twain's reluctance to stop the narrative flow of his books by describing the weather conditions therein.

Summers of sun, sea and swimming pools had been potent pleasures in my childhood and I welcomed them back into my life with something like ecstasy in the Spanish coastal towns where the bullfights often took us. At the Hotel Miramar in Malaga I would lie contentedly by the pool after a long swim, drying in the sun, and Ken would say in surprise, 'It doesn't take much to make you happy, does it?'

The overall atmosphere of these yearly fiestas, when we were part of the *afición*, was rife with boisterous high spirits, lots of jokes, hotly held opinions, short tempers, lengthy insults, and hurt feelings. Loving loyalties were followed by betrayals, then exchanges of letters full of accusations and apologies, and subsequently reconciliations, before the cycle began all over again.

In my mind all those hundreds and hundreds of corridas we saw have now melted in my mind so that now they are all one bull, one bullfighter and one bullfight.

Sometime in '53 we were invited to Chertly Court, the country estate of Lord Beaverbrook. He was a small gnome-like man and I was most impressed when, upon greeting me, he held on to my hand, asked me three easy questions about myself and then, as if apologizing for the presumption, said, 'When I'm nervous I always ask questions; it's a good rule.' It was as if he'd been all this time waiting in tense antici- pation for my arrival. So that's the way the big boys break the ice, I thought, and forthwith I felt at ease.

I took away only two wisps of the conversation at dinner. I was seated next to him and he started off with, 'Do you see that painting on the wall to your left? That's my wife, who died many years ago. I adored her. I have a granddaughter who's the living image of her. Her name is Jean Campbell and I'll see that you meet her. She is the apple of my eye and she can have everything she wants.' I liked him for saying that. I already had a weakness for short, straight-backed, suc- cessful grandfathers (like mine) who indulged their grandchildren.

I remember asking Beaverbrook if he was Catholic. This provoked his merriment and he wanted to know what made me ask. 'I was look- ing out the window behind you at the field with a huge cross blazing with electric lights.' He said it was to illuminate his cows in the evening. 'They are the most peaceful and serene animals in the world,' he said. 'I contemplate them for hours and it soothes me.' I looked closer and, sure enough, there were some calm Cuyp-like cows linger- ing around the cross.

I took in the rest of the dinner guests at some point and, though their names didn't register, Ken later told me that they were Labour politicians whom our host, a Tory, kept under his thumb by giving them space as writers on his papers. I had thought they were pretty rude to the old man, contradicting him at every turn. I actually felt sorry for him. Boy, was I lost. After dinner we went to his projection room and saw a movie, an Ealing film. There he was at my side again, asking me – not Ken, *me* – what I thought of it. I said I liked it because when I first walked around London everyone I saw looked exactly like a character in an Ealing comedy, and that would never be true of a Hollywood comedy. He seemed delighted. How could I not like him? Ken didn't. He was a much feared man, he said, and didn't trust him.

A few nights later we ran into Beaverbrook at the opening of *Porgy and Bess*. He did it again, asking me – not Ken – for my opinion. 'I know what I'm supposed to feel but I'm not sure I do.' A minority report, but honest. He nodded approvingly. Ken was annoyed. 'He treats you as if you're the power behind the throne,' he said. 'Sure,' I replied, 'I'm American. He thinks I'm Wallis Simpson.'

Twice afterwards we dined at Chertly. Same routine: different Labour politicians attacking Beaverbrook over the dinner table, Beaverbrook still courtly to me.

Early in May I started to rehearse for an official BBC TV Coronation play called *All on a Summer's Day* written by the popular author R.F. Delderfield. I played the daughter of the family, married to a GI. Ken told me I was working with some of the most versatile character actors of the British theatrical profession. They were in the comical/tragical, urban/rural, middle- to working-class category: Charles Hawtrey, Henry Oscar, Alison Leggatt, Gladys Henson and Eliot Makeham, as well as sturdy young rising actors such as Thomas Heathcote and Muriel Pavlow. From then on it seemed I kept seeing one or another of them whenever I turned on the TV, listened to radio, or watched a certain kind of English film or play.

I came in one day to overhear Ken talking on the phone; he hadn't seen me enter the room. It was immediately apparent that something of a sexual nature was going on. He hung up quickly when he saw me. I accused him. He confessed. He was having a fling. The woman turned out to be a new acquaintance of ours, a married woman on the verge of divorce. My first reaction was strong and simple. 'Okay,' I said, 'that's it. We're finished. It's over.' I was not unfamiliar with this aspect of male behavior. I had often enough been on the receiving end of unwanted passes made by young married men confronting fatherhood during the first year of their baby's life and feeling trapped or neglected because of it. I was also aware of the wives' reactions upon discovering their husbands' wanderings – they were to a woman passive and put upon.

I was not going to have a marriage like that. I was shaking with rage, but there were no tears, just angry shouting and threats to leave. So Ken called the woman up, said I'd found out, and dropped her.

Then, as so often would be the case in the future, the march of events seemed to require the two of us to show up at places together. Marriage, I was realizing, had a life of its own.

In June we met Gene Kelly and his wife Betsy Blair, who were to stay in England for a year. Every Saturday night they gave parties that lasted till 4 a.m. We played games, lots of different kinds but mostly the Game, that form of charades so popular in its day. That's how they spent their Saturday nights in Hollywood too, we learned. We went to Stratford with the Kellys to see *King Lear*, visited Edward Montagu, an Oxford classmate of Ken who though still in his early twenties was *Lord* Montagu already. I wrote my parents on his blue writing paper, headed *Palace House, Beaulieu, Brockenhurst, Hants*. In the New Forest, Edward reigned over a kingdom all his own. Besides the stately home (open to tourists on the weekend), he presided over a car museum, a yearly jazz festival and a ruined abbey. Early one morning I heard the sound of monks singing Gregorian chants and when a cock crowed they stopped. I told this to Edward at breakfast. He showed no surprise. His sister Elizabeth always heard them when she slept in that room, he said.

The placards by news-stands selling the *Daily Express* or the *Evening Standard* usually announced the results of a closely fought election, or a rugby match win, or a Duke's hotly contested divorce. Suddenly at the end of June they blazed with the provocative, if perplexing, question: 'Another Shaw?'

The mystery revealed itself to be a publicity campaign to further promote the *Standard*'s new drama critic. Both papers began to run ads with such excited headlines as 'Not since Shaw was young': 'Not since the time of young George Bernard Shaw has there been a theatre critic like Kenneth Tynan . . . he is the voice and spirit of youth . . . he has delighted theatregoers and infuriated those producers who have come under his lash. He has done a brilliant series of articles which will begin today in the *Evening Standard*.'

That this kind of hyperbole would set up exaggerated expectations of Ken's forthcoming articles was quite enough to put considerable pressure on him. He was discovering how deadly a weekly deadline could be with the additional workload of five long articles on top of his weekly reviewing.

Around this time the *Standard* chose to pull one of its mischievous Beaverbrook stunts. Much to the irritation of Ken, the paper would print letters attacking him. Simultaneously undermining their critic while puffing him, one day it even ran a whole page of letters under the heading 'Who's for Tynan? Who's for Baxter?' (its former critic).

For a while a running telephone conversation between feature editor Charles Curran and me had been taking place weekly at some time during the evening that Ken's piece was due. 'Mrs Tynan,' he would say his voice at once stern and supplicating, 'you *must* see that he gets his copy in on time!' And I would reply that it would be a lot easier if he stopped running letters attacking Ken. 'Don't let it worry him,' Curran would say, striving to minimize these snipes, 'you know how Beaverbrook is. He likes controversy.' And I would reply, 'It's hard for a critic to write with authority with all those letters denouncing him.'

One evening, in the middle of writing what would be Ken's last piece for the *Standard*, he took a break and we ate in a small local restaurant. He was exhausted and upset. Those letters really distressed him. 'I know they're all written in the office,' he kept saying. I said, 'Why don't you write to Percy Elland [the editor] and explain to him how you feel. I keep telling Curran but obviously I get nowhere.'

When Ken finished his review he gave me his copy to take down to the *Standard*. I asked if he'd written the letter. He put it in the envelope. I was to post it separately, he said before collapsing on the bed.

Soon after, on a summer morning, Ken looked up from the letter he'd been reading, turned to me, and said, 'Now look what you've done!' Crisis!

He thrust the letter at me: a curt note from Elland saying that in reply to Ken's letter his contract with the *Evening Standard* was hereby terminated. I was stunned. 'What did you write him?' I asked. He went into his study and came back with a copy of it. Arrogant and angry, with none of his famous acerbic wit and charm, it accused the *Standard* of printing adverse letters about him invented by their staff. He ended by warning that if they printed another he would sue them for libel and slander. When I got to that part I gasped.

Before I could utter a word he repeated that it was all my fault: I had insisted he write Elland. Thanks to me his career was in ruins. Once you got on the wrong side of Beaverbrook your name would never be mentioned in his papers; you became a non-person. Then, in the next breath he groaned that Beaverbrook would now hound him for the rest of his life.

I felt a physical jolt, as if I'd jumped off a merry-go-round before it stopped. Finally I caught my breath and said he ought to be glad of what had happened. Wasn't it just what he wanted?

I pointed out that over the past months we had discussed how his journalism was preventing him from doing things he really wanted, such as working on a book about his Oxford days, or a play he'd adapted with Peter Wildeblood of the Stella Gibbons novel *Cold Comfort Farm*. Wasn't this the very time to break away from bonds of weekly criticism? Together with his income from his father's trust and my own income we would have enough money to swing this. Let's take a year off, I urged. At least it would give him more time for his planned book on bullfighting. 'We could live in Spain for six months.' I said.

Ken saw things differently. He was out of a job. He would never get another. I was to ring Curran immediately and tell him Ken was sorry about his intemperate letter and that he would apologize. And, he added, I was to tell Curran that I'd put him up to it. I called Curran but the best I could do was to say it was partly my fault by encouraging Ken to write that letter. 'It's no good,' said Curran. 'It's done. Beaverbrook isn't going to change his mind. Let it go,' he urged me. 'The whole episode will only be an amusing footnote in Ken's biography.' I reported back to Ken, who called Elland, only to be told orders would not be rescinded.

Then he said I must write to Beaverbrook – he'd easily believe I'd put Ken up to it. So I sent Beaverbrook an awful cringing *mea culpa* letter. From the minute I posted it, I was sick with self-loathing. I could picture him reading it gleefully to his cronies. At the same time I asked myself why I'd found what I'd done so hateful.

Because I loved Ken. I had pledged myself to support him in every way. I did not type out his poems, or copy by hand his masterpieces, like Vivien Eliot or Sonya Tolstoy or other wives did for their great writer-husbands. Nor did I wash and iron his shirts or work as a secretary to earn the money we needed for him go on with his art. So this was the least I could do. He had raised me. Why was I dragging my feet?

My self-esteem, my sense of self, which I'd paid very little attention to since my marriage, was non-existent. In fact, Ken *was* my self-esteem. No illusion was more crucial to my belief system, even to my stability, than that Ken remain the sun around which I revolved.

This is not just a figure of speech. I was his satellite, contentedly spinning around him. I had written to Beaverbrook in Ken's study because I had nowhere else. I'd sat down at Ken's desk because I didn't have a desk of my own. I'd used Ken's writing paper because I didn't have any of my own. And I failed to notice I had none of these things because I didn't need them.

I began to think about the fact that I never talked over with Ken the roles I was playing on TV, never asked him how to play them or what he thought of my performances, wasn't even sure if he'd seen any of them. Perhaps he was always at the theatre at that time? My roles had not seemed significant enough to be worth his time or consideration.

It was confusing to stay in orbit around a sun that was now skidding around the sky. Strong conflicting air currents seemed to change his course without warning. He now desperately wanted the job he had for so long hated. He needed to be in sole control in steering his course but, when that went awry, he needed someone to blame. Some attacks against him he predicted and even looked forward to; others hurt him so badly they paralyzed him. And as he never gave me any indication which would do what, I too was thrown off course.

But my shame had most to do with my awareness that I wrote to Beaverbrook because I was too weak with love, too scared of falling away from Ken, of falling out of our heaven and crashing down to earth. All that seemed to matter was that I continue to spin safely around him forever.

My best response to the immediate situation was to resume drinking. There was nothing like a drink to reconcile opposing emotions colliding inside me. After my nine-month abstinence I seemed able to hold my drink as well as I had when I first began. If once in a while, I did get very drunk – well, so did every one else.

I didn't hear from Beaverbrook and, as Charles Curran had predicted, Ken stayed fired. Or rather, as the news was released, he 'resigned'.

I must take credit for twice helping Ken that year in ways that would have a lasting effect on the rest of his life.

The first had to do with the *Observer*. Ken had asked a mutual friend to sound out David Astor, the newspaper's publisher, about the possibility of Ken taking over from their critic Ivor Brown when he retired. When the friend reported back Astor's reply – 'Why would someone like Tynan want to work for the *Observer*?' – Ken gathered that Astor viewed him as all flash but no substance. I suggested that he send him *He That Plays the King* to change his mind. On that particular day, Ken was in one of his passive, hopeless, defenseless moods. He was looking very young, very much as I imagined he must have looked when hurt as child, so I mailed Astor a copy of Ken's book with the author's compliments. Then Ken, feeling a bit better, wrote Astor a letter positively demure in its modesty, indicating he would enjoy writing occasional theatre pieces for the *Observer*, or reviews of plays not covered by their present critic. Astor let Ken know he was most impressed with his book, and he began to write pieces for the paper. By December of '53 Ken and the *Observer* were in negotiations for him to become their main drama critic in 1954.

The other thing I did to change his existence was present him with a filing cabinet, an object seemingly unknown to Ken. Filing cabinets were among the office metal furniture my father's Universal Fixture plant manufactured, and a shining new four-door cabinet was sent to us. It reorganized Ken's public and private life, compacting and safeguarding his articles, correspondence, contracts and diaries. Just as important, it protected his secrets. From the very first, everything in it was kept under lock and key. Up until then, Ken had kept all his papers in a big laundry basket in our narrow hall, where everyone always bumped against it. Once, when for some reason its lid was left open, a dignified guest fell into it.

Ken was twenty-six years old when he signed the contract with the *Observer* that signified he'd attained his dearest wish, the pinnacle of his career, as he thought. His reaction was a sigh filled with divine discontent. He mourned, 'Now I'm just a critic.'

14

Life With and Without Ken

Early one Saturday morning in January of 1954 the telephone woke me. It was Peter Wildeblood. He was sorry, he explained, that he would not be able to take us to the ballet that evening as planned; he was being held at the police station, having been arrested for committing homosexual acts. 'Right now,' he went on without a pause 'I want to ask Ken to stand bail for me.' Ken took the phone, instantly said yes, dressed, went down to the police station and returned with Peter, who told us the whole story.

Two police officials had arrived at his door that morning before dawn, roused him out of bed and pressed their advantage over their half-asleep target. The older of the two, playing the sympathetic, caring father, began to interrogate Peter, throwing a lot of leading questions at him, always starting with, 'You know, you'll feel a lot better when you've told us all about it.' It seems three Royal Air Force enlisted men had been questioned and confessed to engaging in unlawful – that is, homosexual – activities at a certain time and place when on leave. Peter clearly had been identified by them as one of the participants. He immediately saw that the officer had the goods on him and, thrown off guard, confessed. Strangely, he did feel better.

He had long before come to abhor concealing the fact that he was gay.

Peter once told me he had always wanted to disclose to his mother that he was gay but found it hard to bring the subject up. He invited her to spend a weekend with him in Paris, where he took her to gay clubs hoping it would lead her to comment on them and then to Peter's revelation. Mrs Wildeblood immensely enjoyed herself and saw nothing out of the way. She would know now, said Peter, though not quite in the way he had wished.

Lord Montagu and Michael Pitt Rivers were also indicted in this case. All parties concerned were consenting male adults; no one was accusing anyone of having forced him to commit criminal acts. The three stood trial, were convicted and served sentences. To many people these arrests plainly looked not only discriminatory but political. It was this case that first called the public's attention to the fact that this law was outdated and unfair. In 1957 the Wolfenden Report recommended legalization of same-sex acts for consenting adults over the age of twenty-one. Not till 1969, however, was the Sexual Offences Act passed, repealing the original law.

Ken's response in agreeing to stand bail for Peter had been instant and whole-hearted, and when the storm broke around him so it remained. After the case hit the headlines, Ken was inundated with letters. Some called his action rash and unthinking and, many urged him to remove himself from it or be tainted with guilt by association. Others worried about its effect on his career, and some just took the occasion to attack him. These letters made me very uneasy. We knew many victims of 'un-American' McCarthyism. But Ken took it all in his stride.

Rebecca West's letter arrived almost the day the story broke. She commended Ken on his bold and noble action, counseled him to beware of the attendant dangers that would beset him, and then, with the shamelessness of a world-class journalist, demanded Peter Wildeblood's whereabouts as she wished to contact him. The other reaction I remember was that of David Astor who, just as swiftly, let Ken know how much he approved of him standing by his friend.

The beginning of that February found me as happy as I had ever been. Ken was the object of my admiration, and Tracy was romping up to the age of two.

I had never been aware of young children – had never known for instance, that when the infant feeds, the milk goes right down to her wiggling toes. Tracy was, daily, a most profound illumination and revelation. She understood that you waved and said bye bye to people to underscore their departure and so she waved and said it only after they were out of her sight. 'Where gone the ball?' she would ask. I thought she got to the crux of the matter quicker than grammar could. 'Where gone the phone?' she would ask after it stopped ringing. A good metaphysical question. A phone that stopped ringing was no longer a phone.

She soon learned the most important words of all: 'I want.' She said it with a vengeance. 'I want,' she would say, then point to an apple, a pencil, a penny, whatever. She was a reasonable child and most things she wanted we were able to supply. At five, however, I remember her asking me in March when her birthday was and when I said May, she burst into tears. 'It's too far away,' she sobbed, 'it's too far.'

Besides looking at Tracy, that February of '54 I looked at our calendar and was thrilled at the listing of the events the next months would unfold. As Ken did not start on the *Observer* till September, he had many months free. In March we would go to Hollywood; at the beginning of May we were going first to Rome for a quick tourist look, then on to Madrid for the *feria* of San Isidro. After that we were going down to Seville, then to Huelva, where Ken would again interview the bullfighter Litri for his planned book *Bull Fever*.

So why was it that three and a half years into our marriage I found myself in a supermarket deciding not to purchase a large jar of peanut butter? I was the only one in our household who ate it and the thought struck me with force that our marriage was not going to last before I finished it. What had happened?

Specifically, the Tot of Destiny had turned into the Marquis de Sade. And I, in response, had become a virago.

Prior to our marriage Ken had once confessed to me that at Oxford he had indulged in certain sadomasochistic practices that had been much in vogue at the time. He skimmed lightly over the subject, dismissing it as a part of his sexual education that he had no desire to continue. If I'd had a better understanding of exactly what was involved and how dedicated to these practices he had been, though, would it have stopped me from marrying him? *Of course not*. With the innate fatuity that has been the portion of lovers since the world began, I knew my love was powerful enough to keep him from slipping back into such undesirable behavior. It never occurred to me he'd intended my love for him to be powerful enough for me to submit to it.

One morning he announced that he was getting bored with our love-making and wished to return to his Oxford practices. I was a naive American who didn't understand the sophisticated joys of sado-masochistic sex, so he gave me two books to read. In the first the author said that it was a fact that sexual flagellation has been practiced in England with greater frequency than anywhere else. The second was convinced that the 'English vice' was not simply sadism but flagello-mania. I was, apparently, up against a revered British institution.

From his filing cabinet Ken unlocked his treasure of pornographic photographs and writings for my edification. There was a series of rit-ualistic sadomasochistic games he was determined to initiate me into.

I agreed to try, but it was not a success. The headmaster's cane was his weapon of choice. To cane a woman on her bare buttocks, to hurt and humiliate her, was what gave him his greatest sexual satisfaction. The session ended with my grabbing his cane and breaking it. The proceedings were so distasteful to me and my rage so complete that it was the last time he invited me to share these 'pleasures' for a while. Nowadays, when kink is king, my objection may seem quaint and out-dated. The fact was, however, that before Ken's idea of beating as foreplay I had never had a bad lay in my life. In short, I felt cheated.

Although I deeply hated it in theory and in practice, I submitted to his flagellomania on several different occasions, some lasting over the course of a week. And there were times when I submitted, that some-thing far worse was happening to me than the physical and moral pain. In the sexual excitement these acts produced in Ken, I was beginning to feel in myself a lickerish sense of excitement, the thrill of an accomplice collaborating at her own ruin. And then my rage would crash through again and the ordeal would be over. After that some time would elapse until he brought the subject up again – always dangling an 'either-you-do-or-I-know-someone-who-will' tag. And again I would discard reason in favor of self-destruction.

Abusive men, however, risk facing abusive wives. Ken found in me a wife not slow to hit back. Soon after the humiliations and punishment he would mete out to me while indulging in what he called his 'pastime' I would rally and with adder-tongued invective let him know how vile and evil I thought him. I was first at a loss to know where this fathomless fury came from. Then suddenly it became quite clear. It came from my father. I had inherited his rage.

Talk about appointments in Samara! I had fled my father and come all this way to fall in love and marry the one man I saw as the least like my father: physically, mentally and emotionally; the least like him in nationality, background, education, opinions, goals and occupations. My husband was as unlike my father as possible. Or so I'd thought. Now I had to face the bitterest irony of all: I'd married a man who in one fatally important aspect *was* like my father. Both men were violent towards women.

That February things took another frightening turn. Ken would stand on the ledge of our living room window at Hyde Park Gardens and threaten to jump if I left the room without agreeing to do something he wanted. We were disagreeing all the time now, and it would usually happen when I was going off to rehearsal, so I'd be ready a good half-hour in advance, allowing time in case he got on the ledge again. Ken's ledge-standing, which he used as a tool of persuasion, continued throughout our marriage, both at home and in the hotels where we stayed. On each occasion I was faced with the certain knowledge that he would *not* jump. Nevertheless I knew that he might *slip and fall*. And that his blood would be on my hands.

I cannot say if while I was married to him Ken ever had a sexual relationship in which his flagellomania did not play a part. But certainly my refusals to submit to it, he made clear, justified his infidelities. Inevitably it became a reason for me to justify mine. Now we had a solid rock upon which to build our fights.

Ken became highly critical of me, objecting to what I wore to the theatre with him as being too conservative. I said that because of his own resplendent clothes I dressed down because I didn't want us to look like a circus act. He liked to accuse me of being a Puritan. Almost everything I did or said showed I was a prig, a prude and a Puritan – especially about sex. I said no man I'd ever slept with would underwrite that remark. I accused him of being the Puritan. Who else but a Puritan would first have to punish a woman for arousing his sexual instincts before he could have sex with her?

Sometimes I felt like Sisyphus, ceaselessly rolling a huge stone of blame up a mountain. Just when I got it to the top and perfectly aimed to come crashing down on Ken, it would come rolling back on me. If I had plenty to be angry about Ken, he had plenty to be angry about me. I mean my drinking. If Ken didn't say enough about his sexual problems, before we married, I'd said nothing about my drinking problems – even after I saw they weren't going away. It had taken me only a year to catch up to where I'd left off before I was pregnant – brownouts, blackouts, the lot.

Now that the Hollywood trip was nearing I saw yet again that the march of events seemed to require the two of us to appear places together.

Before we went Arnold Weissberger, a well-connected theatrical lawyer, asked me if there was anyone I particularly wanted to meet. I'd heard that the playwright George Kelly now lived in Los Angeles and said I'd love to meet him. Easily arranged, said Arnold.

Soon after we arrived we were invited by Mr Kelly to his home in the Hollywood Hills. He was a bachelor, elderly and dignified. He had a male companion, and wore a hearing aid. We had tea and conversation. He said the hills were full of gangsters and the evenings were made horrendous with gunfire. Then he invited us to come back again next week and have tea with his niece, an actress whom he would like to meet Ken. To our astonishment she was Grace Kelly. Demure in a little white halo hat and little white gloves, the model of a respectful young actress meeting an English drama critic.

At Ira and Lee Gershwin's dinner for us were probably assembled the star intellects of movieland. I say probably because I do not recall who was there. The last thing I remember was sitting next to Oscar Levant, who kept saying, 'Why are you giving me such a hard time?' The hangover the next day lasted till noon. Ken gave me the silent treatment, so I never did find out what happened.

Judy Garland was fat in a caftan but talked easily and wittily and, for a lovely half-hour, allowed us to be intimately acquainted with her. She'd recently done A Star is Born, directed by George Cukor. She loved George, she said. We met George Cukor. He loved Judy, he said. He took a great shine to Ken and we both kept up our friendship with him. We stayed for hours at his house that day, walking around his beautifully landscaped gardens full of marble statues. Cukor said he wanted to work with Marilyn Monroe because 'she doesn't censor her thoughts'.

Jack Benny urged us to meet George Burns, who was smooth and growly, smoked a cigar and urged us to go to Vegas. There we watched Don Rickles famously insult his audience, his friends and one or two people in recent front-page scandals. We met Buster Keaton and his wife. No longer a headliner, he was doing a sad Vegas act at a minor hotel. We met George Stevens and became friends with his friend, scriptwriter Ivan Moffat.

We saw Gene Kelly again. We visited a very civilized Nunnally Johnson, who had scripted The Grapes of Wrath. We dined with Billy Wilder (looking very Hollywood) and his partner, Charles Brackett (looking very bank manager), at Chasens. We met Christopher Isherwood and Don Bachardy at their house amid a rustic setting seemingly miles away from Sunset Boulevard.

'Oh by the way,' Ken said to me one morning in May, 'since you refuse to join me in the sex practices I like, 'I've found someone who will.'

A protective numbness descended on me. 'Good,' I said. At the time I was standing by our closet in the bedroom, wondering what to wear to the rehearsal. By rote I chose a skirt and a sweater and slowly my mind began cranking up again. Thank God I have an acting job, I thought. It was the first day of rehearsal. Who would be there that I might be attracted to? At the end of the day I went out with some male members in the cast. We made the pub/club scene and I stayed out late. The excursion had provided me with plenty of high spirits but no flutters of expectation, not a spark of romance. I did get home late, though. Ken was asleep.

A day or two later, I found not a perfect lover but someone who was to become an important friend. Coincidentally, at the same time so had Ken. And curiously our friendships with each of these people had their foundations in *Persona Grata*.

Marlene Dietrich had come to London to make her highly publicized personal appearance at the Café de Paris, opening on June 21. She had read Ken's adoring lines about her in *Persona Grata*: 'She has sex but no gender . . . Dietrich's masculinity appeals to women, and her sexuality to men.' Dietrich was intrigued. She wanted to meet this man, and Ken wished for nothing more in the world than to meet her. They met, and clicked. Immediately she put him to work – along with Noël Coward – to fine-tune her coming performances in every single detail, from the running order of her songs down to the last spangle of her gown and the final cue of her lighting board. Ken was with her constantly night and day, so much so that Marlene actually rang me to say she would be glad to babysit, that I must be sure to call her when I needed someone. 'And when I babysit,' she added, 'I wash the dishes and clean the flat as well.' These words were the very same she was giving out in interviews about babysitting her grandchild. I was amused at her call – it was sweet – and I tried to reassure myself not to be jealous of her. After all, Ken liked them young and impressionable.

It was through *Persona Grata* that I became acquainted with Henry Green. Ken would grumble that in Cecil Beaton's selection for their book he very often simply chose people he had photographed before merely because he could use shots of them that had not already been published. The novelist Henry Green was one of them. Ken was not a keen novel reader so he had to go out and buy a Green book, chosing *Party Going*. I had never heard of him before but what Ken – and then others – said interested me.

Henry, a businessman as well as a writer, after a certain time, never allowed a photograph to be taken of his face. And, in Cecil's photograph in the book, there was Henry seated on a chair with only the back of his head, ears, neck and a portion of his suit visible. He was of the same literary generation as Evelyn Waugh, W.H. Auden, Christopher Isherwood, Cyril Connolly, George Orwell, Graham Greene, Nancy Mitford and Anthony Powell, all born between 1903 and 1905. In this bumper crop of Edwardian baby boomers, Henry Green was one of its brightest, most original, and most admired. He had written some nine books when, in 1952, he suffered what would be an almost terminal writer's block.

While authors as disparate as John Updike and Eudora Welty derived inspiration from his work, my experience was different. I derived inspiration from Henry himself. Right about the time Ken met Marlene, I first met Henry at a party given by Hilary Mackendrick. When I arrived, the first thing I saw was the back of a man seated on a sofa looking, in outline, exactly like Beaton's photograph of Henry Green. Upon being introduced I saw a man of about fifty with triangular eyes, a small mouth and dark hair that came to a widow's peak at his forehead. His expression was both amused and amusing. I sat as near to him as I could, listening to him talk.

He was describing how all the family members of his business, realizing he was now hard of hearing, had been told that the higher you pitch your voice the easier it would be for Henry to hear. From then on, at every board meeting his ears were assaulted by the screeching of grown men.

Hilary had met Henry because they both frequented the same pub for lunch, the Wallace Head near the Wallace Museum in George Street; their offices were nearby. Why didn't I join them sometime for lunch? I soon did and after that Henry and I met often at another nearby pub, just the two of us.

These lunches were among the most enjoyable I've ever shared. Henry laughed easily; you wanted to make him laugh. He was hard of hearing, but very cleverly overcame this by manipulating the conversation so that he somehow preset its limits, not so much of time and place, but in subject matter and mood. He was someone with the highest gift for drawing you out and staying in step with you, which I am sure is consistent with there never being an intrusion of the author's voice in his novels. As it has been noted, Green kept his face out of his novels just as he turned his back on the camera.

I told him about some of my misadventures in Paris. I described how I met James Bond's creator Ian Fleming at a party and how he'd advised me never to drink anything but Gilbey's gin because it was double distilled, therefore you never got hangovers. I called up my wineseller and asked for Gilbey's gin because I'd heard it was double distilled, and was told *all* gin was double distilled. So much for 007, connoisseur.

I began to recognize that I was hearing a voice that was me but that wasn't me. It was a voice Henry gave me, yet I'd heard it before. But never this clearly. It let me play the screwball again. It went back to my mistaking the Avenue d'Iena for the Champs Elysées, to growing aware of having this intrusive, alter ego inside me, this comic character whose presence I had to give space to. With Henry I saw it as a release from the ever-lurking depression that threatened my existence. Henry was just what I needed: an enheartener magically capable of cheering up a lonely, distraught and rudely awakened wife.

Years later, in 1980, when dining with a good friend, Cole Lesley, who had been Noël Coward's long-time associate, confidante and biographer, he told me his story about what happened after Dietrich's opening at the Café de Paris on that long-ago evening in June of 1954. It had been a triumph for its star. Noël, Cole, Noël's companion the actor Graham Payne, and Ken gathered at Dietrich's suite at the Dorchester afterwards to toast her success and replay her triumph. As it was getting late, Noël and his contingent said their goodnights and left. Significantly, they noted, Ken had stayed behind with Dietrich. In the hall they found themselves waiting for the elevator for some time.

'Poor little Mrs Tynan,' said Noël, 'she must be putting her head in the oven by now.' No sooner had he uttered this than Ken appeared. The elevator arrived and they all descended together. 'There was a most embarrassed silence,' said Cole, 'because of the discovery that Dietrich and Tynan were *not* having an affair after all.'

'Poor little Mrs Tynan,' I corrected, 'was – at that very moment – on the town with Henry Green. The great English novelist,' I added for dramatic effect.

Henry and I had been lunching together the day of Dietrich's opening and I had mentioned that I didn't much like the idea of sitting around at home by myself while Ken was out. He said that his family had gone to Ireland and that he was alone too. We decided to go out together. He'd been invited to a roulette party at the house of Mark Boxer, an attractive young man we both knew who would have several claims to fame. (Among them was being rusticated from Cambridge for printing a poem in *Granta*.)

The reason for the roulette party was that Mark hoped to amass enough money from it to pay for a trip to the South of France. It was fairly chaotic as Mark was croupier and sometimes mixed up the commands '*Rien ne va plus*' for '*Faites vos jeux*', with the results that no one knew whether to put down their chips or pick them up, or whether they'd won or lost. So they'd have to start all over again.

After a while Henry and I left and went on to a couple of expensive nightclubs such as the Embassy and the 400 and then, having closed the last one, we went over to Henry's house at 16 Trevor Place. At some point I decided not to go home. It was too late and I was too drunk and did not relish the sight of an empty bed. If Ken did come home and I did not, the sight of an empty bed would serve him right.

In his den Henry and I improvised a bed for me. The next thing I knew it was morning and Henry was at the door – Ken was on the phone, did I want to speak with him? I said no but Henry came back and said, 'He's calling at eleven thirty.' I went back to sleep.

It seemed only two minutes later that Henry was at the door again saying, 'Ken is here.' I sat up in bed, naked, and said, 'I thought you said he was calling me up.' What he meant by the word 'calling' was that Ken was coming over. I said, 'Only in English, not American.'

I got dressed, starting from scratch, thinking how like me – the Henry me, in my screwball mode – to get something like the English 'calling' mixed up with 'calling up' so that I would have to come face to face with Ken when I had not the least desire to.

Henry and Ken were talking pleasantly over drinks when I came in. Ken rose and looked at me as I had not seen him do so for a long time. He made as if to come forward then stopped and said humbly, 'Skippy, darling, I was so afraid something had happened to you. Thank God you're all right.' Henry was all jolly urbanity and Ken all respectful tenderness, and I joined them in a drink in the convivial atmosphere. Henry said that about this time he always went to the pub in Montpelier Square to meet Arthur Koestler – would we care to join him?

The double eye string had threaded itself again between Ken and myself and I didn't even have to look at him to feel its tug, which said how eager he was to meet Koestler, one of his idols. But when we got there and had a drink, Ken didn't touch his but kept playing with my hand and looking at me questingly until I looked back yes. He stood up, still holding my hand, and said he was sorry but we really would have to go.

Back home we went straight to bed and made love in all our lovely old ways. Afterwards he said, 'I'm not having an affair with Marlene, you know.' I said I knew. And I said, 'I'm not having an affair with Henry,' and he said he was so afraid I was. I asked about the girl he'd found who liked what he liked? And he said there wasn't any; he'd just made it up because he felt lonely because I was leaving him to go to rehearsal.

One evening Ken took me to the Café de Paris and before the show we went to Dietrich's dressing room and I met her. Later he stopped by alone to compliment her or whatever. When he returned he told me she'd said, 'How dare you introduce me to your wife!' He seemed as surprised as he had been the time when Orson threw him out of his dressing room.

July was peaceful. Almost perfect, it seemed. There was Ken and Henry and Tracy.

I went on lunching with Henry, and Ken kept on seeing Marlene. We had arrived, it seemed to me, simply and legitimately, at that time of a marriage where we could sometimes prefer to be safely with someone else.

Around July, I did an episode in *Fabian of Scotland Yard*. I did a sketch with Bernard Braden, the popular Canadian comedian on *The Vic Oliver Show*, which was known as the English equivalent of *The Milton Berle Show*. Oliver, the compere and a dance band leader, was then married to Sarah Churchill, the actress daughter of Winston

Churchill. She invited us to a cocktail party where I found myself standing in a group composed of herself, Natasha Parry (married to Peter Brook) and Suzanne Cloutier (married to Peter Ustinov). Suzanne, noting we were all actresses with one thing in common, suddenly said, 'I wonder which of us has the hardest time getting parts because of our illustrious connections?' We each had our own war stories. I described theatre auditions where I was told, 'You read well but if you don't get the part I hope your husband won't give us a bad review, ha, ha.' I said I got so tired hearing this that I stopped going to them and stuck to television. The others commiserated. Having to reroute my career in this manner was a minor pitfall compared to others that had developed in our marriage though.

In August we returned to Spain to stay ten days for the San Sebastian and Bilbao *ferias*. We invited a new friend, a young American woman, Margot Scadron, to come along. Ken made an ostentatious play for her in front of me, and the next afternoon, also in my presence, she berated him for following her to her hotel room and propositioning her when she was retiring for a siesta. She told him she thought his behavior disgusting. I went to my room. Ken came after me, bad-mouthing her, swearing she was lying. Shortly thereafter she left for England. Our recent armistice was definitely over. I too planned to leave and was packing when Ken came up from the lobby and said that Orson was there. I unpacked.

We spent the next week in Orson's company. It was not only the first time we had been to bullfights with him but also the first time I was exposed to the full blast of the charm and scope of his conversation. It was also the thousandth time (since my early teens) that I'd fallen under the spell of the indescribable melodies and phrasings his voice played upon – Miles Davis had cited it as one of his main musical influences.

It is still hard for me to believe that Orson was only thirty-nine at the time. He had a way of making extraordinary sweeping statements that seemed to cry out for rebuttal. He told us, for example, that when he was in South America at the beginning of World War II, as a special emissary of President Roosevelt, he met and dated as a call girl a young radio actress named Eva, who later metamorphosed into

Argentina's beloved Eva Peron. He informed us that in the twenties Budapest and Peking were the two great artistic centers of the world. (These assertions, I would discover later, turned out to be not untrue.) Playfully, he would imitate a typical Frenchman's reaction to a bull-fight; while the rest of the crowd yelled their *olés* he would content himself with a Gallic '*Ah, quelle jolie passe*'. He regaled us with his treks from Harlem down to the Stork Club in Manhattan and back up again during his acclaimed black Macbeth production in the thirties. He described how he won the veneration of the young Frank Sinatra by his easy friendships with the great black musicians, and his easy use of the black vernacular, dropping such remarks as 'Dig you cats later' as he took off from one spot to the other.

When we returned to London I was forced to face how important to me was the life that Ken led, how willingly I danced attendance on it and how completely I owed him the sort of existence I had always promised myself.

What it always came down to was my making the effort to detach myself from him, of that I was fully aware. What I was only half-aware of was that I'd better make something of myself too.

Ken's first article in the *Observer* came out the first Sunday in September 1954. Though he still shied away from telling the plot of a play – that would always be his weakness – he remained matchless in describing a performance on a given night. No matter how severe his criticisms, they still disarmed by their wit. No living drama critic would outdo him in his arresting opening sentences or the compelling summations of his closing ones. He wrote with growing authority and growing use of an empowered first person, lengthening his column and widening his scope to include world theatre. He traveled incessantly to compare and contrast every country's theatrical contributions, meet-ing with all the heads of these theatres for discussions on its drama. No critic was more actively concerned with the fate of the theatre.

Late in November, I auditioned for an interesting stage play called *The Ghost Writers*, about American blacklisted writers. It was to be directed by Bernard Braden at the Arts Theatre and the part I read for was a good one – the young female lead. One of the producers called me a week later to say that they liked my reading and would be deciding on the cast sometime in the next month. As I was planning to be in Paris over Christmas (the *Observer* was sending Ken for a fortnight), I gave him the phone number at the Hotel Louis Le Grand.

I hadn't wanted to go to Paris. I'd wanted to stay and see if I got the part, but when I objected to going, Ken staged another ledge standing. I agreed and arranged to have Tracy stay with her nanny, Elizabeth, at her home in Salzburg.

Christmas Eve we arrived in Paris. We must have gone to any number of plays, but what I remember is the nightly visits to the Crazy Horse Saloon, a popular Parisian cabaret of beautiful girls, scantily clad or nude. From this an idea began to obsess Ken. Why not put on a sexy sophisticated nude review in England or America? Out of this grew *Oh Calcutta!*

On January 7, 1955, when we returned to London, I found three telegrams waiting for me. The first two offered me the role I'd read for in *The Ghost Writers*. They hadn't been able to reach me by phone either at the Paris hotel or at our flat. The third wire said they'd had to start rehearsals and had given the role to André Melly. I was flabbergasted.

Then I realized what had happened: another difficulty in getting parts because of my illustrious connection was traveling under my married name and forgetting to leave my professional one at the hotel desk.

15

I Was Walking Down the Street
One Day When Suddenly . . .

Around mid-March of '55 we went to New York, staying at the Buckingham Hotel in the West 50s, in the heart of everything.

Our friend Johnny Marquand Jr threw us a party on our arrival. We met writers who would become the nucleus of the *Paris Review* parties I would regularly attend in the late fifties and the sixties, including George Plimpton, William Styron, Norman Mailer, Philip Roth and James Baldwin.

As I was heading for the exit a slim, young man with a sharp nose, a prominent flash of teeth and floppy hair falling over his brow waylaid me and said, without preamble, 'Do you know Henry Green?' When I replied yes his whole body seemed to relax as if his long search was over. 'Can we talk about him?' he asked. I said I was just leaving and he looked crestfallen, so I told him I was staying at the Buckingham but he shouldn't phone me right away because I was busy. He gave me his name, which I promptly forgot.

During the fortnight Ken was there we saw lots of plays. The last one we saw together was Tennessee Williams's *Cat on a Hot Tin Roof*, an immediate and immense hit. A couple of days later Ken flew back to London. I was having a good time, so I stayed on.

That next Sunday, in celebration of its success, Tennessee gave a tea at the St Regis Hotel for his mother so that she would meet what would ultimately appear to be the first thousand people who most wanted to be in her company.

I had invited Johnny Marquand to go with me and by some miscalculation we arrived on time. This meant that there were only a few people present, so I was able to watch and listen to the rhythm of the party as it swelled and yelled to its peak.

I got to say how d'you do to Mrs Edwina Williams. She was wearing a Hat – not a hat, but a Hat. It was a perfect garden party hat, straw and suitably festooned. She was also wearing a garden party gown. She definitely stood out in the crowd, delineating to perfection her role as the mother of the South's most famous playwright.

As I watched the profusion of American Greats milling around I commented to Johnny that everyone, absolutely everyone in the theatre, was there.

'Some writers too,' he said. 'There's Gore Vidal.' He explained that Gore was one of the new young novelists, bracketed with Truman Capote but tough rather than tender.

I didn't hear any more for at that moment a buzz and a rustle ripped through the crowd. Everybody stopped what they were doing, freeze-framed with their drinks, hors d'oeuvres or cigarettes halfway to their mouths.

They were all looking in one direction. A path had been cleared, and walking through it was Marilyn Monroe. She was wearing what anyone else would have called an underslip, a simple, unadorned black silk slip with thin shoulder straps and clearly nothing under it. Her skin was a luminous alabaster with pearly blue and rose tints such as I have never seen outside paintings by the Old Masters. She was more astonishingly beautiful in the flesh than on celluloid and we all stared silently in our reverence.

Eventually the party started up again. By then I had worked my way around to her part of the room and was rewarded with the following *tableau vivant*: blonde Marilyn was seated in an armchair. On one of its arms perched Carson McCullers, her brown hair chopped short and uneven as if she'd taken an ax to it, her body fierce in tomboy tension and twisted like a pretzel. Sitting in a chair on the other side of Marilyn-in-her-slip was Edwina-Williams-in-her-Hat. They were conversing with each other, all three with heads inclined. The Three Fates, I decided; Beauty, Brains and Motherhood. Whose destiny were they spinning out at that very moment?

Among the many people I met and remet was the formerly brown-haired and now very blonde Maria Britneva. She was playing Blanche in *Streetcar* at the Actor's Playhouse, an off-Broadway theatre and would put two tickets in my name at the box office.

He didn't telephone, but suddenly the young man who wanted to talk about Henry Green began appearing in front of the elevator in my hotel lobby waiting for me. The first time, as I was stepping out, he was holding tulips that were slightly droopy so he must have been waiting quite a while. Couldn't we talk for a few minutes? I said I was late – sorry, some other time? He was there the next day just as I was coming in. The tulips, still in his hand, flopped like his floppy hair. I was late for an appointment, sorry. He turned up a third time. I was going out to buy liquor for people dropping in for drinks. I asked him if he could come along and help me carry them. He said yes. I asked him to tell me his name again. It was Terry Southern, who would become a very successful screenwriter.

Back in the hotel room he helped me arrange the liquor and the ice and glasses and all, then we sat down and he talked a little about himself. He was a writer, originally from Texas, a town called Alvarado. He told me that as a boy he had copied out word for word stories by Edgar Allan Poe. I thought this was very peculiar and interesting and I thought, This guy is serious. He worshipped Henry Green's work yet few people in America even knew it, and I was the first person he'd found who knew him.

I talked about Henry until my guests arrived. There was something I began to like about Terry. He'd been so quietly efficient in helping me prepare for my guests. Not only was he easy at helping me with the drinks, but he got along easily with my friends. And then, when they left, he was still there, unobtrusively helping me tidy the place up.

I found myself inviting him to see Maria in *Streetcar* two days from

then. I had never seen her act and thought she was all wrong for
Blanche Du Bois. Terry – who obviously belonged to no theatre
clique – would be the least likely person to spread the bad news of her
performance if, in fact, that's what it was.

So we went. To my surprise, Maria was *good*. For the first time I was
able to see Blanche play the scene with the beautiful young man selling flowers as if wanting to make love to him was not a case study of
sick compulsions but, from her point of view, the most natural thing in
the world.

After the play we went back with Maria to Tennessee's apartment,
where she was staying (the playwright had skipped town, as he usually
did after a play of his opened). Maria calmly took out of her deep rain-
coat pockets a door knob, some screws, a screwdriver and a dead bolt,
then proceeded to unscrew all the locks on the front door. Apparently
some undesirable person had managed to make duplicates of
Tennessee's keys and was always attempting to get in the apartment at
odd hours. With Terry masterminding the operation, the locks were
swiftly changed.

I was to see more of Terry during my stay. He had not a trace of a
Texas accent but instead a very funny, very catching sort of clipped
delivery, peppered with meaningful italics. It was Terry who coined the
phrase 'the Quality Lit. Set' to define the literati at *Paris Review* parties. 'Cooling it somewhat off the scene,' was another phrase of Terry's
that was to install itself in my vocabulary as an adroit description of
one's action in avoiding potentially embarrassing encounters. I also
found useful Terry's description of the art of editing as a 'tightening
and brightening' process. If he was particularly pleased with something you'd done or the way you looked you were in his phrase 'a
perfect darling'. I also liked him addressing me as 'Miss Smart'.

Shortly after I returned to London I received a letter from Terry
describing a weekend in Fire Island. Henry was in Leeds at the time,
and, thinking the letter very funny, I sent it to him, having already
mentioned the young American writer who was passionate about his
work. I was certainly not prepared for Henry's reaction. 'I know nothing
about your friend,' he wrote, 'except that he is a genius.' I immediately
relayed this to Terry and put them in touch with each other.

Letters went back and forth between these two and a friendship developed. A year or so later Terry married and moved to Switzerland and Henry went to Geneva to visit them. Terry showed Henry his novel *Flash and Filigree*; Henry considered it 'dazzling' and sent it off to the publisher, André Deutsch, who said he would publish it with the proviso that Henry would write a review of it. Henry's review in the *Observer* ended: 'Let everyone salute Mr Terry Southern, who with only his first novel already has a winner.' Thus Terry, like many other American authors, was first published in England. Terry and his singular talent went from strength to strength: the screenplay for *Easy Rider* (for which he received no credit), the screenplay of *The Loved One*, from the novel of Evelyn Waugh, and my favorite, *Dr Strangelove*.

Sometime after their historic meeting in Geneva, I lunched with Henry and we talked of Terry. 'We're going to resurrect me,' said Henry happily, and he spoke about a play he was writing. The play didn't happen but their longtime friendship did. I thought with immense satisfaction, had I not been anything less than a 'perfect darling' in bringing these two writers together.

On my return from New York in April, Ken had been very glad to see me. Our separations often had that effect on him. This time he lay ill with hepatitis. The doctor had prescribed bed rest, a special diet and no drink but champagne, so I lay beside him blissfully happy while we drank champagne, rented a projector and watched movies we wanted to see. Cocteau's *Les Enfants Terribles* was our favorite. Brother and sister were in love with each other and for that moment in time we too felt this consanguinity.

After Ken recovered, the oasis that had been for us such a refuge of happiness vanished as we started back to our routine of theatre-going and social activities.

How drearily my life seemed to stretch out before me. In the midst of all the rich full busyness I felt a gray everydayness, a monotony, a sinking into depression that was always close to the surface. A dismal scene from my past kept coming back to pull me further down. I kept remembering one particular lunch in my junior year at Sweet Briar when I'd looked at my plate filled with soggy string beans, lumpy mashed potatoes and a tomato concoction we called train wreck. I had looked around the table and realized my lunch mates and I had nothing to say to each other. One and a half more years of this, I had thought.

I played another small part as a nurse in a segment of the TV series called Douglas Fairbanks Presents. I told the costume woman that the shoes were much too big for me but she said they were all they had and to put Kleenex in them. I wondered what the hell I was doing after all these years as an actress and then as a mother having to put Kleenex in my shoes? They began shooting my scene and they were in a hurry. 'C'mon, we've got to get this scene in the can before lunch,' the cameraman was told. Finally we broke for lunch, I changed into my street clothes and went off shopping in Oxford Street. When I got home there were urgent messages. They needed me to reshoot the scene. I didn't ring back. Neither did they.

I began to think that maybe forgetting to give my professional name at the hotel in Paris had been some kind of signal I was sending myself. I seemed to be withdrawing from acting. I worked regularly and steadily, but the parts were *nothing*.

My depression turned to resentment and my resentment landed on 'them' out there who kept giving me those nothing jobs. I was above that now. I stopped phoning my agent, perusing the *Stage* for possible jobs, having new glossies made, keeping my ear to the ground trying to catch some whisper of activity, calling directors and other actors I'd worked with to see if they knew of anything that might be right for me.

I said to Ken, 'Either I'm giving up acting or it's giving me up. It just doesn't mean anything to me anymore.' He suggested that I write a novel. The letters I'd written him during my stay in New York showed him I could write a very good novel. He said it seriously, emphatically. Ken could be a great encourager. It was part of what made him a great critic. He also set me an example as a hard-working and dedicated writer.

Ken didn't want to see the novel he said until it was finished because he would not know my story's intentions. That made sense. It would also make me want to finish it. I decided I would write a wonderful novel and that he would be proud of me. And all would be as it so beautifully had been once upon a time.

I'd also made a profound discovery: one thing you can do without being asked is write a novel.

To begin with there was that persistent feeling of never coming across a part that was right for me. Or for any of my female friends, or any young female I had struck up an acquaintance with next to me in a café or at a hairdresser's.

Ken's praise of American playwrights in writing roles for the unique girl, who exists in her own right, independently and eccentrically alive, was bullseye, but I felt that even American playwrights and novelists didn't go far enough. They didn't get into all those complications and contradictions going on inside the contemporary girl as I knew her. They never showed that, in spite of her wit, intelligence, education and ever-present self-awareness, these complications and contradictions could lead her into many comic situations as well as life-threatening ones. I would tell it all in the first person, in the voice I'd been polishing up on Henry. In short, I would write a great part for myself.

Then there was my hangout – the Buckstone, where young creative people met to exchange ideas and stimulate each other. Every good young English actor and actress turned up there. Peter O'Toole, Albert Finney, Tom Courtenay, Robert Shaw, Denholm Elliott, Jill Bennett, Maxine Audley, Vanessa Redgrave, Maggie Smith, Claire Bloom, Virginia McKenna, Siobhan McKenna, Rosemary Harris – all came and went. Young playwrights such as John Osborne, Harold Pinter and Sandy Wilson went there as did *Intimate Revue* writers such as Peter Myers, Alec Graham and David Clime, and Sandy Mackendrick and other English film directors. The list is endless. Every young actor playing in every West End theatre and the Old Vic went down those stairs.

They were a group of diverse young people from every background, loosely tied together by a consensus that they were all equally brilliant at doing best what they liked to do most. For very little money, which I think was an intrinsic part of it. The Old Vic, for instance, was not paying £30,000 a week for Richard Burton to play Hamlet or Claire Bloom to play Juliet. Thirty pounds was more like it. It kept them all hungry, alert, willing to take chances, and made their art a main consideration. I'd sit watching them wearing their accomplishments so effortlessly, and was inspired and reassured. I felt I would succeed because they had.

One morning I opened a notebook and wrote 'I was walking down the street one day when suddenly—'. A good beginning, *in medias res* and all that. What street? As the street grew clearer I saw it was in Paris, so it was a boulevard. (And some months, or maybe a year later, those first words would finally become: 'It was a hot, peaceful, optimistic sort of day in September. It was around eleven in the morning, I remember, and I was drifting down the Boulevard St Michel, thoughts rising in my head like little puffs of smoke, when suddenly . . .')

The only person I knew something about was the heroine. Her name was Sally Jay Gorce, because Gorce is the name of a Thurber character I loved in *Men, Women and Dogs*. 'Miss Gorce,' says another Thurber character, 'is in the embalming game.' And I chose Sally Jay because it sounded so American. Sally Jay was walking down the boulevard and I knew she was wearing an evening dress in the middle of the morning because I'd worn one for a couple of days in Paris before I managed to get to the cleaner to retrieve the rest of my clothes.

Somebody stopped Sally Jay, of course, the man she would fall in love with. Would he be the hero, or the villain? Undecided. He was called Larry, like Larry Olivier, and looked like Jonathan Miller, whom I'd seen in the Cambridge Revue, *Out of the Blue*, in 1954, and whose looks I liked a lot. For some reason I gave him a scar on his forehead. Sally Jay was an actress and Larry was an actor and they already knew each other and went to a café when suddenly – what? She saw her lover, an Italian diplomat called Alfredo who looked like Rafael Ortega, the bullfighter we'd seen at our first bullfight in Madrid. I gave him the nickname of Teddy to make him seem slightly ridiculous. When I got stuck I would say to myself, 'What would I *not* do?' and then I would have Sally Jay *do* it, and I would be off again.

Events from when I was single in Paris were mixed in with events in Spain when married, and characters popped up from all periods of my life. Sally Jay's beloved uncle had characteristics of Maxwell Anderson plus his telescope. I kept my friend Judy's first name and most of her history, but I gave her a Spanish father. With enormous round eyes and a slender stem of a neck, she looked like the adorable young Anna Massey, who had made a sensational debut that May in *The Reluctant Debutante* in the West End. Left Bank ex-GIs got mixed up with actors from the Dramatic Workshop. A bullfighter and his entourage that I'd spent some time with in Seville surfaced. A photographer suddenly made an important appearance. He looked like Ken and I gave him some of his background, but his ethos and life experience were based on the great war photographer Robert Capa, and the house he inhabited in Greenwich Village, with the tree growing through it, belonged to Dick Avedon.

Writing instead of acting gave me more time for Tracy. I watched as she grew ever more fascinating with each year. We would have people to drinks several times a week, and Tracy aged four or five, fresh from her bath in a blue wool bathrobe with a white bunny embroidered on it, would come rushing in, her shining dark brown hair cut short with bangs clinging to her beautifully shaped head like a helmet.

She would shake hands with everyone, dropping a quick curtsy at the same time, as she was taught in dancing school, then she would sit quietly listening to our guests. And when I'd say it was time for bed, she'd rise and kiss everyone goodnight and bound out of the room. I'd think how unlike either of us she was in every way, happy, sensible, reasonable. How relieved I was, thinking she'd not inherited our quick tempers or impatience. I prayed for her to be as little like me as possible. What an admission to make. I tempered it by deciding that the combination of Ken's and my genes had produced this wonder.

I discovered the wonderfully comfortable and excellent American Library in Grosvenor Square. It was there, in the peace and quiet, that I got down to work and the book became a reality.

Late one afternoon, after I'd come home, Ken followed me into the bedroom and closed the door. We were in for another crisis. He was about to be prosecuted by the Post Office for sending pornographic material through the mail. He'd received a letter that day with an official statement.

It turned out that for some months Ken had been exchanging letters with a correspondent whose name he had found through a personal column in a porn magazine in a Soho bookshop specializing in sadomasochistic material. (He thought he was corresponding with a woman when, in fact, it was a man.) He'd just been to his lawyer, who said it must have been part of a clean-up drive by the Post Office to find out what was in the letters set up by pornographic magazines and told Ken to leave England for a fortnight. If they couldn't find him, he assured him, it would blow over. Ken's plan was to call Johnny and Sue Marquand, who were now married and living in a villa in Los Palamos, outside Barcelona. He would ask them up to put us up for that length of time, saying he had to leave the country on account of some fiddling he had done with his income tax, which could only be righted if he were away for the specified time. Of course I would go with him. I said no.

I was deeply shaken. I could see as clearly as if I'd been there in Ken's study late some night when his work wasn't going well or when he was bored that his need for some gratification of his sexual desires was so strong, so uncontrollable, that in lieu of the real thing he could only assuage it with this outlet. With my interest in my novel and with Tracy-watching, I'd found I could push this problem away, even think that since it hadn't come up for a while it was gone. Yet once more I saw the power of his sexual needs. I understood his predicament and was horrified.

Ken insisted I go with him to the Marquands', and in the end I gave in, saying goodbye to Tracy with a pang. I took the chapters of my novel with me and worked on them.

The Post Office scare went away. Life settled down again as we found a focus for our mutual energies. We'd been finding Hyde Park Gardens too small for us, and begun flat hunting.

When Ken went to Paris to review its theatrical season I went with him. One evening the play was Bertold Brecht's epic *Mother Courage*, staged at the huge Palais de Chaillot, the home of the Theatre

National Populaire. Suddenly I thought of Piscator and his Epic Theatre: big topics, large casts, actors coming out of the audience and so forth. I passed on it.

As a result I missed being on the spot at Ken's conversion. By the time he arrived back at our hotel room, his views were in place. 'I have become a Marxist,' he announced. He went on to describe the extraordinary experience he had just been part of. He had never seen *Mother Courage* before, (a contemporary classic acclaimed everywhere in Europe *except* London, he would always say.) In a magnificent performance of this epic of the Thirty Years War, Brecht had compressed the squalor of all wars. Ken had never before seen an audience of a thousand people in one theatre rise cheering and weeping from their seats. Its Marxist message was glorious to him. He was its latest recruit.

While I did not bounce up and down hugging him with tears and laughter and congratulate him on his transformation, neither did I have the reaction to his statement that caused our ex-Marxist American friends to cover him with derision. Wasn't Ken just a little late to take up the Marxist banner? Ken, as they never tired of kidding him, was either an innocent or a fool, a throwback from the thirties.

I found his Marxism interesting, understandable, even logical. Early enamored in his Oxford days with the exalted theatre of stars playing kings, Ken had for some time seen that it was only their heritage or chicanery that allowed them the throne in the first place. Nor was he happy with the facetious and fairly meaningless metaphor he used in one of the first columns he wrote for the *Observer* as its drama critic, when he defined his role as that of being a lock waiting for a key – the work of art – that fit snugly into his bias or prejudices. What he'd needed was a larger, clearer point of view: a focus, a standard, a point of departure. A life-long atheist, he needed a belief, a philosophy, a cause.

Being a Marxist gave his criticism what he most wanted. The socially conscious plays of Brecht and Arthur Miller were now the keys that unlocked his heart. All drama was political, he insisted, and what was happening on stage had to connect with what was happening in the world. Plays, he now contended, must make people face today's realities, even if they exceeded the worst nightmares of Hamlet or Oedipus.

I welcomed his new social consciousness, because I held a mistaken idea that his metamorphosis meant that the more he became involved in humanitarian causes – whether the plight of migrant workers or nuclear disarmament – and the more egalitarian he became, the more likely he would drop his desire to inflict physical and mental pain on another member of the human race. Specifically me!

He picked up the phrase 'It is a sin to make money breed', which became one of his slogans. It put him on sticky ground. Not only was he living off his father's investments, but my money, of which we freely availed ourselves, came from my father's and my grandfather's investments.

Every man to his own Marxism. Not for Ken the Orwellian journey down the road to Wigan Pier. Not for him actual contact with the people whose lot he was throwing himself in with. As long as I knew Ken there was never a man of the working class inside our home. He marched to Aldermaston for nuclear disarmament, marched to Downing Street in aid of civil disobedience. He and his chums wrote strong letters to *The Times* against the Suez crisis and any other Tory proceedings. He took instruction from seasoned left-wing activists such as Doris Lessing and Christopher Logue. Didn't that make up for a lack of prole pals?

16

Life in Mount Street

At 120 Mount Street we finally found the flat we'd been looking for and by the autumn of '55, with workmen still around
us, we moved in.

From the outside you would have said our life there could not be
improved upon. We were in the heart of Mayfair, one of London's most
luxurious districts. The antique shop and auctioneers Christie's, with
its opulent windows, had its shop on the ground floor next door to us,
and several steps further toward Park Lane was Farm Street, with its
miniature jewel of an emerald green square presided over by the
centuries-old Farm Street Catholic church, headquarters of the Jesuits,
and of Father D'Arcy, converter to the faith of such famed brains as
Alec Guinness and Evelyn Waugh. The butcher shop on the corner
and the stationer's across the street were both By Royal Appointment.
We were no distance from Curzon Street, which boasted of the art
cinema, the great restaurant the Mirabelle, and the superb Heywood
Hill Bookshop, all so close together as to seem to be jostling one
another. And we were always dropping by the cocktail lounge at the
Connaught Hotel, across from us, to join friends staying there.

We had a large eight-room second-floor flat in a street with a famous Victorian façade of rosy fog-stained brick houses. Winding through its middle our wonderful, rambling, gothicky apartment had a spiral staircase with a small round elevator placed in its center. In consequence the walls in some of the rooms and parts of the hallway were beautifully curved. It had sky-high ceilings and two of the rooms were enormous. The rent was low, especially for that location, but there was no central heating and it needed renovating throughout.

We worked with a young architect and decorator, Peter Miller and decided, in order, as Ken said, to impose ourselves upon it, to cover an entire wall of the living room with a huge soft-focus black and white blow-up of Hieronymus Bosch's *Garden of Pleasures*. It was, to be sure, a conversation piece.

The two largest rooms overlooking Mount Street became the living room and the library. The small room in between Ken chose for his study. Peter Miller led me into junk-cum-antique-shops that had good finds and I went crazy. I bought eight graceful chairs for a pound each and had them lacquered black and upholstered in the same cloth as the sofa in the library. What a bargain! They looked wonderful. The trouble was they broke when anyone an ounce over a certain weight sat down on them. I would have them repaired with steel reinforcements but still they broke, maddening the fallen guests, and still the chairs were repaired and returned. I'd become so attached to them that I couldn't let them go.

My parents were breaking up their apartment at 1185, distributing most of its furnishings. I was very surprised to find I wanted the large baroque Poseidon turtle lamp I'd stared at listening to my father as I was to about to make my final getaway. They sent me a beautiful French antique desk, a graceful chaise longue and an octagonal table as baroque as the lamp that sat upon it.

We had sufficient means, we had health, a beautiful child and lots to occupy us. Instead of counting our blessings, though, our days did not get off to their once happy start.

Developing a social conscience had heightened Ken's dissatisfaction with the way things were going on in the world.

When we woke up I would make a pot of tea and he would lie in bed reading the newspapers. We subscribed to two, the liberal

Manchester Guardian, with which Ken mostly agreed, and the conservative *Daily Express*, with which he violently disagreed. Together they produced a set of symptoms in him that grew into a syndrome I called Making It Worse, shortening it to MIW. Ken would point out all the awful things that were happening in the world and how they would affect him, and us, and all humanity, expounding on them darkly, making everything sound worse and worse. Sometimes even a headline in the *Daily Express* was enough to raise his indignation to the level where it literally shot him out of bed. I noticed more and more that I was joining in. Thus we got ourselves out of bed: Ken ready to take on the world, I ready to escape from it to my novel.

Novel-writing did help to cut down on my drinking. I never drank before or during writing. When I went to the theatre, though, I still welcomed every opportunity to drink. Then, more and more, I found myself declining to go with Ken to openings. I was finding I had a one-track mind. I was an amateur; I could not put down my writing and concentrate on other things that now presented themselves as annoying interruptions. Ken, on the other hand, had a many-tracked mind. He could write and drink, he could write and leap onto any number of bully pulpits and hold forth on all of them. What worse for a married critic than not having his wife – probably one of the reasons he married in the first place – accompany him to the theatre?

One opening wild horses wouldn't have made me miss was *The Chalk Garden* at the Haymarket with Edith Evans and Peggy Ashcroft, directed by John Gielgud. The playwright was Enid Bagnold, I loved her novels – *National Velvet* and especially the outrageous *Serena Blandish*. The play was the kind of upper-class stylish West End H.M. Tennent production that Ken routinely attacked as the arch-enemy, but in this case he surrendered completely to the perfection of its patrician acting folding seamlessly into the wit and eloquence of the writing. He added, however, that he hoped it signaled the end of this kind of play forever. Miss Bagnold was enchanted with Ken's review and invited us for the weekend to her house in Rottingdean, near Brighton.

Back home in Mount Street the Tynan quarrels continued. They often began in restaurants after the theatre. During one such meal at the Caprice, Leyland Heyward, superagent to the stars turned producer, stopped by our table to say hello and have a drink. He was full of trim Ivy League charm, from the top of his brush-cut Ivy League pepper and salt hair to the soles of his well-shod Ivy League feet. When he left, Ken said to me, almost as a rebuke, 'He's the sort of American I thought your parents would be like.' 'What a snob you are,' I snapped. 'Would they have been as generous to you if they were like Leyland?' 'They can't buy me,' he replied, his standard Marxist answer whenever a rich person expressed an interest in him. 'I thought you liked my mother.' 'She's all right, but she's a bit of a bore,' he replied. I said nothing. I stopped eating but went on drinking, and when we got home I told him what I thought of *his* mother, also questioning what she had done to make him so screwed up sexually. How conventional this quarrel was: the old in-laws fight.

As he headed towards his thirtieth birthday, Ken had aged. He had gained weight and he wore glasses. He had developed a sense of responsibility that went with his role as the *Observer* critic and his new job as an Ealing Films script editor, a post he held from 1956 to 1958. In 1956–1957 he organized the *Observer* Playwright Contest, with the Royal Court committed to putting on the plays of the winners. He also began to work on television specials. One program was on the Actors Studio and the Method, and another was called *We Dissent*, made up of American dissenters from Eisenhower's current Republican reign.

Ken had also developed a deadening coldness. I tried to match it, but was never able to.

Soon after his book *Bull Fever* was published I happened to open a copy again. Looking at its dedication to me, I felt a rush of love. 'I've never really thanked you properly for dedicating *Bull Fever* to me. It was darling of you. Thanks.'

'Why shouldn't I have?' he replied. 'You paid for it.'

Determined to hit back, one day I said to him, in a voice as neutral as possible, 'Please be sure to remove my name from the dedication of your book if it goes into a second printing. And while you're at it, you might take my name off that moldy pun you have me say on the first page. I find it forced and unfunny,' I continued, 'and when people comment on it I assure them I never said it.' 'When I'm not sure of a joke I give it to an American,' he replied. 'Give it to another American, there are plenty around.' By then I was shouting.

In public I wished to be seen as separate from him. I disassociated myself by disagreeing with him often, especially on such over-the-top comments as 'Bertold Brecht is the greatest living European playwright,' or his view of the importance of pornography for the masses.

When people came back to our flat late in the evening, conversation, under his direction, now became one continuous quiz game. His role was that of commissar. Once, in Malaga, sitting at the Miramar with Orson and some others, he started in with his current favorite quiz game: 'Where would you rather be right now?' When it was my turn I looked at Orson and said, 'Right here.' Orson laughed, 'Oh no, you'd rather be with Tennessee or Truman Capote.' 'No!' I said, 'I'd rather be with you but somewhere else.' This sort of thing always made for a congenial atmosphere.

In spite of it all Ken could also be kind and loving and generous and fun and charming, suddenly piercing my heart by doing things such as taking dancing lessons because he knew I loved to dance. And we had some wonderful, unforgettable times in London, Spain, France and America. And throughout he wrote like a fallen angel. My emotions were a battleground between 'Now I can love him' and 'Now I must hate him'.

In Barcelona in '56, we ran into Tennessee at the Hotel Colon. He showed us something we'd never seen before – the town's thriving gay side. Twice he took us to see a South American ballet company, which danced *Swan Lake* and other classics. The members of the ballet corps were all young, with beautiful hard, compact bodies. Suddenly I realized they were all men. Tennessee took us to a party that the company was giving at an apartment house the architect Gaudi had built – the one paved with cobblestones on all the hallways. We entered a strangely shaped apartment lit by candlelight and filled with the beautiful young men and women dancers who were all men. Tennessee went out on the balcony and dimly I saw his pudgy silhouette, so different from the others.

He also took us to a gay beach called San Sebastian. Later, in 1958, I saw a preview of the film of his play *Suddenly Last Summer*, where the character driving the plot is a homosexual called Sebastian who is eaten by starving boys on a Spanish beach.

One Sunday in October we found ourselves about to give a dinner for Marilyn Monroe and Arthur Miller. Marilyn had finished filming *The Prince and the Showgirl* with Laurence Olivier and the Millers had remained in London during October for the production of the playwright's *View From the Bridge*. Paula Strasberg, Lee's wife and Marilyn's acting coach, was leaving London but urged me to invite Marilyn and Arthur Miller to dinner; she was sure we'd like each other. She gave me their phone number, and Ken spoke to Arthur and together they fixed a date for a dinner party. For the other guests we invited John Osborne and Mary Ure, who were, or were about to be, married. We also asked Peter Hall and his then very pregnant wife, Leslie Caron, and Maria Britneva, now Maria St Just (who had recently married Lord Peter St Just), and Cyril Connolly. It would be an intimate dinner for ten.

When I invited these guests, I not only told them the date but added that Marilyn and Arthur would also be present. All of them immediately said yes. Not one of these busy, in-demand people said, 'Let me just look at my book and check.'

We hired a recommended caterer. A special man arrived on the night, along with a waitress. The menu consisted of a simple but sumptuous fare: for starters a deliciously rich pâté; as the main course pheasant with all the fixings – chips, currant jelly, bread sauce, small French peas and small roast potatoes; a salad of sliced oranges, baby lettuce leaves and watercress; crème brûlée for dessert; a cheese board. All with the choicest wines throughout and the best brandy afterwards.

One hour before the guests were due to arrive, Arthur Miller was on the phone to Ken. He was sorry, but Marilyn was just not able to come. But he was. Fifteen minutes later Arthur rang again, this time saying that Marilyn *would* be coming. Five minutes later he rang once more: neither of them were coming. 'My wife', said Arthur, 'is hysterical.' 'So is mine,' replied Ken. I loved him for that, but I wasn't. I merely said, 'Good, now there'll be more for us to eat.' Ken thought about canceling the dinner, but I strongly vetoed the idea. Our guests were on their way. Also, except, for Cyril, they were theatre folk and there is no group of people in the world more used to last-minute catastrophes.

Cyril was the first to arrive. Cyril Connolly's reputation as a mid-century intellectual institution and *monstre sacré* is still vibrant: a bon viveur, gourmand and gourmet, as well as editor, critic and sometime novelist. His uncomfortable non-fiction works *The Unquiet Grave* and *Enemies of Promise* earned him the distinction of being called the greatest living authority on reasons for not writing. One of the brilliant literary Edwardian baby boomers, he was at Eton with George Orwell and Henry Green, both of whom outstripped him as novelists. When I knew him he was the powerful literary critic on the *Sunday Times*. Sometime during '56, among the literati, Cyril spread it about that he had tired of his old set of friends and wished to cultivate the Tynans. He said the amusing party life now revolved around us. He even went so far as to announce this to Ken himself, who, as a great admirer of both Cyril's work and his persona welcomed him with open arms.

That Sunday was my second encounter with Cyril. (The first had been when we took him to a Duke Ellington concert, which, he assured us, he enjoyed immensely.) Cyril took the bad news of our celebrity no-shows philosophically. A similar thing had happened to him before on a BBC talks program, when Arthur Miller, at the last minute called it off with the same excuse – the sudden nervous collapse of his wife.

As a *monstre sacré* Cyril was licensed to enter any literary household and stir things up. He took his job seriously and always gave value. When being shown around our flat the characteristic first words out of his mouth were those inspired by Ken's study, the small room Ken had chosen himself. 'Ah,' he breathed, his voice full of gentle exhalations working in direct contrast to the sharpness of what he said, 'I see your wife allows you this space.'

It was a good party. As I predicted, all present received the news gracefully. High spirits prevailed. Suddenly it was as if we were a bunch of school children who, instead of having to face a dreaded exam, were given a day's holiday. We dined and wined and talked till late. I registered I was getting very drunk, and almost removed my clothes, something I had taken to doing when I thought the party needed livening up. This time, however, I thought the better of it and went to bed. Shortly after, Cyril followed me to say goodnight and thanked me for the evening. He saw that I was naked under the covers, put his arms around me and kissed me goodbye. He also asked if I would have lunch with him on Thursday of the following week at the Coq D'Or. I was ready for it, surprised by how easily, in marriage, I could be seduced.

If only there were an accurate word to define my relationship with Cyril. We coupled but were not lovers. We had a friendship but not an affair. I suppose a friendship that occasionally became sexual is the fact but not the feeling. Actually, it became sexual right off.

In her autobiography Barbara Skelton (Cyril's second wife) writes that Cyril had been 'seeing a lot of Elaine Dundy', and that is much closer to the truth. I further noticed that, often in her book, when Barbara begins 'seeing' various men there follows a scene that makes it clear they are sleeping together: a trip they take together, or a squabble in a hotel room. I find her choice of the word both accurate and delicate – 'seeing' certainly covers what a man and woman do together at both the most casual and the most intimate level.

That Thursday Cyril was seated at a banquette at the Coq D'Or when I arrived. 'I was so afraid you wouldn't come,' he breathed. After we lunched we went back to his room at Chesham Place, the hotel where he lived, and tumbled into bed. There was a bookshelf beside his bed filled with books. He hated books, he said. He was always being sent books. He sold the ones he reviewed but he kept accumulating others. 'They pile up until they are heavy enough to go through the floor and wreck a house, they gather dust and get mold and bookworm.' He offered to give me as many as I wanted. I chose a couple. Sometime after he gave me a copy of *The Unquiet Grave* in which he inscribed:

> Here lies one of happiness bereft,
> Money he loved and after money sex.
> No flowers culled he from the Garden of Eden
> Neurosis gripped him in a vice of Auden.

We lunched. We went to art galleries, antique shops, an antique fair. We walked in the park and talked and talked. I spoke freely of my marriage problems. 'Of course Englishmen love flagellation,' he said. 'It's the only time they ever get touched as children.'

Cyril called me his Boucher Girl. Familiar with the painter's eighteenth-century cavorting nudes, I nevertheless went to the Wallace Collection to study his canvases. The same model kept popping up. She did look like me: small, large-eyed, with a short nose that, like mine, went on a straight line from the forehead without indentation. She had, I must confess, rather the look of a hoyden. Intrigued, I read up on Boucher. A court painter of Louis XV, his canvases were 'steeped in gaiety, licentiousness and fashion' and filled with 'deliciously curved young women of easy virtue'. Okay, I thought, off with my clothes. If my face and form are good enough for the eighteenth century, they are good enough for the twentieth. Away with concealment, disguise, camouflage, welcome disclosure, exposure, the natural woman.

Cyril's emotional life was in a much worse mess than mine. He still loved Barbara Skelton, whom he had finally divorced, naming George Weidenfeld, his publisher, as correspondent. It had been soul-wrenching. Then Barbara had married Weidenfeld, and the result for all three was soul-wrenching. Then, most soul-wrenching of all, Weidenfeld divorced Barbara, naming Cyril as correspondent. The newspapers had a field day.

Now Cyril was mad to marry someone else, thereby breaking the cycle, and finding him a wife was the order of the day for his friends. Without having met her, he fell in love with the actress Rosemary Harris just seeing her on stage. Knowing she was a friend of mine he showed me his letter inviting her to dine with him. I okayed it. But when I asked Rosemary she said she'd never received it.

Cyril was the most gluttonous, envious, lustful and slothful man I have ever liked. It was amazing that all those deadly sins should add up to a likeable man. He was charming, sophisticated, immensely knowledgeable, divertingly expert on all sorts of subjects. He was vulnerable, human, ready, in fact, eager to ask your forgiveness for his character defects as they manifested themselves. I found him easy to forgive.

After all, I wasn't married to him. He possessed a radiant smile that enveloped you. 'Enter my life,' it said. 'Enter my life, *please*.'

On the other hand, 'he's not as nice as he looks' was the way someone had once described this *monstre sacré*, a remark frequently referred to by those who knew him best. The truth of it hinged on the fact that Cyril was quite ugly as well as quite malicious. He was fat, and his face was wide and flat with small eyes, a pug nose and a wide mouth. Like many other women I found him very sexy though. My seeing Cyril, which lasted for about a year, was neither ground-breaking nor chapter-making, but a logical transition. I was settling into the English literary life, as rife with liaisons as theatre life.

When I think back to the first months in 1957, my strongest memory is of me even more feverishly working even longer hours on my novel. What had spurred me into this rush of activity was Spencer Curtis Brown, chief of Ken's literary agency, who had read the three chapters of my novel and asked to see whatever material I had. I kept sending him chapters as they came out, and he was most encouraging. He invited us to his country house in Surrey for a weekend, and one afternoon asked me to come for a walk with him. As we sat on a hill overlooking gentle rolling green fields for miles around, not a soul or an animal in view, he began talking about my book, mentioning the things he liked, finally asking when I was going to finish it. I said Sally Jay was at present in Biarritz, and then she was going back to Paris, and then I thought I'd take her to England. 'No,' I remember him saying firmly, 'she does *not* have to go to England. Be thinking about the ending now.'

So I spent my time on our long, low, black and white sectional sofa in the living room, hunched over a portable typewriter on my knees, typing and typing and typing. I hurt my back badly and it may have been the beginning of my subsequent back troubles. Someone told me of a ladies' Turkish baths at the Dorchester Hotel, close by and surprisingly inexpensive, and I went twice a week. It was the most wonderful regime in the world, first the dry heat room, then the steam room, then a blissful massage, after which the masseuse scrubbed you down briskly with a loofah under hot then cold showers. I would emerge refreshed and energized and ready to go back to work.

A month or so before I completed the book it was still untitled. One evening we dined with Sandy Wilson and his companion, Jon Rose, at their house. This time it was our hosts who were scrapping, so to change the subject I commented on the wonderful avocado plants they'd grown. I told them how I'd kept sticking an avocado pit in a yogurt bottle with toothpicks and nothing happened. Sandy said, 'What you have is a dud avocado.' Ken remarked, 'That's a good title for a book.' It was an observation that Ken, a writer for all seasons, often made when three or four seemingly incongruous words came out of someone's mouth.

'That's my title!' I yelled happily. Avocados, I instantly realized, had a symbolic significance for me. They kept popping up in my life, first with my year at Mills, where I first ate them, then at the dinner party where Harold Nicolson's mention of them were the first words of his I understood. It culminated in the fact that now they were the vogue fruit in English cuisine and house plants. It struck me that I had come to regard this fruit as a symbol for all things American exported from their native soil abroad – and that Sally Jay was one such export. Were avodacos indigenous only to the Western hemisphere? I found out they were.

I opened my book to find where to work in my title. I saw the place that was crying out for it. In went the reference.

By June I had completed the novel. I had it typed and sent it off to Spencer. He rang to say he had asked Juliet Hay to handle it. She asked me my first choice for a publisher. I immediately said Victor Gollancz, thinking what a great job he'd done on Kingsley Amis's first novel *Lucky Jim*. If he didn't like it, I was not to be discouraged, she warned me. It was only Gollancz's highly personal reaction. She would send him the manuscript with the understanding that he agree to read it within a week.

The Hustons, John and Ricki, were settled in Galway; Ricki and I had become friends while they were living in London. I took up her invitation to visit her to wait out the Gollancz decision.

At the end of the week Juliet Hay telephoned me in Galway saying that Gollancz had accepted my novel with two provisos: one, that I use my married name Elaine Tynan, and two, that I change the title, which, he said, sounded like a cookbook. I said no to both conditions and Juliet conveyed this to Gollancz. He promptly dropped the first stipulation, though, as it turned out, still brooded over the second. I flew back to London.

At last Ken was ready to read the book. I gave him a typescript and he went into his study. Some hours later he emerged. 'This is going to be a colossal bestseller,' he said. Only then did I realize how anxious I'd been about him liking it. Only then did I feel that *The Dud Avocado* was indeed going to be a hit. I thought, he is pleased and proud of me – just what I'd hoped and planned. Now I could love him again.

'However . . . ' Ken began (I braced myself), 'you've left it too late to explain Sally Jay. You have to move the flashback of when she is thirteen from Chapter Five to Chapter One.' He saw my face. 'Look,' he said, 'I've done it for you. It fits right in. You only need a couple of connecting sentences.' He showed me. And there it is, now and for-ever in Chapter One, where it belonged.

A short while after, Ken went on some writing assignment to New York and Los Angeles and came back with a present for me from Jax, the California boutique where Marilyn Monroe bought her clothes. It was a cocktail dress, of beautifully cut black linen, sleeveless, with a high round neck but a daring bare midriff connected only by about seven inches of the dress material in front, exposing a provocative expanse of skin on the sides and back. I put it on. It was sensational.

Unfortunately along with the dress came Ken's announcement that he was going to Valencia for the *feria* with an American actress, Carol Grace, who had been married to William Saroyan (she subsequently married the late Walter Matthau). Ken said he'd met her when we were in Los Angeles that first time and he had been increasingly drawn to her over the years. They were, he emphasized, sexually com-patible, and now he simply must go with her to Spain. It was the only way to get her out of his system.

It was a body blow but I didn't fall apart, didn't rage against him or plead with him to stay with me. Perhaps it was because the day he'd left for America I'd had some sort of premonition and rang Cyril and told him to come over. It could have been the lighting, or his smile, or the dapper way he was dressed, but that evening he looked very good to me and within moments we were in each other's arms. His timing was perfect. Afterwards we went out to dinner at the French Club, where he told me he was glad to see that I wasn't drinking. I remember feeling somehow very satisfied with myself. And somehow my casual dalliance with Cyril never 'counted'. I was discreet. Ken knew nothing about it.

In any case, there it was: in 1957, the year Ken turned thirty, the year he had reserved for his death, he was, instead of dying, going off to Spain with another woman.

I told him that if he went I would divorce him. He kept begging me not to, imploring me to understand that it was something that would only last a fortnight. I walked out of our bedroom, rang Maria St Just and went over to her house. An expert on English divorce, having contemplated it several times in her own marriage, she gave me the name of a lawyer, who told me that in accordance with English law there must be an injured party. Even if both parties agreed to divorce, it could not be granted. He agreed I was the injured party, but I must have irrefutable evidence of adultery. I gave the lawyer several photographs of Ken and the date of his leaving for Spain and other details. A detective was hired.

I noted the following juxtaposition of dates: On July 18 I signed my contract with Victor Gollancz. On July 20 Ken left for Spain.

The night before Ken left I stayed with Maria to avoid any last-minute skirmishes. The next day she came back to the flat with me. We found scraps of paper taped to the furniture in the bedroom and library, some fifteen of them that I've saved all these years. Each carried a separate message: 'My life turns on you only my love', 'You are everything beautiful', 'I have nothing to do any more without you my darling', 'Please do not leave me today. Not today please my love', 'There is nothing without you except absolute darkness', 'Please or I shall die', 'Please Skip', 'Oh Skip stay with me please'.

Maria and I looked at each other. What was going on? We are all guilty of rewriting history, self-justification is one of our survival tools. But only Ken was able in one fell swoop to rewrite the *present*. Those bits of paper belonged to an entirely different scenario, the one in which the *wife* deserts the husband and he leaves messages hoping they will make her return to him. Or was he writing them with his fingers crossed?

Two days after Ken left I gave a party. I wore my Jax dress, which strangely had now taken on the significance of my Schiaparelli dress, making me look the way I most wanted to. I announced to the gathering that this was to be a double celebration. First, I was celebrating signing my contract with Gollancz and second, I was celebrating getting a divorce. The person I remember distinctly was Robert Kee, a novelist who was soon to become famous as a prominent political analyst on TV. Devastatingly handsome, with dead black hair and rugged features, he was one of the few people I have met to have mastered the difficult art of holding stimulating conversations at cocktail parties – which were the only places I ever saw him. Now I wanted to know him better. A lot better. When he invited me out for the next night I felt something like pleasure for the first time in days. I told myself it was going to be all right.

In the early hours of the morning the phone rang. It was Ken calling from Valencia, sounding very rattled. The detective had caught him in bed with Carol in their hotel room. We both started talking at once. To my surprise I was horrified at what I'd done and began crying and explaining it was the only legal way to get an English divorce. At the same time he kept pleading with me not to divorce him, saying he was coming home on the earliest flight the next day.

Reluctantly the next morning I rang Robert Kee and canceled our date, explaining that Ken was returning and I didn't know why but I guessed I was taking him back. He said that some people are destined to stay in our lives forever. I said I supposed so, but I wanted to add that I hoped not.

Ken arrived in the early afternoon. Over and over again he said he loved only me. He had been miserable the whole time he was away. Couldn't we take a trip together and make up? I said only if we were with other people: I somehow balked at us being alone.

Cyril spent his summers in the south of Spain, in Churriana, just outside Malaga, with Annie and Bill Davis at their house, La Consula.

Annie's sister, Jeannie, had been Cyril's first wife, who died. She had been a wealthy woman, and Annie inherited her money. What could have developed into a hostile relationship was circumvented by the fact that the Davises liked Cyril and looked up to him, reveling in meeting all the fascinating people he knew. They installed him in their beautiful house, where he presided as house priest, carefully choosing their guests, while they offered a hospitality that was known far and wide. Cyril had wanted Ken and me to visit them that summer. When I told him I planned instead to divorce Ken, he gave me his telephone number there so I could keep in touch.

That afternoon I telephoned Cyril at La Consula and explained that Ken and I would like to visit the Davises if possible. I next went to see my lawyer to call off the divorce. He was furious. 'You intellectuals,' he barked, 'you're supposed to be models for other people and instead you behave like spoilt children. Look at the Weidenfeld-Connolly scandal! It's a disgrace! They're a laughing stock.' I said something about being serious about trying to give our marriage another chance. 'I wouldn't put your divorce off if I were you,' said the lawyer shrewdly. 'You'll only have to do this again.' Then he insisted I listened to the detective's report.

I came home and told Ken I was not going to Spain with him. The detective's report had painted a clear picture of two people happy in each other's company on holiday.

No, no, Ken insisted again; it was not true that he had been happy. He had been most unhappy, missing me dreadfully the whole time. And then he proceeded to bad-mouth his recent companion. This was to become a pattern. Whenever he wanted or needed to get me back he would bad-mouth his current girlfriend. As I was to discover, while he was saying awful things about her and beautiful things to me, he was also saying awful things about me to her.

What I kept forgetting was that a critic basically succeeds not only on his ability to criticize but on his ability to convince. As I was finding out, I wanted to be convinced, to believe that, as he kept saying, I was the fixative of his memory. That things that happened when I was around stayed happened, and the rest faded. That experiences he had without me were like smoke and didn't last. That I was the source of his excitement, the fuel of his engine and without me there was no reason to survive. Over and over again I wanted to hear and believe that.

So I dropped the divorce and we went to La Consula. A hired car met us in Gibraltar and we drove to Torremolinos then up a winding path to Churriana, to a gate that had to be unlocked. Passing through, we finally saw a beautiful white house with wide white verandahs on a hill in a setting of trees and flowers. Inside were spacious white rooms hung with fine paintings and furnished with solid pieces of carved mahogany. Semi-invisible servants were there to make your beds, to wash and iron and put away your clothes, to attend your every need and desire and to cook delicious meals. There were two semi-hidden little Davis children, a boy, Teo, and a girl, Nena, who lived on the other side of the house in a nursery where the doorknobs were placed too high for them to open the door leading out. The swimming pool, in its beautiful setting, was redolent of the sweet, dry smell of the trees mixing with the flower-scented breeze.

And our hosts, Bill and Annie Davis – so charming, so informal – welcomed us into their lives as well as their house. Unquestionably they were the Gerald Murphys of the fifties, transferred to the new high bohemian playground of the Mediterranean Gold Coast of Spain. Or had we died and awakened in the Murphys' villa on the Riviera in the twenties, with Scotty and Zelda about to come rolling in any minute?

There being no Scotty and Zelda, it was left to Ken and me to supply the fireworks. Our late-night fights often shattered the well-organized serenity the Davises worked so assiduously to create to soothe the spirits of their guests in Shangri-la.

Soon after we arrived Ken announced that he was reinitiating his sadomasochistic sex practices. He hadn't come back to me to be deprived of those, he said. For a week, after lunch, we retired for the siesta and he put me through his punishment routines. The night of the seventh day I got very drunk and we had a huge row at the dinner table, which ended with me overturning a plate of food on him in front of Bill, Annie, Cyril and other guests. The next morning Ken told me he'd apologized for my behavior to the Davises and said that we must leave. After packing I went weeping to Annie in her room and told her of Ken's sex acts so she'd understand what was going on. She was sympathetic.

Ken and I returned to London barely speaking. I now registered his activities only out of the corner of my eye. The beginning of August – five months before my book was to be published – found me embarking on what I believed was surely the smoothest, fastest, most exhilarating ride anyone had ever taken from novice to novelist.

It was blue skies all the way, and one negative event showed me how lucky I was to be living in England and having my novel published by Gollancz. Before its publication in England *The Dud Avocado* was rejected by fourteen American publishers. Juliet would ring me each time the manuscript bounced back; once I said, 'Please don't let Victor Gollancz find out about this.' She replied, 'You don't know him. It'll just make him surer of his decision.' On the other hand as soon as it went into proofs, foreign translation rights were sold: Dutch, Scandinavian, German, English. *Harpers Bazaar* would be printing an excerpt of my novel, and made an appointment for Tony Armstrong-Jones to come to Mount Street to photograph me.

John Gross was my editor. Over the years he was to go on to a distinguished career as an author, a literary reviewer for the *New York Times*, and currently the drama critic of the *Sunday Telegraph*. He was Gollancz's most recent staff acquisition, and *The Dud Avocado* was the first book he was to edit. Working with him was an enjoyable experience. I liked the way he unsnarled sentences, making several sentences out of ones that went on forever, correcting my grammar and punctuation. I was especially impressed at his ability to pull meanings out of my vaguer convolutions, and how he scrupulously challenged me on words he didn't find in the dictionary until I said I'd made them up. Then he okayed them. I felt he was allowing me to succeed or fail on my own merit. And for this first-time amateur, who was sure she was saying something no one else had ever thought of, it suited me fine.

Then he gave me the bad news. He told me Victor Gollancz had deleted the word 'come', which I had used in describing the orgasm that Sally Jay experiences at the mere touch of Larry's hand in the first scene.

Gollancz had finally accepted my title but insisted on adding what I felt was a hideously coy and unnecessary subtitle – *The Vie Amoureuse of Sally Jay in Paris*. After an exchange of letters, a compromise was struck. Gollancz kept the offending subtitle on the cover *but* inside the jacket was added: 'The eight words printed in black on the front of this jacket are ours, not Miss Dundy's.' Then he invited me to lunch at the Savoy. Gollancz, upon meeting, was an impressive presence. Bushy black eyebrows, piercing eyes, ruddy complexion, tufts of white hair surrounding his baldness, peppery, arrogant, opinionated . . .

I came prepared, bringing *A Leftover Life to Kill*, the recently published book by Caitlin Thomas, Dylan's widow. I was completely bewildered when Gollancz spent the beginning of the meal complaining about the servant problem as it concerned his house in the country. Having got that off his chest, he suddenly became much more interesting in his remarks pertaining to publishers, novels and critics, explaining how just the *right* quote from just the *right* person on a book cover would boost its sales. He also told me that if Cyril Connolly reviewed a book in the *Sunday Times*, even if it was a bad notice, its sales immediately went up, and if Harold Nicolson reviewed a book in the *Observer*, even if it was a good notice, its sales immediately went down.

In the caesura between the main course and dessert I gave Gollancz *A Leftover Life to Kill*, calling his attention to Caitlin Thomas saying that she is the least spontaneous person in the world but that she always 'comes' when she dances. After he read this, I said, 'There! A respectable publisher has allowed the word "come" in the same sense I use it so why can't my book have it in?' Gollancz said merely, 'Out of the question, our printer wouldn't print it,' and went right on reading the book. I thought I'd lost him forever, but he finally looked up from it and said, 'She's a good writer. She has real compulsion.'

So the word was cut from the first few editions; with the American publication by Dutton, in July '58, I got it put back in again, and it has remained there ever since.

17

Success and New Friends

The Dud Avocado was published on January 12, 1958. That Sunday it received two excellent reviews. 'As delightful and delicate an examination of how it is to be twenty and in love in Paris as I've read . . . ' began John Metcalfe in the *Sunday Times*. 'A champagne cocktail . . . best of all noonday refreshers. Just such a draught has been prepared by Miss Elaine Dundy . . . One falls for Sally Jay from a great height from the first sentence . . . ' said John Davenport in the *Observer*. And during the next weeks more flooded in.

In an English world without the Sunday papers running bestseller lists, the *Sunday Dispatch* had this item: 'In the week's Best-Selling Six (our analysis of leading booksellers' sales throughout Britain) Elaine Dundy's *The Dud Avocado* hits the top.'

Good reviews were supposed to unhinge you, either making you so swollen with pride as to be unbearable or plummet you into inexplicable fits of despair. One of the reasons I was able to avoid these pitfalls was that I had been trained by example in the Buckstone School of Accomplished Feats. It taught you how to succeed, but it also trained you to think there was no such thing as failure – only setbacks. So what I felt was that I had finally joined this group no longer as a bit player, but a full-length one. This had some kind of stabilizing effect on me, enabling me to maintain my cool.

There were pinpricks of course. I heard that Cyril, when asked if my book was any good, was replying, 'Just another wife trying to justify her existence.' When I took him to task, he said it was simple envy and jealousy that made him say that. Barbara Skelton's *A Young Girl's Touch*, about her affair with King Farouk, had recently been published, and Cyril had worked closely with her on it. Though it had attracted some notice, it hadn't made the same splash as my book. Could I forgive him? Sure. As I said, I wasn't married to him.

Besides, he was right about me being 'a wife trying to justify her existence'. Of course I wanted to justify my existence, not just as a wife but as a person. After all, what had I been doing all these years as a small-part actress? Furthermore, I very much wanted to justify my existence to Ken.

Another pinprick: I had thought that, mission accomplished, I could sit back and enjoy it, but this was not the case. I told Rod Steiger, now in London doing a film, 'Do you know what's happening? The book's been out less than a month and everyone wants to know what I'm *going to write next*. I mean, don't I get a minute to rest on my laurels?'

'No,' said Rod, who with several great performances under his belt understood the ins and outs of success. 'Succeeding only means you get another chance to try to do it again.' A daunting prospect for me, especially since I hadn't intended to write another book.

Every Friday Ken went down to the *Observer* to confer with the literary editor, Terry Kilmartin, about his column, and afterwards they would join their colleagues at one of the pubs in Fleet Street. One Friday evening Ken, on returning home, marched into our bedroom, where I was lying on the bed reading, grabbed a typescript of my novel that happened to be on a chair and flung it out the window.

Turning on me he said, 'You weren't a writer when I married you! You were an actress!' as if accusing me of deliberately deceiving him.

'What's got into you?' I asked.

It transpired that some of his pub buddies had been enlivening the evening by baiting him with such barbed commiserations as, 'Poor old

Ken; poor old sod. Here you are, slogging away week after week to stay where you are, then along comes your wife and does it in one.'

This was mischief on a large scale. Seeing how it hurt Ken I was for the moment far angrier at them than at him, but the awful truth was not so much that his tormentors had pressed upon him the idea that his wife had 'competed' with him and 'won' but that he was buying into it. Except for the screwball comedies, where women were allowed some equality in regard to jobs, professions and careers, we females were taught by endless example never to seem to have even the appearance of 'competing' in any way with our husbands.

I said truthfully that I wouldn't have written the novel if it hadn't been for him. This was the wrong thing to say. He withdrew into his study, where he remained for the rest of the evening. I remained in the bed – shattered. I had failed by succeeding. Bitterly, my thoughts went around in a vicious circle, blaming in turn Ken, his tormentors and myself. I was asleep by the time Ken came to bed and still pretended to be when he left in the morning for Ealing.

He rang me later that day. 'Now what?' I said defensively. His voice, when he replied, took me by surprise. Unexpectedly it became the voice I loved. He'd just this minute finished reading my book again. 'And Skippy, it's wonderful,' he said. 'There's love on every page.' He was having a copy of it specially bound in leather as his present to me.

I loved him again at that moment. What clearer proof could he have given me that the night before had been nothing but a temporary aberration. And I loved him again when the red leather-bound copy of my book arrived, edged in gold, and I saw on its right-hand corner my musical notes signature also engraved in gold. His inscription read: 'From the Critic to the Author'. When I first looked at this message, I wondered if it cost him a lot thus to define ourselves. Today I look at the book with its happy notes and its inscription and I think, We had our moments. Full-blown and unforgettable.

But as my book caught on, it would not go away, and neither did the ribbing meted out to Ken. We both suffered from it. Being a best-seller, there was a movie sale. Penguin issued it in paperback. Somewhere along the line the *Financial Times* headlined a news item that such-and-such stock was 'No Dud Avocado'. On September 30, 1959, Groucho Marx wrote to me:

Dear Mrs Tynan,

I don't make a practice of writing to married women especially if the husband is a dramatic critic, but I had to tell someone (and it might as well be you since you're the author) how much I enjoyed *The Dud Avocado*. It made me laugh, scream and guffaw (which, incidentally, is a great name for a law firm).

If this was actually your life, I don't know how the hell you got through it.

Sincerely,
Groucho Marx.

Things like that kept happening but at the same time I was having to move people out of Ken's earshot at a party if they complimented me in order to spare his feelings. Appalled, I caught myself acting as if I were embarrassed by my success when really by now I was mad about it and as a result was a much nicer person. To everyone but Ken. He may have loved the book but he hated its success.

One night he said to me coldly 'If you ever write another book, I'll divorce you.' That did it. Early next morning I sat down and started a new novel. For the first and only time in my life, the entire plot unfolded before my eyes. An American girl plans to kill an Englishman. Why? He has the money that by inheritance should belong to her. The man would be considerably older than the girl. He would be very, very English, an English *monstre sacré*. In fact, like Cyril Connolly. I would call it *The Old Man and Me*.

I met Gore Vidal in London shortly before my book was published. He was working as a screenwriter on a film about to be shot at Ealing Studios. Staying at nearby Claridge's he and Ken would go out to Ealing together in Gore's chauffeur-driven car. ('He speaks in whole sentences at 7 a.m.,' Ken would say wonderingly.) We saw a lot of him. He was cool, collected, funny and heartless, but also, for me, something I was now missing dreadfully in Ken: playful.

It wasn't long before I realized I'd met Gore just in time. Looking back it is impossible to imagine what my life would have been like without him. What I had to hide, or downplay, with Ken, I didn't have to with Gore. He took my writing seriously, he followed my book's progress from English to American bestsellerdom, then through to the movie sale, and he applauded all the way.

Beginning in 1958 Gore became part of my life. For short spans we were part of the same story. I came to prize the constancy of his friendship and reaped the benefit of his amazing mind. Being his friend however also meant that, like his other friends, I had generous doses of critical Attic salt rubbed in my wounds by this elegant, scholarly and acerbic American Atticus. When he left London in April, I missed him. Both Ken and I looked forward to seeing him again.

In January, soon after my book came out, I met Mark Culme-Seymour at a party. I quickly noted that he was attractive, in fact ravishing. Instinctively I knew he was single and invited him to come to the party we were giving to celebrate my novel. It never hurt to have an attractive extra man around.

Later that week Mark invited us to dinner at the Caprice. Once there he asked us if he could bring to our party his sister, just divorced and feeling a bit lost. At some point Ken went to the men's room and wasn't halfway there when out of the blue, lazy-eyed and laid-back with only the merest inclination of his head, Mark said, 'I asked you both to dinner because I particularly want to go to bed with you most awfully.' It was a pounce without a preface. I couldn't decide whether to be offended, or – what? If your manly beauty is as highly charged as Mark's and you're sending out all kinds of sexy signals, the pounce is not ineffective. Still, I was annoyed at the crudeness and decided to put him down; he deserved it. Well, maybe not exactly put him *down*. Rather put him *off*. 'I don't know. I'll give you my answer at the party,' I said, still startled by our conversation, just as Ken came back.

At our party I wore a very twenties short white dress I bought at the inexpensive dress shop Fenwicks. It cost whatever would be the equivalent then of $19.95 today. Another one of the dresses I remember with pleasure, it was completely made up of rows and rows of tasseled fringes that moved when I moved (and I moved a lot). There was dancing. Ken had hired the band of street musicians we used to hear playing New Orleans jazz outside the Yorkminster pub in Soho, and they were a great success. Every American we knew in London was there, as well as the new English literati of the left that Ken's new conscience had attracted and theatre and film people. Gore Vidal came with Lillian Hellman. Donald Ogden Stewart, one of the better-known Hollywood exiles from the McCarthy political climate and screenwriter of our favorite film *The Philadelphia Story*, was, with his wife Ella Winters, the first to arrive. New friends Alan Sillitoe and Ruth Fainlight were there, as were usual suspects such as J.P. 'Mike' Donleavy, Christopher Logue, Doris Lessing, Clancy Sigal and Tony Crosland, Labour MP. So was Tracy, as always, meeting everyone in her new quilted bathrobe and having a lovely time.

Then Mark arrived and I wanted to be wicked. I went with him into the bedroom, where the coats were left. Tense but determined to speak before I changed my mind, I said, 'Yes.' We fixed the date and the time.

Two days later I turned up at his flat. He looked at me as I settled into a chair with the drink he'd offered me and said, 'I see you're no longer nervous.' I wasn't. In fact, I was very much at ease. The Boucher Girl was in the ascent.

Thus began a perfectly normal, perfectly conventional yet exciting ex-marital affair. I was able to blend it into my life. I was feeling my oats, feeling I'd earned the right to do anything I felt like. I was changing from a pre-*Dud* reflector to a post-*Dud* generator.

Mark belonged to neither the literary nor the theatrical category, but he was a recognizable English type. In fact he too, like Cyril, was a British institution. In Mark's case he was a splendid example of the man-about-town. Women were his real career and he was very good at it, but nothing prepared me for how deeply he *needed* women as when we went to bed; at orgasm his face was wet with tears.

How many people we knew in those days had carnal knowledge of each other? The thirty-year period that existed after syphilis was under control and before the outbreak of AIDS was the time certain men and women with certain careers had sex not for favors, nor for second-hand fame, but for curiosity and attraction, for fun and for free.

18

Larry and Viv

In February the theatre director Peter Brook and his wife actress Natasha Parry invited us to dinner at their house. On arrival we found Laurence Olivier and Vivien Leigh there. It was the first time I had ever met them. Ken had, but only briefly upon finding them at the same official theatrical party: Olivier grim, Vivien gracious.

I was dazzled by Vivien's beauty. Her face had the kind of delicacy of carving so fine-grained you could not fully appreciate it at a regular distance; the kind that was forever caught in her film close-ups. In contrast Olivier appeared solid, almost stolid. I searched his face for traces of the features of Heathcliff that turned a whole generation of schoolgirls my age into frenzied idolators. I found them in his eyes, still set in tunnels so deep that I got lost looking into them.

There were no other guests. At dinner the talk was general, everyone participating, everyone, to my astonishment, appearing at ease. Ken had never left off attacking Vivien whenever she shared the stage with Olivier. In their 1955 season at Stratford – *Titus Andronicus*, *Macbeth* and *Twelfth Night* – he was either savage or dismissive of her. With his attack on Vivien's Lady Macbeth, I thought Ken was completely off base, as did not only other critics and theatregoers but her theatrical peers. She was the best Lady Macbeth I have ever seen, perhaps because, for once, Lady Macbeth was *married* to Macbeth both off stage and on.

Yet now at the Brooks' all seemed forgiven, or forgotten, or cast aside.

Sometime later Vivien invited us to dinner at their mews house. It was just the four of us and it was as pleasant and without strain as our earlier meeting. Vivien impressed me with her formidable intellect and her knowledge of art, literature, and philosophy. Describing herself as a Zen-Buddhist Catholic, she told us she would soon be going to Italy to visit the latter-day saint Padre Pio, whose stigmata sometimes ran blood, before going into rehearsal for Giradoux's *Duel of Angels*.

Olivier congratulated me on my book, adding, 'I won't read it. I've never read a novel in my entire acting career except for *Sister Carrie* because I was going to be in the film of it.' This pronouncement shed light on Olivier: the actor-manager so dedicated to his calling he read only for work, never for pleasure. Olivier and Ken stayed on the safe grounds of theatre abroad.

Vivien sent us a postcard from Italy and to my absolute delight telephoned me when she returned to London. We began lunching together. The Vivien I lunched with at such restaurants as the Connaught was elegant, cool and self-possessed. Then I took her to a little out-of-the-way Thai restaurant I'd just discovered. It was full of Thai students. Slowly at first, then in increasing waves, they came over to Vivien, bringing paper napkins for her to autograph. Suddenly she became tense and distressed; her body began to tremble and her hands to shake as she strove to sign them. Finally in a barely audible voice, she said to them, 'Please let me eat.' I quickly asked for the bill and we left. Outside she was fine again. I felt badly that I'd let her in for this situation – albeit unknowingly.

When *Duel of Angels* began its West End run in April I was in New York. When I came back and saw it I remembered Vivien telling me about watching the play in Paris and announcing to the producer, Binkie Beaumont, that she would only do it if it was costumed again by Christian Dior. Binkie agreed, but cutting costs planned to use only the Dior sketches and have the dresses of the two leading women made more cheaply in England. Upon discovering this Vivien gave Binkie her ultimatum. Unless her costume was sewn by Dior *in Paris* she refused to do the play. She must have French stitching, she insisted! She got it. Viewing the play I saw what she meant. The costume she wore fitted her like a second skin so that, sitting or standing, her every move was made with grace and freedom. At the same time the other actress was constantly giving her English-stitched costume little distracting tugs of adjustment.

While Vivien was playing in *Duel of Angels*, Olivier was working in the film of Shaw's *The Devil's Disciple* with Burt Lancaster, directed by Sandy Mackendrick. Vivien and Olivier were on different timetables. And so were Ken and I. We were not even talking, and had gone our separate ways again. While Olivier went to bed early to get up early to film, Vivien needed to unwind after her 11 p.m. curtain and held late-night supper parties at their new home in Eaton Square. I sometimes attended and enjoyed them – without Ken.

I hadn't heard from Vivien for a while when I read in the papers that *Duel of Angels* was temporarily closing to allow Miss Leigh to rest from her demanding role. Although she was on stage almost all the time, she seemed to me to thrive on it. But perhaps she was ill? I recalled rumors I'd heard in the past of Vivien's 'spells'. Some years earlier, while filming *Elephant Walk* with Peter Finch in Sri Lanka, Vivien had had a much publicized breakdown, so severe that it had necessitated her leaving the film in mid-shooting, her role taken over by Elizabeth Taylor. Her face, pale and tense in the Thai restaurant as she tried to control her hands, came back to me.

One day Vivien invited me to Notley for the weekend. She would be sending a car for me on Saturday morning. Like everyone in or out of theatre I'd heard about the fabulous magical Notley Abbey and now I would see it with my own eyes.

Saturday morning produced a dilemma. Vivien's invitation had not included Ken. (Olivier would not be there, having gone on holiday in Spain with his older brother, who was dying of cancer.) Ken, who'd been hanging around that morning, badly wanted to come and implored me to ask Vivien. Though she'd sounded fine over the telephone, Vivien was presumably in fragile health. Was Ken, her harshest critic, the ideal house guest right now? The two times they had met, he reminded me, they'd got along very well. So I rang Vivien and with apologies asked if it would be all right if Ken joined us. Yes, said Vivien. It turned out to be quite a weekend.

That beautiful summer day at Notley, Vivien greeted us wearing an organdy full-skirted dress; a large-brimmed straw hat with a blue band hung by streamers down her back. Notley's main halls were dark and imposing, but upstairs Vivien's touch was everywhere, in paintings on the walls and in light airy bedrooms where the eye glanced with pleasure at whatever it discovered: some delicate china figure or a book that Vivien had specially placed on a bedside table knowing it would interest a particular guest. Among other people at the party were Vivien's mother, her father and a man named Bill who turned out to be a sort of general factotum to the Oliviers.

Vivien was in high spirits. It was just the day for a picnic, held on the grounds near the river. With our food we drank a lovely light dry white wine tasting of flowers. Vivien, animated and vivacious, was holding forth until a wasp began to buzz around her. Suddenly the charming Scarlett O'Hara became the harrowed Blanche Du Bois. Her face went rigid with fear, her hands flailed the air. She shrieked 'Go away! Go away!' and, shivering, buried her face in her hands. Bill wrapped a shawl around her shoulders and held her for a moment. When she took her hands away from her face the wasp was gone and all was well again. Reaching for my glass of wine, I saw that I had finished it. Someone poured me another. I finished that one off too.

After the picnic I walked back to the house with Ken. Vivien's outburst had affected him strangely. He walked slowly dragging his feet. He yawned. 'I'm sleepy, I've got to have a nap.' I thought this was his way of disassociating himself, of being disapproving. Fervently I wished he had not come. Back at the house Vivien showed Ken to a room where he could sleep undisturbed.

The rest of us went down to the croquet lawn and were preparing to play when Vivien, turning fiercely on her mother, suddenly cried out, 'You're to blame. It's all your fault! You never wanted me to play Blanche. You tried to stop me!' If her first outburst over the wasp had distressed me, this one made me want to cheer. Vivien was doing what

I'd never been able to do for myself: she was telling off a parent. Instinctively I knew that Vivien's mother had been the cause of deep conflicts in her nature, and later I would find out more. Vivien's mother, Gertrude Hartley, had uprooted her six-year-old daughter from her home in India, dragged her crying into convent school in London and returned to India not to see her daughter again for eighteen months. Although for the next seven convent years she saw her daughter only sporadically, in Vivien's adulthood she remained forever at her side, always ready with a reprimand. She was a great disapprover: of Vivien's first marriage, of her engagement ring, of her attitude towards the Catholic Church, of her liaison with Olivier, of her choice of roles.

'Vivien, behave yourself!' said a mother to a forty-five-year-old daughter that day on the croquet lawn. Vivien turned and ran into the house. The rest of us carried on playing.

Then it was teatime. The other guests had departed and Vivien had gone to wake up Ken and I was sitting in the grand baronial hall with Vivien's mother having tea. 'I'm so glad Vivien has you for a friend,' she said. 'She needs intellectual stimulus.' Perhaps her mother felt the need to present her side, for she went on, 'There is nothing the matter with Vivien. She does not need all those psychiatrists. They just try to make trouble. Why, as a little child at the convent, the nuns told me she loved me so much she used to cover up my photograph with her blanket at night so my picture wouldn't get cold.' This tale was supposed to warm my heart as an illustration of a child's steadfast filial devotion. Instead it chilled me to the bone as an illustration of a six-year-old's desperate loneliness.

At this point Bill came in. Alarmed at Vivien's behavior he had contacted Olivier in Spain, who was flying back. 'We'll wait dinner for him,' said Bill. 'I'll be staying on too. And so will you and Mr Hartley, won't you?' he said to Vivien's mother. He turned to me apologetically. 'I'm afraid with the extra people there won't be much to eat,' he said.

The thought did flash through my head that perhaps Ken and I should leave but I ignored it. Having been drawn into the vortex of this drama, I felt as if I must stay with it to the end. I went up to our room and fell asleep.

When I awoke I couldn't believe my eyes. Ken was sitting on my bed dressed in chainmail armor. He explained that it was the original suit Sybil Thorndike had worn in the first productions of Shaw's *Saint Joan*. Vivien had awakened him and made him put it on. I told Ken about Olivier coming and he took it off and we got dressed for dinner.

In the grand baronial hall, Vivien, stunning in a red and gold sari, served us sherry. 'Larry is coming back tonight,' she said. 'Ken, put Sybil's chainmail back on. It always makes him laugh.'

Some time later Olivier arrived. We took our seats at the long candlelit dinner table in the huge dark dining hall. Way up at one end was Vivien in her sari with Ken next to her in chainmail, which I noticed hung miles too long in the sleeves, which dribbled over his fingertips and made it difficult for him to eat. Way down my end I was seated next to Olivier. Vivien's mother and father and Bill sat somewhere in between.

As I had been forewarned there was not much to eat, though the food was doled out very grandly and stately wines flowed freely, changing from course to course. I realized, however, I could not just sit there silently guzzling.

'How was Spain?' I asked an unsmiling Olivier. He let the question go. 'How's your book selling?' he asked instead.

'Oh, great.'

'When it makes enough money we can run away together and you can support me.' As he said this I felt a kind of anger coming off him, as though he were demanding that I rise above the awkwardness of the situation and respond to him, flirt with him, do anything to keep up my end of polite dinner chit-chat.

I said something like, 'Oh, sure. Yes. Ha ha,' and, as before, got lost in the deep tunnels of his eyes.

After dinner we retired to the study. In the ever-expanding and contracting numbers of the Notley house party, I noted there were now only four of us: Ken and myself and Olivier and Vivien.

Over brandy, Ken suggested we play one of his dreaded games, and the Oliviers agreed politely if not enthusiastically while I registered my feelings by making a face. Clearly Vivien was soon as bored as I was, for she said, 'Come with me Elaine, I know a better game than this.'

We went up to her bedroom, where, seated at her dressing table, we began splashing ourselves with her various rare and expensive perfumes. And here came euphoria. The simple fact of being away from Ken and his party games, of being with a dear friend I loved and admired, gave me a glorious sense of freedom. I loved my world, my world loved me. Vivien and I went downstairs to another room and listened to records. We danced and giggled a lot and just generally behaved like happy tipsy schoolgirls. Again there was that feeling of weightlessness, of soaring free from fetters as in those periods of gaiety my sisters and I shared as children.

When we finally returned to the study Ken and Olivier were deep in an intense discussion. Or rather, Olivier was doing most of the talking and Ken, having divested himself of his chainmail, was listening as if to the music of the spheres. Olivier now seemed a different person, full of high energy. Clearly the two of them had struck some chord of harmony. Olivier looked up at us when we came in and smiled. 'A good time was had by all?' he said. Playfully I perched on his lap for a moment. He chuckled and squeezed me. I thought: what bliss to be here at Notley. Soon after the party broke up.

Next morning dawned grey and drizzly. I asked Ken what he and Olivier had been talking about so intently. 'An English National Theatre,' said Ken. 'It's not just a sometime-in-the-future project to Olivier. He wants to be its head and he's taking steps toward it.' Ken began to stammer in his excitement. Olivier had talked to a lot of people already and had done a lot of planning. Olivier wanted to know Ken's thoughts. A National Theatre, Ken assured him with passion, was his most cherished dream. 'No one else c-can make this h-happen but L-Larry,' Ken finished ecstatically.

Vivien came into our room looking fresh as a breeze and bearing a breakfast tray of tea and toast and soft-boiled eggs; an exquisite vase held a single rose. 'Larry wants you to take a walk with him when you're dressed,' she said to Ken. Minutes later Ken was ready.

I was still dressing when Ken returned. Instantly I saw that he had bad news. Though I'd awakened brightly, at just that moment a hangover began to press itself down on my right eye. As if in premonition there had been a spider in the washbasin in our bathroom.

'Larry's kicked me out,' said Ken. 'He wants me to leave immediately.

He says I'm having a bad effect on Vivien. She's having one of her spells. He said they were cyclic but that ever since that piece I wrote about her in the *Evening Standard* the cycles have become more frequent.' He paused while we both digested this. Larry was in his rights of course. His only interest was Vivien's welfare. 'He wants you to leave too—' said Ken attempting a smile. 'Well, you're my wife. I'm sorry. I really shouldn't have come.'

I began to pack. I couldn't begin to sort out all the clashing social forces, trigger points and power bases that had been spinning around that weekend. The next bewildering spin for me was that I felt sorry for Ken. And I felt sorry for myself too. Because we, like the Oliviers, were a marriage, we found ourselves facing events together again.

And that wasn't even the final spin. We returned to Notley the next Sunday at Vivien's invitation and in Olivier's absence. She was shaky with a nurse in attendance. We listened to the new album Noël Coward had sent Vivien of his recent performances. Ken held Vivien's hand and they both wept. Tears of joy? Of sadness? Probably both.

While at the Edinburgh Festival that summer Ken received an unexpected phone call from William Shawn, the editor of the *New Yorker*. Their drama critic, Wolcott Gibbs, had died that summer and Shawn was offering Ken Gibbs's job. The more Ken thought about it the more he liked the idea. He accepted a two year contract.

Nine years before I had left New York harbor on the *Ile de France*, a solitary figure, alone and unknown, standing by the ship's rail staring thoughtfully at its receding coastline – or something like that. Now I would return under circumstances bright with opportunities. As always, changing towns activated me.

I went to Eaton Square to say goodbye to a restored Vivien and immediately afterwards I ran into Cyril on the street and said goodbye to him too. One afternoon I went over to Mark's flat and said a sentimental farewell to him.

Then, having sublet Mount Street for the next two years to Melvin Lasky, one of the editors of *Encounter*, Ken, Tracy, Dolly (our new au pair) and I boarded another French ocean liner, the *Liberté*, and I sailed back across the Big Pond.

19

The American Experience

'And how are you finding the American Experience?' a friend of Gore's asked Ken one afternoon. His raised eyebrows put silent quotes around this figure of speech. Ken, referring to the deafening cacophony caused by the destructions and constructions in New York blasting away on practically every street of the city, replied, 'The noise in New York is the sound of the city tearing up yesterday.'

New York, at that moment in '58, was still undergoing drastic revisions that, along with the ear-splitting noise, sidewalk blockings and traffic snarling, seemed to have gone on for years without end. New Yorkers viewed these serious inconveniences as yet another chance to display their grit under pressure as they went about establishing meaningful relationships with the workers. Spectators and building crews engaged in snappy dialogues. Citizens in a rush nevertheless stopped and gazed upwards at the rising skeletons of things to come as if deep in uplifting meditation.

I too was all for tearing up yesterday. On Madison Avenue, near where we lived, I would pass a large hole being gouged out in preparation for the next new edifice. One day, walking on the gray planks laid over the torn-up sidewalk, I tripped and found myself sprawled flat on the ground. I tried to rise but couldn't until a man came by and helped me up. In those moments before getting back on my feet I stared with horror into the black hole beneath me. The excavation seemed to expose the old city I used to live in. I had the weird thought that if I got a divorce, I would have to go back and live there with my parents again. In future I avoided the excavation whenever possible.

We had settled down in a furnished flat at 56 East 89th Street, where we were to live for the next two years. The flat's decor was dowdy Mittel European, its good point being its convenient location. My only contributions to it were Bloomingdale's linen, bedspreads, quilts, towels and a couple of my parents' gold-framed mirrors on the living room wall.

Ken worked first in the dining room then preferred the bedroom where he could close the door. On nights he wrote his *New Yorker* pieces I slept on the sofa in the living room. During the day he worked with a secretary in our living room.

The American publication of *The Dud Avocado* had occurred in July and it was on the bestseller list from mid-August. By the time I arrived in New York everybody I met at parties had read it, or read of it. For a while this deluded me into thinking I had written a new book, an experience similar to my New York clothes looking new to me in Paris because no one had seen them before.

When reality took over I discovered that in trying to write a second novel I'd already said everything I had to say in the first one. The well was dry; how to fill it up? I purchased a journal. I took notes on everywhere I went and about everyone I met and ended up with a lot of notes all irrelevant to the novel.

I attended W.H. Auden's fiftieth birthday party. He lived in St Mark's Place in the East Village with his companion Chester Kallman in a walk-up flat. In the bathroom the bathtub was filled with champagne cooling in ice and surrounded by a dirty bath water ring. One room had a wall with a sinister bulge the size and shape of a man walled up in it. Assorted poets were all drinking Auden's health, with Marianne Moore to the forefront.

Auden, his face with its well-known cross-hatched complexion suggesting super-intense reactions to life, sported a black velvet jacket for the occasion. In a revelatory manner he began grandly, 'I'm really a Victorian at heart. I love luxury. Private railway carriages, that sort of thing.' I gazed around at the rumpled room in which we sat and thought of the bathtub with its ring around it and the bulging wall next door. Perhaps he had a country seat somewhere? When I tuned in again the poet was on another topic: 'No matter what the weather, I cannot sleep without the weight of a blanket over me.' A pause. Ken ventured, 'Is it true the *New Yorker* proofreads your poems and even suggests grammatical changes?' 'Oh, yes,' Auden replied. 'Don't you *mind*?' Ken pressed, 'you don't think them impertinent?' 'Not at all,' said the poet, 'at least it shows that they *care*.'

It was a trying time for Ken at the *New Yorker*. Given this opportunity to review Broadway, seated on the throne that both Robert Benchley and Wolcott Gibbs had graced, and with *tout* New York's eyes on him, Ken had the bad luck to sit through two of the most dismal seasons in history. Plays opened and closed so fast Ken had me check before writing about them to see if he was to compose a review or an obituary. In *Curtains*, his selected writings on theatre from 1951 to 1960, he found only twenty-three plays worth including in his section on American theatre.

In his first column, writing about the French revue, *La Plume de ma Tante*, Ken ran smack into *New Yorker* prudery. In a skit taking place at that Parisian institution the *pissoir*, where a man can take a quick pee, it was decided that the actual word was too vulgar for the *New Yorker* to print. Along the way, however, in the two years of his tenure on the magazine a great deal of horse-trading successfully went on between him and William Shawn, who traded leniency on his part for constraint on Ken's. They worked well together, and in spite of the sorry seasons, Ken was writing as well as ever. The good working relationship he developed with Shawn grew into a warm friendship.

The American Experiences that Ken and I did share with enthusiasm were the new comedians on display at New York nightclubs. Satire, contrary to George Kaufman's dictum, did not close on Saturday night, but played to standing room only. In fact satire was as much of a force in directing the course of the sixties as were the Beats, the Beatles, hippies, cool jazz and hot protest. The sixties, above all, was the age of disrespect for the old established hypocritical order. Right alongside the Theatre of the Absurd stood the Theatre of Disrespect.

Two of the most popular nightclub acts transferred successfully to Broadway, its members being physically attractive as well as awesomely intelligent. The first was called *An Evening with Elaine May and Mike Nichols*, in which the two took audience's requests and did hilarious satirical skits in the manner of a variety of authors from Pirandello, to Dostoyevsky, to Conrad. The second was the political satirist Mort Sahl, dressed in a red sweater holding a rolled-up copy of the *New York Times* on whose articles he commented with extreme wit and disrespect. Along with the comedian Lennie Bruce, whose humor was the darkest, these performers spawned a dozen more and were followed by satirical TV shows such as *Laugh In* and later *Saturday Night Live*. Simultaneously in England the success of the satirical revue *Beyond the Fringe* led to a new club named the Establishment, whose entertainment was entirely given over to irreverent young comics and satirical skits, as was the enormously popular TV show *That Was the Week That Was*, which began the career of David Frost.

One thing that Ken poured his energy into with a vengeance was developing his idea of a nude sex show. His interest having been stimulated by the Crazy Horse Saloon in Paris, he expanded the concept of a sophisticated revue to consist of a series of sex sketches written by well-known playwrights and authors and to be performed by players in the nude, an idea finally to crystallize as *Oh Calcutta!* Among the writers I remember he asked to submit sketches at the time were Jules Feiffer, Jack Gelber, Norman Mailer and Terry Southern. Tennessee Williams, too, was invited, and he submitted a sketch about two lovers who only get roused sexually by quarreling. It didn't make the cut.

Ken's nightly coughing, which had started in Mount Street, became worse in New York, sometimes lasting for half an hour during the early hours of the morning. Glasses of water helped some, and I always kept a water carafe on the bedside table. Over and over again he refused to go to a doctor knowing he would have to confess to at least a three-pack-a-day habit and well aware of the warnings he would be given.

We went to parties non-stop. The parties given by the Lumets, Sidney and his then wife Gloria Vanderbilt, and by George and Joan Axelrod were the largest and had the best mixtures. At the Lumets' you met theatrical stars of the hour, such as George C. Scott, as well as the likes of Izak Dinesen and Carl Van Vetchen. At the Axelrods' you met Hollywood stars as well as the political historian Theodore H. White and Random House's publisher Bennet Cerf. At Lennie and Felicia Bernstein's you met Stravinsky. And whenever you went to any of these parties you met Adolphe Green and Betty Comden, collaborators on such musicals as *On the Town* and *Singing in the Rain*.

Then there were the *Paris Review* regular parties. At that time Stephen Spender had remarked that the English literary scene resembled not so much a battlefield or a jungle as a cozy conspiracy; the *Paris Review* parties bore strong resemblances to the battlefield and the jungle. Norman Mailer told me what he most recalls about the parties was their charged atmosphere. All the writers – himself included – walked rigidly through the packed room, heads erect, only eyes swiveling sideways to identify the enemy. I too remember the parties as filled with dangerous, challenging, near-fatal fusions of novelists, critics, editors and publishers stewing together in the pressure cooker of that long narrow room. Antagonisms were based on warring philosophies. Hip, Beat, and Square were philosophical concepts that translated themselves into literary styles. Mailer declared himself hip, Styron declared himself square. As each participant passionately stood for something, it followed that each must be passionately opposed to something else.

Every morning, everyone in New York talked on the phone to everyone else about the parties they'd been to the night before. It made you feel we all lived next door to each other. I talked to Mike Nichols, to Terry Southern, Howard 'Doc' Humes, and Judy, my friend from Paris who was now living in the city. (Sometime in 1959 Judy came home with me one afternoon. Jules Feiffer was there with Ken and so they met. Soon after, at a party, Jules told me how much he liked Judy. They were married three years later and although I was in London at the time I made a point of returning for it.) I was also on the phone often with Johnny and Sue Marquand, with Jean Stein, who soon became Jean Van den Heuvel (then Jean Stein again), with Maria St Just, with Gore, with James Baldwin, with whom I'd become friends while doing a David Susskind *Open End* TV program on expatriates. He'd got the bit between his teeth and talked and talked and eventually out-talked everyone on the show. When I complimented him on this he told me he'd gotten his training from being a boy preacher in Harlem.

Tracy, now in first grade, went to Brearley, known for a rigorous curriculum matching that of an English school. Tracy loved school and her new friends, livening up her school uniform by hanging rabbits' feet of all colors on her school uniform belt. Best friend Susie lived next door, and they went to school together. Driving with them in a taxi through Central Park once they suddenly recited, with synchronized gestures, a nonsense poem about a mysteriously sullen girl called Cecilia, who reluctantly opens the front door to a 'tall, fat, skinny, little man' (repeated three times). He falls on one knee and thrice proposes marriage to her. Thrice she turns him down, then on pure whim she accepts him. It was good to find first grade at Brearley alloted time for poetry as well as the rigors of the three Rs.

We lived near the Guggenheim Museum – cultural opportunity. Tracy and I went over. The big hole in the middle was mesmerizing, the ramp winding upwards then downwards around it. I grew bored, imagined skiing down it. The paintings were only abstract and action stuff. Afterwards I interrogated Tracy. 'Well, did you like it?' 'Oh, yes.' 'You didn't mind that the paintings didn't tell stories?' After all she was only six. She explained patiently, 'No, because I can make up my own.'

Also Tracy had caught on to us. 'Oh, we're not a real family,' she said calmly. 'Real families have meals together.' I explained this was because we went to the theatre.

One Sunday morning in the middle of '59, reading the *New York Times*, my eye happened to fall on an ad saying, 'Are You An

Alcoholic? These test questions are used by Johns Hopkins University Hospital in deciding whether or not a patient is an alcoholic.' Then followed twenty yes or no questions. I filled them in. Ten yesses. Then I read the print below: 'If you have answered yes to three or more you are definitely an Alcoholic.' Now it was official – I was an alcoholic. Today's memoirs present this moment of self-discovery over and again as a road so well traveled by both men and women in the Arts that their autobiographical confessions are surprising only in their similarities. Far from addiction being a shocking admission, the reader feels cheated in a memoir without this disclosure, even if the writer in all honesty cannot, without lying, confess to it. In '59 I felt a freak: in 2001 I feel positively mainstream.

I sat there and knew I must get help. For the better part of my life the struggle went on in earnest as I began to look in all the places conventional and unconventional for a cure. I would stop drinking for months, even years, at a time and then I'd slip without warning, unfortunately sometimes just when a large number of people were around to observe the serio-comic results.

20

Hem and Tenn

In April of '59, when Castro had been in power for some two months, Ken, on assignment for the magazine *Holiday*, went to Cuba to write about it. In a holiday mood ourselves, Tracy (on her spring break), Dolly and I went along too. Ken, looking forward to seeing what the revolution had produced, was eager to meet Castro. In ousting the corrupt Batista regime, with its reign of terror and its ties to the Mafia, Castro was a hero to a large number of Americans and Europeans. We would be seeing Hemingway too, at his estate in a suburb of Havana. Having met him in Spain and again in New York at the Harvey Breits' and discovering that he and Mary would be in Cuba when we were there, Ken asked if we could visit and he invited us to lunch at their home upon our arrival.

That Tennessee Williams would be in Havana at the same time was unforeseen. We stumbled across him quite by accident when we were gawking around the famous Hotel Nacional.

In the late fifties and at the beginning of the sixties I knew both Tenn and Hem (Tenn better and longer than Hem). I observed them closely, listened to them carefully and wrote it all down afterwards. In the dry heat of a Spanish summer I ran into them at bullrings and at bars where Hem drank vin rosé and Tenn dry martinis. I met them in luxurious hotels like the Palace in Madrid, the Colón in Barcelona and the Miramar in Malaga – though never at the same time – and I sat with them in the best restaurants. Tenn was often alone; Hem was always surrounded by an entourage. With one exception they never met. And so I kept them both in the mutually exclusive worlds to which they belonged.

But the exalted place these two giants occupy today in world literature gives me a different perspective. Now my mind insists that I look at them together and that by comparing and contrasting them I sharpen and deepen my perceptions of their characters. By defining one I can define the other, and finally it enables me to see their commonalities. No two writers living at the same time and sharing equal fame and celebrity were less alike in their work and their personas than Ernest Hemingway and Tennessee Williams, the yang and yin of American letters. They complemented each other so neatly as to seem preordained.

The genius of Hemingway flared brightest when exalting his characters' hard-won self-controlled courage; the genius of Tennessee when exposing his characters' nerve-wracked, out-of-control terrors. One was master of the stiff upper lip, the other of the lip that quivers and the soul that quakes. Heart-wrenchingly, Hemingway wrote of grace under pressure; heartbreakingly Tennessee wrote of *dis*grace under pressure. The world still knows what is meant by a Hemingway hero and a Tennessee Williams heroine (and writers in particular still know what it is like to fall under their influence). Time has not dated them. One reason for this may lie in Max Beerbohm's assertion that 'realistic figures perish necessarily with the generation in which they were created, and their place is taken by the generation which supervenes. But romantic figures belong to no period and time does not dissolve them.' He might have been talking about Jake Barnes and Blanche Du Bois, or Nick Adams or Amanda Wingfield, or any number of either authors' romantic creations.

Looking over the last half of the twentieth century, these twin peaks in literature, Hem and Tenn, seem to tower so high above others as to suggest that their volcanic eruptions have flattened the field.

What writer alive today will inspire contests in newspapers and magazines all over America, year after year, with prizes for the best imitation of his style decades after his death? What living playwright will have festival after festival held in his honor long after his death? Whether with contests or festivals, we cannot get enough of them. Equally remarkable is the fact that their popularity suffered no sharp decline after their deaths, which is usually the case when the Legend is no longer around to stoke the fires of our insatiable curiosity.

Biography after biography uncovers their secrets, rakes them over like dead leaves to find more secrets below. Their illness-wracked final years, their numerous hospitalizations, their increased pill and booze intake: all raised questions of their sanity as well as their physical ailments. Their tragic endings – Hem in suicide, Tenn choking to death on the cap of an eye-drop bottle – contribute rather than detract from their legends, for we know they were the real thing and I speak for a whole generation when I say we miss not being able to pick up a paper and read the latest bulletins of their triumphs or disasters. Hem was an impressive six-footer, Tenn barely five foot seven. Hem's eyes looked directly into yours when he conversed, while Tenn's slid over you and then favored the middle distance. Hem tended to kiss and snuggle you in a taxi; Tenn put his hand over yours when he sensed you needed it.

I first met Hem in Madrid when we were invited by George Plimpton to a luncheon party he was giving for him. In a sunny restaurant Hemingway sat at the center of the long table and held court. Such was the potency of his presence and the skill of his storytelling that we all – about fourteen of us – sat in a happy mesmerized silence. With the arrival of coffee and brandy George began to rearrange the guests to give Hemingway fresh partners. I had been sitting a safe five seats away when George approached to say he was putting me next to the great man and hurriedly whispered that if he called me 'daughter' I would be *in*, but I must respond by calling him 'Papa'. My quick rebellious feelings – *this is too silly!* – vanished the moment I found myself next to him, looking into his watery, somehow pleading eyes. Straightaway I entered into his aura, and when he called me daughter I responded with a blissful 'Yes, Papa'.

Nevertheless I'd found Hemingway's voice very much at odds with

his persona. It was a light voice, pitched rather high, with flat subur-
ban Mid-western pronunciations unchanged from childhood. How
further to define it? The word 'coddled' comes to mind. A voice cush-
ioned against raw nature by good plumbing, warm clothes, hot food
and worried mothers, not what you expected to issue from his monu-
mental build. From such an edifice you expected nothing less than the
thundering sonorities of Orson Welles.

Tennessee's voice, on the other hand, with its supple, insinuating
Delta rhythms, perfectly expressed his persona. Echoes of it would
stay in my ear after an evening in his company, and before falling
asleep that night I would hear its sinuous sounds like waves plashing
against some distant shore. I can still hear the gusto of his rhetoric, the
juiciness of his delivery, the orchestrated fluctuations of his rhythms,
and the way he would pounce on certain words – tackle them, play
with them, squeeze and stretch them until the words themselves
seemed surprised at being infused with so much passionate intensity.
Remembering him talking over martinis in a bar in Barcelona in the
summer of '55, I can still hear his extended 'OOhhhh?' if anyone told
him something he found interesting. I still hear him telling me that no
matter where he was he had to swim every day of his life 'just to fee-
yul [deep diphthong] aliivvve? Yuh knowww?' Even his famous laugh –
three short staccato barks – belonged only to him. Marlon Brando had
pointed out to him, 'You used to laugh heh, heh, heh, and now you
laugh [pitching his voice a precise octave higher] Hee, hee, hee.' To
which he had replied, 'Of course my laugh is higher. It stands to reason.
I am older and more nervous.'

Tennessee's voice, with its Southern upward inflections at the end
of a sentence, seemed to be pausing to give you the opportunity to
agree or disagree. Hemingway's pronouncements were strictly ex
cathedra. It was rather as if Tennessee, as Everyman, proposed, while
Hemingway, as God, disposed.

During the time I knew Tennessee I never heard him disparage a
fellow writer. Indeed he seemed to be more interested in praising those
he admired, like Pinter and O'Neill and Beckett, and to enjoy elabo-
rating on their virtues. In this connection, and going forward in years
to 1967, I am reminded of him taking me up to his apartment in a high

state of excitement to hear 'the most original, the most beautifully poetic album of songs' he had ever heard. It was the Beatles' *Sergeant Pepper's Lonely Hearts Club Band.*

In Hemingway's work he found much to admire too. 'He writes about the quest of honor among men,' he said in my presence. 'I know of no quest more dangerous than that.' Much later, in *Clothes for a Summer Hotel,* Tennessee would give these words an ironic twist in a powerful scene between the 'ghost' characters of Hemingway and Scott Fitzgerald, which climaxes when Hemingway reveals to the latter that some day he'll write about a man who will be: 'completely you Scott, and it will appear, this portrait of you, in my last work *A Moveable Feast.* In it, aspects, embarrassing aspects of you, will be suggested clearly to the knowledgeable reader. You see, I can betray even my oldest closest friend, the one most helpful to me in the beginning. That may have been at least partly the reason for which I executed myself not long after . . . by blasting my exhausted brains out with an elephant gun . . .'

Hemingway did not give me his assessment of Tennessee's work but he was certainly, by any standards, a harsh critic of his contemporaries. Lest these words appear judgmental, let me quickly add that in the Quality Lit. Game, as correctly played, savaging one's competition is considered not only acceptable and legitimized by tradition – but *fun.* Hemingway, however, may have been too enthusiastic a player. Dawn Powell, whose writing Hemingway admired – he once said to her, 'You are the best woman writer I know and I don't mean woman writer' – told me she had stacks of letters from him she wanted to sell – she badly needed the money. 'But I wouldn't dare to,' she sighed. 'He said such really awful things about other writers.'

One balmy tropical evening in Havana, after drinking Papa Dobles at the Floridita as we dined with Papa and Miss Mary at an outdoor restaurant, high in the hills under a black sky bright with stars, Hem took deadly aim. Of Faulkner he said, 'He is a sauce writer. You can smell the sauce coming off every page of his writing.' He went on to equate what he considered Faulkner's failure as a writer with a bull-fighter who performs ninety-eight passes with a bull but doesn't know how to finish off the series. Graham Greene received these bullets: 'He

Lollipop summers on the New Jersey coast. Shirley on far right. Elaine third from right.

When we were very young. Betty, Shirley and Elaine.

Elaine as a baby, gazing into the future.

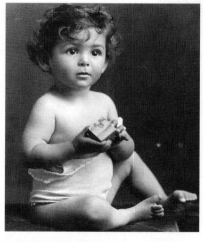

Elaine in the middle, crowned with a wreath, on her fourth birthday. Shirley has got one too. Deal, New Jersey.

Father, third from left and mother on the far right, strolling down the board walk with friends in Atlantic City in the 1920s.

Grandparents, Jennie and Heyman Rosenberg. Their crystal wedding in 1907.

Grandpa: an amiable genius whose revolutionary screws fastened together some of America's most beloved landmarks.

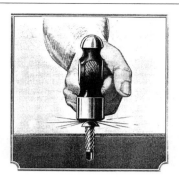

Parker-Kalon

Hardened Metallic

Drive Screws

PATENTED JAN. 29, 1924 — No. 1482191
OTHERS PENDING

For Making Permanent Fastenings to Iron, Brass and Aluminum Castings, Steel, Bakelite, etc.

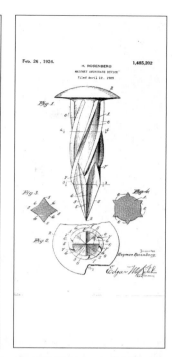

TOP LEFT: Grandpa's Parker-Kalon screws did away with nuts and bolts and with two men working on one fastening. One man with a hammer or similar assembly-line device now drove the hardened Self-Threading screws through sheet metals and fastened together the new inventions of the 20th century.

TOP RIGHT: A 1924 patent of a Parker-Kalon screw.

RIGHT: When Parker-Kalon joined forces with Nettlefolds, English major steel products, George V and Queen Mary showed up, 1935.

Their Majesties visit Exhibition of Screw Products
NETTLEFOLDS–PARKER-KALON
Associate Manufacturers

Greta Garbo, who became Elaine's imaginary companion as she enraptured her on the cover of *Photoplay*.

Elaine's sister Shirley, dark haired, sitting centre, Captain of the Green Team at Camp Fernwood. Standing farthest to the left is her other sister Betty.

TOP LEFT: Elaine's mother at a charity do in the 1940s.

TOP RIGHT: Shirley, Betty and Father around the same time.

RIGHT: Betty in her early teens. She was the beauty of the family.

The Brimberg Girls in their grandmother's silk, satin and lace boudoir. Betty, Shirley and Elaine in 1939.

TOP: Off to college, 1939.

CENTRE: Shirley and her husband Bert Clarke at their wedding, 1942.

RIGHT: Betty and her husband Boris Lorwin, 1946.

TOP: Transformed in and by
Paris, June 1950.

RIGHT: South of France
house-party. Friend Tessa on
balcony.

Wedding day – January 25 1951. Tessa Prendegast was maid of honour and Peter Wildeblood, best man. CENTRE LEFT: Delighted with Tracy, 1952. CENTRE RIGHT: Tracy at three and a half: a magical child. FOOT: Photographed by Henri Cartier Bresson at a bullfight, Pamplona in 1952.

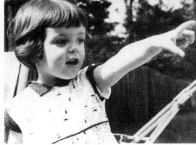

Shirley's camera catches a
serene mood in a hotel in
Paris in 1955.

Elaine, taken to mark *The Dud Avocado*, 1958.

Ken, at launch party in Mount Street.

Tracy enjoys the festivities.

TOP LEFT: Mike MacDonald, 1964.

TOP RIGHT: Richard Avedon photo for the cover of *The Old Man and Me*, 1964.

LEFT: Cyril Connolly presides as House Priest at La Consula, 1958.

BELOW LEFT: With Tracy and Peter Combe after the near drowning, 1963.

BELOW RIGHT: With Rosemary Harris outside the Caprice in the 1950s.

LEFT: Gore Vidal in a sun god mode at Edgewater in the late 1950s. CENTRE LEFT: Francis Wyndham, outstanding as features editor on Queen Magazine, 1960.

CENTRE RIGHT: Pauline Rumbold, a lively friend. With her brother David Tennant and mother, Hermione Baddeley.

BOTTOM LEFT: Rosemary Harris as Desdemona for the BBC in 1955. BOTTOM RIGHT: Henry Green: pub lunches in the 1950s.

Three of the 20th Century's Legends in their Time
Ernest Hemingway   Tennessee Williams

Hem and Tenn: The Yang and Yin of American letters.

Orson Welles. Throughout her teens Elaine held imaginary conversations with him. Later she had real ones.

Shirley as she is best remembered. Experimenting on video tape for television.

Shirley in action in the 1970s.

August 16 1987 – the year of Elvis Presley's deification. Elaine is one of the speakers. Not bad for someone who didn't know Elvis was alive until he was dead.

With Lillian Fortenberry, Elvis's aunt and Gladys's oldest sister.

Corene Smith and Reverend Smith, Elvis's first preacher.

With Roy and Debbie Turner.

Elaine's son-in-law Jim McBride and daughter Tracy Tynan with Ruby (11) and Matthew (13). November 2000.

Today and then
(aged twelve in a
swan dive)

From here to there
and back again.

was going pretty good there for a while but now he's a whore with a crucifix over his bed.' Reloading, he fired off another salvo at Greene for only spending ten days in Havana before writing a book about it, getting everything wrong – mixing up all the street names and buildings and then trying to deflect criticism by calling it an 'entertainment'! That right then and there in Havana the hilarious, hugely successful *Our Man in Havana* was being made into a major movie, starring Alec Guinness, Ernie Kovacs and Noël Coward and directed by Carol Reed, may not have improved Hemingway's temper.

Yet he highly praised Izak Dinesen and with genuine fervor urged me to read *Out of Africa*. About my novel he said, 'I like the way your characters all speak differently,' and then, quite casually, proved he could be as tough on himself as on others: 'My characters all speak the same because I never listen.'

Some days before we'd had lunch at Hemingway's *finca*. At one point he rose, magisterially proclaiming, 'Now you have been sitting in the living room a while. It is time we show you the house.' It is impossible to conceive of Tenn thus organizing the troops. Hem tried to contain chaos, Tennessee surrendered to it.

Hemingway showed us around. At one point he stopped in front of a door and when he opened it I was confronted with the strange sight of a room filled with letters still in their envelopes. It contained no furniture; there was nothing but the letters, fan mail from around the globe. They seemed to spill out of the room as if by opening the door he had loosened a flood. I swear you could not enter without wading waist high through them. 'Don't you read them?' I asked. 'I can't,' he said. 'I wouldn't get any work done.'

Something about the way he looked at all the letters held my attention. His face had an expression of annoyance, of frustration, as if he were brushing aside something – some burden he kept trying to shake off. Perhaps some vague moral duty to read and answer these letters nagged at him from time to time, so he kept them but didn't open them. He's protecting his talent, I thought. It was the first time I had put it in those words. Something in me shifted and I vowed hereafter not to make value judgments on how people of extraordinary talent should or should not be conducting their lives – a vow I did not always keep.

Did Tennessee get fan mail? He must have. Sooner or later most writers refer to the mail they receive, but Tennessee never did. Perhaps that was one of his ways of protecting his talent.

Each guarded his talent in different ways while trying to relax and get some fun out of life to make up for the long hours of hard work. At the height of their fame they were not only reaping the rewards of their celebrity but its penalties as well. The people they chose to relax with were chosen primarily to protect them from the world that had bestowed upon them so much hostility as well as so much admiration. The atmosphere surrounding them often became volatile: fights often broke out in their celebrated presence, some they would eventually be drawn into and others they themselves would create.

Age and success had not mellowed either Hem or Tenn. Instead it had increased rather than diminished their need to gratify their appetites. It had also made these desires both easier and harder to gratify with the world looking on. It seems to me that each assumed a public persona close enough to his interior self so that he could feel comfortable with it. Hemingway's persona had undergone a sea change in the post-war world. Shifting from his belligerent heavyweight boxer stance, he had begun, at the end of the Second World War, to call himself Papa. By 1950 he was bearded and his hair was grizzled, and by 1954, at fifty-five, his hair and beard were white and he resembled an Old Testament prophet. Inwardly he had cast himself in the iron mold of Colonel Cantwell in *Across the River and Into the Trees*, the pater-familias of the world, who knew more about everything than everyone and did everything better than any one else. Thus Hemingway spared himself the humiliating uncertainties of a mid-life crisis by leaping from virile youth to wise old age.

While Hemingway donned his Michelangelo robes, Tennessee donned the motley. The cap and bells he assumed were those of long standing. As Tom, his alter ego in the *Glass Menagerie*, he explains it was a role conferred on him by 'the only one in the warehouse with whom I was on friendly terms'. This friend, whom he calls Jim O'Connor (whose real life name was Jim Connor), 'called me Shakespeare. And while the other boys in the warehouse regarded me with suspicious hostility he took a humorous attitude toward me.

Gradually his attitude began to affect the other boys and their hostility wore off. And so, after a time they began to smile at me too, as people smile at some oddly fashioned dog that trots across their path at some distance.' This, with certain amendments, innovations and adjustments arising from the power invested in him as our premier playwright – he could, without warning, harden into steel – was the basic personality in which he felt at home. To be regarded humorously as an 'oddly fashioned dog' – or a sort of idiot savant – was something he had decided from youth upwards was the best way for him to get along with people. It fit his floating walk and abstracted air and finally it became his way of fending off people's importunities and their envy. All I can say is that it worked.

Hemingway, in order to protect his talent, demanded in his leisure hours a kind of willing sycophancy from people – needed it, craved it, enjoyed it, reveled in it. I have seen quite well-known people sitting at his feet, and A.E. Hotchener once balanced on the edge of a chair, one foot forward, one foot back, ready to spring at Papa's command. Spending time with Hem I realized he had rules for every hour of the day: for how you sat and walked, what you ate and drank, what you saw and how you saw it. It was as if he felt that only by strict adherence to this code could you get through the day with honor. Being with Hemingway meant joining in his elaborate game-playing as a necessary mark of respect. On the surface, his Papa/daughter gambit was a playful conceit: a wise, loving Papa and his well-loved daughter. But it was also a relationship that implied, because of the biological roles assigned, that the daughters would be forever adoring and submissive, would always listen agog as he recounted his war stories, exclaiming at the end, 'Oh, Papa, you're wonderful!' rather than saying, as a son might, 'Hey, Pop you're full of it.'

Tennessee, on the other hand, asked nothing but that you be yourself. Though yourself had better be colorful. And yourself had better be honest. Tennessee was suspicious of sycophancy, disliked it, detested it. When the playwright Peter Shaffer fell to his knees before him and kissed his hand, he responded by telling him to rise, saying coldly, 'Peter, you are up to *no good*.' I have heard him reduce a well-known actress to tears at a party as he berated her for her fulsome adulation.

'I came here to enjoy myself, to have a good time, not to listen to you carrying on about my work. I am so tired of your insincere praise. I am so tired of you calling me up the morning after every one of my flops raving about the play when all I want to do is just to be left alone. Go away, will you? I don't want to hear anything you have to say.'

He made demands on his own honesty. When he had met Princess Margaret at Gore Vidal's fiftieth birthday party he said to her politely, 'I'm afraid we can't talk to each other, ma'am, because we live in such different worlds.' What world did he live in? she wanted to know. 'Are you acquainted with the opera *La Bohème*, ma'am?' he said. 'That's my world.' His world as I knew it was redolent of lunches on Hal Wallis's yacht, cocktails on Sam Spiegel's, and the high life and night life of Rome with Magnani, Visconti, Zeffirelli, Fellini and assorted members of the *Dolce Vita* set. It was hardly the world of unknown artists starving in garrets, yet when he talked of *La Bohème* I think it was in remembrance of a world he lost – and deeply missed, one of artists among artists, filled with all the passion, excessive romanticism and idealism he had once experienced with the little St Louis theatre group called the Mummers, about which he has so feelingly written.

One thing Tennessee did ask of me was to call him by his rightful name, Tom, but there was no penalty involved if I forgot and slipped back into the more familiar Tennessee. I was not drummed out of the club, as I might have been with Hemingway had I failed to call him Papa. In keeping with this honesty Tennessee made sure that you knew his correct birth date was March 26, 1911 and not the official 1914, which for various reasons had been given out early in his career and kept appearing in print.

In '61 I spent a day with Tennessee in Madrid that was not without incident. We were staying at the same hotel and had planned to meet at noon. He called me at ten that morning. He was about to be interviewed by a Spanish critic and he wanted me to turn up at his room at 11.30 on the dot. 'So that when the man sees you he becomes aware I have other things to do today, you know?' When I arrived there was Tenn – having discarded the idiot savant pose in favor of the real savant that he was – winding up an astute analysis of Arthur Miller as a Northern and classic playwright, in the manner of Ibsen, as opposed to himself as a Southern and romantic one, in the manner of Lorca. Smoothly, he rose to greet me. Smoothly and politely, the Spanish critic was thereby dispatched.

A rich businessman had invited Tennessee and me to his house for lunch and a swim that day. The Japanese ambassador and several diplomats would be there and were eager to meet him. About half an hour into the occasion Tennessee suddenly pulled me over to him and said, 'I want you to hear what I'm going to say.' Having been engaged in conversation with the ambassador and his emissaries, he turned back to them , his voice steely with rage: 'I have been trying to hold a literary conversation with you. I have tried several times to talk to you about the Kabuki theatre which I admire. I have tried to talk to you about your brilliant director Kurosawa, and about that fine Japanese novel *The Key*, which I have recently read. But all you want to talk to me about is which bullfighter is homosexual. You are extremely rude.' And then, turning to our host severely: 'And you sir, have been listening to all this and have done nothing to stem the interrogation which you saw was so distasteful to me. Come on, Elaine, we're leaving.' In the car he said, 'If the rich and powerful aren't kind and well mannered they're just vulgar.'

He was in the midst of strangers and they should have treated him with kindness. I do not believe he could have written that most famous of all his lines – about depending on the kindness of strangers – had he not spent long periods on the Mississippi Delta in Clarksdale with his beloved grandfather, an Episcopal minister. Not since Homeric times has a people placed such emphasis on kindness to a stranger as in the Deep South. It is not only thy neighbor who must be loved as yourself but the stranger as well.

For Hemingway any challenge to his authority was inadmissible behavior, and for this reason in the summer of '59 Ken ran afoul of him in Malaga. Seated around a table of aficionados at the Miramar, listening to Hemingway praise the kill of the matador Jaime Ostos in the third bull, Ken was overheard to say that on the evidence of *his* eyes the kill was three inches off. Words were exchanged. 'I advise you Tynan,' said Papa at one point 'to take your fucking eyes and stick them up your fucking ass.'

There is a coda to this. The next day, after the bullfight we were seated on the terrace of the Miramar. Papa approached and said to me, 'Did you like Jaime Ostos's kill this afternoon?' 'Yes, Papa,' I said, acquiescing to him as I always did, 'very much.' 'Jamie Ostos *es numero tres*,' he pronounced solemnly. I concurred. He turned to Ken. 'Sorry about last night,' he said gruffly, 'too much vino.' Ken rose and faced him. 'Thank you, Papa,' he said. Papa extended his hand and Ken shook it. Hemingway moved on. Ken sank limply into his chair and said in tones of awe, '*I've been apologized to by a Nobel Prize winner!*'

They seemed poles apart, Hem and Tenn. But were they? In certain significant ways they were arrestingly alike. At important points of their lives they each chose Key West as the place in which to house their talents and write many of their major works. As can be seen by their novels and plays, Hemingway and Tennessee also shared a mutual love of Italy and Spain and were profoundly influenced by Latin culture.

Both were attracted to the Catholic Church. Hemingway informed me that he looked upon himself as an 'honorary Catholic'. Tennessee, when suffering from a bout of flu and convinced he was dying, allowed his brother Dakin to talk him into being baptized in the Catholic Church, thereby ensuring his entrance into heaven. One evening over drinks at the Plaza, Tennessee described this as a hilarious scene. In its aftermath, restored to health, he went to Rome intending to meet the Pope but was only met by the Jesuit luminary called the 'Black Pope' surrounded by his cabal.

There were other striking similarities. Both had domineering mothers – that's no news. Both were second children with older sisters. What I find most interesting is that they both had grandfathers they were proud of and fathers of whom they were eventually ashamed. The simple fact of Hemingway's both being officers in the Union Army fired young Ernest's imagination to the extent that he vastly exaggerated their brave exploits to his schoolmates. And by the same token, Tennessee's oeuvre, filled with religious symbols, can be accounted for by the fact that young Tom from childhood on had accompanied his grandfather, the Reverend Walter Dakin, in his Episcopal duties as he went among his parishioners. It was these grandfathers, it seems to me, who inspired the young boys with a sense of purpose that went beyond everyday existence, an ideal of service with all its noblesse, pitfalls, betrayals, sacrifices and glories. In Hemingway's case the ideal was the military; in Tennessee's the spiritual.

And finally they met that April in Havana. Ken and Tenn and George Plimpton (also in Havana at the time) have all written about it, each seeing it from his point of view.

From my own notes I recall that Ken said to Tenn at the Hotel Nacional, 'We are going to have lunch with Hemingway. Have you met him?' Tenn said that George Plimpton was arranging for them to meet. 'I – ah – gather he is not overfond of people of my persuasion,' he said, then with that upward inflection, 'but I hear he's very courteous?' I said, 'Yes,' which was true, and added, 'but he can be fierce,' which was also true. I was remembering some remarks made to me by Hemingway in Spain that could definitely be construed as homophobic. Specifically Hemingway had told me of an incident that took place on an ocean liner when a famous actor, Frank Vosper, a homosexual, went over to Hemingway's table with the idea of joining him for a drink and Hemingway smashed his glass 'to indicate that I did not wish to drink with a pederast'.

The evening before the meeting I tested the waters on the subject by reminding Hem of our conversation in Spain. 'I am for normalcy and against homosexuality,' he said mildly enough, 'because sexually there are infinite variations for the normal person but none for the homosexual one.' This indicated to us that Tenn would at least not be subjected to a salutation of smashed glass.

They met late one morning at the bar of the Floridita, Hemingway's favorite haunt – Hem and Tenn, George and Ken. I heard both Tenn's and Ken's versions of the meeting later that day, and I was to hear Ken's account of it many, many times, refined and honed and embellished to a brilliant set piece. I don't think Ken and I discussed any other two people as much as we did Hem and Tenn during our stay in Cuba – going over and over who said what *exactly*. And exactly what did it mean.

Ken and Tenn's stories did not tally. At the time I favored Ken's version because he imitated Tenn so wickedly, but I think now it was a

...turned Tenn into a buffoon while Hem deadpanned caus-... monosyllables and elaborately pulled his leg. Ken established his ...by describing Tenn as wearing a yachting jacket, as if to convince ...em that 'although he might be decadent he was decadent in an outdoor way'. In fact it was a navy blue blazer I had often seen him wear. George also commented on Tenn's costume, adding to it a yachting cap and white flannel trousers. Could Tenn have retreated for safety into his original persona and donned the motley? Or is it not probable that Tenn – however ludicrous the results seemed to the others – had decided to dress up to for occasion as a mark of respect? We know that he was not infrequently a guest on certain yachts and his gear must have been something he had to hand.

In Tenn's version the meeting was a pleasure. He found Hem sensitive, gentle, and kindly disposed towards him. Besides the two of them agreeing that it was essential for a writer to keep his liver and kidneys in good shape if he wanted to stay the course, trading recipes to help achieve this goal, the main topics of discussion were: Key West and its landmarks and how it had changed; Hem's late wife Pauline, who had been a friend of Tenn's; and the bullfighter Antonio Ordonez. In Ken's version Tenn told Hem he had met Ordonez and found him a fine young man, personable and charming, to which Hem responded all mock innocence, including the other two, with, 'Do you think *we* would like him?' And Tenn, with genuine innocence, assured him that they would. Tenn's version, which appears in his memoirs, states that he told Hem he knew nothing about the technical aspects of bullfighting but he had become friendly with Ordonez, whom he liked very much, and Hem replied that he was glad Tenn liked him. I give Tenn's version the edge simply because in 1959 anyone *not* having heard of the much publicized friendship between the bullfighter and Hem would have had to have been living on the moon. Tenn's demeanor may have suggested that he visited the moon from time to time, but his mission was Broadway, and he loved the gossip columns. And, like all celebrities, he kept a close watch on the doings of his peers.

Further, at that meeting it transpired that Ken asked Hem to write a note of introduction for him to give Castro as he had an appointment to meet him that afternoon. Tenn said he wanted to meet him too. In Spanish, Hem scribbled to Castro his introduction to 'the English journalist Kenneth Tynan' and 'the great North American playwright, Tennessee Williams'. Reading that must have told Tenn something.

All things considered, for several reasons I am now inclined to take Tenn's version, which suggests the two met as equals. For several reasons. First, both men would honor each other for having reached the very pinnacle of their art – the more so as they did not impinge on each other's turf. (George says that afterwards Hemingway characterized Tenn as 'unpredictable', commented humorously on his outfit and then cast his vote: 'Damn good playwright.')

Second, in Ken's account of the meeting he has Tenn inquiring if Hem's wife Pauline had died painfully. (She died in 1951 away from Key West, where Tenn had known her.) Ken takes Hem's reply – 'She died like anyone else. And after that she was dead' – as a rebuff to Tenn, though it could just as easily be argued that Papa was merely being Papa. But Tenn, upon reading Ken's version, immediately wrote to Hem to apologize if any remarks he had made about Pauline had offended him. That was a letter Hem did read – and answer. He assured Tenn that he had not taken offense.

And finally, we must not overlook the profession of one of the participants of the meeting. Not two weeks before Ken, in his column in the *New Yorker*, had savaged Tenn's new play *Sweet Bird of Youth* and Hem would have been aware that any day now he might feel the stab of Ken's pen. Is it not possible two authors would be more on the same wavelength, finding a fleeting sympathy, feel closer to each other then they would to their natural enemy, the critic?

But – *did* Hem and Tenn really have that feeling of closeness? Maybe not. After all, they never met again, which suggests these two shining celestial bodies were wrenched off course for one puzzling moment before resuming their parallel paths. But we are told parallel lines do meet in space. Therefore I think Hem and Tenn did meet once again, in their work. Our two legends were drawn to another legend, a woman who fascinated them both. She was a real woman and – although she primarily belonged to yet another and equally famous writer, F. Scott Fitzgerald – they each appropriated her for their own use. Their treatment of her is significantly different. In *The Garden of Eden* (another of Hemingway's posthumous works) he creates a wife crazily bent on destroying her writer husband. In *Clothes For a Summer Hotel* (Tennessee's last Broadway play) he creates a wife who has been driven crazy and destroyed by *her* writer husband. Hem called his woman Catherine. Tenn called her by her rightful name – Zelda.

Dead Hemingway and dead Tennessee are now both respectable United States postage stamps. Late in his life, Tenn said to an actor appearing in one of his last (and badly received) plays, in reference to the audience sitting out front: 'They can't wait for me to die so that they can commemorate me.'

I wonder if Hem didn't sometimes feel like that too.

21

Gore

'When I signed my contract with the Devil, bad reviews were not part of the agreement,' Gore Vidal said to me soon after our arrival in New York in November of '58, in reply to my question about how his latest film was doing. As I got to know him better I would recognize that such wrap-up statements announced the closure of one venture and the beginning of the next. What I could never guess was what would be next.

My younger self accepted all Gore's activities from the time I first knew him when he spun out films and TV plays while keeping his opinions, thoughts and views on a variety of topics flowing lava-like through outlets that included *Esquire*, *Partisan Review*, the *New Republic*, the *Nation* and the newly started *New York Review of Books*. He also served for a while as theatre critic of the *Reporter*. Furthermore there were numerous television talk show appearances in which the actor in Gore displayed that this medium was an agreeable place for his wit, wisdom and iconoclasm.

I regarded his multitudinous activities with curiosity and admiration, but I took them all for granted, just as I took for granted the achievements and successes of all the talented people I knew because

I believed they would all go on forever. My basic attitude to the diversity of his labors was something like, 'Well, Gore's a writer so that's what he does, he writes.' I thought of it simply as his intellect's random outpourings. Later I was to see it as a well-thought-out, orderly planned progression. Orderly, but filled with risks.

Gore had thrown the first party we went to in New York. It was held at his apartment on East 55th Street, which was small and impersonal and had an off-hand feeling about the way it was done up. The next day he drove us across the Hudson River to his place in the country, where we were to stay for the weekend.

And there, upon arrival, virtually without warning, was Gore's secret weapon laid bare – Edgewater, his stately Greek revival house in the Hudson valley, with elegant yet comfortable appointments within. He had bought it for a song in 1950 and spent the next eight years singing for it by using the money he earned to fix it up. I sensed almost immediately how essential were the roots he'd dug there for himself. I saw I was wrong to imagine him as one of those rovers of the world's capitals, those elite gypsies who spent their lives living it up at international first-class hotels or lodging places. I'd got it back to front. Edgewater was where Gore lived; everywhere else was where he stayed. I now understood the off-hand look of the apartment in New York.

By his own account Edgewater had released a new energy in him. It also served as a perfect place for him to relax in needed peace while getting ready to jump back into the fray.

I see him as he was back then, so many years ago, relaxing in the autumn sunlight on the lawn. In an ecstasy of unconditional love he is slobbering over his two spaniels, Billy and Blanche, and receiving their licking-wet kisses while in return he prattles away to them in some arcane version of baby talk. He is handsome, yes, I had long conceded this point; there was no denying his crisp good looks, his well-defined eyebrows, his sharp straight nose, the curve of his mouth, the quiff of his brown hair and his dimpled smile.

I see him also around this time standing in the front door at Edgewater trying to herd us into the car. 'C'mon, c'mon, let's *go*. Like, *make tracks*,' he briskly encourages us; baring his teeth in statesman-like smile while giving his jacket a statesman-like tug. Instead of affecting the lounging, lanky, slouch of the upper-class Easterner, as his years at Exeter might have predicted, his stance – shoulders back, chest up, chin tucked in – is more in the manner of a graduate of a Southern military school, a salute perhaps to his West Point father.

Gore, unlike many writers equally intent on being controversial, did not telegraph his punches clotheswise. They were not so much understated as not stated at all; they were close-mouthed clothes. There were such items as a perfectly silent brown tweed jacket, a hushed red tie with quiet little amoebas swimming on it, unexceptionable trousers of khaki or gray flannel. If he appeared without a tie, he was tieless in a clean white shirt and navy blue blazer, and his brown loafers were always polished. There was no rebellious statement in his attire as with other male celebrities who, beginning in the fifties, were strenuously into self-expression.

Gore's outside didn't match his inside. He looked like a young Republican. Until he opened his mouth. Although his society friends could always count on him to pick up the right knives and forks at a formal dinner party, by the end of it they would be made several shades greener (or redder) by the wrongness of his dinner conversation, most of which was spent in attacking their treasured convictions.

Gore, who made an amusing, if provocative, if *provoking* guest, came into his own as a host. It is one thing to throw good parties, as Ken and I did, and have your guests (figuratively) swinging from the chandeliers for three or four hours. But it is quite another to have them (literally) underfoot for a weekend and to keep them as Gore did, in a fairly blissed-out state of satori.

The weekends I spent at Edgewater in '58, '59 and '60 were luminous. Just the sight of Gore standing at the Rhinebeck station as I got off the train on Friday evening had the effect of instantly cleansing my palate, like some tart lemon sorbet, of the toxic fury I had ingested all week at the moveable feast it was my lot to share with Ken. I always returned from a weekend at Gore's rested and refreshed and restored to sanity. Evenings there were enlivened by the company of Gore's neighbors, such as Fred Dupee and his wife Andy, the political journalist Richard Rovere and an assortment of the more interesting professors currently teaching at the nearby college, Bard. Eventually the guests would depart, leaving the world to darkness, to Gore, to his young red-head companion Howard Austen, to Billy and Blanche, and to me.

His Atticisms on themes dropped from his mouth like so many pearls; real, cultured, or faux, it didn't matter. They all came tumbling out, a ceaseless raillery, scattering all over the floor, and we would laugh and laugh until I felt the laughter break loose, become palpable, and roar around the room like a ten-force gale, rattling the windows and banging the doors. I was choking, weak, gasping for breath and clutching my sides. And finally it would subside, but only till I caught my breath. And then he would start it up all over again.

I saw in the novels that he calls his 'inventions' – such as *Myra Breckinridge*, *Duluth* and *The Smithsonian Institution* – that Gore flew into the wild blue yonder of what is termed 'thought uncontrolled by reason' with the greatest of ease. In spite of his boast of being a third-generation atheist, no one is more at home in the mythical, the supernatural, the paranormal, the metaphysical and even what might be called the spiritual.

I was, I suppose, the designated laugher, a role I enjoyed playing to the hilt. As the hours and the drinks progressed certain signposts would regularly appear. Howard, who aspired to be a pop star, would try out a few songs on us. Gore would balance a half-full glass of whiskey on his head, which was never referred to and which, miracu-lously, never spilled. I, enveloped in this ambiance of warmth and ease and gaiety and, feeling at once both liberated and cozy, might near bedtime, divest myself of my clothes (also never referred to).

And once, and only once, Gore and I went to bed together. Next day everything was back to normal. Let us say we chose to bathe in the pure, refreshing streams of friendship rather than shoot the perilous rapids of physical love. Which is not to say I wasn't in love with Gore, because I was. I saw nothing odd about this. If Platonic love is not based on passionate feelings, how can it sublimate itself and ascend the heights?

I remember the high-ceilinged living room of our revels and later, in bed, being aware of that powerful sound of country silence broken only, if I was still awake in the early hours of the morning, by the click-clacking of the world's longest freight train, which ran forever behind Gore's property. Its sound had for me that soothing quality peculiar to train locomotion.

Another soothing quality of the Gore–Howard ménage was its notable lack of the sexually driven spats that made the company of so many couples (myself and Ken included) heavy-going for guests. 'It's always the way with me,' Gore said of his alliance with Howard. 'What might begin as sex often turns into a father-and-son type relationship.' Gore was the father of a bright if wandering boy, for Howard at the time was having a fling with Rona Jaffe, at the beginning of her bestsellerdom. As Gore and Howard's partnership developed, so did Howard's ability for organizing and administrating every aspect of their existence, including their finances. 'Gore does the writing,' Howard said, 'and I do all the rest.'

'What've you been doing?' I always asked Gore when I hadn't seen him for a while. His answer, though consistently opposite to what he'd been doing before, would seem just right for him. But in the summer of '59, when he visited me at Martha's Vineyard, his answer made me wonder. 'I've just written a play about a presidential election,' he'd said. And though my response was, 'Great,' my unspoken words – 'Why would anyone want to see a play about that?' – were what he picked up on. He reminded me that we were coming up to an election year in '60. 'Ah,' I said, 'timely.' Said Gore, 'I'm getting interested in politics again.' I was surprised. I didn't know he was interested in the first place.

Gore, in fact, talked very little about his play The Best Man until it was at the casting stage. 'We want Leora Dana for the wife of one of the presidential nominees. She's the only actress on Broadway I know who can play a lady. But she says the part's one-dimensional as is. I'm going to fix it. Call her and tell her I mean it.' Leora and I had been friends since my earliest acting days, so I called her and repeated Gore's remarks. The next thing I knew she was cast in the part. When I asked her how Gore fixed her role, she replied, 'He gave me a sense of humor.'

The Best Man opened on March 31, 1960, a few months before the presidential conventions, and it was a solid hit. It was revived in 1962 and in 1976 and again in 1987 at the Ahmanson Theatre in Los Angeles and in New York in 2000. It is all talk, but talk that demonstrates the political skullduggery that is part and parcel of choosing a presidential candidate. It is so savvy and credible, so insidious and outrageous, and it remains absolutely pertinent to this day. The play is as full of surprise and suspense as a courtroom drama and the twist at the end is worthy of Agatha Christie. What consolidated its success on its opening was the return to the stage of two well-loved veteran actors: Melvyn Douglas, who played the good Adlai Stevenson-like candidate, and Lee Tracy, who played the Truman-like former president. They both gave star performances, holding the audience transfixed without seeming to do a thing except inhabit their roles with total authority.

Not till that summer was I to understand that the play served as Plan A to the much larger Plan B. If it had flopped it would have had far greater consequences for Gore than receiving awful notices and closing on Saturday; the master plan would have been infinitely harder to implement. Yet not even when Gore began talking about his new friendship with Eleanor Roosevelt, who happened to live in the same county, or when he introduced us to Jackie Kennedy, with whom we spent an evening, was I prepared to receive – upon returning to London in 1960 – letters from him on writing paper headed: 'VIDAL for CONGRESS HEADQUARTERS, Washington St., Poughkeepsie, NY.

Late in September, by which time his campaign was well under way, he wrote me:

. . . SO ANYWAY AFTER Summer came Autumn in New York and all the squares do tiny rectilinear things to each other, you can guess like what, and Dundy is still a name on a lot of lips some chapped others merely bruised from life's battle, and all in all OLD GAUZE [my name for him, based on a garbled message I received that 'a gauzy doll called'] is making concentric rings hell-wise with the speed of forenamed said bat out of. The candidate gets up at seven, does seven coffee hours

with groups of like forty fifty women a crack, goes through two
factories shaking hands, meets the farmers, and ends the day
with a speech before shrieking crowds not since the early
revivalists has there been anything to compare this to . . .

Gore had asked some of his theatrical friends to stump for him:

INGE (William Inge) hates OLD GAUZE, no word from 10
WMS (Tennessee Williams) . . . I guess I'm just not going to be
the best loved lil' ol' writer-man who ever came down the pike.
I don't write, I don't read, I don't think, I just talk.
The NEWMS (Paul Newman and Joanne Woodward) are all
that's left and they have been valient little soldiers invading
the District to speak for OLD GAUZE which they do with
great passion and craft and much effect . . .

   So why haven't you written a book or anything? Why don't
you come home? Why don't you do a lot more adultery, I mean
golly it's not like you've got all the time in the world with
nuclear fission the way it is. I know what a grind adultery is but
you've just got to put your mind to it and grit your teeth . . .
no! No, don't do that but you know what I mean metaphori-
cally. You can't let the team down.

   Aren't you ever coming back? Jack, Jackie are doing well
and he will win though the press has come out for Wm.
McKinley and will not back down.

   I am in terrible danger of winning myself.* I've never
worked so hard at anything.

                COME HOME, Love
                Gauze

*When I win me I will use it as a doorstop—

It turned out I happened to be going to New York in November. As
part of a surprise birthday party Dick Avedon was giving Mike
Nichols, he arranged for Ken and me to be flown over and pop out of

the birthday cake, so I was able to accept Gore's invitation to come up to Edgewater at election time and witness the proceedings. This was, of course, the same year as the Kennedy–Nixon race.

Gore was running for Congress in the 29th District on the Democrat ticket. The incumbent was a Republican who, though he had been voted in for years, was virtually unknown to his constituency. The district, which included Dutchess County, had always been a stronghold of Republicans, but with the growth of cities in the area and the infusion of a new population composed of industrial laborers, who traditionally vote Democrat, change was possible. Also, never before had the natives had a Democrat candidate with the high profile of this novelist/playwright/screenwriter/TV performer aged thirty-five. Although in those days scrutiny of a candidate's private life had not become the routine matter it would later, Gore had been subjected to a small pry on the part of an interviewer from the *New York Times*, but that had fizzled out.

I arrived in the evening on election day and took a taxi from the station to Edgewater. A young couple connected with the campaign and Howard were waiting in the living room and Gore had gone out with his father for a walk. I had not been there for many months and I immediately sensed a change. The House of Mirth had been transformed into the House of Purpose. The different arrangement of the recently polished furniture seemed to proclaim it. Even the dogs Billy and Blanche seemed more focused, more sober. Instead of frisking around and tripping you up, they were now sitting demurely on chairs or stairs or dead center on top of beds.

Finally Gore and his father came back. This was the first time I had met Gene Vidal, a trim military-looking man, his skin tanned, his features evenly cut. I saw a relationship between father and son that was at once easy-going, intimate and respectful, revealing a side of Gore I had never seen before. We talked unmemorably, all eyes on the clock. As the hour approached when polls in various districts had been closed and a sufficient amount of time had passed for the results to start coming in, we got into cars to drive to election headquarters in Poughkeepsie. On the way there with Gore and his father, talk was confined to road information and driving directions, but as we arrived

I witnessed a short but noteworthy moment: Gore's father placed a paternal arm around his son's shoulder and said, with attempted cheerfulness, 'Well, it's just like another opening night, isn't it?' 'With this difference,' replied his son, tight-lipped. 'This means more to me than any opening night ever did.' The remark startled me for underneath I had always assumed his running for Congress was just a lark. It put us in a somber mood as we walked into election headquarters to be met . . . by the buoyant spirits of the people assembled.

Quite a crowd was milling around. At a glance the women looked like Vassar girls, which they were, as the college was in the 29th District and Gore had organized a number of them to work for his campaign, while the men looked like old-time Democrats. The returns had started coming in and the news was good. With every further announcement of the counted votes chalked up on the board, hopes were raised higher. The first returns were the big city votes, and in Poughkeepsie and Kingston, the industrial centers of Dutchess County, Vidal was running well ahead of his Republican rival, so far ahead that a landslide seemed possible. More returns went up on the board to the jubilation of friends and party workers, and there were happy hugs all around as the Vidal numbers rose. Something interesting caught my attention: in proportion to the swelling numbers of votes were the swelling numbers of people into the room. The population had doubled, I was seriously forced to consider the reality of Congressman Vidal.

A fresh urn of coffee broke out as we settled down to watch the rural votes stagger in. Slowly, inexorably, in all the rural areas, the farmers reversed the numbers as they voted solidly in favor of the Republican candidate. The room quietened down and shrank back to its original population. The party workers anxiously looked to their leader, pleadingly it seemed, as if hoping he would do something about all this. Finally he did. He studied the numbers for the last time, checked on the few still uncompleted scores from outlying districts and calmly made his decision. He gathered the troops around and crisply conceded the election. He thanked everyone, shook hands all around, and before I knew it we were in our cars and back in Edgewater. While the rest of us settled down in front of the TV for the long night's vigil until it seemed certain that Kennedy was our next president, Gore, to my astonishment, retired to his room and went to bed.

Mid-morning, next day, on my way downstairs, as I passed his open bedroom door I saw him talking on the phone. He was asking to speak to his agent. There was a pause and then I heard him say, 'Okay, I've lost the election. Get me a movie.' By which graceful note he won by losing.

22

Shirley's Cool World

'You have vindicated me!' said my sister Shirley, laughing wildly over the phone the very day I landed in New York in '58. Then, dropping into her serious mode, she continued, 'Your review in *Time* magazine has vindicated me. I now feel free to go forward, backed by your success.'

I was dumbfounded. True, under the heading of 'Tender is the Fulbright' *Time* magazine had given *The Dud Avocado* a pleasant and provocative review, also running my photograph and an interview. But Shirley, iconoclast and rebel, had already established herself as an independent filmmaker, whose short films from the very start were greeted with prize-winning acclaim at art festivals from Brussels to Toronto to Venice to Los Angeles to New York. *Skyscrapers* had even captured an Academy Award nomination in '57. So why, I wanted to know, would her main criterion for success be the seal of approval from an establishment magazine such as *Time*?

What better a place, she replied, to receive confirmation than from establishment magazines with huge international circulations like *Time* or *Newsweek*? And receive it, moreover, for doing precisely your own anti-establishment thing? 'Every serious artist knows the importance of getting his work into the market place.' Shirley was, among other things, a realist. Three years later she would get recognition from *Time*, *Newsweek* and the *New York Times*, as well as from one even more relevant source. And it would be for doing her own anti-establishment thing.

In 1942 Shirley had married Bert Clarke, originally from Baltimore. He was a charming man, a gourmet cook who had his own printing press and was a book designer of repute, especially noted for producing beautiful art books, including those of Georgia O'Keeffe. They lived in a brownstone in New York on East 87th Street near Gracie Square, and in 1944 their daughter Wendy was born. From the outside they seemed a happy nuclear family. In the early fifties Shirley came across an old wedding present: a camera. It gave her an idea. Enlisting the aid of Bert as her first cameraman, she produced an extraordinary dance film, and from then on she transferred her allegiance from dance to film, giving to the latter the same passionate dedication as she had the former. Like the magic box my grandfather had advised everyone to carry with them, Shirley carried her camera wherever she went. Their home became a center for independent filmmakers and film critics the world over.

Until Ken and I moved to New York in the autumn of '58, Shirley and I saw each other only briefly when I was in America or she in Europe. Now that I was living in New York, we met more often.

One day in '59 Shirley announced she was going to take a big step. Up till then she had only made short films; now she felt ready to take the plunge and do a feature film. Could I help her? Could I think of any book I'd read, any play I'd seen, a short story, or anything that could be adapted for this purpose.

I didn't even have to think. Something that would suit her right down to the depths of her avant garde soul was the off-Broadway play *The Connection*. It was written by a new playwright, Jack Gelber, and stunningly performed under the direction of Judith Malina at the Living Theatre. The plot was simple: a playwright rounds up a group of drug addicts in a shabby loft in order to write a play about them waiting – like Godot – for their connection, called Cowboy, to arrive and give them their fix. Unlike Godot, the connection finally comes. He turns them all on, with one near-fatal result. It had pulverizingly authentic street dialogue plus a group of superb musicians as part of the cast playing be-bop in a taut, strung-out way that made you hear their craving for a fix become an almost spiritual yearning. It had the actors, still in character, haranguing the spectators for money during the intermission so convincingly that they left profound doubts in the audience as to whether or not they were the real thing. It was, to use a word just gaining favor, a happening.

It also had a history that was the stuff of which avant garde dreams are made. It had opened in July 1959 to hostile reviews but the producers kept it on until it won raves from such quality lit. weeklies as the New Yorker, the Village Voice, the Nation and the Saturday Review, whereupon it became the off-Broadway sensation and most discussed play of the season.

After seeing the play Shirley was fascinated, but . . . The but was a big one. She couldn't see how to solve it for a film. I said that didn't matter a damn and reminded her of the market place, saying The Connection came with built-in publicity that would precede it wherever it went and whatever form it took. I also said it had the advantage of a superb, ready-made cast.

She saw it a second time and had a complete change of heart. She was now wild to do it. Jack Gelber was a friend of ours but I left well enough alone. It was now between the two of them. They clicked and decided they would co-write the picture. 'Shirley was like a rushing river,' was Jack's first impression. 'Warm, quick, garrulous, laughing at the slightest provocation, she seemed ready to jump at any new experience out there.' If Shirley was new to feature-filmmaking, Jack was new to screenwriting.

It was also to be a new experience for Lew Allen, a successful backer of Broadway shows now wanting to get into films. Getting it all together in record time Shirley began shooting the film and completed it in an incredible nineteen days.

Shortly after the actors had finished their roles in the movie in 1961, they were flown to England by the producer Peter Daubeny to play *The Connection* in London's West End for a foreign theatre festival.

I was in London at the time and attended opening night with Richard Buckle, ballet critic of the *Sunday Times*. During the performance some boos were heard from the gallery first-nighters, and at the end as a group they booed a great deal louder. In response Buckle, who had risen and was giving the play a standing ovation, looked up at the balcony and called out in the clarion tones, 'Fuck the gallery!'

Among those who would first see the film and become its staunch supporter was Gene Moscowitz, *Variety's* top man in Paris. Through his good offices the film was chosen to go to the Cannes Film Festival '61 in the out-of competition category. Shirley went with it. 'Oh my God!' said Shirley in an interview, 'It was just extraordinary what happened in Cannes. We were the absolute hit of that festival. There was not a girl in a pink bikini with a pink poodle and pink hair that got photographed that year in Cannes. All the "Beat" Americans in Europe came to Cannes to support us in their Volkswagens buses and cars – their "look" was the hit of the festival . . . They enchanted the European press . . . The festival gave us a villa to live in, and we just took over . . . [They] gave us a place to sleep but hadn't given us very much money to eat with. Allen Ginsberg became our Jewish uncle and showed us how to hustle. It ended with the head of the festival, Monsieur Fauve-Lebret, giving a dinner party for me. All the Cannes critics had been invited to dinner and they came to meet me. And in [his] after dinner speech, he said, "Any film you ever do Madame, from now on is invited to play at Cannes". I mean I was insane. I was out of my mind.'

At Cannes Shirley's hour had come. She was heroine of the Beats, the Queen of Cool. And she had found her Prince Charming. She and the young black actor, Carl Lee, who played Cowboy, the Connection himself, had fallen in love. She would later tell me he was the only thing that mattered to her in the world, the great love she had been waiting for all her life.

I'd known Carl Lee when he was a student at the Dramatic Workshop. He was a good-looking polite youngster, eager to lend a hand at any theatrical task. After I saw the play of *The Connection* I went backstage to congratulate him. He seemed to me to be the same young man as ever – but he wasn't.

Shirley had married young and in those first years I saw her trying hard to be the model young wife. She wore flowers in her dark flowing hair, like a sort of South Sea island bride. Bert adored her and with his help her involvement in films could be total. Along with their loyal housekeeper he performed every function needed to keep the family going, including bringing up their daughter Wendy, whom Shirley loved passionately but was too deep in her art to attend to.

When Shirley began filming *The Connection*, she had been married for eighteen years, but after the film's triumph in Cannes Shirley, now in the throes of love, took off with Carl for a year in Europe. When she broke the news to me I think she expected me to be overjoyed or at least understanding. It was, more of less, the type of thing I'd done with Ken. But I was less than thrilled. I was in fact alarmed and dismayed. So was Jack Gelber, now living in London, when I told him. Though I'd known nothing about Shirley's affair with Carl, I'd known for some time that besides being an actor (and maitre d' at the Café Bohemia, where Miles Davis played), Carl was now a drug dealer who was himself on hard drugs. Such information was readily available to those frequenting hip circles in the sixties.

That good-looking, polite, well-mannered youngster I'd known at the Dramatic Workshop now lived in two worlds: the bohemian world of white artists and black musicians in the East and West Village and the black underworld of Harlem. In the drug culture of the sixties you could say he was a bridge between the two. It was also known that he was a pimp. Jack Gelber remembers visiting Carl one day in his pad and meeting stunning-looking call girls who bought their drugs from him. In his autobiography Miles Davis talks about a call girl who subsequently became his girlfriend and says they were introduced by Carl.

Irony upon irony piled up around the meeting and mating of my sister and Carl. First irony: if I hadn't urged Shirley to make a film of *The Connection* she would never have met him. Second irony: After completing *The Connection*, which carried with it a decided anti-drug message, Shirley threw in her lot with the hipsters of the drug culture and under Carl's spell insisted, so she later told me, that he turn her on to drugs so that she could be on his same glorious wavelength. Third irony: Shirley was a highly independent woman in every sense of the word, in her time one of only a handful of women filmmakers in the world. She was a woman who gave orders to tough male crews, who led and inspired a generation of film students. I couldn't bear it that she had chosen an evil punk for the love of her life, that I was inhibited from expressing this forcibly to her by my awareness that I myself had slept with the enemy for so many years.

Her relationship with Carl would last, on and off, for some twenty years. As I saw it, Carl satisfied her need to rebel against bourgeois morality as she'd done as a young communist in the thirties and a post-war anti-nuke marcher. I think his outlaw activities must have excited her. She would see them as her chance to enter into the lower depths and outer limits of a world she longed to explore. But there was another side to her. She genuinely worshipped black genius (as did we all growing up in nightclubs and dance circles in New York). A political activist from her teens, the injustices suffered by American blacks had always been a cause close to her. To Shirley, black was beautiful; negritude spoke to her soul. It also spoke to her filmmaking. Three of her major films – *The Cool World*, *Portrait of Jason* and *Ornette Coleman: Made in America* – are about black people.

The Cool World (1963), shot on location in Harlem, was a devastating inside look at teenage gang life in the ghetto. It was Carl who gave her the special entry into this world, where he was a man of substance, a respected presence in the cool black underworld. Without his endorsement of her, Shirley would not have had access to record it so intimately. In the neo-realism mode she used a handheld camera and mostly non-actors. Among the few professionals was Carl, who also shared credit for co-writing the script with Shirley. Adapted from a novel by Warren Miller she credited Carl with 'ironing out the novel, changing the dialogue and putting characters together', but the power of the film, I thought, lay in Shirley's camera.

What made Carl? He could hardly claim to have grown up on mean streets. Of his background it is often mentioned that he was 'raised like a prince'. In any case his background was middle class. His father,

Canada Lee, was a distinguished actor who played Shakespearean roles on Broadway at a time when, apart from Paul Robeson, black actors in roles of stature were unique; Canada played a priest in *The Cool World*. His princely son Carl was to die of AIDS in the eighties from a contaminated hypodermic needle.

The summer of '63 *The Cool World* was chosen as an entry in the Venice Film Festival, at whose invitation Shirley and Carl attended. So did my mother, who brought Wendy and Tracy along with her. Shirley had decided to tell Mother about her and Carl, then she changed her mind. She was separated from Bert and living with Carl in an apartment in the West 90s. When I came to New York and visited the two of them in her new apartment, I brought a friend along with me. When we left, he said of Carl, 'He has beautiful manners.'

Before entering the cool world of Harlem, Shirley had visited a wholly different universe and made a documentary that paired her with a legend. *Robert Frost, A Lover's Quarrel with the World* won her the Academy Award for Best Documentary in '64.

In '65 Shirley told me she'd been ill. She named the upscale rehab facility in Connecticut where she'd spent some weeks (she didn't have to spell out why), and added that she'd closed down her apartment and broken off with Carl. She wanted to live in a hotel. I had written, as my first article for *Esquire*, a long piece on the Chelsea Hotel. She read it. Should she stay there? I phoned them right away.

I told Stanley Bard, who, with his father, owned the hotel, that my sister wanted to stay there; she was very special and I wanted him to look after her. Most important, she was to have a large spacious room on one of the top floors. (I had discovered during my stay that they were the best.) He assured me he would personally take care of it, and he gave her a good room on the tenth floor. Soon after he let her take over the penthouse as well as the Chelsea's roof, and it became her home for some thirty years. She used it as the base for much of her important film work, and it was there that she met, mingled and merged with the other extraordinary denizens living or hanging out at this hotel. In the seventies she taught how to extend their personal visions via the sensational new invention, the video camera.

Shirley was happier there than any other place in her life. She

owned two beautiful Morris poodles, whose meals, I remember, she
ordered daily at the adjoining restaurant, El Quixote, picking up the
phone and saying, 'Two large hamburgers, hold the buns, hold the
onions, tomatoes, lettuce, and fries.'

23

My Place

Throughout our American Experience, the combat between Ken and me had continued. Looking back it is often where our fighting took place that I remember rather than what those rows were about. One particular altercation, at East 89th Street in the winter of 1959, began in the living room and rapidly accelerated to the stage where we were looking for things to throw. When we saw that the maid was trying to get in to clean the room, without missing a beat we moved into the bedroom she had just finished putting in order.

Had we a penchant for theatrics? What did you expect? We were at the theatre every night, watching plays that dealt mostly with the ever-popular subject of marital strife (what Ken called domestic anecdote). At some point during one particular domestic anecdote, I saw that Tracy had come into the living room and was watching us as if at a tennis match. When it was over and Ken had left I said to her: 'What did you think of that?' She replied, 'You've had that row before.' It stopped me dead in my tracks. As well as pointing out that we'd said it all before Tracy also made me recognize that this didn't lessen our need to keep on saying it.

'Why do people often feel bad in good environments and good in bad environments?' the philosopher-novelist Walker Percy asks. 'In fact, why do people feel so bad in good environments they prefer bad environments?'

It is a point worth pondering. In '59 we agreed to spend the summer safely, serenely and sanely apart – I with Tracy and Dolly in Martha's Vineyard, he in England and Europe writing about theatre. No sooner were we settled in Vineyard Haven than I received a letter from him in Berlin saying he absolutely could not write without me. Then followed pages detailing everything and everyone he had seen and met in Paris. Now that I was no longer with him, he saw all the annoyances that triggered off his temper when traveling would – had I been with him – provoked us to a fight. Our trouble was that we expected each other to be perfect and he realized now he wanted me the way I am. 'You are the only proof I have that I exist. I am in love with you in the same way that the earth revolves around the sun. If I don't see you within a few weeks I shall take to my bed and have one of those wasting diseases people died of in Victorian novels'. He died when he thought I might be utterly happy without him. Writing the letter was like a drug, giving him a temporary hallucination that I was there.

I later without a qualm lifted these words out of his letter and put them into the mouth of a character in one of my novels. Nevertheless I wrote him back that I had decided not to go to Malaga.

On June 26, Ken called me from the Connaught Hotel that he had looked in vain in my answering letter for clues that I was responding to his entreaties but he had found none. My resolve not to go to Malaga dipped him into a two-martini sadness. If only I would come to Spain, he promised to revive my trust in him.

I wrote back that one reason for my not going to Malaga was that I was tired of the social game-hunting and the hanging around Big Personalities these *ferias* always involved. In reply he promised there would be no more of that. He didn't need them. He only needed me.

After this letter I agreed to go to Malaga, then changed my mind again, wrote saying I wanted to put off meeting him until September as we'd first planned. He called me, saying Spain without me would be a nightmare. My refusal devastated him, made him cry. He was thinking of me most of the time and for the rest was stumbling around as if paralyzed. Two articles written in my absence had been turned down, both editors characterizing his performance as half-hearted. It was because he needed me so. He begged me not to sigh hopelessly.

It was those last words, begging me not to sigh hopelessly that did it! I had taken to sighing hopelessly instead of giving us one more chance.

In the summer of 1960 Ken, deciding that his future lay in England, left the *New Yorker* and returned to his post as drama critic of the *Observer*. Back in Mount Street we now had what I supposed is called an open marriage, that is, a closed one. It meant keeping our private lives and private thoughts closed from each other. It was the kind of marriage in which both partners openly seek and respond to the attractions of other people while rejecting those of their spouses. It didn't stop the rows from continuing.

Nor were we ever sure how any altercation might end. It might terminate in two weeks of sulky silences and bruised feelings – or in each other's arms. A row in our library had reached the boiling point when suddenly Ken held up a copy of *Picture Post*, as he might a white flag and, pointing to a headline on its cover, exclaimed, 'Look! Read what it says'. Advancing several paces I read, 'There is Hope for France's Drunken Children.' We paused, caught each other's smiles mid-air, broke down and laughed. Perhaps it was true what Ken used to say: we were so close 'a small frown could make us savagely resentful and a small smile could dissolve us in fits of delighted tears'. We had become representatives of our warring nations, England and America. I said it was 1776 all over again, 'the part where the British are winning'. We thought that was funny. It wasn't.

The permanent solution would be for one of us to go Juarez and get a Mexican divorce. There you could obtain a divorce simply on grounds of incompatibility. People we knew in America were doing it, and this divorce, we were assured, was valid in every country. I was pushing for it. Ken kept refusing. The Band-Aid solution was to stay under the same roof, but as far away from each other as possible. The Mexican divorce discussions would be a leitmotif that ran through our lives for the next few years.

Unlike Ken, I'd been discreet about my sexual adventures, but that summer in New York I'd had an affair with Bill Becker, whom I'd met in Paris when he was a Rhodes scholar and whom Ken had known at Oxford. He now wrote theatre criticism for a literary review and was also in real estate. Ken found out about us and flew into a rage, promising to start a divorce action against me, conducting his own defense. Like his ledge-standing, I knew he wouldn't go through with it. It blew over. In reality it was just part of our endless business of keeping the pot boiling.

To stop all that I began taking definitive steps towards self-rule. At the beginning of '61 I spent a fortnight over the New Year on my own at Klosters in Switzerland. I had long been curious to see this particular playground of the western world. Into this small meritocracy, internationally fashionable figures in society and high echelon diplomats mingled with internationally known figures in the arts as they gathered together to ski and après-ski during the holiday season. Irwin Shaw and his wife Marion, with whom I'd become good friends, had often urged me to come. I didn't ski, but London that season had been exceptionally damp, and I welcomed the thought of a cold, dry, bracing climate with lots of sun. Why not take my two main characters in my novel which I was working on again to Klosters and see what they'd get up to?

I arrived in Klosters the day before New Year's Eve, checked into my hotel and went to meet the Shaws for drinks at Chesa Greshuna's cocktail lounge, where everyone gathered. Among the people who dropped by our table that evening were: (I am copying down their names from my journal) Alan Lerner, whose musicals included My Fair Lady and Camelot, and his French wife, Michele, a lawyer; Dorian Leigh, supermodel and older sister of super-supermodel Suzy Parker; Winston Churchill II, grandson of the renowned elder statesman; Peter Viertel, screenwriter on The African Queen, and his wife, Deborah Kerr; Peter's mother, Salka Viertel, who collaborated on the screenplays Queen Christina and Anna Karenina for Garbo and remained her close friend; Swifty Lazar, demon Hollywood agent, and his wife Mary; Gene Kelly and his new wife, Jean; Elsa 'Gogo' Schiaperelli; Anatole Litvak, the director of *The Snake Pit* and *Anastasia*, and his wife; Don Stewart Jr, a reporter on the *New Yorker* and son of Donald Ogden Stewart; Ella Winter, Mrs Donald Ogden Stewart; Lex Barker, ex-film Tarzan and ex-husband of Lana Turner; Terry and Joanna Kilmartin; a French ambassador, Monsieur Hervé, and his wife.

During my stay, perhaps because I was in Klosters by myself, or because not skiing gave me a certain amount of availability in the day-time – or perhaps I was communicating subliminally that I was *in* Klosters but not *of* it – I had somehow been elected to fill a much needed service. I listened to women crying in their unhappiness.

The first one cried over her husband's infidelities while we were having lunch.

The next cried when we were alone in the ladies' room because her husband insisted on maintaining a lifestyle they could not afford. 'We must get at least within *spitting* distance of our income,' she said half sobbing, half laughing. To this day I remember their tears; and how, with the release of their feelings, their voices went up an octave and their eyes grew shiny and their tears began to flow.

One day at tea, Salka Viertel cried softly over the recent harrowing death of her former daughter-in-law with alcoholic problems in a fire.

As we sat in a bar, Marion Shaw wiped away her tears as she talked of how Irwin's drinking was ruining his health.

And then there was Kelly, who told me that she'd quit the Sorbonne for a lucrative career as a high-fashion photographic model. She had been married and divorced. Her husband had obtained custody of her son. Now he was seven and she didn't even know where they were. She began crying as she talked, crying hard; she took out her handkerchief and pressed it in her mouth and bit on it.

Was unhappiness endemic to these privileged slopes? It was not one or two but five encounters I'd had with women that ended in tears. All were charming, busy, intelligent, cultured, knowledgeable in the arts, some had houses full of fine furniture and fine paintings, and all were laid low by domestic crimes. All those magnificently answered prayers were ending in tears.

Back in London I reread my journal. The stories were all there but they weren't ones I wanted to tell. Nor did I want to involve the characters in my novel with them. It was all too gloomy, too depressing. I didn't want to draw that stupid, smug, self-righteous moral about the price we pay for answered prayers. I knew life was a struggle, knew how deeply flawed the whole social system could be. The characters I wanted to write about were those who beat the system.

Now I found myself running with a whole new set of theatrical friends. Their effect on me was so invigorating it spurred me into putting aside my novel and writing a play. They proved to be a strong centrifugal force in spinning me away from Ken.

Lionel Bart's musical *Oliver!* had opened at the New Theatre in the West End while I was still in New York. It was a huge hit and the actress, Georgia Brown, in the role of Nancy, the prostitute murdered by her lover, scored a personal triumph. I'd known Georgia for years and after seeing the musical I went back to her dressing room to congratulate her; I fell into the habit of frequently returning.

Oliver! had settled down to a long run and Georgia's tastefully decorated dressing room was filled every night with new young style-setting friends. Lionel Bart, was there, of course, and so was one of Georgia's close friends, the young dress designer, Kiki Byrnes, who, with Mary Quant, was one of the first new wave couturiers to make London the sixties fashion center. The new young hairdresser Vidal Sassoon, whose distinctive straight-hair cuts were copied internationally, would drop by, as would the new young lions Peter O'Toole and Albert Finney, and the revolutionary stage designer Sean Kenny, who'd done such an extraordinary job with the *Oliver!* sets. Upon arrival in London visiting film and theatre celebs from America made a bee-line for *Oliver!*, ending up afterwards, as if propelled by a divining rod, in Georgia's dressing room. There would be drinks, then all assembled would progress to the White Elephant for an after-theatre supper. It was Georgia herself, with her earthy humor, her intelligence and her enjoyment of her success, who was the central force around which this ever-changing group revolved. I was fascinated by how she existed at the cutting edge of the present while at the same time retaining her connection with the strong East End roots of her past.

Quickly my play began making popping sounds in my mind. Combinations of the new people I was meeting would appear in it. The central character, modeled on Georgia, was Annie Fox, the young new wave star from the East End, now inhabiting the West End dressing room so recently occupied by the grand theatrical knights and dames. My play would be a backstage comedy about the new generation of theatre people who came from the lower-middle or working classes and, rather than concealing their roots, were proud of them. What was happening in London theatres was basically what I had seen happen in post-war New York, where 'proletarian' actors had moved into what till then had been the province of the middle classes. Also a first: the producer of Annie's play would be gay, but not the usual 'pouffy-for-laughs' gay, just simply an other acceptable character in the diversity of theatrical life. Annie would have as a lover Paddy, an equally successful North Country working-class actor in a West End theatre near hers. They love, squabble, part and reunite by the irony of both having accepted high salaried roles in a big international blockbuster film. During the play Annie makes the discovery that, in her own words, 'I am my own understudy.' In the end, she can depend on only herself.

Reality kept helping me out. While writing the play the real Georgia was moving from her old flat to a new one and found herself flatless for a week, so she actually lived and slept in her dressing room. It had become her pad; her place. As it was one of the main themes in the play, I called it *My Place*. Then I realized it was mine too.

One Sunday in July Donald Albery, the producer of *Oliver!*, held a reading of *My Place* on the same stage where the musical was playing. That afternoon I lived out a playwright's dream. I heard my play read with Georgia Brown, whom I had written it about. She read beautifully and I thought: *I've got her right!* I also saw that the play needed a lot of fixing. By the end of July I sent the play to Gore for his comments and advice.

Back came a letter beginning, 'Well old trout, the play's arrived and a gaggle of laughs titters and snorts – not since *The Kid from Colchis* has there been such a laffriot, romp and frolic . . .' Then, as always with the American Atticus, the letter while playful and hilarious was filled with sharp doses of Attic salt. He had also taken the trouble to give me a detailed critique of my play, act by act, scene by scene.

I began rewriting.

While I was happily involved with my play, Ken was under considerable stress. On October 22 there appeared a very bitchy, personal and intemperate attack on *Curtains*, his book of collected writings. It was written by that literary serial killer, Mary McCarthy, and appeared in the *Observer*, the same paper where Ken's column appeared every week. Those *Evening Standard* letters that had so upset him in the past were mere sheep bleatings: this was more like the savaging of a wolf. Under the headline 'Curtains for Tynan', Mary's piece started off with a faux innocent query to Ken: 'Is the title of this collection a pun (It's Curtains for me, pal)?' Allowing him his gifts of wit, humor and parody she affirmed that 'this is not criticism', that 'rational discourse is not Tynan's strong point', and further condemned him as not being able to 'reason or analyse'. On his 'positive' side, she sneered, he 'tends to write advertising copy'. She called his 'reiterated thoughts not so much ideas as middle-aged crochets', and gave a list of critics – mostly unknown – who were better critics than Ken, concluding that she thought better of him when she began reading the book than when she finished it.

Terry Kilmartin expressed his dismay to me over the review. I expressed my annoyance at him for inviting Mary to write it in the first place, knowing exactly what to expect of her.

On the same page the *Observer* ran a rebuttal from critic Alan Pryce-Jones: 'Steady now. Here is a very clever lady writing about a very clever gentleman. Adrenalin flows like the mill race at Rosmersholm. Anyone falling in will get drowned; and someone has fallen in; and it isn't Kenneth Tynan.' It left a lovely image of Mary drowning in her malice. Then point by point, he masterfully demolished her mode of reasoning and analysis. But the truth was that Mary's piece had profoundly hurt Ken.

Ken's mother died in November. She had been confined for some years to St Andrew's Hospital in Northampton in the psychiatric ward. In her seventies, she may have been victim of the then unknown Alzheimer's disease rather than the senile dementia that had been diagnosed. We became aware of her condition before we left for New York in an alarming and horrifying way.

Rose Tynan was a devout member of a Methodist church in Birmingham. In the fifties she became devoted to its new minister, Frank Thewlis, and his family, and when they moved to a parish in Keighley in Yorkshire, Rose would visit them. On one occasion she set out to visit them and, according to the Reverend Thewlis, who telephoned Ken, was picked up by the Keighley police, who had found her wandering the streets lost and confused before managing to discover her destination.

Ken brought his mother back to Mount Street and, seeing her in a state of serious disorientation, we asked Dr Cane, our family doctor, to give us his opinion. Under his encouragement she talked of Ken as a youngster in a detailed and loving way. When Dr Cane said, 'You must be proud of your son now,' Rose replied, 'Who?' The doctor indicated Ken and repeated, 'Your son.' She looked carefully at Ken and said, 'Oh that's not Ken!' And with these words of sanity, by which I mean words that conveyed to me a higher truth, she condemned herself. By her lights, I understood that grown man – whom she'd had no contact with for so long, who was now a public figure – was not the son who lived in her mind.

Ken was to blame himself entirely for his neglect of her. After undergoing tests it was clear that Rose needed hospitalization and Ken arranged for her to be placed in the highly recommended hospital. When we returned to London he sent her gifts and paid for her relatives to visit her. While he often planned to visit her himself there always seemed some deadline that made it necessary to replan it sometime in the near future.

In November of '61, her doctor contacted Ken to tell him his mother was terminally ill. Ken visited her on November 12 and returned deeply shaken. She had stopped eating and was emaciated. She did not recognize him, but he'd sat on her bed holding her hand and together they'd sung hymns. It was a flash of his early churchgoing days, hitherto unknown to me. She died a few days later and was cremated at the Northampton Crematorium. I said something to Ken about it being for the best and how she was no longer in pain. He said,

'You don't understand. You have a family, parents, sisters. I have none. Now I'm really an orphan.'

It was also during these months that Ken was producing a television series on contemporary culture called *Tempo*. The many programs and the various problems surrounding them took up a great deal more time than he had bargained for since he also went to the theatre every night for his *Observer* column.

For Ken it all came to a head during one particularly trying week. He had been ingesting huge amounts of deximyl and drink to keep going. On Thursday he sat down later than usual to write his theatre column, and in the early hours of the morning I had it delivered to the *Observer*. Sometime later that day Terry Kilmartin rang Ken to say the column made no sense and quoted some of it. Ken looked at his first and second drafts of it and said they made no sense either. He showed them to me. They were filled with odd unrelated references, some about the Earl of Harewood, a colleague of Ken's on *Tempo*, and Orson Welles, whom he'd invited to appear on it. *Tempo* was obviously on his mind, but how had it bled into his theatre piece in this weird way? I asked if he felt anything strange while writing it. He'd had a feeling of complete arrogance, he said; he felt he only needed to make it *look* like his column for it to be it. It was as he said: the pages were as always neatly typed, single-spaced, with a few legibly penned corrections in the margin. But the text was nonsense. I went to the *Observer* and brought back his final draft. It was crazier than the other two, with Harewood, Welles and *Tempo* all over the place.

He needed to see a psychiatrist, he said. Jonathan Miller recommended a Dr Paul Senft, and soon Ken was telling anyone who would listen, me included, that he was being analyzed so that he could rid himself of the guilt that prevented him from divorcing me. I riposted by telling him and the same people that the truth was that I *wanted* a divorce and he was trying to get himself to the point where he could *consent* to one.

At the beginning of January Ken left Mount Street and took a furnished flat in Groom Place in Knightsbridge, a step we both knew was in the right direction.

More important for me was that in November *My Place* had become a reality. Donald Albery had turned it down and Georgia opted to stay in *Oliver!*, for which I did not blame her. But Oscar Lewenstein, once general manager of the Royal Court and subsequently one of its producers, had bought it and would be presenting it under his own banner. Diane Cilento would be playing the lead. Diane, a young actress of striking blonde good looks and ability, had played on Broadway as well as the West End and the Royal Court, often choosing unusual roles over less challenging ones. John Dexter, a highly in demand Royal Court director, then specializing in Arnold Wesker's working-class plays, would be directing.

On November 22 I wrote my news to Gore: 'tomorrow at 10.30 at the Cambridge Theatre we start casting.' He replied, 'Dear Dundy, well there you are a dramatist just like the big guys and gals who dance and play in the streets of every capital in the world. Oh, I hope it won't turn to ashes in your *bouche* I do and work hard on that last scene so important to ring that curtain down on a well rounded ending with a surprise or two a catch in the throat a breaking of wind oh will any of us be the same after *Luther* yes absolutely the same . . . So now you are a playwright and it seems like only yesterday you were a girl. Come back to NY after play opens . . .'

During the first day of casting *My Place* an incident occurred that showed me John Dexter was not exactly single-mindedly devoting himself to my play. He'd asked his secretary to take down the name of an actor who'd just read and when I inquired what part he had in mind for him, he replied, 'Nothing in this. I want him to read for the Wesker play I'll be doing next.'

One of the reasons I wrote the play was that I thought the cast, the director and I would all be one happy family and once again I would slip comfortably into the bonhomie of my acting days. Except for my friendship with Diane, it didn't happen. In December, when rehearsals began, I attended them until John told me not to. 'Why?' I asked indignantly. 'I haven't said a word.' 'Yes, but your face is an explosion,' he replied.

I had dinner that night with Harold Clurman and, expecting sympathy, told him my story. Instead he laughed. 'Give them a break, stay away for a while. You know a lot of actors feel the only good play-wrights are the dead ones.'

So I stayed away for two weeks, then in the third week I showed up again. One of the actresses came up to me, smiled and said, 'Can I see you after the rehearsal?' Thinking of tea and a cozy chat, I replied yes, but all she had to say to me was, 'Tell the director I will *not* wear that dress.'

On January 29, My *Place* opened its pre-West End tour at the Shakespeare Memorial Theatre in Stratford (whose Shakespeare season in those days ended in September). I went there by myself and sat in the theatre that was the same theatre where I had gone for the first time in '51 and seen, also for the first time, Richard Burton become a star. Now, eleven years later, here I was in that barn of a the-atre with a play of my own.

The high point of the week at Stratford came the morning after the opening. 'Miss Dundy,' said a voice on the phone, 'you don't know me but I'm Jack Priestley [J.B. Priestley! I inwardly exclaimed]. I saw your play last night, and liked it—' then, after a small pause, 'I imagine you must be getting a lot of advice.' 'I'm not getting any advice,' I moaned, 'not even from the director, who's off doing another play.' He said there was still time before the London opening on February 13. He invited me to lunch that day at his house in Kissingtree, a village near Stratford.

When I arrived he greeted me in a friendly, jolly way. We went to his study and sat down. 'Your stage managing is terrible,' he began, so right away I saw it was going to be nuts and bolts time. Cues had been missed, he pointed out, and the loudspeaker didn't function to get the audience back in for the second act. 'Always have a woman as stage manager,' he cautioned me, 'because they have a sense of responsibil-ity. Men in that position tend to be found in a pub when most needed.'

About the opening scene, he continued the audience needed to know specific facts about the actress. He enumerated them: how much does she earn a week? How long has she been acting? When and how did she get her break? I eagerly agreed to write all those details in, but wouldn't it make the play too long? 'Plays may differ according to the fashion of the time, but audiences remain the same,' said Priestley, and he went on to make an interesting point: when the audience is first seated waiting for the play to start, they are alert and in a frame of mind to receive every bit of information you offer. Towards the end of the play, however, their concentration is split between the play and what they will be doing afterwards. Where will they go to eat or drink? What mode of transportation will they take? They begin to think of their handbags, scarves and umbrellas. So the last act had to be cut ruthlessly. Then, almost casually, he said, 'By the way, in the scene when the understudy refuses to go on, Annie should be drinking through it and getting tight.' 'Of course!' I exclaimed.

After a very good lunch, where I met Priestley's wife, the archeologist Jacquetta Hawkes, who said of my play, 'I just loved it,' for which I had to restrain myself from kissing her in Kissingtree, I flew over (so it felt) to Diane's dressing room at the theatre and told her that Priestley said she should be getting drunk during the understudy scene. Right! said Diane. Then I went out front to watch the matinee and saw Diane now drinking through the understudy scene. Voom! How it came to life.

I do not remember Ken making any suggestions about My Place. I would have said he'd never read it were it not that I remember him dropping over to Mount Street briefly the evening of its London opening at the Comedy Theatre and saying, 'This is a good play. And if you get any bad notices, it's because the critics are getting back at me.' He would not be reviewing it, but he was there.

So was Dr Roger Gilliatt, husband of Penelope Gilliatt, who had eloped in a blaze of publicity not too long before with the angry young playwright John Osborne. Roger had once chided me for assuming Penny and Ken were having an affair which – in the face of all evidence Penny and Ken vociferously kept denying. When Penny eloped and Roger saw the light about his roving partner, he rang me up to apologize, and we became friends.

I spent most of the time on the opening night at the cinema near the theatre. I have no idea what I saw. I caught the tail end of my play and the curtain call applause seemed fine, then I went backstage and all seemed pleased. No party though. The production budget did not run to such frivolities. I had dinner with Ken and Roger that night, after which Ken went back to his flat, Roger to his, and me to Mount Street.

Having accompanied Ken on his theatre rounds for so many years I'd gotten to know all the other critics well. I was familiar with their likes and dislikes and thought I could predict which kind of play each would admire and each would not. I figured on *My Place* being attacked by the middle-aged critics but thought it might win praise from younger ones. I was partially right. Middle-aged intellectual Philip Hope Wallace was particularly offended by it, but middle-aged Harold Clurman, writing for an American paper, liked it, and Tom Quinn Curtis in the Paris *Herald Tribune* gave it a glowing notice, as did T.C. Worsley in the *Financial Times*. The young Bernard Levin, then drama critic at the *Daily Express*, predicted it would run a year with coachloads of people attending its every performance.

It ran only five weeks. Before it closed I went to a Saturday matinee. There the audience would not be composed of contemporary bright young things who thought and talked like the characters in the play but mainly of middle-aged, middle-class matrons whose attendance and approval I knew happened to be the life blood of the theatre. These are people who love and respect theatre, and to whom it has become a way of life. Surprisingly they are eager to grasp any new experience a play might give them; if properly presented they are willing to reach far out to get it. This matinee audience is the same in London as it is on Broadway. I watched them, anxious to see if they would get it, and, to my sorrow, they didn't.

I would have loved for my play to have been a success but I was new to writing and my defenses in this area were surprisingly strong. It was not a failure I told myself, merely a setback. True, as most of the notices pointed out, it had been hideously undirected. I had been hideously betrayed by the disappearing Dexter and I should have complained loudly to Lewenstein about him. But I hadn't. Too many things could go wrong with a play, I thought, so I went back to my novel, where I could have more control.

Immediately after my play had opened I skipped town to join Gore and Howard in Athens and then Rhodes. Alexis Solomos, the Greek director whom I'd known during my Dramatic Workshop days, had found out through Gore that I was arriving and I spent a day with him. At his house in the hills of Hymettus we talked of our time at the Dramatic Workshop. He said he had something to show me, something he'd saved all these years, and went through some papers and handed me a sketch of himself. I looked at it and said, 'What about it?' 'You drew it, don't you remember?' I looked again and was about to insist I hadn't when I saw scribbled on the lower right-hand corner the musical notation of the three-note phrase that I'd used as a signature. I thought: I'm beginning to have a past, some of which I don't even remember.

Ken at Groom Place had publicly taken a mistress, the portrait painter Brenda Bury, so before I left for Greece I set a detective on his trail again. Now in Athens I received a letter from my lawyer saying I had grounds for divorce. I read it to Gore, who read me a letter he had received from Ken.

It was a masterpiece of dissimulation. No mention of the detective. In his letter Ken was all concern about me. Did I seem to be under a strain? Was I tense? Was I sleeping well? Did Gore think there was a chance for us? If he didn't it would be kinder not to reply because Ken felt wretched enough already. As for his feelings about me, if there was the slightest chance of our being fully reunited he would walk across Greece to grab it. Gore answered Ken's letter by saying, 'Elaine wants something that neither you nor anybody can give her. She wants herself.'

One Sunday when Tracy and I were lounging around reading the papers I came across an article by the writer Penelope Mortimer. Married to John Mortimer at the time, they had lots of children and she had come to believe that raising adolescents in London was not best for their well-being. They needed round-the-clock country life, with fresh country air, regular schedules, the company of friends, regular mealtimes, the development of discipline and habits. In short they needed boarding schools. There were splendid ones of the liberal, experimental and progressive kind scattered around England. She said boarding schools for her children had been a success. The holidays became lovely events with the parents spending much more time with their children than before.

Tracy was at the time attending St Paul's School for Girls, which she liked, but when I read her the article to see what she thought, she all but shouted that she would love to go to boarding school. No, she was not too young at age eleven. In fact that was why she wanted to go now, while still young enough to enjoy climbing trees, things like that. This could be a good solution, I realized. Certainly family life *chez* Tynan was hardly an ideal setting for her to grow up in.

I called Ken at Groom Place about our plan, which he concurred with and then Tracy and I set off on weekends to various recommended boarding schools. Bedales and Cranbourne Chase were two I remember, but when we got to Dartington Hall in Totnes in Devon we knew we had found the right one. In its favor was the beauty of the countryside and of the local architecture. We wandered over the grounds, impressed by its splendid theatre, its Arts and Crafts building, its library. I remember particularly a warm happy dormitory filled with the warm happy students who poured out of it and down towards a shed near the river where, that Sunday, they were building a canoe. Another plus: it was co-ed. What adolescent would not want to go there? Equally to the point was its reputation of having a first-rate teaching staff. What first rate-teacher would not want to teach in these burgeoning, bountiful surroundings? And I remember that at Lincoln we took the same tests as the English students at Dartington Hall. It was my early hands-across-the-sea bonding with it that made me feel it so doubly right for Tracy to be at Dartington. She started there in September of 1963. It was to become her security and her continuity for six years.

24

The Injured Party

In my resolve to divorce Ken I had papers served on him. Hysterical scenes followed, with ledge-standing and threats of suicide. I suppose it was inevitable that he would drag his shrink into the act. Ken implored me to hear from Senft himself how precarious his state of mind had become.

When I visited his psychoanalyst I told him right off that whatever tale Ken was spinning him, *I* wanted the divorce and was going through with it. He assured me he understood my determination but gave it as his opinion that Ken at this point was suicidal. He asked if I could give Ken a little more time in his therapy to enable him to accept the situation.

Feeling emotionally blackmailed and angry at myself for submitting to Ken again on his terms, I nevertheless agreed to put the divorce on hold. The strain of my unsettled relations with him was taking its toll. I was restless, irritable, disdainful and bitchy. To act weary of everything was my way of taking out my disaffection on others.

I was constantly changing my mind. When Jimmy Baldwin arrived in London he came over to the flat and, after teaching Tracy the twist, turned night into day as he and I twisted at the Saddle Room, after which Jimmy, lying on someone's sofa, read to a group of us his long essay on the Black Muslims until seven in the morning. Under the title *The Fire Next Time* it created a sensation when it ran in the *New Yorker* and again in book form. But my mind, invaded by a thousand clashing thoughts, was a perpetual snowstorm. I couldn't concentrate on what Jimmy was saying.

In April I gave a party that, with blasé disdain I later referred to as having 'the dullest thirty-eight people on earth'. In fact neither the people nor the party could have been called dull by any standards. The action began with Dominic Behan (Irish actor, writer, one of Brendan Behan's brothers, known for brawling), threatening to punch Alan Brien over some disagreement. Ken, who had crashed the party, rushed into the fray and begged Dominic to punch *him* instead. Dominic turned down his request and punched out a windowpane. Having grabbed everyone's attention, he was looking around for his next candidate. A scary moment. I saw that my guests were not happy to be there. Then one of them, Sean Connery, appeared at Dominic's side, took him by the arm, gently sat him down and quietly talked him into going home. Dominic, though drunk, was not so foolhardy as to disagree with Connery. It was a subdued brawler who followed Ken downstairs to the mini-cab I ordered. As they left, his countrywoman Siobhan McKenna, in her best St Joan voice, called out after him, 'Dominic! You're such a . . . you're *such a bad actor*!' – to her the lowest form of humanity. According to Ken, when he returned, Dominic, rambunctious again, had shoved his face into the cab driver's and snarled, 'I'm going to bloody Balham. D'you even know where it is?' The driver looked at him with weary recognition. 'Get in Dominic,' he sighed, 'I'll take you to bloody Balham.'

Though I told myself I couldn't care less about the broken windowpane and the chaos Dominic had caused, in fact on some rational level I *did* care. And I very much cared that Ken showed up uninvited. He was not supposed to be there.

I'd made it clear to him that I wasn't stopping my divorce action, but merely putting it on hold. Was it because in spite of everything I hoped we would reconcile? More likely it was because I had a new agenda. I was looking for Mr Right. My recent sexual adventures had been like brief encounters of two whims simultaneously zapping together at a party, a club or a restaurant, desiring only transient carnal knowledge of each other for fun and for free. But I just wasn't up to it anymore. Nor was I up to Ken's pranks. I dreamed of finding a new and greater love who would do battle for me, deal with Ken, get him off my back. Then I would glide smoothly out of Ken's orbit and into my lover's brave new world.

Some two and a half months later this scenario would begin playing itself out.

At the end of July Tennessee was in London and we had dinner together. He asked where Ken was. In Malaga at the bullfights. Why wasn't I with him? It was a pattern, I explained. Ken would go off somewhere and after a while cables would plead with me to join him. Whenever I did so the fights would start at the airport. Only not this time, I emphasized. The cables had come but I was staying put. As of a week ago, they'd stopped.

'Of course you're both very much in love,' Tennessee said. 'I see it every time I'm with you two. You must go to him.' As he continued in this vein I started thinking that maybe Tenn was right. After all, who knew the secrets of the human heart better than he? Finally I said I'd go. 'But I'm going because I'm tired of making my own mistakes,' I said. 'Why not let you make them for me?' He patted my hand approvingly.

I cabled Ken at the Miramar that night and asked him to reserve a room for me (since I filed for divorce we had not shared a bed). He cabled me back his pleasure.

Meanwhile the lunacy of turning my life over to Tennessee forced me to look at the fact that, despite my brief encounters, despite being in divorce proceedings, I was still ready to come when Ken called. On the other hand I had known for a long time that it was essential for Ken always to be at the apex of a love triangle consisting of a husband, wife and mistress. Since I, as his wife, was not fulfilling his requirements as a partner, he needed a mistress, went his thinking, but somehow the more he was with her, the more she became his wife – and I his desired mistress. What I also suspected was his growing need for me not only as part of a triangle but as a victim.

Arriving in Malaga it took me just one day to see I'd waited a week too long. Ken's entourage now contained an incipient, if not actual, mistress: his public update of the old love triangle. But this time, instead of noisily suffering, I went off with another man, a house guest of an English friend in Torremolinos.

His name was Peter Combe, and I hardly knew him. I would see him at the Savoy Hotel whenever a film company or a new American musical was putting on some big promotional bash in London, because he did some of the hotel's public relations and I saw him occasionally at theatres too, usually with some titled beauty on his arm. He was probably in his late thirties, charming and good-looking, his face alive with expression, his brown hair crisp with highlights. Thick eyebrows and thick furry eyelashes framed his penetrating blue eyes. He had the strong trim figure of an athlete. In fact he was handsome in a way that once seen is not soon forgotten.

We sat next to each other at the end of a large table on the Miramar terrace after one of the bullfights. Ken sat at the other end engrossed in his girlfriend. At some point I became aware that Peter and I were talking only to each other and when he suggested that we go somewhere to eat we simply slipped away. It was a very simple coming together. We ate, we went on to a nightclub, returned to Torremolinos and the house where he was staying, and on arriving went straight to his bedroom, where I spent a happier night than I had for a very long time.

Peter and I spent the next day together. After the cacophony of the day before, being with Peter was like listening to chamber music in sunlight. Driving around with him the countryside looked fresh and new and full of bright colors. We stopped somewhere at a café and talked about ourselves. I told him Ken and I were at the end of our marriage, living apart, and I was here because he'd asked me, but I'd seen immediately I'd made a mistake. Digging through memories, Peter remembered he'd been a guest at the wedding party given for us at Oxford by the Peels. When introduced to me he'd had the distinct feeling of wishing it were under different circumstances. As he said this a clear image of Peter came back to me: of him flashing a very interested smile at me, to which I'd very nearly responded, pulling myself back sharply by reminding myself I'd just gotten married. We'd come full circle.

Peter talked about how completely his existence had changed a short while ago when his father died. He had been the Laird of Strathconon, an estate in Scotland above Inverness in the Highlands and Peter had inherited the title. It meant, for the new Laird of Strathconon, a rearrangement of his life. He'd given up his public relations work in London and now lived much more of his time in Scotland. It was for him a serious rite of passage, with responsibilities for all his land and tenants. When he talked of falconry I fell into a Brigadoon swoon.

Peter existed in another world from me. I'd never met a landowner under fifty – much less been intimate with one. I thought of Ken as 'indoors' as opposed to Peter's 'outdoors'. I was fascinated to hear him explain how he was able to identify and fix the knock in the carburetor of his sports car, and why he thought his host's cat behaved in a certain way. I found him tranquil yet energetic, philosophical yet sensual. When he picked up a pebble there was something about the way he rubbed it that made me feel as if he was stroking me. His perception of people was quick and accurate, and he seemed to have a burning curiosity about all kinds of natural phenomena.

However, there was one bar to his tranquillity. He was being named as a co-respondent in the divorce case between the Duke and the Duchess of Argyll. He was contesting his alleged part in it. He had not been her lover but her friend, he said, and he was determined to clear his name not only for himself and the Duchess but for the people of Strathconon.

Peter dropped me at the Miramar late that afternoon. I told him Ken was leaving in two days but I'd decided to stay on, and we planned to meet the next day. At the hotel desk I was handed a thick envelope. A letter from Ken. One of his position papers: pages of professions of love followed by pages of accusations mixed in with threats to kill himself. I must meet him on the terrace that evening. I must tell him where I'd been last night. I needed help.

I sought out the one person I knew Ken would listen to: Orson Welles. He had rented a house not far from the Miramar and I walked over. I asked him to talk to Ken and tell him how I seriously felt we must divorce. He was reluctant. He said Ken was not a person he could ever be with on intimate terms. However he went over to the Miramar and shortly returned. He'd tried to talk to Ken about me but Ken refused. When I left the Welleses after dining with them *en famille*, Orson's final words were, 'You'd better divorce him because he's destroying you.'

Later Ken came into my room demanding that I tell him where I'd spent last night. I refused. He left. Sometime later he returned. He had been in Torremolinos to find out who I'd spent the night with. Later I was told he had been running up and down the cafés trying to find someone who'd seen me last night. By this time everyone apparently knew the answer, but nobody was talking, except for one woman, a house guest where Peter was staying, who told Ken that I'd spent the night with Peter. She was shunned for the rest of her stay for her role as informer.

Upon finding out Ken accosted Peter in the café where he was sitting with friends and loudly declared, 'I'm divorcing Elaine and naming you.' Peter replied, 'I think you should divorce. You're no good for each other. But will you give Elaine this message? Write it down because I want her to hear it accurately, word for word.' I could picture Ken pulling out his small black pocket diary and the others at the table falling silent at this. They were about to get an earful. And so was I in my hotel room as Ken, diary in hand, dutifully recited to me Peter's words. 'About the divorce. Tell Elaine I will do only whatever she wants me to do and *nothing* else. And will you tell her I loved sleeping with her last night and that I can't wait to do it again.'

A pause while we thoroughly digested how thoroughly Ken had been outclassed. The supposed cad had behaved honorably; the cuckolded husband had behaved like a cad. I had liked Peter very much before; now I was prepared to love him. I told Ken to get out of my room. He complied only saying – with new civility – that he'd made an appointment with Peter tomorrow on the terrace of the Miramar to talk things over, and please would I come?

We met at the siesta hour, when the terrace was empty. Peter spoke first and repeated that he would be willing to be named in our divorce suit only if I wanted him to be. He would, however, prefer the case not to come up until after the Argyll case was settled. No wonder English playwrights were still kept in champagne writing drawing room comedies with the plots turning on the absurdity of English divorce laws. Such things still happened, and I was in the middle of one. Then it was my turn to speak up. I pointed out that Peter needn't be involved at all. My divorce papers had already been filed; I had proof of Ken's infidelity and proof that we had not cohabited since.

Ken said nothing. He had gone pale and was looking extremely unwell, sweat pouring down his face, his shirt sticking to his chest, his whole body drooping. He said, 'I can't stay here any longer. I have to go back to my room.' He got up and left.

Peter was silent for a moment, then said, 'I've just learned something I didn't know. He's still in love with you.' I dismissed his idea with a laugh and secretly hoped it was true. I wanted Ken to suffer.

'Let's go,' said Peter. We walked out to the front of the Miramar, where his car was parked. 'Come on, get in,' he said, kissing me lingeringly. I turned towards the hotel entrance and saw Ken on the steps. He had seen us and the look on his face was awful. Some people in their grief look old. Ken looked young – like a child of five who has been told by the other children they are never going to play with him again. This should have been my final triumph, my final revenge, and all I could feel was sadness for him. 'I'd better stick around,' I said to Peter. 'He's leaving the day after tomorrow.'

Ken followed me back into the hotel. Would I do him one last favor? Would I go to the bullfight in Ronda with him the next day? He was leaving early the day after. If he promised not to name Peter in our divorce I would go. He promised.

I ran into Peter in Ronda at a bar. He was surprised to see me with Ken. 'It's going to be all right. He's not going to name you.' I said. 'But will *you* be all right?' asked Peter. I was to remember that.

Ken and I spoke very little. At one point he said he felt humiliated that everyone knew about me and Peter. I thought of all his blatant infidelities and said, 'Now you know how it feels.' At the end of the day back at the Miramar I went straight to my room and checked that the door between our rooms was locked. I took a sleeping pill. As I dozed off, Ken knocked on the door. Wouldn't I let him in for just a moment to say goodbye? Knowing I was too drowsy to get drawn into a fight, I unlocked the door.

That night Ken brutally assaulted me, leaving me unconscious on the bathroom floor with two black eyes and a broken nose while he escaped to London on the earliest plane.

The next morning I went over to the Welleses. On answering the door, Orson looked at me and said, 'Now will you divorce him?' His wife Paola took charge, put me to bed and I slept for the rest of the day. The next day Orson took me to a doctor and the X-ray of my nose confirmed it was broken. Orson insisted on sending me to London to see a specialist.

I called Peter and told him what had happened. He came to see me, but I didn't want him to see me the way I looked, so Paola sent him away. He came back, of course, and left flowers. Orson arranged for my flight back to London and I returned to an empty flat. Tracy was still at summer camp.

A specialist confirmed that my nose was broken, though not badly, and that nothing should be done. 'The face is forgiving' was the way he put it.

I stayed in the London Clinic for a week resting, then returned to Mount Street. In my forgiving face, my black eyes went from purple to brown to yellow and healed amazingly fast. So did my nose.

One day Ken came over to Mount Street. I warned him that I'd called the police and had a restraining order put on him. On the whole he downplayed what he'd done – no apology, only an off-hand mention that his shrink had dismissed it, merely saying it was clear that he'd kill me or I'd kill him if we stayed together. He was neither ashamed nor sorry for what he'd done. Nor did he seem embarrassed that I'd told people about it. There was always part of him that gloried in his reputation as a lady-killer, the sinful, depraved Don Juan. The mad, bad, dangerous-to-know sadist.

I was about to ask why his shrink hadn't pointed out the connection between his sexual sadism and beating me up but I got smart; I took a step forward instead of back into the old quagmire of wrangles and just mentioned the Mexican divorce again. This time he agreed. He was going to New York soon and would talk to our American lawyer about it. That finished off that encounter.

With or without Ken I'd always loved Mount Street. It was my home. Now its personality had changed. It looked worn and sad and crumbling. It was sick, dying, without virtue, integrity or novelty. I wandered through the rooms, the bedroom, the living room, the library, all filled with remembered scenes of crises and betrayals. I wanted out.

25

The Stars Are Not Fixed in Their Courses

Shortly after I came back to London I began seeing Peter. He had a house in a mews near Cadogan Street. For the first time in years I was being made love to by someone I loved, and the storms of emotions it unleashed in me were as intensely painful as they were exhilarating.

Then he returned to Strathconon and I first went to visit him in mid-September. He met me in Inverness, wearing a kilt, and the sight of him looking so positively ceremonial against the perfect setting left me dumbstruck with awe. A moment later, sitting next to him in his jeep he put my hand under his kilt and said, 'No, we don't wear anything under it.' At once the atmosphere became remarkably more informal.

We drove north for a while, and when we stopped I got my first look at the Laird's life. In a house set high on a promontory with a panoramic view of the surrounding area, Peter lived alone with two dachshunds and two white Eskimo dogs. There were also two birds: a peregrine, a species of falcon that he trained for hawking, and a wounded eagle he was nursing back to health. His main room had a large window almost extending to the length of the wall. Every day I would sit in front of it watching the Scotch mist bathing the landscape from one minute to the next in all colors of the rainbow – blue fading into pink turning into gold.

Peter often walked around the house with the peregrine on his shoulder or his wrist. It was important for them to become friends, he said, to have a working relationship, for the bird to trust him. I worked hard at conquering my fear of a bird without a cage indoors, though I jumped every time it flapped its wings. Peter favored falconry over shooting game birds, he explained, as it was nature's way of continuing the life and death cycle. It was also more sporting.

With Philip Glasier, a leading falconer, and his girlfriend, a pretty American, we went hunting on the moors for grouse. It was quite an operation synchronizing the dogs and the falcons and the grouse: if one of them didn't perform exactly as they were supposed to the game was lost. Grouse must fly, dogs must point, falcons must leave Peter's and Philip's wrists and fly after prey and get there fast, for if the prey flies over water, scent is lost and grouse are gone; also falcons must kill grouse mid-air and deposit them on ground. Dogs must instantly retrieve grouse from falcons before they eat them and, their hunger slaked, they fly away forever, and falcons must return to falconers' wrists to be made ready for the next assault. This was done by whirling a piece of meat on the end of a string. I was particularly struck by Philip's ability to see and hear the birds long before anyone else.

I loved walking in the heather. It was so soft; so *bouncy*. To my astonishment I would occasionally find a grouse walking along beside me. Someone – not me – could almost have picked it up, wrung its neck and popped it into the bag. Instinctively I did not call attention to the bird walking when it should be flying towards its destiny. Not sporting.

After a day on the moors Peter and I toured his vast property in his jeep. It was the rutting season and we watched two stags lock horns in their primordial fight to gain sovereignty and with it, said Peter, the winner's privilege to look after the huge harem of hinds for the rest of his life.

Peter's factor came round each day and they went off to attend to the estate's business. Whenever Peter left I was sad. When he came back a few hours later it was as if he had been away for as many months. As I sat waiting for him to return, one of the Eskimo dogs, sensing my mood, would sympathetically pat my arm.

Evenings were still warm so we could be outside under the blanket of bright stars. To my astonishment they were in all the wrong places. The Cassiopeian chair was now upside-down, the constellation I've always called the 'W' was now an 'M'. And the North star was not where I'd left it in other climes. I thought with elation: the stars are *not* fixed in their courses! I didn't have to keep on repeating my mistakes.

Visiting Peter over the next few months I found my stay at Strathconon in February particularly special. The contested Argyll vs. Argyll divorce case was being given enormous publicity and was about to explode in Edinburgh. Soon Peter would arrive in that city to defend himself. Even in faraway Strathconon some paparazzi had descended to close in on him as a potential star witness. Peter treated them with courtesy. One morning I looked out the window and saw Peter in his kilt chatting amiably with a bunch of them while being photographed. Discreetly I withdrew from the window and stayed indoors until they went away.

You would never have known by the way we spent our days that Peter's ordeal was getting nearer and nearer. Although he was not looking forward to the trial and the notoriety that would attend him, he barely mentioned it. In the eye of his cyclone all was calm. The weather was perfect; the winter sun shone every day, the sky blazed blue. We breakfasted at ten followed by a leisurely lolling around, then Peter got out all manner of reference books from the *OED* to road maps to the Bible. We used them to settle various questions we'd raised the day before, which ranged from the sublime to the ridiculous. We indulged in no gossip, nor did we burden each other with the rigmarole of our respective childhoods. I did not plow through my long list of grievances against Ken; Peter did not hash over past loves. Our talks were strange but agreeable and refreshing, all somehow at one with the boundless space and splendor of his land. There was little reference to the Duchess of Argyll except for Peter repeating that they had *not* been lovers.

Later we would go to the village hall that was built by Peter's grandfather. I counted thirty-six stag heads on the walls, shot by him, and we pored over history lessons of photograph albums of the Combes in the Edwardian era. The village hall was going to have its village amateur society drama competition soon and Peter was actively working on it. In fact he mostly built and painted all the sets himself, collecting or inventing, seemingly out of bits of muslin and old tin cans, all the props. I helped when possible, spending lots of time in cold toolsheds while a saw buzzed angrily through numerous pieces of wood.

In the evening from 7.30 to 9.30 Peter went off either to take over the rehearsal of the play or to piping classes. He was learning to play the bagpipes but, thank God, hadn't got to the bags yet, only the pipe, which made a rather lovely melancholy sound. Argyll case or not, I noticed with admiration, Peter's priority was the people and customs of his country.

When he returned home, Peter would whip up a delicious dinner that we ate on trays in front of the television set warmed by the fire flickering merrily away and surrounded by the dogs. Then to bed . . .

And on this blissful note I would force myself down to earth to conclude that if it weren't for the sheer impermanence of the situation I would probably be screaming with boredom. I discovered that, having found someone as perfect as Peter, he was, perhaps, not perfect for me. I feared I was getting entangled in one of those agonizing one-sided relationships that I thought I'd put behind me in my teens. Confronted with the truth and consequences of this I had, self-protectively, slipped back into my role of sophisticated disconnection.

If Ken living out his life in public had cut one kind of historic figure in post-war Britain, Peter, whose deeds were barely noticed by any but the immediate few whose destinies they affected, had cut another that, in its own way, was just as extraordinary. It was that of a Tolstoyan landowner who, overturning long traditions, waived his rights of ownership of his tenants' land by selling it to them for the token sum of £100.

The longer I stayed there the more I became aware of the reality of Peter's ancestral position in Strathconon, not just by how the villagers and tenants related to him in spite of his democratic presence, nor by the fact that he was amongst them longer each year than were the former Combes. Although he was doing for his tenants what past

Combes on his paternal line or past earls on his maternal side would never have, he was still doing it from a *noblesse oblige* that had been bred into him, and everyone knew it. The more I saw his heritage bolstering him up, the more I felt it bearing down on me and wondered how I would fit into all this in the long run. It was disconcerting, discouraging. The role called for a woman younger than me, someone who would produce an heir and enjoy spending time serving the community. Knowing this did not make me want Peter any less. Hence the ambivalence; hence the conflict.

Back then, at the end of my fortnight stay, in February of '62 I drove with Peter to Edinburgh. I walked with him into the hotel lobby swarming with paparazzi and reporters and became uneasy. Though I hardly expected to be recognized, my picture had appeared quite a few times in newspapers and – you never knew – a photograph of Mrs Kenneth Tynan with Peter Combe, co-respondent in the Argyll trial, might have had unsought ramifications. I flew to London that evening.

Historically the Argyll divorce case was the oral sex trial, foreshadowing the oral sex trial thirty-six years later that almost got the US president impeached. Instead of a stained dress, the Duke of Argyll lawyers presented the court with photographs of fellatio taken by the Duchess herself. She lost her case. Although there was very flimsy evidence, and no overt signs of affection, as the judge said in his summing-up, Peter was found to have been one of her lovers – good old guilt by association.

Peter felt very down about the whole affair. He told me he was planning to go to York to be a French teacher at a boarding school. He felt he must do something to restore his self-worth and his dignity.

In January I had left Mount Street and moved into 31 Devonshire Place Mews, at which point Ken moved back to Mount Street. It was not an ideal situation, my being semi-separated from Tracy, and I kept popping back there two or three times a week. But it would not be for long. In September she was to go to Dartington Hall.

In April, for the first part of her spring holiday Tracy and I stayed with Gore and Howard and their dogs Billy and Blanche at their flat on the Via Giulia in Rome. One of the dogs kept stealing Tracy's socks, storing them in its own private cache, which Howard finally discovered. One afternoon Paolo Milano, a distinguished Italian critic, began talking to Tracy and they got along swimmingly. After he put his arm around her and she fell asleep on his shoulder, he said to me in French, 'She has much need of a father.' He was right. All this back and forthing between Ken and myself in Mount Street was not doing her any good. Falling back on the old scenario – in which, upon finding my new and greater love, I glided smoothly out of Ken's sphere forever and, taking Tracy with me, into that of my new lover – I cabled Peter and asked if Tracy and I could stay with him for the rest of her spring holiday.

I received no answer during the rest of my stay. Back in London and still not hearing from Peter, I decided he had lost interest in me. After all, his letters to me, which were few, were puzzling. They would start with 'Darling' then blow hot and cold, sending out mixed messages. So I did the stupidest thing I could. I got in touch with Ken, who was covering some film or theatre festival somewhere and, deceitfully, told him how much I wanted us to be together again under no matter what conditions. Ken agreed and I went back to Mount Street, casting a cold eye on my decision. It was true that Tracy and Ken loved each other very much, but after he began instigating his sex games – which started up our rows again – it was also true that I had had no intention of staying with him. My Devonshire Place Mews flat, which I'd kept on, was at the ready. When Tracy went to Dartington Hall, I intended to leave for New York. I had thought this through and decided to put an ocean between Ken and myself and see about settling down there. Then I would go to Juarez for the Mexican divorce.

While still at Mount Street there was one hell of a star-crossed mix up in the works for me. Peter had sent a cable to Gore's saying that he would pick up Tracy and me and take us skiing. Gore had seen Terry Kilmartin in Rome, and asked him to tell me to ring Gore, but Terry forgot to pass on the message.

By the time I got Gore's letter enclosing Peter's cable I was in Mount Street. If only I had stayed on in Rome *three more days* and received the cable . . . I really do wonder if it would have made a difference in my life. Peter, understandably, reacted to my return to Mount Street rather coldly and asked if I hadn't better make up my mind.

I moved back to Devonshire Place Mews and began seeing a psychiatrist, Dr Charles Rycroft. Forced to look at how loony my life was, I fell into a deep depression. Curiously, one side-effect was that I was working well. I had gone back to writing *The Old Man and Me*. Mysteriously, my novel seemed to have come along on its own in my absence, and it looked as if it could be finished in a couple of months.

But I was physically – not to say psychologically – run down and when Dr Rycroft suggested I go to a health farm, I found his proposal so unpsychiatric and sensible that I went to Enton Hall in Kent at the end of May for a fortnight. Its salads, leeks, parsnips, nursery puddings, fresh air, daily walks, massage and hydrotherapy pulled me round.

I was grateful for my restored health when late at night on June 12 my mother called me from New York to say that my father had died that day of a heart attack. He was seventy-five years old.

My first reaction was relief: he's finally made it, he's at peace at last. But on the plane going over to the funeral, a flood of memories tugged me back to my old nursery, there to be greeted by a series of emotions so unfamiliar and bewildering that it was as if I had never been in that room before. There was a large bear on wheels that Daddy gave for my fifth birthday. I loved riding around the nursery on it, pulling on the ring on his back that caused him to make growling sounds. There was a father who always held my hand when I was learning to walk down steps, who gently stroked my hair. I seemed to hear him say, 'How about a kiss?' I recalled his special armchair in the living room, where I would sit on his lap. Covered with deep gold velvet pile it had once been for me the comforting symbol of his beloved presence and I recalled how, in his absence, I used to rub my hands over its surface as if it was an Aladdin's lamp and I could make Daddy magically appear.

At this point my memory swerved and in its place Daddy's chair came to represent his frightening presence. Once more I went back to that evening in 1929 when Daddy came home and suddenly began to cry. And then, when I tried to comfort him, slapped my face.

In New York I stayed with my mother at the Lombardy for a week. She was surrounded by her sisters, their husbands and some of their progeny, as well as my sisters. I saw the healing that was effected by my mother telling us over and over all the details of my father's death, the hour before his attack, his attack, the ambulance taking him to hospital, the hospital's announcement to her that he was dead. At one point she said he would have been glad he died on the 12th and not the 13th, which would have been bad luck. Then came the reading of the will. My father left us, his children, substantially well off, though certainly not as rich as to be called, as I read somewhere, 'heiresses'. Our money was tied up in trust funds, which I thought sensible but which infuriated Shirley. She stormed angrily out of the room saying, 'He always hated me and this will proves it.' It was a matter of different professions. As a writer I didn't need the same kind of ready money as Shirley, who had hoped to invest it in various film projects.

26

The Drowning

Shortly after I returned to London, shockingly I found myself accepting Ken's invitation to go on a gastronomic tour of France. 'Not without Gore!' I said. I invited him and listed the proposed route: Paris, Avallon, Lyons, Vienne, Lac D'Annecy. From June 21–26 we would enjoy three-star restaurants all the way. 'It could be great fun. Please come, Please come!' I implored him in a letter. He came.

Ken and I went on to Pamplona, which was exhausting and filled with endless rows. The last one, which seemed terminal, came one night when Ken wished to 'punish' me for my 'treachery' in telling author Jim Jones and his wife Gloria about his type of sexual mania. I countered that all his friends knew it anyway and that Kingsley Amis referred to him as 'an old-fashioned British flogger', a remark I had been saving up for some time. Ken did his Proud But Broken Man thing and went off into the night. I changed my air ticket and left the next day.

That year of '63, while I had been loving Peter, Ken's heart had not been idle in its affections. First came the Chinese actress Tsai Chin, followed by Rita Moreno, and finally Kathleen Halton, the woman he would marry in '67 and remain married to until his death in 1980. Both concurrently and intermittently Ken and I went through our paces.

He had gone through a major career change as well. 'If I have to review another production of *A Midsummer Night's Dream* at the Old Vic I will go crazy!' he said one day during a period when we happened to be talking to each other. He was explaining why he was leaving his post as drama critic of the *Observer*. He had chosen the perfect play at the perfect theatre to balk at having to write about one more time. Tradition held that an Old Vic production of no matter what quality must be reviewed. For him the *Dream* had become a nightmare.

It was Senft himself, Ken continued, who had found him his new job! He'd counseled Ken that he should be the dramaturge, or, literary advisor, later literary manager, to the National Theatre. It had finally gotten underway, with Olivier at its helm and its repertory season had debuted in Chichester in a specially built theatre. Ken must simply write Olivier asking for the job. He did so, and Olivier hired him.

After our gastronomic tour, Ken met with our lawyer Aaron Frosch. The Mexican divorce was in readiness, and all I needed to do when I arrived in New York was meet with him and go over it. Passively I had left the details of the divorce to be worked out by Ken and pragmatically I accepted as fact that the divorce must be seen to be Ken's decision. No fights for women's rights. I knew it was the only way not to get it bogged down again. Even so, there was plenty of foot-dragging on his part.

My passivity plagued me. That year, as a result of conversations with my new friend the novelist Emma Tennant, we reached the firm conclusion that in the 'War Between the Sexes', as the situation was then called, women at present were losing – *badly*. We thought we should call attention to this state of affairs and decided *Queen* magazine, would be the best place to disclose the information about the second sex becoming second-class citizens and the downward plunge women had taken since we got the vote. Jocelyn Stevens, *Queen*'s publisher, agreed.

I became the guest editor for the first section of the July 1964 issue of the magazine. Between Emma and me we had assembled a roster of eight impressive names to elaborate on the subject.

Elizabeth Smart, well-known Canadian poet and novelist, then *Queen*'s chief editor, wrote the editorial for my section, which I had titled 'Woman: A Special Kind of Hell'. The text of the section was printed not in the usual black type but in what Emma called 'menstrual red'. Beside me the list of contributors included Kingsley Amis, Clancy Sigal, the seventeen-year-old Polly Toynbee, the poet Ruth Fainlight, novelist Maureen Duffy and the highly esteemed psychoanalyst R.D. Laing; Gerald Scarfe did the illustrations. All of us tried to figure out why or point out how women were getting such a bad deal as of 1964. Then came Women's Lib.

In contrast, the second section (after all, it was a fashion mag) was titled 'Paris: A Special Kind of Heaven'. It was entirely devoted to the sensational new Paris couturier André Courréges, and gave his collection an unprecedented thirteen-page photographic spread. *Queen*'s cover featured a model stretched out flat, every inch of her submerged in the master's total look: not only her thickly drawn Courréges penciled eyes and eyebrows but the never-before-seen cut, shape and material of her red pants suit, her strange headgear – a sort of tailored babushka tied under the chin with a tailored bow – as well as her boots, gloves, accessories and makeup, also in shapes and materials never before seen. Courréges had his time of glory throughout the sixties and into the seventies. I can never see that sign, which so resembles a paper doll cut-out, stamped on the entrance of Ladies Restrooms in public places without thinking of him.

'You *must* take Courréges,' ordered the magazine's fashion police in the second section. Entirely by happenstance, *Queen*, in simultaneously publishing 'Woman: A Special Kind of Hell' and 'Paris: A Special Kind of Heaven', had pretty well covered two major aspects of the female dilemma. Then and now: what rights to fight for and what clothes to wear.

Sometime in July I finished *The Old Man and Me*. Victor Gollancz read it immediately and liked it so much he chose to do the editing himself. I felt a huge surge of confidence. My American publisher, Dutton, had a similar positive reaction and was confident that it would also be a bestseller. At last the signs were good: now, it seemed, was the right time to head for New York.

In a buoyant mood I called Peter to tell him my news. He invited me to Strathconon in mid-August, and we arranged that I would bring Tracy, whom he had never met, and her nanny, Moira.

Peter collected us in Inverness in his jeep and drove up through the magic Highlands to his house. It felt good to be back.

That evening when we sat down to dinner we were joined by Philip Glasier, the falconer, who'd arrived that day, Alistair, a Scottish journalist who had become friendly with Peter during the Argyll trial, and Flutey, a geologist, a short mild man obsessed with the rocks on Peter's land who came every summer to study them.

It was one of those improvised dinner parties that absolutely took off. Philip and Tracy, seated next to each other, were instant soul mates, continually giggling over their private jokes. Then someone said, 'It's almost midnight!' in a challenging sort of way, as if to say, 'Let's top this.' Someone suggested a midnight sail. The night was warm, the air was soft – a wonderful idea, we unanimously agreed. All but Peter. He objected to sailing at night. In the end he reluctantly gave in but insisted we wear extra clothes for warmth. We ransacked cupboards for sweaters, socks, scarves and jackets.

Tracy begged me to let her go. After all she was eleven and she knew how to swim, so why couldn't she? I relented. And since Tracy was coming, Moira, though she'd been complaining of sniffles all day, came along too.

Soon we were seven people banded together in the beautiful adventure of sailing in the middle of the night, in the middle of a loch, in the middle of summer, with enough of a breeze to speed us on our way until we decided to return.

Then in a split second everything went from being all right to being all wrong. A squall blew up without warning and water lashed against the sailboat, which first rode the waves and then began to heel over. Peter gave the tiller to Alistair, who was closest to it. Then came Peter's voice, 'Now you've done it. You've let go of it.' 'It' was the centerboard, which had dropped out of the boat and down to the bottom of the loch.

Peter said, 'Now stay calm everybody. Everything's going to be all right,' at which point the boat capsized and we all landed in the water. My first reaction was acute annoyance at getting wet. Then a scream froze my blood. 'It's Tracy!' I shouted, and a moment later a voice said, 'She's all right. I've got her.' I could see nothing. Suddenly a torch flashed on and dimly I could see Philip astride the overturned boat holding Tracy in his arms.

Quickly he took charge. He made Flutey straddle the boat at one end and Alistair at the other. Moira and I, now hanging on to the boat, both mostly in the water, were told to stay put. We would be held onto whenever needed – me by Alistair, Moira by Flutey. 'All right,' said Philip, 'she's balanced. As long as everyone remains strictly at their stations she'll keep us afloat.' As we heard splashes he announced that Peter was going to swim to shore to fetch a rowboat from the dock. After hanging on to the boat so he could take off his clothes to swim, Peter splashed off, naked. Faintly I heard him intoning words that sound strangely like: '*J'ai, tu as, il a, elle a, nous avons . . .*'

Someone laughed, sniggered rather, and said, 'That's Peter pacing himself. It's what we're told to do in very different circumstances.'

The squall, which had died down, blew up again, then died down again. My body rocked with the waves. Flutey had the other torch. It didn't work. Too wet, he said. He was dismantling it, trying to dry the batteries.

I marveled how naturally Philip had become our skipper. All questions would now be addressed to him; all assistance was expected from him. The squall blew up again and we all rocked with the waves.

The current, Philip told us was pulling us downstream over to the left shore. His voice confident, he said he shouldn't be surprised if we drifted to shore 'before Peter even got to the rowboat'.

I wanted to believe this. I willed myself to believe it. 'Well, if we're going downstream, the loch will end on a shore, won't it?'

Flutey said, 'Not necessarily. This particular one goes past Dingwell into the North Sea.'

'It won't come to that,' said Philip quickly.

'Tracy, are you all right?' I asked. 'Of course I am,' 'she replied, 'Philip's holding me.' With Alistair's help I hoisted myself up a little to see Tracy folded in Philip's arms in such a way as to keep her, as much as possible, from the water. Thank God for Philip.

Time passed. There were silences, then talk would start up. Then die down. Someone found something to say, then there was silence again.

Suddenly Flutey said, 'What's going on at the boathouse? Some lights went on, but now they're flicking off and on.' A pause. 'Now they're on, now they've disappeared.' 'Peter's probably going for help.' Philip said confidently. 'It may take a little longer but in the end it'll be a lot safer.'

My thoughts grew antic. During one of the silences I found myself speculating on which of us had the right to be the most pissed off at landing in his blasted loch. I went down the list – Philip the Falconer, Alistair the Journalist, Flutey the Geologist, Moira the Nanny, me the Mother and Tracy the Child – and discovered that there was one of each of us, just like those movies about a group of people trapped in a prison camp, shipwrecked on a desert island or held hostage in a hotel. I'd always dismissed the-one-of-each formula as an obvious plot contrivance, but now I knew that any group anywhere was always made up of one of each. My discovery was accompanied by a sudden gush of love for all the others. They were all different yet they were all behaving so well. They seemed to be instructing me to behave well too. My mind went back to who was the most pissed off. I chose Moira. She'd never been out of Australia before. Little did she know that when she signed on to be Tracy's nanny at the beginning of that summer she'd end up in the middle of a loch in the middle of the night. 'Moira, you okay?' I asked. 'You seem lower down in the water even than me.'

'Oh, I'm fine Mrs T. Truly I am,' she replied cheerfully.

'Oh Moira, *please* call me Elaine,' I said, thinking this was getting more and more like a movie, showing how under stress social barriers break down and we are all equal in the eye of God.

'Oh may I? Oh, thank you very much, Elaine,' she said, as if conforming to the script. 'How pissed off are you at being here?' I asked her. 'Well, I mean, it's just one of those things, isn't it?' she replied. 'It might happen to anybody.'

I was not cold in the water. Were Peter's woolens protecting us? Was I in shock? I do remember peeing and welcoming the stream of warmth that ran down between my legs.

Conversation had become important. Someone asked Flutey exactly what he was doing among the rocks in Strathconon, and he explained that he studied the formations of rocks here as well as the similar ones in parts of Scandinavia, proving that the two continents had once been one. And he went on about how the British Isles were tilted up in Scotland and down in the southeast of England like a pile of books fallen over. Geologists knew it because the oldest rocks were found up here in the northeast, where they couldn't get washed away. 'So why are we getting so wet?' asked someone.

'Well, anyway, we are getting closer to shore all the time aren't we, Philip?' I urged in my frantic need of reassurance.

'That's right,' he said. 'Closer all the time.' I heard something in his voice that sounded abstracted, something that did not reassure me.

That was when I stopped believing him. I decided to take matters in my own hands and said to the others that Tracy and I were going to swim to shore. I needed someone to help – who would come with me? No one volunteered. I asked each of them separately if they could swim. Improbably – to me at any rate – each said no. I told Tracy we were going anyway. She said, 'All right, if you say so, Mummy, but I'm so sleepy, and I don't want to get any wetter.' Instinctively I turned to our leader. 'Philip, shall I try it with just us two?' 'I don't know,' he said, 'I just don't know. It's up to you.'

Suddenly Philip cried, 'Swing your torch about Flutey! And everybody start calling for help. All together now and at the top of your lungs.' We yelled and yelled. There was another silence.

Then Philip said, 'I hear them coming.'

A wave of hysteria swept over me and I lashed out at him, 'Philip, don't do this to us. There's nothing out there and you know it!'

He ignored my outburst. After a stretch of infinity he said, 'It's the rowboat. Two men and Peter.' We yelled again and after a while I too could hear the muffled sound of oars and the cries of the men and see the rowboat.

Philip, wishing the evacuation to take place in an orderly fashion, said, 'Elaine, you go first.' The danger over, I managed to pull myself together. I said that Tracy must go first, then Moira, then me.

I don't remember anything about the rowboat part of our deliverance except that we got to shore and that the two men with Peter were shepherds. Later Peter told me that at one point the rowboat, which had never held more than four people before, with nine of us had almost sunk. I knew nothing of this. I only knew how good it felt with all of us bunched together in a heap with our arms and legs tightly wrapped around each other for warmth. I discovered we had been out there a good hour and a half.

When we arrived at the shepherd's cottage, we were received by the women, who had been reading up on first aid in preparation. They undressed Tracy and me — we were shaking too hard to do it ourselves — and dried us and put us in warm clothes. Then they put us together in one bed, wrapping us in a blanket, then one blanket at a time pulled other blankets over us. After a while they gave us tea with lots of sugar, holding the cups for us while we drank because we were still shaking.

I remember that Tracy stopped shaking in about twenty minutes and that I took much longer. I eventually sat up. There was an open fire. Moira, seated next to it, draped in a blanket, was jubilant. She said the dunking in the loch had completely cured her of her cold. For some reason this filled me with pure joy. The room was warm and glowed in a Scottish Rembrandt light. I looked at the others, grinning in the borrowed clothes of our rescuers. We all knew we hadn't just endured, we had prevailed.

We went back to Peter's house and talked some more about what was going through our minds as we hung on to the boat waiting to be rescued. Tracy was thinking about her gumboots, wondering if she should remove them because they might be weighing the boat down, and then she thought, 'But if I take them off I won't have them when we get to shore.' One lesson I'd learned was that I would never again think I was safe in water just because I could swim. I could swim, but not at night in the middle of a loch in blackness where you don't know which way you're going. I thanked them all for discouraging my mad idea.

Peter's tale, which he'd begun at the shepherds' cottage and continued in more detail in his house, was terrifying, filled with risks and perils and obstacles upon which hung our lives. Things had almost gone fatally wrong. Three-quarters of the way through his swim to shore the current was running strong against him and he was tiring fast, so much so that he didn't think he'd make it. He almost hoped he wouldn't because he thought we'd had it out there. Arriving at the boathouse he was too exhausted to manage the rowing and decided to get the help of the shepherds living nearest the loch.

Naked and wet he got into his jeep and tried to start it. His wet feet kept slipping off the pedals and 'the damn thing stalled'. The lights that Philip and Flutey had seen flickering on and off were from his jeep as he kept trying to jump-start it. Oh God let me die, he thought once again. Finally the engine connected and after a couple more false starts got going. He drove off to one of the shepherds' cottages.

He stopped his jeep outside it and staggered to the door. The family were confronted with the sight of Peter, stark naked, panting hard and just able to gasp, 'There're six people drowning in the loch,' before fainting dead away.

When they revived him and clothed him, he enlisted their help and Peter and two of the shepherds drove to the loch. 'What you have to remember,' said Peter, 'is that shepherds hate the loch. They never go near it.' When they reached the rowboat, Peter had to teach them to row.

I asked Peter why he was declining French verbs as he swam. I said that someone mentioned it was done in other circumstances. Peter replied, 'Yes, it's schoolboy lore. It's to pace yourself, to stop you from coming too soon.'

Finally, when we were all ready for bed, I took Peter aside and said, 'I'm sleeping with Tracy tonight.'

Next day someone dropped by to tell us that the boat had drifted to shore. 'There,' said Peter, 'nobody has ever drowned in the loch. I expect the loch doesn't want us.' This example of British phlegm or Scottish whimsy caused me to explode. 'The loch doesn't want us?' I repeated incredulously. '*We don't want the loch!*' I simmered down and we all went to the Highland Games in Dingwell.

When the time came for Tracy, Moira and me to leave, Peter drove us to the Inverness airport. We bade each other friendly, unmemorable farewells. There were no curtain speeches, and we made no plans for the future. Peter had saved our lives but I never wanted to see that loch again. Our journeys lay in such different paths. We were never again to meet.

Some years later Peter married a young woman who had fallen in love with him 'at first sight' at the age of eighteen. They had three children and were happy and loved by all of Strathconon, where for twenty-six years he had set up their popular Highland Games. In October of 1987, aged sixty-two, he died of cancer in his home there. His widow, Carola Combe, now lives in Dingwell with their children Karina, Tabitha and Matthew. Peter is buried on a hill overlooking the loch.

27

Hollywood '63

Returning from Strathconon and happy to be alive, my life was now all circumstance. It led me east to Austria and west to Hollywood.

Out of the blue the *Manchester Guardian* asked me to cover an international writer's conference in Salzburg that had become a cultural media event, with prizes awarded among others for the best novel of the year. The two main contenders for the best novel that year were Nathalie Sarraute and V.S. Naipaul.

One morning Mary McCarthy invited me to share a taxi with her to the conference. After I got in she looked me straight in the eye. 'Elaine, is it true what I've been hearing about you?'

I'd decided it was the right time and place and Mary was the perfect person to receive my long-awaited message to the literary world. I took a deep breath. I said, 'Yes, it is true. Ken and I are divorcing.' Mary looked at me perplexed, then, with a flicker of irritation, as if she'd asked for champagne and I'd given her ginger ale, rephrased her question. 'I mean,' she said, 'I heard that you are against giving the prize to Nathalie Sarraute.'

A few nights later I ran into Christopher Plummer, who was making *The Sound of Music* in and around Salzburg. He'd been there for months and was at the point of feeling – as he later expressed it – as if he were being beaten to death with a Hallmark card. Glad of a new scene, he accompanied me to the conference to hear the lectures given by internationally eminent writers. There he had a fine time proclaiming, 'That's a star,' or 'That's not a star,' at the end of each lecturer's performance. Mary McCarthy, as always severely coiffed and gowned, with her fierce somewhat unsettling delivery as she heaped praises on Nathalie Sarraute, he declared a star. 'She has attack,' he noted approvingly.

The next speaker after Mary was Jonathan Miller. 'Not a star – or maybe he's miscast,' said Christopher. Jonathan talked very fast, his stammer intact, about the comedian Lenny Bruce, a surprising choice for this gathering. His reception was mixed. Christopher and I later mingled with the crowd, picking up on the buzz. Frankly, people were baffled by what they'd just heard, or as it turned out, misheard – they had mistaken Jonathan's pronunciation of 'Bruce' for 'Proust'. And though tolerant of English intellectuals, they were sceptical of his theory. True, Marcel Proust had been dependent on drugs, true he was a superb mimic who often performed his imitations of well-known people for the delight of an assemblage, but that Proust had 'invented a new kind of black comedy that was the inspiration of a whole new school of American *comedians*' was, they felt, going too far.

Back in London I saw Tracy off to boarding school. I had been afraid she might be tearful upon leaving, but she was delighted. She had instantly made friends with other Dartington Hall children on the train's platform; I was the one who cried.

I went to New York. I planned to stay at the Algonquin for a while, laying the groundwork for the big move. I was determined to approach New York as a brand new country with new horizons rather than a retread. Still, I had to contact old friends to get started.

Back in June, when in New York for my father's funeral, I went to a *Paris Review* party and met a tall fresh-faced young man in his early twenties who bounced up to me with such an affable, outgoing, confident-diffident glow, with such smiling determination, that the jaded reveler who'd been haranguing me about his publisher fell back in mid-harangue. The young man quickly presented his credentials. He was Mike Macdonald, son of the formidable critic Dwight Macdonald whom I'd met during his stay in London. Mike submitted that he knew my sister Betty from summers on Cape Cod and that he had taken a film course from my sister Shirley. It also turned out he had gone to Lincoln for a couple of years. This shared background gave me an immediate sense of familiarity with him.

Now two months later, back in New York again, I attended a party in Irving Place where Mike was also a guest. This time we struck sparks and the next night he picked me up at a mutual friend's apartment. In the elevator on our way out to dinner, he kissed me.

So I began seeing Mike, walking straight into a new romance. The rugged path I'd recently trod in England seemed miraculously smoother. I congratulated myself on my versatile heart and at never making the same mistake twice. For as different as Peter Combe was from Ken, so different was Mike from Peter. Had I consciously been searching for Peter's diametrical opposite I could not have found anyone who more perfectly fit the bill. If I'd considered myself too old for Peter, who was close to my age, I considered myself just the right age for Mike. I felt that, as *une femme d'un certain age*, I was ripe to play Colette's Lea to his Cheri.

Adding to the equation: as firmly as Peter was set in Strathconon, so firmly was Mike set adrift. Aged twenty-four and having 'beat it out of Harvard' (his phrase) a couple of years back, he was undergoing, according to the mutual friend who was acting as Cupid, a sort of nervous crisis brought on by seeking but not yet finding what to do for the next years of his life. His problem was perhaps exacerbated by having always before him the example of his father, a model of industry and literary achievement. Dwight in the past had edited such bastions of intellectual thought as *Partisan Review* and *Politics*, and now kept busy as lecturer at universities, a book reviewer for the *New Yorker* and film critic of *Esquire*.

It was with a sense of recognition too that I noticed in Mike, who grew up in the company of such well-known members of the

American intellectual aristocracy as Mary McCarthy, Edmund Wilson, Delmore Schwartz and Fred Dupee, the same charm and social ease I'd seen in the offspring growing up in Paradise-on-the-Hudson.

Mike's last job had been working in publicity on the film *Lilith*, starring Warren Beatty, and he was leaning towards further involvement with films.

At this point entered Gore, working in Hollywood on the film of *The Best Man*. Gore had previously met Mike through Dwight and liked him, and as a result talked his producer into giving him a small part – a send-up of his old foe William F. Buckley. The idea was that Mike could spend further time in Hollywood to see if he could find a good job there.

Mike left for the West coast in high spirits. Once there he checked into the Montecito, a well-known actors' hotel in downtown Hollywood, where a bulletin board daily posted the arrivals of actors staying there so everyone knew who was in town. He bombarded me with letters and telephone messages full of his comings and goings and declarations of love. In the beginning you could positively feel his energy and euphoria springing off the page.

It was so cheering to come back to the Algonquin late at night and have a message handed to me by the desk clerk that read that Mike was on page 14 of *Dud Avocado* and was already aware that I was a GENIUS. Or another: 'Am now seeing *Gathering of Eagles*. It's a GHASTLY picture. Nevertheless I love you.'

Mike's adventures and misadventures in what was to him a foreign country also gave me a sense of familiarity. Allowing for male/female differences it reminded me of my early days in the foreign country called Paris.

Mike's letters were filled with descriptions of various studios as he went from one to the other learning his way around them and looking for potential jobs after his movie stint. The back lot at Warner's rendered him rapturous, with a mean street he recognized as having serviced the entire Raft–Robinson–Cagney–Bogart output of crime pictures. The day he did his first scene with Cliff Robertson in *The Best Man* he kept upstaging himself until Robertson deftly turned him around during the shooting. He did a tour of art galleries, mentioned a new show by 'a friend of Marguerite Lamkin's, Andy Warhol, a Pop Art leader'.

That was the letter that began: 'A brief note as I'm bedridden for next few days . . . feeling very low – physiologically.'

I replied I was sorry to hear he was ill. Since he didn't say with what I assumed it was the flu bug, and went on about taking massive doses of vitamin C. 'A genial, jocular Mike is what we're after, his naturally loving heart full of sunshine and exhilaration.'

His next letter spelled it out, describing the states of mind he had been going through since his arrival: loneliness, boredom, irritation and anger, ending with just wanting to be alone. Today was the worst he could remember.

This was the first time Mike talked to me of his 'illness'. I had not seen him in that mood. I thought it took honesty and courage to list the irritations that caused it, and humor to admit that not one of them was catastrophic and they all added up to one big overwhelming over-reaction. I was no stranger to depressions, having experienced them myself as well as watching them at work on Ken. It made me wonder if everyone I knew who was sensitive, intelligent and prone to great enthusiasms was not subject as well to black gulfs of despair.

One day my London agent called me at the Algonquin to say that he thought The Old Man and Me had great potential for a movie sale and that it would be handled by the Frank Cooper Agency in Hollywood. Although the novel was not coming out until March, I found out copies were already being distributed to the major studios. I told him I was coming out to Hollywood. I had friends there, contacts there; I needed to tell them about my book, and to be an actual person to the Cooper Agency. And it would be great to see Mike.

I flew to Los Angeles early in October. Driving from the airport to the Chateau Marmont, where I was to stay, I opened the taxi window to enjoy the soft Southwestern night in its eerie, almost holy, silence. Cars flashed silently by on broad boulevards, city lights sparkled without city noise. There was a hush and tranquillity in the wide open western spaces of this sprawling town. It's God's country, I remembered someone saying of Southern California; that's why there're so many crackpot religions out here.

I arrived at the Chateau, majestic in the moonlight. Floating through the archway beside the flower-scented courtyard, I opened the huge oaken door of the castle, halted in front of the desk clerk – and came down with a thud. There was no reservation for me. The travel bureau at the Algonquin had made the reservation. I insisted and repeated my name, spelling it out. The clerk shuffled through some papers. Nope, no Dundy. I sat on my luggage and paused for a moment, revving up for a big scene. Dimly I became aware that the piano playing in the lobby had stopped and the pianist was coming towards me. It was someone I knew – Miles Davis. I told him my sad story, and he said to the clerk, 'You sure there's no reservation for Mrs Tynan?' 'Oh, *Tynan*. Yes,' said the clerk, handing me the key. I'd done it again. The closer I got to divorce the more I forgot I had to register at hotels under Tynan because my passport was still in that name.

A youth in jeans and a T-shirt materialized to take my bags and show me to my room. It was large and high-ceilinged. A light kept flashing on outside the window, and I looked out to see the revolving forty-foot likeness of a Las Vegas showgirl advertising the Sahara Hotel spinning in circles on top of a large silver dollar. She was the eyesore made legendary by Gore in *Myra Breckinridge*. My room had three beds in it: one double, one single and one divan. I looked at them and told the boy I'd only reserved a single room. He said all the rooms had lots of beds in them. This is Hollywood, I thought, always ready for an orgy.

As a hotel aficionado, I knew something of the Chateau's history. Beside all the famous people who had stayed there it had a ghost. Its high vaulted architecture had been copied from the Chateau D'Amboise in France where Leonardo da Vinci had spent his last years. When the Chateau Marmont was completed in the twenties, went the legend, Leonardo's ghost had gone west to lodge in the hotel and inspire its clientele. Where else would this Renaissance man go after inventing the airplane but to Hollywood, home of the most important new artform since his time? Artists producing the very best kind of art, music, theatre and film the world over regularly chose to stay at the then *modestly* priced Chateau rather than the more expensive showy hotels. It more than lived up to its reputation during my stay.

I called Mike at the Montecito and he came over. We were hungry so I rang downstairs, but the Chateau had no restaurant. It had, instead, what were called the Chateau Irregulars, a band of boys, around fifteen years old, who had apparently abandoned school as too tame and liked the glamour surrounding the celebrated denizens in the hotel. They hung out in the Chateau garage where, it was rumored, they also slept. They were world-class gofers, who could find anything you needed, no matter how exotic, in record time. Much of the time they were sent zinging directly across Sunset Boulevard to the famous Hollywood drugstore, Schwab's, which opened early and closed late and sold everything that a self-respecting super-American drugstore stocked at the time as well as running a terrific counter and coffee shop. From there the Chateau Irregulars delivered every morning to guests large paper cups of freshly squeezed orange juice for breakfast along with sweet rolls and coffee and, for the rest of the day, such American staples as hamburgers, sandwiches and milkshakes. That night an Irregular took our order and swiftly returned with sandwiches and cokes.

Next day I was busy on the phone. I was amazed at the warmth with which my calls were received. These were people I'd met in my Kenelaine days and I suppose I was testing the water to see how I'd come out by simply being me. I'd come out okay, it seemed. I also got a strong sense that in those days anyone who could bring first-hand news of the great world outside to these natives in their desert playpens was welcomed. My engagement book was quickly filled.

The first people Mike and I visited were the Oscar Levants. Levant – concert pianist, film actor, quiz show expert, professional neurotic and wit – had by the sixties developed rather problematic behaviour, veering from charming to alarming but never dull. He entertained us to tea wearing his signature pajamas and dressing gown in which he now spent most of his time. The day we came was defi-nitely one of his good ones. He was delighted to meet a son of Dwight Macdonald. He was an admirer of the latter's writing and was fasci-nated to know more about the man behind it. Mike obliged, following his thumbnail bio on Dad with a hilarious imitation of him. Goddard Lieberson, RCA's classical music magnate, had come to tea as well and was a fund of over-polished anecdotes. Suavely Oscar let us know he preferred the more improvisational style of conversation that Mike and I were serving up. When we left I felt triumphant in the afterglow, fully aware that being with Mike had made the visit doubly enjoyable.

One day Mike and I had lunch with George Cukor in the dining room at Warners, where he was directing *My Fair Lady*. He himself brought up *The Old Man and Me*. What he did next was so surprising it took me a while to figure out what was happening. After assuring me of his interest in my novel, he went on to *tell its story back to me*, beautifully, excitingly, hitting all the high points, putting each of them in its proper dramatic setting. I was overcome with admiration. 'How did you find time to read it?' I asked. 'I didn't,' said Cukor. 'I read the studio's synopsis.'

Footnote: Hollywood – a generic tale. A year and a half later I received a call from Cukor, who said he wanted to make *The Old Man and Me* with Warners! 'Rex Harrison is crazy to do it!' he enthused. I said 'Dammit, George, it's already been sold to MGM.' He said, 'MGM just bought it to keep anyone else from buying it. They're not interested in making films anymore. Warners is the only studio who still is. Which producer has it?' I said his name was 'E. Ronald Lubin.' 'Oh,' said Cukor, 'that's Al Lewin's nephew,' (profiling by nepotism). End of story.

Next stop: in 1967, at his invitation, I went to meet Cary Grant at the Plaza. Outside his suite I heard a male voice raised in song. I rang the bell and he opened the door and stood there fresh from singing in the shower with only a towel around his middle, looking devastatingly like Cary Grant. He welcomed me in. He got dressed. Showed me pictures of his daughter. Said LSD would do me a lot less harm than the cigarettes I was smoking. E. Ronald Lubin arrived. Both assured me they were keen to make the film of *The Old Man and Me*, changing its title of course. I looked at Grant and said, 'Of course!' That week Cary Grant was in a bad car accident on Long Island. End of story.

Last stop: David Niven was keen to do it. I exchanged letters with him. He finally wrote me that the trouble was that MGM was asking 'an arm and a leg to sell it'. End of that story. *The Old Man and Me* is still somewhere in the MGM archives.

In '63 Geraldine Page and Rip Torn (then married) were also staying at the Chateau. The Hollywood Hills were sparsely populated with humans, but filled with wildlife. Rip, a Texan, would go out in the hills behind the Chateau with his gun and shoot quail, then on Sundays he and Gerry would roast the birds and give a big party for *le tout* Hollywood. There I saw Miles Davis again, with his wife Fran. I'd gotten to know them both in London and New York. I was a major fan of Miles, both of his music and his blunt, prickly personality. I loved it when he said he thought the Beat Generation was 'a lot of white shit'. In fact in *The Old Man and Me* a character named Jimbo (his face, like Miles's alternating from a mask of comedy to a mask of tragedy) was based on him. On reading the novel his sole comment was astute: 'Watch out for slang; it dates fast.' His wife Fran was a charmer. She moved with the grace of a dancer, which in fact she was, trained by Kathryn Dunham. Miles had first been captivated by seeing her dance in a *Porgy and Bess* production in New York, and he composed the piece *Fran Dance* for her.

It was at Gerry and Rip's that I also ran into Hermione Baddeley, mother of my friend Pauline Rumbold. Hermoine was living in a poolside bungalow at the Chateau, and had an adoring klatch of British pop singers.

One night Mike and I came back late to the Chateau. As we walked through the courtyard in the fragrant night air someone on an upper floor was leaning out a window singing a haunting Cole Porter ballad. As in a movie musical, Mike joined in on the last stanzas. Coming closer, we recognized the singer. It was Elaine Stritch. We introduced ourselves.

'Come up here,' she said, giving us her room number. 'I'm so angry I can't sleep!' When we arrived she began pacing the floor. She was in a play soon to open called *The Time of the Barracudas*, and her anger was directed at her leading man, Laurence Harvey. 'Every bit of stage business I've invented that gets a laugh *he copies later on*! I've called him on it and he just denies it!'

The next day in the Chateau lobby I ran into Laurence Harvey himself. Our friendship dated back to '51, and since then Larry's career had sky-rocketed. Now he was well known as an actor and a heart-throb both on the stage and screen. His lifestyle too had soared. He'd been married to the English stage star Margaret Leighton, and was now married to Joan Cohn, the wealthy widow of Columbia's boss, Harry Cohn. Larry had just dropped Miles Davis off at the hotel after listening to the musical score the latter had composed for *The Time of the Barracudas*. 'He admires my music and I admire his acting,' said Miles, in one of his rare positive, and therefore noteworthy, statements about a fellow artist.

Larry drove a long, mean, killingly expensive sports car. Mike and I spent an evening tooling around in it with him. First he took us to dinner at the Bistro, which he and some other actors, including Paul Newman, owned. It filled their need for an easy informal place to drop in for a good meal or a drink, day and night. After that he took us on the town and gave us a fabulous time. Wherever we landed Larry would telephone his wife, Joan, assuring her he would be home any minute. Much later he dropped Mike back at the Montecito, where he made another phone call, and then he drove me back to the Chateau. 'She's locked me out,' he said. 'Why not sleep here?' I suggested. 'I'm sure there'll be a room for you.' 'No,' he said. 'It's three in the morning. I think I'll sleep in my car. Hell, I've slept in worse places.' I woke up next morning thinking how odd that I had not remembered that he and Hermione Baddeley had once been lovers; Ken and I had met the two of them together at that memorable polo match with Tennessee and Maria. There had been so many changes in his life, each more startling than the one before, as to wipe out all memory of the previous one. A free spirit, he'd been a lot of things to a lot of people – male and female. If he'd slept in worse places than his custom-made super-charged sports car, he'd slept in better ones too.

Of all the people I saw when I was in Hollywood that month, no one had come from further away nor had so short a time to stay than Larry. When he died of cancer in '74 he was only forty-five. Gore saw him when he was dying and reported that Larry was somewhat amazed at this turn of events because, as he explained, 'I thought that only good guys got cancer and died like this.'

Touching base with the English while there, I also spent an evening with Christopher Isherwood and his companion, painter Don Bachardy. When I'd first met them some nine years before, Christopher had an English accent, while Don, an American, had what sounded to me like a Southern one. Now Christopher had superimposed Don's accent on his English one while Don superimposed Christopher's accent on his American one, with the result that they both sounded alike. Don later did two charcoal drawings of me which still hang in my living room; in both I am holding a cigarette. I also lunched with Gavin Lambert, whose book *Inside Daisy Clover* was at the time being filmed by Alan Pakula with Natalie Wood. Gavin, who along with Lindsay Anderson had been responsible for making the British film magazine *Sight and Sound* such an influential organ, adored Hollywood without reservation. When in New York he liked to sit at the lounge of the Algonquin in the early evening, shocking the rest of the cocktail crowd by ostentatiously reading the *Los Angeles Times*. Also he would say, 'Well, of course, New York's climate is wonderful, but the city is too spread out. There is no there there.'

Mike and I went to a party at the Paul Newman's. 'I'm not a great actor,' Paul said to me (standard modestspeak that the better type of actor always affects), 'but I'm a good enough director to get me out of any hole a director gets me into.' From then on, watching him on the screen, it does seem to me I sometimes catch him nimbly ducking around hazardous director-placed holes. This is one of the things that has kept Paul around for so long: he looks out for himself. Though he insists his stardom is based entirely on the exact shade of his blue eyes, he takes care of himself in many clever ways, like regularly keeping up outside interests, whether racing cars or inventing a salad dressing, and not least in having his brother as business manager. By keeping his career a family concern, Paul insured himself against waking up one morning to learn, as stars do, that their managers have been embezzling their money for years. Paul's brother himself bore a strong family resemblance to him, yet Paul looked like a magnetic movie star and his brother like an ordinary businessman. Did they look like what they'd become – or was it the other way around?

Producer Sam Spiegel's wife, Betty Boo, was a gorgeous brunette with alabaster skin and a long willowy body. She looked like a high fashion model, which she probably once had been. An important hostess in Hollywood and New York, she gave a variety of parties, from intimate dinners, to larger formal ones, to even larger, even more informal ones that were – or so I'd heard – orgies.

Early in my stay I had been to one of her small dinners. I asked this most sophisticated of ladies what one thing she thought I must see during my stay, she replied, 'Do yourself a favor – see Disneyland.'

So Mike and I went. How comfortable we were that day, both with it and each other. Reality may give me troubles but I can handle unreality with aplomb. I loved all the rides. A submarine trip was so realistic that even though it hadn't moved and was all done electronically coming back up to the surface gave Mike the bends. An early American Main Street with an ice cream parlor made me nostalgic for the American past I never had. Finally there was the monorail which zoomed over the site. Had the city been visionary and sensible enough to adopt this mode of transportation it would have solved all future Los Angeles traffic problems before it became gridlocked forever.

One day Betty Boo invited me to a party that same evening. It was just a spur-of-the-moment thing, she said, informal – come around nine. Intrigued, I asked if I could take some people with me, so I invited Fran Davis who brought along Chita Rivera (then appearing with Alfred Drake in the stage musical Zenda). Arriving at Spiegels' vast mansion we went into the dining room, where there was an elaborate buffet. I could tell I was at an orgy because the first person I saw was a highly recognizable young blonde star with a wild reputation and the face of an angel, and she was wearing a brown silk dress that zipped up the back, only it was unzipped. I deduced therefore that her most recent lover, the famous photographer standing next to her, had apparently not bothered to zip her dress up for her. I thought this casual of him in the extreme. I also registered what not to wear at an orgy: a dress that zips up the back.

So at last I was at an orgy. But it was a Hollywood orgy – laid-back, non-confrontational, cool to a fault, with neither a sense of danger nor embarrassment. You didn't have to orgy if you didn't feel like it, you could just sit on the floor of the living room and talk with other non-orgyists and work your way through boxes of delicious chocolates. As I wasn't drinking, that is what I was doing. I ate chocolates and talked with some good-looking gay guys who turned out to be actors who played cowboys on some of those western TV series. Chita and Fran were sitting with another group of people and I could see they were getting bored. From where I sat I could see doors open and doors close and people going up the staircase and people coming down. I began to feel lonely, then somewhat priggish.

Albums of musical comedies kept being played. Someone put on *West Side Story*. I saw Chita and Fran perk up, look at each other and smile. When the Latin rhythms of 'I Like To Be In America' came on, the song that Chita had originally stopped the show with on Broadway, the two of them rose and began dancing together not touching but enveloped in the luminous radiance of the pounding beat. Fran, the inspiration of Miles's *Fran Dance*, and Chita, the eternal showstopper, performed a dance that got wilder and wilder and more and more wickedly exquisite until it was like an explosion of erotica.

People began drifting out of their rooms to see what was up. They remained, transfixed. Chita and Fran were bestowing upon both participants and non-participants of the orgy the thrill of a communal aphrodisiac.

Under the spell of the dance I found myself (a) starting to unbutton my blouse, and (b) looking around for a partner. Then probably for the first time I was clear enough in my head to be aware that logically this sequence should have been reversed. But, as I was not drinking, my standards were impossibly, prohibitively high. So I sat buttoned up but enraptured, and when their dance was over, it was as if our whole purpose for coming was over. The three of us left together and went home like good little girls.

As we left Betty Boo said to me, 'The women tonight are so much more attractive than the men, aren't they?'

*

I didn't know it but I had arrived at the end of an era: the last of that cycle of Hollywood's solid gold days. Though to me it shone brightly as ever, I didn't realize the luster was its evening glow. And the people I saw and the films they'd recently made also shone bright as ever. I thought Paul Newman at his best in *Hud* and *The Hustler*. *The Manchurian Candidate* is a perfect example of the sort of picture that Hollywood used to make: a thriller that tells a complex story so clearly and cleanly it frightens you *into* your wits, not out of them. *My Fair Lady* won twelve Academy Awards, including Cukor's as its director, and it deserved every one. Now thirty years later a regular on movie channels it sits secure in that most splendid of all categories: a hugely *popular* classic.

The Hollywood I saw in '63 would soon be gone forever. Never again would I see a large sign outside a Hollywood hotel heralding the Doris Day Look-Alike contest, or, going into its lobby, watch hundreds of young women hopefulls milling around, all looking and dressing exactly like Doris Day. Gone forever would be what I saw when Tinseltown, pushing the holiday season as early as mid-October, sported glorious Christmas trees in pink and blue and silver nylon, with equally unconventionally creative wreaths, Santas, reindeers, crèches and other decorations adorning doorways and lawns of the big houses on Sunset Boulevard. These displays seemed to carry with them a prideful scorn of the trite, tree-green and Santa-red Yuletide decorations of the rest of the tradition-ridden world that Hollywood would soon succumb to.

Footnote: By the end of 1963 Mike and I had walked out of our romance and into a long friendship which continues to this day. For the rest of the sixties he worked in films and television, and in the seventies he wrote for the *Village Voice*. His interests shifted from entertainment to sociology and politics, and in the eighties he wrote a well-received book, *America's Cities*, and gained a reputation as an urban expert. He has worked on political campaigns including those of Bella Abzug and he served as deputy campaign manager for Herman Badillo in his run for New York mayor in the nineties. The *New York Observer* ran a long article on Mike that year describing him as 'dressed in a black turtleneck and tweed, his dark hair slicked down, looking every bit the Village Bohemian he has been for years', calling him 'a throwback to a time when intellectuals like himself were as much part of the city's political culture as today's special interest groups'. At present he is writing his memoirs.

28

Breaking Up

At the end of October I went back to London. Tracy was having her mid-term break and I planned on staying at Devonshire Place Mews. I was returning also because of Ken. The Mexican divorce had run aground again, with him backing off and seeking reconciliation.

Like Hollywood, Ken and I had come to the end of our era, but not before the luster of Ken's epistolary verve was spent. His letters, as always, had the ability to astound by their very lack of restraint. His over-the-top portrayal of a husband driven to distraction emotionally and physically by his wife's desertion, which should have been ludicrous given our recent history, was instead, disarming. He dared not look at the commercial channel because the ads made him cry. He cried watching cheerful married couples and their kids and their animals and their breakfast foods and their delicious smokes. He wept when they got loans to buy their homes and when they came up beaming out of the pool to have another of those satisfying smokes. He shed tears over our lost youth and the family life we never had. How much he now yearned for domesticity with me!

These letters came as a surprise. When I'd left London that

September we had agreed on the Mexican divorce. We were both
having affairs. At first I regarded the letters as another instance of his
wife/mistress syndrome, but a new and worrying note was struck – his
health. His letters began to be those of an aging man, a dying man. He
complained that although his National Theatre job actually consisted
of very little, it left him exhausted all the time. He was afflicted by a
series of ailments, all caused, apparently, by my absence. To sum up: he
shook inside all the time; without me it was as if he'd had a frontal
lobotomy. Then he began talking not only of his mortality but of
mine. To paraphrase: our youth was over, our capacity for feeling anything in the future would naturally dwindle. For what remained of our
good years we must reunite in order to experience again the great
emotions we'd felt together. Apart, we'd both become a pair of eccentric zombies. He was afraid of everything, he looked forward to
nothing. He was thirty-seven years old.

   This sudden swerve into our creepy old age annoyed me no end. My
youth was *not* spent! My capacity for feeling was *not* dwindling! But his
letters did revive in me the memory of Ken predicting his death at
thirty. He'd survived that deadline, but for several years there had
been the coughing fits, sometimes lasting all night. Often at the end of
a day he was sweating and his color was high, as though he had fever.
There was no question that he was run down, but was it something
more grave?

   During the time we lived together neither of us took care of ourselves in the health-conscious way of today. We didn't work out, we
didn't eat regularly, and though we had delicious meals in restaurants
they probably would not have received a nutritionist's seal of approval,
especially since for further sustenance we regularly added generous
infusions of deximyl, cigarettes and gin. What exercise we got came
from running around to all those places, with all those people, doing
all those things. We kept going fueled by nervous energy. But now Ken
was sounding like a burnt-out case, a dying man grasping at his one
chance of survival. He began phoning me: everything without me was
a void of loneliness and masturbation.

   He was really letting out the stops this time. He had found a new
flat to offer me in that venerable English institution, Albany. My

mother was in London staying at the Dorchester and he enrolled her help to convince me he was in earnest. To my astonishment I received a letter from her along those lines – poor Mother, unable to withstand Ken's supplications, although after my father's death, she had remarked, 'Is there really any *reason* for you to stay married to Ken?'

In the beginning I dealt with his paper assaults by not answering them. Later, on the phone, I was pretty nasty. He asked me once if, just out of politeness to a sick man, I could lay off the hard bright venom. At some point I did. I also agreed to come back to our flat in Mount Street one more time.

The week before my departure I phoned to give him my flight number and time of arrival at Heathrow. His last words were: 'Please don't let's hurt each other anymore.'

I arrived in London on a foggy November morning with these words foremost in my mind. Ken met me at Heathrow. In the taxi to Mount Street we chatted amiably – so far, so good. We were barely through our front door when Ken said, 'Come into the library, I've found a new singer I want you to hear.' This was something Ken would often do when we'd been away from each other for a while. He would produce a record of a singer, or a band, or whatever interesting performance he had discovered in my absence, and play it for our shared delectation. So I looked forward to it. He played the record, and a young girl began singing.

I wish I was making the next part up.

'Listen to her,' said Ken, 'listen to the lasciviousness, the utter debauchery in her voice.'

I said, 'I don't hear it. I hear a rather nice girl singing a love song.'

Then Ken, in his iciest and most contemptuous tones, replied, 'That's it. I've had it. I'm tired of you casting yourself in the role of a fine, noble, upright character, and me in the role of a pervert.'

I said, 'I've been up all night, I need some sleep,' and went into the bedroom. When I awoke he was gone. No note. Nothing. All that had happened was one brief conversation during which the few mild words of disagreement I'd uttered had caused Ken to turn on me in a rage and leave the house.

I sat up in bed and looked around our bedroom. It looked even sadder, more worn, more crumbling than when I'd left. It seemed covered with dust. Dusting had never been one of our cleaning woman's strong points – did Ken still have her? I ran a finger across several surfaces. They were coated with grime. I approached the hanging bookshelf, which had a ridge running along its edge, and as I drew nearer I saw that a schoolmaster's cane was lying along it. Ken's weapon of choice. I wondered how long it had been there, whom it had been used on, whom he intended to use it on.

In one of his phone calls to me in New York he'd told me he was devising a Pax Tynanica, a list of rules for us to abide by to stop hurting each other. One was that Ken would agree to confine sex to bed and stop punishing. No hidden meaning there. Sex out of bed referred to S & M procedures; no punishing meant no flagellomania. What could be clearer? So what was the cane doing on the bookshelf? Our Pax Tynanica had gone up in smoke over an absurd disagreement of what a singer's voice conveyed to each of us. Only I'd disagreed with Ken because I'd decoded what his words were leading up to: the cane.

I wasn't here to have another terrible fight with him. I was here to see Tracy and my friends. For the rest of my short stay Ken and I more or less went our separate ways. The few times we bumped up against each other we were back in the old war zone. Each encounter became progressively more acrimonious.

That first day I had a bath, dressed, and phoned my friends to tell them I was in London. I was particularly blessed with some new non-Kenelaine friends I'd made in '62. They were and are the same people whom I have loved, cherished and admired all these years, the same whose careers I still follow with pleasure, including Emma Tennant, the actor Peter Eyre and the writer Francis Wyndham.

I state categorically that I never met a Tennant I didn't love. (Francis is also closely related to the Tennants.) Of the Tennant women, the one I know best and longest is Pauline, daughter of Hermione Baddeley and David Tennant – now Pauline Rumbold, widow of Sir Anthony Rumbold, fiercely intelligent, generous and plain spoken. I first met her at a small literary gathering in London. Sonia Orwell, George Orwell's widow, wrapped in Parisian chic made a grand entrance then sat down, drink in hand, and began rattling away in French. Though several people, among them Pauline and myself, wondered quietly whether Sonia was aware that she was in England, only Pauline was brave enough to confront her with the fact. At which point Sonia calmly explained that she did know where she was, but that living in Paris had convinced her French was the only possible language in which to discuss literature and that she simply would not talk about it in any other tongue. Pauline returned and repeated her words to me. Sharing a laugh over someone else's intellectual lunacy is always a good way to speed along a friendship.

Tracy came back from boarding school the next day, looking healthy and happy, her conversation sprinkled with school argot such as 'gack' for ugh and 'grockel' for gawk. With her I finally saw *The Mousetrap*, still running in its eleventh year, because of our shared passion for the great Agatha Christie. Another time that week we went to a matinee to see Laurence Olivier in *Othello* at the Old Vic. Backstage in his dressing room, Olivier, still in makeup, met us at the door and swooped Tracy up with a hug and a kiss from which she emerged sporting chocolate-colored greasepaint all over her face and dress.

After Tracy left, Ken and I spent one evening together. I was leaving the next day for New York. I was waiting in the library for my dinner date, my old friend, Julian Jebb, a BBC documentary producer and literary critic, when the au pair who had stayed on for Tracy's return came in and said she'd just heard on her radio that President Kennedy had been shot. I called Ken from his study. We switched on the TV and saw only a blank screen. Then, after a long while, we heard the words 'President Kennedy is dead'. And the screen went blank again. By the time Julian arrived the BBC had pulled itself together and we heard parts of the horrifying story. Then the three of us went out to dine. Later we went to the Kilmartins', where it seemed the entire political staff of the *Observer* was glued to their TV set.

One good thing came out of my Mount Street visit: our Mexican divorce was definitely back on track again and, through my own lawyer, I arranged to go to Juarez in May. Another good thing: on the recommendation of English friends I began to stay at the Chelsea

Hotel on West 23rd Street. It took just a week for me to enjoy its lobby, hung with the work of contemporary artists; my room, with the sun streaming down over the parking lot; the Notice of Inspection in the elevator that listed, along with the usual signatures of inspectors, those of 'Santa Claus December 25, 1963' and 'Barry Goldwater', which date was given as 'February 1875'; and its Landmark of New York plaque, which listed the artists and writers who had lived there, including O. Henry, Robert Flaherty, Thomas Wolfe, and Edgar Lee Masters, as well as more recently, Dylan Thomas (who died there from what the coroner's report called 'severe insult to the brain'), Brendan Behan and Arthur Miller. I knew that this extraordinary hotel would be my next piece of journalism. I wrote it that winter for *Esquire*. What I didn't realize was that I was entering my journalist period and that for the next years I would be writing articles extensively for *Esquire*, *New York* magazine, and *Cosmopolitan* in America, and for *Queen* which at some point became *Harpers & Queen* – the *Sunday Times Magazine* and *Vogue* in England. I would be working with two outstanding editors, Clay Felker and Francis Wyndham.

My social life got an unexpected lift that December when I met the painter Larry Rivers in one of the Chelsea elevators. A dark-haired man with bold sharp features giving him the aspect of a pirate had been staring at me. He finally spoke: 'I'm admiring your coat,' he said. 'It's terrific.' I replied I was delighted someone had noticed. It was an old coat of dark Alaskan seal I'd had made over by adding to it a beige mink collar, beige mink cuffs and a red satin lining. We introduced ourselves and he invited me to step off the elevator at his floor and into his studio, where I met his English girlfriend, Clarissa. It was the Christmas season and suddenly I was going along with them to all the parties he'd been invited to.

On January 6 I received a phone call from Ken. He wanted to tell me about the poem he dreamed the night before. It was about us. He recited the poem, about a beloved dog who was dying because he could not love just one of us. It must be both or neither. It had us biting our knuckles till they bled while standing at the graves of various death symbols of our marriage. In the end Ken told the dying dog 'journey for me, usher me the way I shall go'.

I found it moving, chilling. It disturbs me still, Ken's nocturnal mind creating its dreamscape of our marriage's death and, finally, his own. He would live for sixteen more years but he would die young, aged fifty-three, of emphysema. That day on the phone we continued to talk pleasantly, even affectionately, as in our early days. I said the poem was beautiful and asked him to send it to me.

Another letter from Ken followed. It read as if our being back together again was all that mattered, as if my last visit had never happened.

A few days later I received a formal card announcing that Kenneth Tynan requested the pleasure of Elaine Tynan's company at their 23rd Consecutive and First Permanent Reunion at the Hotel Mency, Tenerife, Canary Islands, January 25, 1964, our thirteenth wedding anniversary.

The letter I wrote in reply showed me as unhinged in my way as he was in his. First I told him the poem made me *weep daily*, that I died a little along with our dear old dog and the death of our marriage. It seemed as if I was going to accept him. Instead I stepped back and brought up his past violence, and declined his invitation.

I came back to Mount Street one more time, three months later, in March. It was for Tracy's spring vacation and for the publication of my novel *The Old Man and Me*. The climate between myself and Ken was wintry. I should have stayed elsewhere, but feared it might start certain English papers sniffing around our private lives. I didn't want the publicity for my book getting mixed up with our impending divorce. In Mount Street I gave interviews and was photographed 'at home'.

The puffs on the book jacket of *The Old Man and Me* were strong. I'd given Victor Gollancz a list of writers whom I thought might like it and they all came through. There were quotes from Gore, Doris Lessing, Penelope Mortimer and Christopher Isherwood. Best was Irwin Shaw's, which went in part: 'Elaine Dundy has done it again and neither the English nor the Americans will be the same from now on . . . It's brilliant, weirdly original, hilarious, and nobody gets away with nothing.'

The first review I read was by Iain Hamilton in the *Daily Telegraph* and it was positive. I felt a huge sense of relief because I was uneasy about the book's reception in England. The different thing about my book was that it featured an Angry Young Woman – an anti-heroine. In fact the 'I' presents herself as 'Betsy Lou, Girl Cad' and adds, 'Is this a first?' Where, I had wondered as I was writing the novel, were the examples of contemporary anti-heroines? Where were full-length portraits of what I called a Girl With a Plan, whose vices and passions were explored and exploited by their authors with the same intensity as those of the men? The truth was you had to leave the twentieth century to find them. In the nineteenth century we had Hedda Gabler, Becky Sharp and the Strindberg shrews, before that were Shakespeare's lively crew, and even further back those legendary raging females of ancient Greece and the glorious long line of colorful anti-heroines from the Bible – Rehab, Jezebel, Delilah, Salome and all. True, in the 1930s Scarlett O'Hara appeared, but her creator's instinct rightly placed her back in the Civil War. All the time I was inventing my adventuress, I was aware the Women Problem of the day was becoming more and more acute as increasingly I saw the female accurately portrayed by our best women writers as anguishedly passive and put upon.

Although I'd unsparingly attacked the Anglo-Saxon attitudes of bohemia and the aristocracy in my novel, I continually showed my protagonist getting tripped up by her adversaries, no match for their sly cunning nor for their sly tolerance. Still, something told me I was going to ruffle some feathers, even though Gollancz had reassured me that the English are famous for being able to laugh at themselves.

Not the two who reviewed it that Sunday for the *Observer* and the *Sunday Times*. Both of them gave it absolute stinkers. Both papers made it their lead novel, and both reviewers dismissed it at length.

Soon the time came for me to go New York for the American publication of *The Old Man and Me*. My publisher was giving me a party and the publicity they had lined up looked great. I took heart again. The English reviews had been mixed. I consoled myself about the bad ones that at least I'd drawn blood.

The day of my departure I left a farewell note for Ken that simply astonishes me today. It answers any questions I might have about the substantial part I was playing in our long dance of death. It had occurred to me then that as long as I withdrew, Ken would pursue. Clear now is that when he withdrew, I, in turn, would pursue. 'I want you and you want me but we never give each other a chance,' I wrote. I speculated that, if one of us died the following week, would not the other drag out the remaining days in despair knowing we'd spent our last years depriving ourselves of each other? I signed myself 'Forever and always'. Now I hear only the false notes. Surely at the time of writing my mind had laid our relationship to rest. Surely I knew it was our quarrels that were real, our reconciliations fake.

I sealed the letter, finished packing, and by the time I boarded the plane I was only looking forward. When I landed in New York at the Chelsea I opened a pleasing note from my editor at Dutton, which had been delivered that day. They had already received advance reviews from important media, then followed positive quotes from *Newsweek*, *Time* and *Cosmopolitan*. The reviews of *The Old Man and Me* in America were much better than those in England, more plentiful too, stretching across the vast continent. They seemed less offended both by the satirical attacks on the English – after all it wasn't their country – and more at home with my American Angry Young Girl. Dawn Powell's review was a cornucopia of delights: 'It's a terrific job – fierce, gamey, vixenish – as if it was bled not written and one is left with a stack of feathers and cracked bones, and witch laughter. Definitely demonic, exquisitely carved, deadly murderous comedy.'

So why a year and some months after publication did I get a letter from Dutton saying they were remaindering it and did I want any copies?

I discussed it with Gore. 'It's not everyone's cup of tea. It's more like caviar to the general,' he said in his blunt, salty way. Was I becoming that dreadful thing 'a small circle writer's writer'? I'd better find out. I ordered twenty copies and sent ten to authors whose work I admired and asked them why the public had rejected it. Among them was Edmund Wilson, who gave it to me straight: 'The reason it doesn't sell is undoubtedly the reason Dawn Powell doesn't sell. The American feminine public doesn't want to read about women who are too tough and with little romantic appeal.'

But I hit the jackpot when I sent it to the comic master of this century, P.G. Wodehouse. More than any other writer he had taught me how to write, and technically, in his Jeeves stories especially, I had studied how the first person – Bertie Wooster – could be used with the greatest freedom and to its fullest effect. I wrote to him that my book was being remaindered 'in great bonfire piles' and wondered if he could tell me why.

In due course the Sage of Remsenburg, Long Island, replied that he had just finished *The Old Man and Me*, thought it was 'terrific' and that it 'ought to have sold as well as the *Avocado* . . .' He wrote that he had to ration himself on it, as he was trying to write a very difficult short story . . . 'but there isn't a dull line in it and I shall read it again many times.' He signed off hoping that I would be writing another novel very soon. 'You can,' he said, 'rely on at least one reader.'

On May 12, in Juarez – you had to book months in advance – I obtained my Mexican divorce. While the presiding Mexican official – who looked all of twenty years old – scanned my divorce papers, I noticed under the glass top of his desk a poem called 'Sí'. It turned out to be the Spanish translation of 'If' by Rudyard Kipling. I read it with avidity. Ah, those Victorian certitudes. 'If—' Kipling promises us, *if* you follow his next five stanzas of excellent advice, 'yours is the world and everything that's in it/and – which is more – you'll be a Man, my son/.' Which is what I intended to be in my brave new world of '64: a Kipling Man.

Back in New York on May 18, 1964 the gossip column of the *World-Telegram* read: 'Novelist "Graduated" from Ace Drama Critic. Mexican Divorce diploma in hand, Elaine Dundy, author, ex of Britain's top drama critic Kenneth Tynan, told us last night, "I feel as if I'd graduated from this marriage."' *Time* magazine in its Milestones column listed that we were divorced after thirteen years on grounds of incompatibility.

In London that June, Sandy and Hilary Mackendrick loaned me their house in Limerston Street. There I stayed until Tracy's school vacation in July. After that we would go together to New York. Ken and I would share joint custody of Tracy and she would spend alternate holidays with each of us while continuing at Dartington Hall.

As a Gay Divorcee I gave a party every night. In the middle of one of them Ken rang. He was furious. How dare I give a party the Friday before, the same night as his own party, and steal his guests!

I said, 'I no longer feel it necessary to check with the Court Circular for the dates of your scheduled events. I give lots of parties. I'm celebrating.'

'Skippy, my party was awful – so boring. It really needed you.'

'Here you go again spinning around in your wife/mistress syndrome. Look, I've got to go. I'm giving a party right now.'

'Can I come?'

I said, 'No!' noting how easily that came now. I also remembered how, in his unabashed way of inviting himself – Can I come? Can I join you? Will you take me along? – he did so well what is one of the hardest things of all. It was a big part of Ken's personality that he could deliver those words without seeming to be losing face. I wonder if all his brilliance would have gotten him where he was in the celebrity world he so cherished without this gift, this ability to announce he would be giving them the genuine enjoyment of having him as a guest, always reserving his right to bite the hand he had so reverently kissed.

Sometime after what should have been the decent burial of our marriage I received a phone call from Ken in Spain saying only, 'Who was that lady I saw you with last wife? That was no lady that was my life.' And straightaway the words set my guts to roiling. Then followed his autumn, winter and spring campaign to get me back, his letters always addressed to Elaine Tynan. But now, at last, divorce papers in hand and in New York with an ocean between us, I finally got it. I understood that it was Ken's manipulative genius ever to pour oil on troubled water and then light it, that any contact with him whatsoever for any reason other than Tracy's affairs would be supping with the devil. We bumped into each other once, inadvertently. Other than that I never saw him again.

Yet in 1980, when Ken was dying in California and Tracy was there spending much time with him, I called her one day and when I asked 'How is he?' she said, 'He's lonely.' With that the reality of the situation hit me, so I asked Harold Hobson, his opposite number at the *Sunday Times*, to write to him, and he did. (I'd asked a lot of other people too but they didn't.) And I was glad I had when Harold rang and read me Ken's reply, for every word rang out with Ken's pleasure at hearing from this old friend and rival.

The end found me at last doing the right thing. I had written a biography of the actor Peter Finch and sent it to Tracy. She rang to say Ken had asked if he could see it. I agreed and said I'd write him. So, after the years of silence, I sent him a letter that said what had to be said because it was the truth. I wrote him that the book would have been better if he'd seen it before it was published, that he would find echoes in it of him throughout, as he would in everything I had written or ever would write. I recalled the time in Paris when we heard Edith Piaf at the Olympia sing '*Je Ne Regrette Rien*' and I thanked him for that. I thanked him for Paris, and for us in Paris, and for the very real beginning of my life.

At the end of May – he had less than two months to live – I received a letter from him indicating he'd read *Finch, Bloody Finch* in just one sitting. He complimented me on the thoroughness of my research and touchingly responded in kind to what I'd said about us in my letter.

His letter ended with a brave postscript – something about how now we could resume normal relations again. And when I looked at those words – they would be his last to me – my angry knee-jerk reaction was: he thinks our relations were *normal*? Nor could I help myself. That was part of our legacy. Nevertheless, in his last days I replied that I too would be glad to resume our relations again. I also sent him a clipping of a periwinkle plant, whose flower, if worn on one's lapel, has the power to ward off evil spirits.

We did bad things to each other, Ken and I, but maybe for me the worst is that even now I cannot let this statement stand without tacking on, in self-vindication, *oh, but he did much worse things to me than I to him*. Isn't it sad that even twenty years after his death I'm still impelled to add that?

Because in the final reckoning, in the adding up of debits and credits, I see that I am more indebted to him than debited. So, really, isn't it absurd that the lesser debt, of gratitude, I pay, but the greater one, of forgiveness, I defer?

PART THREE

DISCOVERING MYSELF

29

68 Charles Street

One day during my last stopover at Mount Street that March (and my last pretense that it was my home), I was walking down the street – like Sally Jay in *The Dud Avocado* – only this time it wasn't the Boulevard St Michel in Paris, but Berkeley Square in London – when I ran into a friend and thus ran straight into a godshot. I call godshots what happens when problems that involve huge amounts of time, trouble, money or frustration, unexpectedly come towards you solved. They are not answered prayers but unimagined favors that leave you loving the universe and all that dwell therein. I was forty-two and, by my out-of-time clock, still young.

The friend was director Sidney Lumet, whose parties with his then wife Gloria Vanderbilt I'd so enjoyed during Ken's stint on the *New Yorker*. I mentioned I was moving to New York but hadn't yet found a place to live. 'Take over my lease in the Village,' he incredibly suggested, 'I'm moving in September.' He was talking about his duplex in a town house where he lived with his new wife Gale (Lena Horne's daughter) at 68 Charles Street, a quiet residential part of the West Village. I'd dined at their home the last time I was in New York so I pretty much knew what it looked like. Even before Sidney ticked off the layout for me – main floor: large room divided into living room, dining room and kitchen plus small powder room; upstairs two bed-rooms, one study and a bathroom – I knew it would be perfect.

Then and there in Berkeley Square Sidney and I closed the deal with a handshake. My lease would start in September. So convinced was I of the all-round rightness of this miracle I did not even bother to look it over until Tracy and I arrived in New York in September.

When we got to 68 Charles Street it looked even better than I remembered. The house was painted pink with white trim, and the empty rooms of my duplex suggested any number of decorating possi-bilities from soft and warm to bright and smart, from woodsy to citified. It had a sweet little backyard, where grew one of those decep-tively delicate-looking New York trees that crash their way through cement. I could gaze at it every day from the long windows in the main room.

We watched the movers unload my goods and chattels shipped from London and as they unpacked I realized there were essential pieces of furniture – like beds, coffee tables, sofas, the chaise longue and various pieces of bric-a-brac – that I'd been unable to wrest from Ken. The living room was empty of essentials. My spirits sank.

Tracy studied the Casa Pupo rug we'd laid down. It had a colorful pink, red and purple pattern. She said, 'Give me some money. I'm going to Woolworths.' She came back with rolls of felt in pink, red and purple and went about cutting and thumb-tacking two empty backing cases into marvelously decorative coffee tables. We then went to Bloomingdales, where she suggested I stay with those colors, and we ordered a long purple velvet sofa and a matching one of red velvet to be placed on either side of the packing case coffee tables. And so I set about – now with gusto – running from Bloomingdale's to the Village furniture and special wallpaper shops decorating our duplex, always guided by my twelve-year-old daughter and, when she returned to her boarding school in England, if not by her presence, by her spirit.

Almost immediately in the euphoria of living in my new place my mind stretched it from being just a duplex into being a whole town house that was mine, all mine. I considered the landlord who occupied the basement flat with its separate entrance to be marginal, and if I thought of him at all it was as an unimportant off-stage character in my unfolding play. Every now and then we might meet when coming or going, or I would run into him when a shop dropped off a piece of furniture or when the decorator came and went. We would exchange pleasantries and I would express my enthusiasm for the thing of beauty I was making of my castle. I wallpapered my bedroom with an old-fashioned print of wild flowers, covering the ceiling with it as well, so that entering it was like snuggling into a quilt. In Tracy's room I loved the roll-top desk and the upholstered easy chair that both rocked and swiveled. I hung my study with blue silk wallpaper after reading that Max Beerbohm papered his various dens with it.

Jubilantly I went on the town, doing all the things to establish myself anew. I was out there, everywhere, meeting everyone, and when I wasn't out there I was at home having everyone in for dinner, or drinks, or after-theatre parties. I met Len Melfi, working part-time at a Village furniture store I used to frequent. He was on the cusp of recognition as one of the new '60s playwrights and we became friends, hung out together, went to lots of parties and plays and enjoyed them all the more because we enjoyed them together. Betty Boo, who had moved to New York, gave her parties. Once Len stayed for the orgy while I left before the party got rough. Later he wrote a very funny play about it.

I would stare at the blue silken walls of my study and try to think up a plot for my next novel. After a while I'd stop trying and write down my dreams of the night before, hoping to dredge up something there. I have journals filled with dreams that made no sense then and make none now: journals that could have been filled with data, crammed with insights and outsights.

Then, imperceptibly, my focus began to shift. In the beginning, while interviewing someone for an article, halfway along I'd be thinking that this person should be interviewing *me*; I was much more interesting than they were. Now I began to see some were as interesting as I was and in certain cases even more so.

Initially I liked doing journalism when it involved theatre or literary people. I was lucky to catch Liza Minnelli and Lynn Redgrave at the moment their careers were taking off, when they were feeling their oats and saying whatever they felt like.

Liza Minnelli was nineteen years old and about to get her big chance on Broadway in a musical called *Flora the Red Menace*, she being Flora. I went to its last tryout in Boston to do a piece about her for *New York* magazine. After the show I went to her dressing room. Also there were John Kander and Fred Ebb, who wrote the score and lyrics (and would also do the same for *Cabaret*). Liza looked like a newly hatched chicken, with a look of permanent surprise: great round brown eyes with wide spaces of innocence between them; a mouth shaped like a slice of watermelon that appeared constantly startled; even her large bunny teeth seemed astonished. Though only eleven days from the Broadway opening, the show was in the typical state of out-of-town madness that never ceases to dumbfound an outsider. Almost immediately Liza asked me what I thought of the show. I answered evasively that I thought the ballet in the second act was very funny.

'That's out,' she said. 'We're rehearsing a new one Monday. The whole second act is going to be changed. Did you like the ending?'

'It wasn't very clear to me. Which of the two men are you going to choose?'

'I don't know yet. It's all going to be changed. For instance Bob Dishy, the one on stage, used to just walk off after I sing "I Believe in You", but now he gives me an apple.'

'No he doesn't,' said Fred.

'He doesn't?' asked Liza in some surprise.

'No, they cut that out on Friday,' replied Fred. 'Now he's going to give you the apple after you sing "You are You".'

'I was very good at the beginning about changes but tonight I opened my mouth to sing a song and suddenly thought, "Oh my God, which one is it supposed to be?" But the right one came out somehow.'

The four of us dined at a Hawaiian-style restaurant. We ordered drinks called Bali Bastards, which arrived in Aku-Aku shaped mugs full of parasols and fruit garbage. Liza talked more about the play. She loved its message: 'For some reason I seem to think that *Flora* has a message . . . though I'm not exactly sure what it is . . .' 'I hope the message is a hit,' said Fred. 'I love the songs John and Fred have written,' said Liza, 'I want to make an album of all the songs that have been cut. The reason I wanted to play this part has all been cut out,' she mused, adding, 'The reason I wanted to sing it has all been cut out too.'

She was frank about the hardships involved in growing up the daughter of Judy Garland and Vincente Minnelli. Moving around with one or the other, she had been to twenty different schools and at last begged her mother to give her a tutor rather than make her face another new school. In this connection she talked about Ayn Rand, whose novels she loved. Once when she was very young she found herself alone and very lonely in Paris and she read *The Fountainhead* and it was the turning point of her life because it made her feel that 'you really didn't need anybody as much as you think you do. Then this awful thing happened,' she continued. When she talked to friends in New York about the book, they sneered it was 'the secretaries' bible'. So Liza had to give it up. But now she didn't care. She thought Rand had written the greatest love story in the world called *We the Living*. 'She writes a rape scene that makes you want to run right out and get raped,' she enthused.

Flora the Red Menace on Broadway was not a smash but Liza made her point: she had arrived. She went on to become a legitimate star in *Cabaret*, both on stage and screen. She is, after thirty-five years of showbiz, one of the few entertainers who have remained household names.

I interviewed the over six-foot-tall Lynn Redgrave for *Cosmopolitan* and *Harpers & Queen*. She was twenty-three and in New York playing in Peter Shaffer's *Black Comedy*. She'd had a great success in *Georgy Girl* as a North Country hulk of a girl, on the surface a pathetic ugly duckling but underneath an emerging swan of a particularly tough variety, with an uncynical force of character that captures the heart and hand of the richest industrialist in town (James Mason). I accompanied her one day on her killing schedule from her apartment to a photographer's studio, to a TV quiz show, to the theatre, to a late-night party, and she kept catching twenty winks in the car driving us around. *Georgy Girl* was a cult film, playing in one cinema for six months, and every time we hit the streets six-feet-and-over girls appeared from nowhere to circle worshipfully around her. Lynn had become their idol and the New York streets were overflowing with them. Of the American fans' reaction she said, 'They're perfectly nice when they come up and talk but there's a sort of American shriek when they recognize me that's unnerving. I get myself up without an *inch* of face showing, but they recognize me anyway.'

The flavor of her talk exuded a special kind of English nonchalance that paints both triumph and disaster with the same comic brush. 'I adored the whole life at drama school,' she said as we dashed into her waiting car. 'I did hate the parties though. Horrid bottle parties where one had one gin, a whisky, some cider and then burst into tears and went home.'

Against all commercial odds, an exalted prose drama about Eleanor of Aquitaine and Henry II called *The Lion in Winter*, taking place in the wigs and costumes of a good many centuries ago was succeeding brilliantly on Broadway. I asked Clay to let me write about one of its stars, the actress Rosemary Harris.

My article for *New York* magazine about Rosemary led off as follows: 'From the minute she hits the stage it is as if she has attained some special state of grace. In point of fact, she glows. And as she picks her way across the scene, whether towards some delightful or some harrowing turn of the plot . . . she presents such a figure of harmony and proportion that it all might be intolerable were it not that it is done with such simplicity and belief . . . No English-speaking actress can rival her portrayal of the Romantic Female Personality in its dauntless pursuit of love, honor, self-sacrifice and the wearing of gorgeous clothes.' As best actress of the year in Broadway in '66, Rosemary won a Tony for this role.

In December of 1999 Rosemary Harris opened on Broadway in Noël Coward's *Waiting in the Wings* and received a superlative review from the *New York Times*. When I called to congratulate her, she replied: 'You know I don't read my notices.' I had forgotten. Down the years she has remained true to this early decision. She never reads her notices until months after they've appeared because she believes critics influence a performance. In proof of this she cites an Old Vic production of *Hamlet* in which she played Ophelia. It received scathing notices. After the second night one of the actors came up to her and said, 'You were the only one I could act with because I knew you hadn't read the critics.' There is to this day a vast army of critics whose praise of Rosemary often brings out their best writing. One recently described a performance of hers as 'a kind of breathtaking work that exhibits both a reverence for language and the human emotion to fill it'. What strength of mind, what discipline must be Rosemary's to deny herself the instant gratification of reading the above in deference to her artistic integrity. 'Even if a review is marvelous,' she says, 'you start playing that review.'

I've known Rosemary Harris since she and Tessa, my friend of Paris days, became roommates in London in the early '50s. This coincided with her acting debut in the West End. In '65, with both of us living in New York, Rosemary and I became closer. Her extraordinary career has yearly produced astonishing surprises, very often for herself. To enjoy vicariously the life of one of the five great living English actresses (the other four: Judi Dench, Maggie Smith, Vanessa Redgrave and Joan Plowright), has been one of the privileges of my own life. Since 1953 not a year has gone by that she has not appeared on the stage mostly on Broadway or in the West End. By '95, when I last wrote about her she had been in sixty-five plays and counting. Besides appearing in new plays she is a consummate interpreter of Shakespeare, Shaw, Ibsen and Chekhov as well as Neil Simon, Noël Coward and Tennessee Williams. Although her record can be explained in many ways, I conclude that, talent aside, it is because she has so successfully balanced her life of fantasy with one of shrewd common sense.

Raised in India at the time of the Raj, Rosemary is very much an English lady. Her saturation in theatre is such that she will say, describing someone, 'Oh, she'd make a *wonderful* Mrs Burleigh,' leaving one none the wiser.

In '66 Rosemary followed *The Lion in Winter* with Natasha in *War and Peace*. These triumphs did not stop her from serving her season in hell. Though they continued to work together, her marriage in 1959 to director Ellis Rabb had been coming apart for some time. As so often with women in the arts, stern destiny levels off their professional success with private distress. Finally she and Ellis separated and she moved to a new apartment on West 57th Street. She was worried about herself, and so were her friends and colleagues. They told her how difficult she had become. She decided she needed help. I referred her to the psychiatrist I was seeing and she began working with him. I paid close attention to her progress, comparing it with mine. She was a very quick study.

A month after starting therapy, she was bicycling around Central Park every Sunday. Several months later, she told me, the shrink having suggested to her – against her flood of rationalizations – that the *real* reason she kept wearing her old shoes, which had constantly to be repaired, was that she was clinging to the old because she was afraid of the new. Rosemary thought this over, then began discarding not only her old shoes but some other old attachments. In '67 she was divorced and married for the second time. It happened in fairy tale fashion:

A close friend of hers was the playwright Bella Spewack, with whom she had a heart-to-heart. To her surprise Bella, dismissing Rosemary's list of woes, asked her to describe her ideal man, the sort of man she wanted. Rosemary warmed to the challenge. She would like him to be in arts, of course. Not in the theatre, but interested in it. A writer, perhaps, a novelist. She would like him to have rugged features, and at this point she even described the color of his hair and his eyes. Bella said calmly that she knew a man who perfectly fit that description, a novelist who lived in North Carolina but came up to New York often because they served on the same theatre committee. His name was John Ehle, and he'd just gotten divorced. Bella introduced them. They fell in love, and married in October of 1967. In due course they had a child, Jennifer. Rosemary's cup ranneth over. They have a house in Winston Salem, a cabin in the hills of North Carolina, a flat in London and an apartment in New York. With industry, application and an ardent enjoyment of their occupations, with natural gifts that include an unnatural toleration of life's calamities, their careers burgeon and prosper. They have been married for thirty-three years.

In April of 2000 both mother and daughter, Rosemary in *Waiting in the Wings* and Jennifer Ehle in *The Real Thing*, were playing on

Broadway. Both were up for the best actress Tony award. Jennifer won. Rosemary was delighted. 'It would have been a nightmare if I'd won,' said the proud mother.

The sixties were not a good time for literature. Rock and pop music and political action were the main cultural concerns. Those writing in the fifties who had made their name at that time got better or worse but remained on the charts. There was, however, one exception.

I met Tom Wolfe in December of '64 and watched him emerge as the new Wild Man of American literature. As we got to know each other in '65 I became fascinated by him, the more so because of the obvious comparison with Ken in their high-decibelled voices in print; in their fame, which all but buried them with adulation, exposure, controversy and deadlines; and in their extreme interest in self-expressing themselves via clothes. For both I think it was an actor-related thing. In both their writings the performer always dances through. Tom was more analytical about the subject of clothes than Ken, who would simply announce he had ordered a new suit – when the startling object appeared on him I always burst into applause.

Initially the article I wrote about Tom was for Francis Wyndham for a new magazine. When it folded he saw to it that the piece got published in English *Vogue*, after which it was printed in American *Vogue* and, through the years, other publications.

The conditions under which I interviewed Tom were favorable. We already knew each other fairly well and the atmosphere was relaxed. As a subject he was fluent, funny and self-exposing, and he neither ducked nor dissembled. Knowing him personally allowed me to find aspects of his personality that were odd and contradictory – in other words, what you find in a person when you delve beneath his surface.

Dandyism in writers is nothing new. Many besides Ken and Tom shared this obsession. Tom showed me how complicated it all is, first demonstrating how he ascribes magical properties to his clothes. 'If that shirt and *that* shirt were running a race,' he once said, pointing to what appeared to be two identical shirts, '*that* shirt would win.' At the same time he bitterly complained about people's reaction to his new overcoat. 'What's the matter with them?' he said. 'Don't they realize the lapels are too wide, it's got too much shoulder padding and more buttons than a policeman's uniform? Why don't they mention it?' In other words, the dandy plans his wardrobe for quite contradictory purposes: to look good and feel powerful in – and to offend people. 'To shake 'em up,' as he put it.

What also separates the dandy from his fellow men is the blind passion with which he pursues this occupation. Tom arrived at my house one day smiling broadly and carrying a package. As he ceremoniously opened it, I prepared to be the recipient of some delightful gift. It turned out to be a tie he'd just bought himself that he hoped I would admire – or perhaps be offended by. The man who dubbed the seventies the Me Decade knew a great deal about the Me Decade himself in the sixties.

Before I began my article, Tom handed me a short poem he had written back in '55 as a graduate student at Yale working on his Ph.D. in American Studies. In doing so he dropped in my lap that perfect piece of information that would both explain him and clarify his goals then and always. It was titled 'I Shall Revolt':

> I shall burst this placid pink shell
> I shall wake up slightly hungover,
> Favored, adored, worshipped and clamored for,
> I shall raise Hell and be a real
> Cut up.

His poem was written under the name of 'Jocko Thor', clearly Tom's jock alter ego: the Scandinavian god of war.

In '65, exactly ten years after his declaration of war, he achieved his ambition. His first book *The Kandy-Kolored Tangerine Flake Streamline Baby* went into its fourth printing a month after publication and in his white-on-white suit its author was favored, adored, worshipped and clamored for.

It is my observation that with writers nobody born and raised in the Big Apple really makes it big hanging out in the city. Only out-of-towners really see Gatsby's green light. Most native literati get in and out of the metropolis fast as possible. I saw that Tom Wolfe, from Richmond, Virginia, by actually living in his green light Manhattan, still retained the out-of-towner's suspicion that he was in constant danger of being sent up, being put on or put down by smart-alec natives.

Tom once told me, noting how little I shared his exuberance for the present, 'You're living in the past. And it won't work.' He was right; I was not 'with it'. I found the sixties unsympathetic. I had come to life in the fifties, in the decade with cultural icons whom I knew and assumed would last forever, only to be greeted by the swinging sixties hot shots Tom wrote about, like Baby Jane Holzer, Phil Spector, Ken Kesey and Junior Johnson, the stock car racer. As a habituée of night-clubs with fabulous entertainers and wonderful jazz bands, hot and cool, I hated the discos, with their screaming music, steaming with people bumping into each other all night long on packed dance floors.

Back into my life came Tennessee just in time for one of my crises. His own mood was not good either. In New York he lived in what he called 'a ghastly new high-rise' in the West 70s near Central Park. He had a penthouse on the thirty-third floor, which I thought odd as he disliked heights. It came as a body blow to him that his producers put off his new play *Slapstick Tragedy*, which was to open in '65 until '66. He said to me he was glad when six o'clock came every evening because it meant 'the day was over'.

One evening he came to see me. Two days before the bottom had dropped out of my life. My landlord, that formerly off-stage character in the basement, moved stage center with the announcement that he was selling the house and when he did I would have to leave. I date this happening, in May of '66, as the exact moment that I seriously began to unravel. I felt victimized, swindled, cheated, betrayed. I felt what he had done by silently watching me fix up the duplex, not saying a word of his plan till I had completed it, was morally wrong. Next day I found out from my lawyer that as I was only paying rent by the month it was also legally right.

That evening with friends I'd had lots to drink and ended up falling down my stairs. I woke up next morning in agony – I would later find out I had sprained my back. I took some painkillers plus a couple of Ritalins to bring me up to speed. By the time Tennessee arrived I was flying around the living room with the combination of pills and gin. Determined to help me, he said he was going to make an appointment for me to see Dr Harris, his psychiatrist. 'Why?' I asked defensively, thinking of the rotten advice he'd given me about going to Malaga. 'Because he is such a *fine person*,' he surprised me by saying. Putting a shrink's integrity of character above his miraculous feats of healing was an intriguing notion, and I agreed.

My regular appointment was the hour after Tennessee's so we often ran into each other outside the office. Once in passing me he said of our man, 'It's okay. He's in a good mood.' It was the first and last time I have ever heard a patient register concern for the *psychiatrist's* mood. He was a very nice man, but I didn't get anywhere. I was dealing with my problems pharmaceutically.

Reality reinforced my despair. When I told people about the treachery of my landlord they shrugged and said the Village was like that. There was a boom in the market and owners were selling properties as fast as they could. Every place I looked at was on a monthly rental basis. My back was killing me. One doctor put me in a hospital for a week with my left leg in traction. It did no good. Harriet Van Horne recommended me to a well-known chiropractor – a godshot who miraculously cured me. But the most unsympathetic of all ailments, the 'bad back', would appear and reappear for many years.

In what seemed to me record time, my landlord sold the house and told me I must vacate my apartment in two months. I took more pills, more booze. In August Tracy came and we went to Aspen. When I returned it was to the basement flat of Charles Street, where my landlord had dumped my furniture. In September, at Tennessee's suggestion, I moved to into his ghastly new high-rise. I hated the place on sight. It teemed with toxic vibes. It had horrible box-like rooms with low ceilings. I hated its bleak streets, its doormen, its rows of mailboxes. But at least I was in the same building as a friend.

30

Valley of the Dolls

I am tempted to say that I moved from Charles Street directly into the Valley of the Dolls. But the truth was far more painful and protracted. In the middle of my life I had lost my way. In contrast to the road up, which had been fast, straight and thrilling, the road down was slow, bumpy, full of false entries, dreary plateaus and no exits.

At times it seemed as if I might halt the descent. I was part of a weekly TV quiz show called *Quote Unquote*. It didn't matter whether you guessed the quote correctly, just as long as you talked amusingly around it. It was fun. It was companionship. Then it went off the air.

My life was episodic. There was no through thread holding it together. I couldn't even thread the needle.

I had long planned to write an article about Dawn Powell. I had the greatest admiration for her books and her wit, which was, as Garrick described Dr Johnson's, 'a forcible hug which shakes laughter out of you whether you will or no'. She was a round partridge-shaped woman with a carefully preserved innocence and impressionability that had stayed with her all during her long years in New York, leaving her both wide-eyed and sharp-tongued. She had remained eternally Village-struck as people remain eternally stagestruck. Each time I was with her

I collected her gems and repeated them all over town, as did everyone else.

'I like rumors,' she once said to me, 'because you can make them up.' I still have her postcard advising me to 'be careful of old friends, be kind to strangers', a nice spin on Tennessee's famous words.

We were having drinks one evening at the Algonquin when my former director John Dexter came over to our table and sat down. 'I hate to table hop,' he said, 'but I wanted to say hello.' 'That's all right,' Dawn assured him, 'who wants to stay with the people you came with?' John's latest play, one of Arnold Wesker's, was a big success on Broadway. John boasted he and Wesker had revolutionized the Royal Court with working-class drama and would be doing the same in New York. Then, as was his wont, he went on to grimly detail his own working-class roots. Finally he stood up. 'Wish I didn't have to leave,' he said. Dawn looked at him. 'Night school?' she asked. 'I'll take that from you,' he said, gagging at the snort of laughter she had shaken out of him, 'I wouldn't from anyone else.' 'He has a store of unearned bitterness,' Dawn remarked after he left. 'I like my bitterness earned.'

One day in '65 I offered Dawn a cigarette. She refused. 'No thanks, I've already got cancer.' I laughed of course. And learned not long after that she did. She died that same year.

Reading Tim Page's biography of her, I came across something I had forgotten. At one of my Charles Street dinner parties Dawn, on a roll, had entertained us at length by describing the Staten Island of her youth. What I didn't know was that another guest, an *Esquire* editor, rang the next day inviting her to repeat verbatim everything she'd said last night in an article for the magazine. And although she replied, 'I wasn't listening,' she wrote it. Her nostalgic vignette of Staten Island was to be her last work.

Flipping through various diaries of '66–'67 I note that I saw Rosemary, Tennessee, Mike Macdonald, Maureen Stapleton, Len Melfi, Severn Darden, Renata Adler and Mike Nichols. I had supper with Claire Bloom and Rod Steiger, who were married at the time. I went out with the actress Patricia Connolly and Danny Kaye, who was enamored of her. He sang in the limo all the way down from the

Sherry Netherlands on Fifth Avenue to Chinatown, where he cooked us a delicious Chinese dinner.

These are among the people whose names I recognize. There are dozens of others with whom I presumably had lunches, dinners, drinks, but they bring forth no accompanying images. I note that I went to some AA beginners' meeting. One entry says: '7.00 p.m. Tim Leary.' This is Timothy Leary in the first flush of the LSD guru-ship that would expand so many minds of that epoch. Significantly, I have no recollection of the meeting.

I note that I went with Shirley to see her new film *Portrait of Jason* at Lincoln Center. I recalled that vividly. Its premise was simple, its result horrific. Shirley in her Chelsea pad placed her camera in front of Jason, a black gay hustler who dreamed of putting together a night-club act, and shot him talking for the next twelve hours (editing it down to 101 minutes). He began on a high: campy, jokey, at ease and eager to please. But as the night wore on he came down off the stuff and, getting drunk his self-mocking laughter bordered on hysteria. His stories of a childhood filled with racial tensions were anything but funny. In the end he emerged as a desperate loser struggling to make something of his life yet knowing he would not. By then Shirley, with the help of Carl taunting and goading Jason on, succeeded in bringing him to borderline breakdown. I was outraged. Could Shirley really imagine for a moment this was 'getting someone to strip bare his soul' or 'giving us deep insight into the Black Condition'? Or that this was Art? For myself, at borderline breakdown as well, it was an inexcusable third-degree grilling any sadistic cop would be proud of. I blamed Carl's evil power over Shirley. Which is nonsense. Shirley knew very well what she was doing; in other words she knew *Portrait of Jason* would score high in shock value. It scored high, period. It has been praised in film circles the world over – 'electrifying' and 'disturbing' are the favorite adjectives – and it remains in the repertory of films shown today in museums and art houses across the country. Pauline Kael, who likes her movies gamy, said to me incredulously, 'How could your sister make such a film?' I shrugged as I slid down a couple of notches more.

Then I made a big effort and went down to Palm Beach to stay with my mother. My diary noted I played tennis, rode a bicycle, got my hair done. I came back to New York. Regularly I got my pill prescriptions filled out by my special prescription doctor.

Tennessee, like many celebrities, was being 'helped' by injections prescribed by Dr Jacobsen, the notorious Dr Feelgood. One day Tennessee took me into his bedroom and showed me his bedside table heaped high with bottles and vials and hypodermic needles. 'Look at that,' he said disgustedly, 'this is what I take every day of my life.' I thought that, except for all the Feelgood apparatus it didn't look that much different from mine. I said, 'I wish you'd get me an appointment with Feelgood. I'm told he only takes people by referral.'

The vehemence of his reply startled me. 'No,' he said. 'I'll never do that to you. No matter how depressed you are, not if you were dying, not if you were on your death bed!' As I said, I had a friend in the building.

One evening in the spring of '67 Tennessee rang my doorbell. He wanted me to go to with him to some big bash. It would cheer me up, he said. It was early in the evening, but I was wearing my nightgown. I said no and went back to bed. He came in and sat on the bed. He was in one of his determined moods and kept on after me to get dressed. I said, 'I've got nothing to wear.' Which was true. All my dresses hung on me because I'd lost so much weight. I knew I should get out, but I couldn't make the effort. Tennessee finally left, but the encounter brought me face to face with how much ground I was losing. Next day I got dressed and began phoning friends.

Some days later Tennessee and his companion Bill Glavin were flying off to Spain. The night before they left they came to say good-bye. Two days later my doorbell rang. It was Tennessee. I feared for my sanity. 'What are you doing here? You're supposed to be in Spain,' Tennessee's four-word reply said it all: 'I forgot my medication.' Collecting the necessary vials, bottles and syringes he was off again. That made sense to me. Have medication, will travel. I traveled a lot that summer: Palm Beach, London, a cruise around the Greek Islands, Dublin to visit Tessa, now living in state with Gareth Browne in a Georgian mansion with peacocks on the lawn.

Four men as lovers came into my life in more or less single file and stayed for different lengths of time in the last days of Charles Street and during those in the ghastly high-rise. Each one was very different from the last in personality and profession. The only pattern I could discern was that although each of them was wrong for me he was not wrong in the way the last one was. Thus a painter who moved in with me but didn't unpack was followed by an actor who spent most of his time in Hollywood, was followed by a writer who was bisexual, was followed by a lawyer who was a conservative. With all these men I felt joy when we met, pain when we faltered, and relief when we parted. I doubled my dose of Ritalin, known as a kinder gentler form of speed than deximyl, to get high, took seconal to sleep and in between scared myself that I might overdose. I dropped out of life and sat in my apartment.

Then it was '68 and I was on my way to my latest psychiatrist ready to throw in the towel. I had just read *Valley of the Dolls*. It made me aware that huge amounts of prescriptions drugs were daily being taken in massive dosages. A growing part of the population was becoming addicted. By vivid examples it showed the fatal grip my addiction was having on my mind and body. It made me ready to take the first step towards saving my life. Far from being a trashy romance the novel was an unflinching, often grueling insider's look at some interesting, gifted, intelligent, flawed women, revealing their answered prayers and the price they paid for them. It included, in horrifying detail, an entirely accurate description of a detox treatment I myself would undergo several times. That it took this book to show me how acutely I was part of the problem and how dangerous it was makes me wonder how many other readers were helped in the same way.

I leveled with my new psychiatrist about my huge pill intake (which I hadn't before), and together we planned to get me out of New York – never a good luck town for me – into some kind of psychiatric setting in order to get me off those pills. We chose Austen Riggs, a therapeutic community in Stockbridge, Massachusetts, where in an open yet protected environment the patients were encouraged to mingle with the normal population in the area to ease them back into life.

Then began for me some eight hard up-and-down, in-and-out years ('68–'76).

At Riggs we patients – some sicker than others, all much younger than I – were housed together in an architecturally attractive New England inn that fed us delicious nutritious meals. I saw a psychiatrist twice weekly and ended up staying at the inn for a year.

I spent the first six months mostly in my room in bed in a paralyzing depression accompanied by panic attacks. I knew it had been waiting all this time to devour me and that I'd been shoaling up drink and pills against it, but I didn't know it would be this bad or this time-consuming. I've been prone to depressions all my life and my expert opinion is that I have never learned a thing from them except that the length of time they last and their intensity prevent you from doing the very things that would cure you of them. I knew that getting out of them had everything to do with physical and mental activity, but I never knew what worked until it was working. There was no foolproof method of getting out from under. When I was up I couldn't remember down; when I was down I couldn't remember up. My journey into my interior disclosed nothing. My search has always been outwards.

The next year, at least physically restored, I moved into a renovated barn on Main Street owned by Dr Campbell. He was the silver-haired reassuring figure who was the original of the famous old-fashioned country doctor immortalized by Norman Rockwell in full color on the covers of the *Saturday Evening Post*. It was to be the home base I would return to for the next seven years.

The depressions continued but they would be followed by months of activity. There was an arts bungalow on the Riggs grounds. I found myself chronologically going back through my life's search for artistic satisfaction and began sculpting heads of friends. I stopped when I reached the excellence of gifted nine-year-olds. Then I began painting and lost interest when I reached the level I'd achieved at college. Then I began acting. There were theatres all over the Berkshires, where the town of Stockbridge was located. I directed too and ran a play contest, the three judges being Gore, the actress Leora Dana and Francis Wyndham.

My closest friend in Stockbridge was a bright, beautiful ten-year-old girl, Brenda Bahnson, whose father was one of the psychiatrists. I had great need of a daughter in my life who I would not let down. We had tea once a week, talking about this and that, including what went on in school. She hated the boys. All the girls did. 'They push you and they pull your hair and call you awful names,' she said, 'but as girls are smarter than boys they're always nice to us around test time so that we'll help them with the questions.' 'So what do you do?' I asked. She smiled and said 'We give them the wrong answers.' I considered how early it all begins.

A couple of years later I embarked upon another novel called *The Injured Party*, a title I'd wanted to use since I'd first heard it on the lips of a divorce lawyer. During this time I also began traveling again. I went to the McDowell Writers' Colony a couple of times, to London, and to see Gore in his resplendent manor, La Rondinaia, in Ravello.

In the first part of *The Injured Party* my heroine is on the staff of a New York magazine. For this section I leaned heavily on my life in the city. There is also a character whose flagellomania I borrowed from Ken as a plot contrivance, though he is unlike him in every other way.

But the part set in a woman's prison was something else. Getting the proper background involved puddle-jumping by plane to land in a small nowhere town that housed a women's Federal prison. Posing as a sociologist, I had been given permission to interview the inmates, the guards and the warden. When I heard the prison gates slam shut behind as I entered I expected to crack open like an egg. Instead the unfamiliarity of the situation energized me and my curiosity shot me forward. I was Columbus without a compass but with land and human life in sight. For several days I was shown around the grounds and buildings of what looked like an underfunded junior college. I had a fine time interviewing everyone, eating meals with the inmates, seeing their rooms, sitting in their recreation halls. I was perfectly comfortable talking to them and envisioning their lives. The odd thought came to me that I *can* go home again – as long as it's someone else's.

After my novel was published in '74 I moved back to London. Mutual friend Jill Bennett told me that Ken, enraged by my novel, held readings of parts of it to prove 'his' character was not him. I replied that of course it wasn't and that I was enraged that he thought he'd cornered the market on sexual sadism. But I had learned something from years of coming up against members of the Riggs community, both patients and staff: other people had a right to hold different views from mine. Privately I granted Ken his right to be angry.

In London I first stayed with Tessa in her house in Paulton Square, then rented a house with some other people on Sloane Avenue. The house was large and always cluttered with people I didn't know or like. Sometime at the beginning of '76 it served as the background for a return bout of disaster. I downed several dangerous pain killing tablets called Heminevren before joining a friend for drinks. When I came to I was in the emergency ward of St Stephen's hospital in the Fulham Road, staring at a priest saying the last rites of the Catholic Church over me. I don't know which of us was more surprised.

31

Starting Over

In the aftermath of the priest and the emergency room and all that I knew, there was nowhere to go but up. But when? My mother came and we flew back to New York where I languished despondent all summer in her apartment and made my will.

In autumn I was saved by a happy confluence of events that grew, one out of the other, with miraculous speed, good fortune attracting good fortune as money is said to attract money.

To begin with I was dramatically rescued from despondency by three electroshock treatments I received at Mount Sinai Hospital. They did for me what years of therapy was not able to. Believe that. I can't think why modern electroshock, which time and again has proved successful in curing depression, gets such a bad rap but this is not the place to argue the case.

After the first treatment I moved to the Stanhope Hotel on Fifth Avenue at 82nd Street. From the minute I walked into its large studio room, with windows overlooking Central Park near the Metropolitan Museum of Art, I knew I was safe once more. I saw old friends, especially Jeannie Campbell and Len Melfi, and found new ones, like the theatre and book critic Rhoda Koenig, whom I met at Plimpton's fiftieth birthday party. Again I was able to give parties.

I didn't know it but I was about to enter my final literary phase. I can track its beginning from the day I went to see Clay Felker at *New York* magazine and asked him for an assignment. He arranged for me to see a preview of Paddy Chayefsky's latest film *Network*. He wanted me to do a piece about its director – Sidney Lumet! We'd not seen each other since he'd given me Charles Street. Now he was again to play a part in my destiny. I saw *Network* and was bowled over by it. Unquestionably it was going to be the movie of the year. Writing about Sidney was a piece of cake. Every fine actor of the time had worked with him so I selected a couple, plus Chayefsky himself and a famous film editor, and interviewed them.

Next in sequence was the editor of the *New York Times Book Review* who asked me to review a biography of Vivien Leigh. When I received the book I saw it was by Anne Edwards, whom I'd known when I was living in Stockbridge. I'd read her book on Judy Garland and thought it excellent. She had known Judy, and this knowledge had gained her many insights, but she had never met Vivien, a fact she mentioned to me when once considering doing this subject. Now I wondered how far wrong she might go.

I began reading it. This is Vivien, I kept thinking, turning page after page. *How does she do it?* The facts were abundant, the interpretations brilliant, but other things went into making this not a 'biography' but an unfolding life. Edwards had written it always keeping in sight the most important thing that marks our daily existence: we never know what may happen. Only by successfully reproducing this built-in suspense is biography most able to resemble life. Added to this Edwards possessed what may be one of the most important virtues a biographer can have: the quality of mercy, a sort of agonized tenderness that she extended to her subject. It let us see Vivien Leigh from Vivien's point of view.

My review came out in May. Anne Edwards's *Vivien* had had an inspiring, galvanizing effect on me. She'd shown me the way a biography could be as exciting as a novel and, best of all, you didn't have to make up a plot. 'For strange effects and extraordinary combinations,' says Sherlock Holmes, 'we must go to life itself which is far more daring than any act of the imagination.'

When I came to Vivien's affair with Peter Finch I found myself thinking of his magnificent performance in *Network* and of his other fine performances in films and on stage, most of which I had seen. That January, at the height of his career, he'd died suddenly of a heart attack in the lobby of the Beverly Hills Hotel. I remember how shocked and saddened I had been. From the '50s on Peter Finch and I had known each other. Once, while explaining to me why he was a Buddhist, he'd told me that aged nine he had been a boy Buddhist in India for two years. When this memory surfaced I sprang into action.

At the Lincoln Center Film Library I came across some surprising biographical data. His father, George Ingle Finch, M.B.S. and Fellow of the Royal Society, was a decided personage. Both distinguished scientist and mountaineer, he had climbed Everest with Leigh Mallory on his first expedition in 1922. Although Peter's parents were divorced, they were both living in England. Why then was he brought up in Australia? Why did he never hear from either of them? What questions that raised. What mysteries to be solved. What a story it foretold.

In August I left for London with contracts from both American and English publishers to do a biography. I got to work, immediately re-establishing old theatre contacts and staying on for five months.

Then in January of '78, leaving from Rome, I flew to Australia where I would spend the next five months on the trail of the wander-lust actor. Revelations of his life and background grew daily more incredible. The last person I had seen before I left Europe was Gore. Just before I boarded the plane he had said 'Remember, Australians are a day ahead of you so they already know what's going to happen to you.' To which I had replied, 'The whole purpose of this exercise is that I don't.'

In September of 1980 I came over from London to New York for the American publication of my Peter Finch biography. I'd left London early because Ken's memorial was being held then and I wished to avoid being asked for comments. I'd sent a cable expressing my sympathy to his wife Kathleen and answered her request to list all Ken's Oxford friends, but it wasn't, so to speak, my funeral: I'd written my farewell to him in May when he was dying. When Tracy called me on July 26 to tell of his death the day before the official announcement, my thoughts were mainly with her.

At any rate, here I was in New York with nothing to do but worry about my upcoming reviews.

Shirley was in town. We arranged to meet one evening at a sidewalk café in the East 50s. The first words out of her mouth were, 'New York is now a year-round summer festival! The arts have completely taken over the city.' Right away I saw this was a new Shirley, and it was not only this exuberant remark or the fact that she now wore her hair gray and had put on some weight (when I'd last seen her she was gaunt). She still sat gracefully, as became a former dancer, and rose in one fluid movement when we finished our espressos, but now it was as if something hitherto wound angrily up inside her had uncoiled. After she promised to show me New York *en fête* we wandered down the streets where we came across a mime group, then a string quartet, then a theatre group wrestling with a Shakespeare comedy. All were receiving the same rapt attention that New Yorkers had previously bestowed upon construction gangs.

Later in my hotel room she looked askance as, confessing to an attack of pre-publication nerves, I wolfed down some codeine tablets, but she made no comment. Instead she produced seven packs of multivitamins to be taken daily for a week. She guaranteed they would cure all my ills. In lieu of the bitter diatribes she'd unleashed in the past against film people in the male-directed industry who'd led her on and let her down, she kept saying surprisingly positive things like, 'New York blacks have successfully moved into the middle class.' When I commented on how upbeat she'd become, she replied with one of the most unexpected remarks I'd ever heard her utter. 'It turns out,' she said, and her voice was clear and sweet and pure, 'it turns out that Dale Carnegie was right. You do need to win friends to influence people.' She was teaching at UCLA and I feared she'd fallen in with one of those self-realization cults and that I was going to get a lecture. But she'd simply said her last word on it.

After she left I felt an enormous sense of relief. Shirley was all right again. She was again the energetic potent self I'd called upon so often in my youth. I recognized the huge emotional investment I had in her well-being. What I felt that night was the peculiar sense of gratification that comes from blood ties and family pride. We might have some crazy addictive stuff in our genes that predisposed us to choose the difficult men that chose us, but we had it in us to pick ourselves up and begin again.

In the past Shirley's relationship with Carl had driven a wedge between us. At some point when with her I would find myself saying, 'You still with Carl?' And if she said, 'Yes,' all subsequent conversation tended to cool off. Then in '70, when she came up to see me in Stockbridge and said, 'Carl's gone to California,' I gathered she'd gotten rid of him by sending him to LA to find film work.

Sometime in the '70s, when Shirley had moved to LA and I was in London talking on the phone with her, I began hearing her bitter tirades spewing out as she described her failure to get projects off the ground with Hollywood producers. Then she would begin to quote the praises Ingmar Bergman and Elia Kazan had heaped on her films to increase her sense of injury. I knew she was with Carl again and with all that it entailed but wanted no part of it. It matched too closely my own mood in the house on Sloane Avenue from which I was about to take my dive into the emergency room.

In '75 Shirley became a professor of film at UCLA. She taught directing and gave a class in the video camera – the first professor to teach the new medium, thereby legitimizing it. Then in '77, while I was working on Peter Finch, I received from her two newspaper clippings: the first was a write-up of an experimental play she'd directed, which the critic panned, the second an interview with her the next day in the same paper saying the critic was right, the play was too negative and that it was no longer the way to go. Soon after she called me to say, 'I've broken with Carl. I sent him back to New York.' There was a pause. Then she added, sighing like a teenager, 'And now I'm not in love anymore.' My heart sank as I tried to figure out if there was more regret than relief in her voice, but afterwards there was a freer flow of exchange than we'd had for a long time. Every now and then friends of hers from California, vague as to how they'd met her, would drop by en route to Paris, or the Lebanon, or wherever, with greetings from

Shirley. I somehow had the sense she'd asked them specially to see if I was all right. This touched me. Probably because I was all right.

So in New York that evening in '80, at the sidewalk café when she told me the city was now a year-round summer festival, I suppose I'd already had hints of the new Shirley. But now there was confirmation; now there was rapprochement.

I saw my biography of Finch through its American publication and – with Shirley's help – arranged a retrospective of his most interesting films to be shown at an art cinema. Then instead of returning to London, where I'd bought a house on the King's Road, I stayed on in New York for a while. Something unexpected, tempting and tantalizing had come up. Something I was giving a lot of thought to.

I was wondering if I should do a biography of Elvis Presley, whom I hadn't known was alive until he died. This statement is always greeted with howls of disbelief. People's memories are short. They forget that back then, before his death, it was quite possible to get through a day without hearing his name. I knew of course there was such a being as Elvis, and had been aware of the tumult he caused in the '50s. But, strange as it may seem today, it was easy then never to see an Elvis movie, or watch him on TV, or rave about his act in Vegas. All that changed for the world when he died on August 16, 1977 and for months his specter filled the airwaves. Curious, I bought one of his gospel albums, He Touched Me, and was instantly struck by his musical genius. I reacted with the zeal of a convert and bought a hi-fi stereo tape deck. With musician friends advising me I bought cassette after cassette of his albums. His voice began singing inside me as it has with billions of people the world over.

But should I write a biography about him? My agent, Mitch Douglas, was urging me to. He had discussed the idea with some publishers and they were very interested. I told him there were already books about Elvis up through the ceiling and many more in the works. But, countered Mitch, there hadn't been a biography by a known woman writer. Good point. Still, my friends thought I'd gone not only out of my mind but my realm. They were not backward in pointing out it was not the right step for me to be taking in my career, given my background and experience.

One day, still dithering, I asked Shirley what she thought. 'You and Elvis?' she said, 'Wow!' That was all. But in my ears it sounded an endorsement and a challenge. It stirred my blood. It tipped the scales. It was the Wow! that carried me to Tupelo.

First, however, more about Shirley, who left this planet on September 23, 1997.

32

Shirley Clarke Leaves This Planet

Deliver Us From Evil Whose Presence Remains Unexplained. In 1986 I sold my house in London and migrated to Los Angeles. That's a lot of migration. However, as Ben Franklin famously said in 1770 in argument that the American settlers had quit their allegiance to Parliament in emigrating to America, 'The right of migration is natural to all men. It is a natural law.' I seem to have used and reused this right, but perhaps I was just going with the flow. My choice of LA was based partly on it being the home of my daughter Tracy (by then a film costume designer and married to director Jim McBride), partly on my lovely memories of Hollywood and the Chateau Marmont in the '60s where I was currently staying, and partly on the climate.

I thought Shirley would be at UCLA but she had resigned and relocated to New York. She wrote me a letter with addresses of her friends in Los Angeles and only when I received it did I understand the changes in her that had so impressed me. She sent me two separate lists of friends. On one she listed those in AA, on the other those who weren't. The puzzle fell into place. Like the increasing number of people I knew, she too had joined the program. So, I concluded, all that hokey shit must really work.

In '86 Shirley came for the Los Angeles opening of *Ornette Coleman: Made in America*, her documentary of the black modern jazz composer and saxophonist. It had been a second chance for her, she told me, basking in its triumph. In the late '60s she'd started the project for public TV. They disliked what she showed them and fired her. Crying as she walked down the street, she was hailed by a cinematographer who showed her a new camera just on the market. It was the video camera, and she instantly fell in love with it. She bought one and took it everywhere she went. She put Ornette aside and moved on. Then in the '80s one of the oil-rich Bass brothers from Fort Worth, wanting to call attention to his town, decided to memorialize its most famous home-grown musical genius, Ornette Coleman. Bass found Shirley with all her previously shot film footage intact and was keen to back her if she would make this feature-length film. This she did spectacularly, consolidating the Ornette then and the Ornette now, his small son then and his toweringly tall son now, all with her innovative mixings of film with video tape. She even made Ornette into a video jazz game.

All the while she was talking I was registering her glorious transformation, so one day I casually mentioned that if she was going to AA meetings she might take me along. We went to a few speaker meetings and lunched with some of her friends. I'd been around this block several times in New York and London and it hadn't taken, but I found LA meetings different. Night or day they seemed to take place in sunlight, while those others seemed to take place in gloom. I was impressed by the numbers, by their Southern Californian go-for-it spirit, by the diversity of the people, which seemed to be a cross-section of the town, and by how many were young. Early on I commented to a friend how wonderfully the young people talked, saying it must be because of all those mind-expanding drugs they'd been doing. He said they were only talking about themselves. I said that was all I wanted to hear.

To me from the very beginning the program was about listening, about being borne away on a magic carpet to the wilder shores of life where one cliff-hanging episode followed another through which I saw that the terrible, terrible things that happened when we were loaded were also terribly funny. Above all, I heard about those close encounters with death through which we had all lived to tell our tales. It was Shirley who opened the door for me. It was the program that kept me there.

Around '88, the Museum of Contemporary Art flew Shirley out to LA to film a celebrated octogenarian dancer's special performance for their archives. They were using the auditorium of an old movie palace and Shirley asked me to be part of the audience. At the second break I saw her sitting alone at the end of a row and went up to her. I'd brought along a friend whom I introduced, she ignored him and looked at me as if I were a stranger. 'Did you actually interrupt me just to say that?' she retorted, sounding as if she could not believe my impertinence. My friend and I backed off. He was embarrassed. I was angry. We left soon after. Next morning I reconsidered. Maybe I'd interrupted an important thought sequence of hers? So I called her. She said, 'Were you there?' I caught my breath but merely said yes and we talked a little longer. Immediately I got off the phone I called her daughter Wendy, wanting to know if there was something wrong. Wendy said that for weeks her mother's behaviour had been truly eccentric – even for her. She was arranging for Shirley to see a new doctor. I felt a clutch of terror as the unspoken lethal word floated in the air.

October 2, 1988 was Shirley's seventieth birthday. To celebrate it she threw a party at the Filmmakers' Co-operative, the pioneer company she had founded with Jonas Mekas in '62. The gathering was attended by friends, colleagues and acquaintances. Our sister Betty was there with her daughter, Liza Lorwin. So was Shirley's longtime friend and fellow Chelseaite Viva, the Andy Warhol superstar, and other artistic types staying or hanging out at the Chelsea who happened to hear of it. It was a blast, I learned two days later, poolside at the Chateau Marmont, from a young actress who'd been a guest. And how was Shirley? I asked. 'Great, just great. Your sister is fabulous!' In joyous relief, I urged pool service on her, fresh orange juice, sandwiches, pastry, champagne – anything.

In today's terms, seventy is no great age. Shirley should have enjoyed the septuagenarian's satisfaction of looking back at past accomplishments while confidently looking forward to future ones. Of her past struggles she was able to say to Professor Dee Dee Halleck, whose mentor she was: 'Things are changing. I recently had five retrospectives. There's a sense of respect when I walk into a room. I was always on my way up and now I realize I'm no longer on my way up.' Shirley had her choice of teaching jobs and projects, but she couldn't do any of them. She was plunging instead into the senseless cruelty of Alzheimer's: the disease that kept her alive while wrecking all her hopes.

During the period of doubt I called Shirley frequently, sending her good luck charms and books of daily meditations with words of wisdom from Orwell, de Tocqueville, Shakespeare and their ilk. After a while Shirley herself began to know something was wrong and went to the Lahey Clinic in Boston for a series of tests. She called me shortly after to tell me they had found nothing. Triumphantly I called Wendy, saying, 'See? She's all right!' 'That means she *does* have Alzheimer's,' said Wendy. 'Elaine, you can stay in denial if you like, but I can't.'

Shirley was to spend her Alzheimer's years with David Cort and his family. Shirley and David shared that special relationship possible between a man and a women who are not lovers but the closest of friends and coworkers. They met in the early '70s through their mutual enthusiasm for the video camera. When David and his wife Piper first came out to Los Angeles they stayed with Shirley and she got him a teaching job, and David and Shirley subsequently worked harmoniously together on many of her projects. In her entry stages of the disease she grew more and more dependent on him, and when it became clear that she had Alzheimer's she was visiting the Corts in Winchester, a suburb of Boston. Wendy and David went to various nursing homes in Boston and New York and LA but found them too bleak and awful to subject my sister to. It was then they mutually decided that Shirley would live with the Corts, who would care for her, while her upkeep would be paid by Shirley's funds.

'It was easy for me to take her in,' says David. 'I worshipped her and her work and in befriending me she honored me, she valued me, and that was enough for me to want to take her in.'

On May 31, 1992 I went to Boston to visit her at the Corts'. On our way to Winchester David warned me to expect changes in Shirley. I said I was prepared. He told me she might not recognize me but she talked a lot about her sisters and growing up together. She had become very particular about her clothes. 'She won't wear anything that isn't black or white or red.' I laughed. Then he talked about the hip replacement surgery she'd had a while back. The surgery was successful, but nevertheless she was in a wheelchair. 'She can't remember how to walk and she can't learn anything new. That's part of the disease.' I sat silent while the enormity of this hit me.

In the Corts' kitchen I sat at the table and David introduced me to his wife, Piper, and their twins Adrienne and Bess, girls aged eight or nine. Then David went to get Shirley and wheeled her in.

She looked so well – slim, her complexion smooth, her chin pointed, her sprite look – and it nearly undid me. She wore a jaunty black felt hat, a red and black sweater. She looked as if there was nothing wrong with her. It seemed to me that she did not recognize me but then I'd only been there about ten minutes. She began talking in a Southern Belle accent, something about going down to the levée or leaving Mississippi. Perhaps she was connecting me with my college days in Virginia or her own in North Carolina.

David brought in a collection of leather-bound photograph albums Shirley had painstakingly preserved for some fifty years. Carefully he placed them on the kitchen table. They had pictures of the three of us growing up together. Wendy had removed them from her mother's rooms at the Chelsea and brought them to the Corts' house so that Shirley might have them to hand.

There were albums of us taken over the summers we went to Camp Fernwood beginning when Shirley was thirteen. There was Shirley, captain of the Green Team, poised and in charge. There I was, skinny, sitting cross-legged, in the front row. There was Betty, our younger sister, a beautiful blonde smiling child. As I looked at the rows of girls in camp uniforms I was surprised to see how easily their names and personalities came back to me. I began naming them aloud and talking about them. I thought she was interested –if only sporadically.

It was becoming clear that she did not know me. She looked at me with relentless non-recognition. She would talk in her Scarlett O'Hara voice and I couldn't follow what she was saying. Before I came I thought that, should this be the case, I, who had spent so many years in close proximity with her, would find the key, crack the code and we'd get through to each other. But I couldn't.

Sunlight made the kitchen glow warm. Piper was preparing us a meal of roast chicken and vegetables, a favorite of Shirley's. My sister had to be partially fed when she ate, but she had a good appetite; she still loved food. Then David wheeled her into her room for a nap – she slept a lot – and I went with her. It was a good-sized room containing her bed and a television set and a tape recorder and all sorts of *objets trouvés* and artifacts and photographs and stuffed animals dear to her. I saw the photograph of Shirley holding a statue of her beloved Felix the Cat made into an Oscar statuette to commemorate her Academy Award. I'd always thought my sister resembled him, sharing his playful spirit. In fact, in her favorite bowler hat and tight smart suits she had been described as a combination of Felix the Cat and Betty Boop.

Piper and I went down to the village to the gourmet delicatessen where I bought things that Shirley especially liked. Then we went to a toy store, where I bought some beautiful small silver jacks such as Shirley and I used to play with as children but I had not seen since. Maybe she would remember them.

When we came back Shirley was in the living room with the Cort twins. Clearly she was comfortable with them. The jacks didn't interest her so I gave them to the twins. There was music playing. David said how much she liked the great thirties and forties show tunes we grew up with, which I knew had formed the sophisticated background against which she played out her teenage popularity.

Late in the afternoon we were all back in the kitchen and when it was time to leave I rose and started to collect my things. David, who was driving me back to Boston, also got ready to go. Perhaps it was the physical action of leave-taking that penetrated Shirley's consciousness, for she flashed into a moment of clarity and wailed, '*I can't do anything!*' And with that awful realization she broke down and cried, 'Isn't anyone going to be nice to me?' I hugged her and left.

When I returned next day she suddenly said, 'You look like me.' A breakthrough!

'Of course I do, I'm your sister,' I exclaimed.

'No. You're me.'

And I resented her saying that! Because somewhere in the pre-reasoning days of childhood that was exactly how I'd felt. I'd had no separate existence from my sister but had been her shadow, who only came to life when she permitted me. And I was still angry about it. I still resented this power she had over me even as I sat before her horrified that I was unable to silence these thoughts.

Back in Boston I thought I should have answered her 'You're me' with 'And you're me'. Because we'd helped each other whenever we could, and now we couldn't anymore. So I was myself again. But I was alone. I never went to see her again, but every time my phone rang in those years I thought it might be the news that she was dead. Every morning I devoted a corner of my thoughts to her. I would pray for her but for what? Peace, I suppose. And I would lash out at myself in guilt and when it became unbearable I would call David, talk to him, send packages of music tapes, including Algerian folk music that Ornette had suggested, and Elvis tapes, particularly his gospel. I sent her the Lincoln School graduating class yearbook hoping she might recognize herself and her friends in it, but she didn't. I sent her woolen socks with booties, scarves, gourmet clover honey, eau de cologne, body lotions for massage. I worked my way through the chain of command at UCLA convinced her professorship had lasted long enough to produce a pension. I was told she had left only months before achieving tenure. I was never to see her alive again.

But I did see Shirley again when I traveled to Madison, Wisconsin, where her archives are housed. I stayed for days, losing myself in her interviews and her work, and came upon a couple of masterpieces. *Savage/Love* and *Tongues* are two monologues written for the stage by Sam Shepherd and acted by Joe Chaikin. For television, using video tape, Shirley reinvented them, taking the highly charged monologues and tripling their effect. While Chaikin talks straight to us, we see the back of his head and his profile as well. Shirley's camera, immersed in the rhythm of the actor's tirades, leaps as the mind leaps, swings to every nuance of his emotion. Boldly it pulls his face this way and that, stretches it horizontally then elongates it. As the text swells so do his multiple images. By the end of these grand sprees I had willingly surrendered my disbelief and accepted Shirley's idiosyncratic vision of truth.

I left Madison gladdened by what I'd seen, knowing I'd missed out on something that had always been available to me: I'd seen her work but I'd never seen her working.

Shirley's last days were spent in the Deaconess Palliative Hospice in Boston. They were, like everything about her, extraordinary. Gravely ill after a stroke that prevented her from eating or drinking, or from speaking, seeing or hearing, she lingered without a support machine for fifteen days. Asleep most of the time, her vital signs were normal.

Wendy, helped by David and Piper, had chosen to transform her mother's impending death into a celebration, and her hospital room into a homage. They filled Shirley's room with flowers sent by friends and relatives, and on its walls they taped photographs that had once meant so much to her and on a table were cherished artifacts. She lay on her special mattress under her red blanket.

When I called on Saturday, September 20, – Day 11 of Wendy's vigil – she and David reported an astonishing event that happened that day. They were unexpectedly joined by some friends, a group of film- and videomakers they had not seen for years who had found her whereabouts through the grapevine. As Shirley lay dying they sipped champagne and reminisced about her and how her work paved the way for the MTV generation.

The next day, when I relayed the description of the gathering to our sister Betty, she said, 'It's so like a film Shirley would make.'

On the morning of September 23 – Day 15, an exhausted Wendy called. Shirley had died in her sleep at 2.00 a.m. When Wendy went in to see Shirley, they had laid her out. 'She looked luminous.'

It was wonderful to see her obituary appear in so many newspapers, in so many cities – at home and abroad. People kept sending me obituaries from London, Paris, Philadelphia. And the obituaries themselves were so special, capturing her so well, her achievements and her strivings, struggles and setbacks. You felt she interested them, that they responded to what one of them called 'this graceful candid woman' who described herself as an 'out-of-the-system person politically and emotionally'. Whether or not this generation of obituary writers – or readers – knew her work or even knew of her before she died, they loved the idea of Shirley Clarke.

A few months later came her retrospectives and tributes. The Museum of Modern Art and the Anthology of Film Archives led the way. Both were presented by Wendy, a video artist herself. I attended the opening of UCLA's tribute and seven-day retrospective in April. Seeing the program that catalogued her films I saw that Shirley had videotaped Beats, Beatles and the Buddhists. She'd videotaped Alan Watts giving a Zen lesson, and Harry Smith being his multiple self: cosmological master, painter, anthropologist, musicologist, linguist, occultist, and anthologizer of the famous six albums collection. One day in November in '70, Shirley, ever given to grand gesture, had presented Harry with her Bolex 16mm camera, declaring she no longer had any use for it. From then on she intended only to use her video camera. Together in the Chelsea they shot a multi-framed version of the Brecht–Weill musical *Mahagonny*. One sequence had Alan Ginsberg hugging a toy lamb on wheels quoting Blake's famous poem.

I read of Shirley's free-wheeling generosity to fellow artists. I read of Shirley teaching her students at the Chelsea, dividing them up into five groups, sending them on a dawn patrol to video day breaking in the city. Then, back in her penthouse they cued up the tapes from each group into her five monitors, and with bagels and champagne they toasted the pink sky and switched on the decks for a multichannel view of morning in New York: steam rising from street vents, bottle collectors pushing their carts, pigeons flying from left to right across the five tapes as though choreographed, pastel skyscrapers with windows reflecting the rising red sun ball. 'We were urban guerrillas of the Chelsea penthouse plotting an electronic coup that would liberate the imaginations of the world,' said one student. Said another, 'She taught me how to be an artist. She taught me how to enjoy not conforming.'

'At this moment, high above us on a flickering celestial screen an imp-like Shirley in a spiffy bowler hat morphs in and out with Felix in a perpetual soft shoe routine. Goodnight, Shirley. May some of us, your students, transmit electric visions as sassy and brilliant as you and Felix with an edge as sharp and a passion as deep,' wrote Professor Halleck, sending Shirley off *not* to rest but to keep inspiring and educating the next generation.

PART FOUR

DISCOVERING ELSEWHERE

33

Anybody Is As Their Land Is

'After all, anybody is as their land and air is. Anybody is as the
sky is low or high, the air heavy or clear and anybody is as there
is wind or no wind there. It is that which makes them and the
arts they make and the work they do and the way they eat and
the way they drink and the way they learn and everything.'

Gertrude Stein, *An American in France*

Chronology notwithstanding, I travel back in this concluding
chapter to my yesterdays of twenty years ago, bringing up to
date the final change it wrought in me. If Shirley's tragedy was
an experience to be endured, discovering Elvis and his land was an
education to be cherished.

In April '81 I arrived in Tupelo. Before I left London I told my
friends I was going to Elvis's birthplace 'to find the source of the Nile
and its tributaries'. But I had no plan. I knew no one and nothing
about Tupelo. That was the way I wanted it. I wanted to come from
what Walker Percy calls 'innocence and distance'. It was the old western movie gimmick: a stranger comes to town. I am that stranger. Let
me take you with me and make sense of it all.

I was staying at the Ramada Inn in a room facing the pool. The boy
with my luggage turned on the air-conditioning and I went from the
oppressive heat outside into a blast of invigorating frozen air. The
room instantly struck me as a marvel of functional design neatly
divided into areas. All this was probably standard chain hotel fare of
the period, but I'd never been in one before and it made me feel very
welcome.

It was afternoon by the time I finished unpacking. I lay down to rest and drifted off to sleep to be awakened by the echoing laughter of children's voices in the Ramada pool. I went outside and in the dusk I saw the pool filled with little black kids. It was the beginning of seeing things that didn't make sense to me. Certainly black families would not be welcomed here. Didn't Mississippi have one of the worst civil rights records in America? I thought of the violent events set off here that summer when blacks sought their right to vote. In pursuing the matter, I was informed at the desk, offhandedly, that Tupelo is a big family reunion town and that black families from everywhere in the country who have their roots in Mississippi choose the Ramada for their yearly gatherings. I realized no matter how hard I'd determined not to prejudge I'd come loaded with prejudice. This one was years out of date. Later that night, in the dark, my city psyche thrilled to the unfamiliar sounds of crickets, whippoorwills, frogs and owls. Still later the noise filtering into my room was that of a combo playing in the Ramada nightclub. The music was so good it lulled me to sleep. This, at least was one of the beliefs I came in with that checked out: no music either played or sung by Mississippians would ever be bad.

My education had begun. The source of the Nile was where I suspected it would be: Elvis's mother. But both the source and its tributaries were an education I was led into by the inestimable help, often the enthusiastic co-operation of many people. I am thinking particularly of Corene Smith, Phyllis Harper and Roy Turner.

I stayed at the Ramada for over five months, with side trips to the University of Mississippi and to Memphis. I had arrived on a Friday and by Sunday I was listening to a sermon preached by Brother Frank Smith, Elvis's first pastor at the First Assembly of God church. His sermon surprised me: impassioned yes, fire and brimstone no. It was on the healing power of tears. His wife Corene, who had been a neighbor of the Presleys in East Tupelo became friends with me. We would meet in the evenings at the Waffle House, where, over hundreds of cups of coffee far into the night, she would describe what Elvis and East Tupelo were like when he was growing up.

My second friend was Phyllis Harper, features editor and columnist of the *Tupelo Daily Journal*, whom I met while I was going through the newspaper's archives. She had been born and raised in Fawn Grove, near Tupelo, and after a cosmopolitan life had returned. She knew the town inside-out. She saw what I couldn't, why I was running into a wall of silence with certain citizens. Experience had turned them suspicious. Phyllis explained that they may have believed there was an Elaine Dundy whose novels were in the Lee County Library, but they just didn't believe it was me. 'I'm going to do a piece about you,' she said suddenly. Her article, headlined 'Established Writer in Tupelo to Research Presley', succeeded in validating me. It opened many doors, not only important ones that might have been shut had I tried to storm them cold, but doors I had no way of knowing even existed.

Tupeloans are in love with words. They easily and enjoyably recalled events for me with a precision that made me see images rising up behind them as they talked.

After about a month in Tupelo I started to feel the need of all sorts of documentary evidence: accurate dates, confirmed facts, family trees with their appropriate backgrounds. What I required was a genealogist. I first met Roy Turner, a brilliant twenty-eight-year-old, that May in his house with his wife Debbie and their children. He was then the Corresponding Secretary of the Northeast Historical and Genealogical Society of Mississippi. His day job was working in public relations at Sunshine Mills. Over the breakfast table Roy and I sat from 4 p.m. till 10 p.m. while he pored over marriage, census, school and cemetery records and crash-coursed me in the arcane ways of genealogy and the intuitive leaps you had to make before turning up a documented solution. It was better than a detective story. It was Roy who discovered that Elvis's great-great-great-grandmother through her maternal line the Mansells was a Native American Cherokee named Mourning Dove.

Back in London I did some sleuthing on my own and discovered another important tributary. Elvis was often quoted as saying that he was the hero of every comic book he'd read. One day I sat down in a comics bookshop to look at those popular when he was growing up and came across all those double identity heroes he must have read from Superman to the Spirit. Then I came across Elvis's face staring at me from its pages: Captain Marvel Jr. Being himself a twin the double identity of the powerful young captain and the powerless Freddie Freeman existing in the same body would have a special meaning for Elvis. Here was the boy he aspired to be and the boy he was. I began to see how Captain Marvel Jr actually formed Elvis's personality, humble and humorous, how subconsciously the grown Elvis copied his hero's glistening black hair and sideburns and triumphant stance. Years later he wore his version of the Captain Marvel Jr cape, and the white scarf Freddie Freeman often wore turns up around Elvis's neck in performance. Most important was Elvis's taking over the lightning bolt emblem that Marvel wore on his chest. It became Elvis's logo, his signature, turning up on his private plane, in his game room, on the jewelry he gave special friends, the gold neck chains and bracelets. All of them were designed with Captain Marvel Jr's lightning bolt in the center.

It was Elvis twinning into Captain Marvel Jr that made me see the powerful twinning tributary that ran through his life. He twinned into all different forms of music, making him a different kind of singer from any other of the great entertainers such as Al Jolson, Maurice Chevalier, Frank Sinatra, Bing Crosby, Judy Garland and Nat King Cole, who sang only in their own voices. He had a whole range of voices that he sang in that were appropriate to the song. As a tour de force Country singer Buddy Bain pointed out that in the hymn 'How Great Thou Art' 'you can hear Elvis go from Metropolitan Opera to country, to folk, to blues, to rock, almost from note to note without breaking the feel.'

My book *Elvis and Gladys* took me four and a half years to write and I wasn't bored for a minute. What I did not foresee was that I had embarked on a journey that would continue to the present day. Also it may be said that it had two lives. When it came out in hardback it was well reviewed and did well enough. Only when it came out in its first large paperback edition did I begin getting mail from all parts of the world. By far the most frequent theme to emerge in these letters was Elvis as Healer, as Saver, indeed as Savior. It was uncanny how often these letters disclosed the same psychological profile and charted the same course. Brutal fathers and frightened mothers produced children who, by their own choice, 'lived almost in seclusion'.

Until, discovering Elvis and his music, he became a major part of their lives. 'Whenever anything went wrong,' a Canadian woman wrote to me, 'I knew I could turn to Elvis's music and he would help me through.' There was also, in late adolescence, a history of near sui- cidal attempts that the children saved themselves from because they 'thought of Elvis' and even 'heard his voice'. His death had not ended his power in their lives and they still call on him in their crises. One young boy wrote he was in a foster home in a small town in Michigan and asked me to tell him where the nearest Elvis Fan Club was. The letters reminded me of what a London psychiatrist had said: 'When Elvis went into the army I had to treat English children for grief.'

Elvis's birthday on January 8, 1987, ten years after his death, was like one of those shots heard round the world. Fans and curiosity-seekers alike overflowed on the Graceland lawn to celebrate it with a birthday cake. This had been happening for nine years but interest was swelling: the increasing numbers in attendance; the TV channels filled with Elvis movies (those most available unfortunately the worst); radio sta- tions broadcasting for a week twenty-four hours a day from all twenty-three years of Elvis music; Oprah's show about the 'Elvis Phenomenon', during which she herself confessed to dreaming that she would marry Elvis until she grew up and knew she wouldn't; a book in which a woman claimed to have a child by Elvis received much attention. The media picked up the message and ran with it. So did I.

By the end of May I realized I would return to Tupelo and Memphis for several weeks around August 16, Elvis's tenth death anniversary. I had to be there. I wanted to see the good friends I had made in those towns, and what the festivities were like. I'd never met a bonafide Elvis fan face to face and I was curious. The media had gone into such a feeding frenzy about Elvis that I wondered how it would all end. And, to be honest, I did just wonder if Elvis might not give us some sort of Sign from Beyond.

Arriving in Tupelo on August 6, I again stayed at the Ramada Inn and spent the first days pleasurably renewing my friendships with people who now felt like old friends.

On August 10 the English Elvis Presley Fan Club, some 2,000 strong, arrived. They behaved not like English soccer fans then banned the world over, but like English people always behave in crowds: jolly and polite. At breakfast the dining room at the Ramada was full of them. It felt as if I had arrived at a popular English seaside resort. The women were dressed in traditional English summer frocks of splashy prints. The men, with their Anglo-Saxon pink complexions, white shirts, gray flannels and navy blue blazers, were smoking pipes and gave an overall impression of representing the conservative element of fans. The young folk – a surprising number of them – went in for the universal punk chic: boots, belts, jeans and T-shirts sporting frisky slogans.

I joined the crowd gathered at Elvis Presley Park for the opening ceremonies of Elvis Presley Week in Tupelo. Standing in the shadeless heat, bright red circles sprang before my eyes. Speeches were kept blessedly short, but even so by the end of them twelve Brits were overcome by the heat and had to be carried off to be revived at the local hospital.

I met Daphne Brown from Wales, who had been to Tupelo seven times. It turned out that we had corresponded. I remembered her letter well, for it contained the information that in the south-western part of Wales lie the Preseli Hills, which figure prominently in the story of prehistoric Pembrokeshire, and that in the Bronze Age the 'Prescelli' tribe was dominant over the whole of southwest Wales. Further, there is a Welsh parish called St Elvis. The coincidence of meeting her reminded me that it is a small Elvis world as well as a wide one. It was extraordinary, this coming together of perfect strangers, finding we had in common not only Elvis and his music, but a shared history of years gone by: of the Second World War, of marriages and births and deaths, of good times and bad times that had marked us all.

That evening at the Ramada Convention Center there was a dinner for the English contingent, followed by an all-Elvis disco that lasted till dawn. If there is one thing no one will dispute, it is the danceability of Elvis's music, but it was the first time I had watched such numbers swept up in it. I was struck by the variety of kinds of dancing the music lent itself to, just as I was struck by the skill of the dancers. They slow danced to romantic ballads, they fast danced to the fast ones, they disco danced. They jitterbugged and jived to his rock, and forming groups of eight did country dancing. In one group a girl wearing a leg brace danced no less spiritedly than the others, and I noticed for the first time two fans in wheelchairs.

Another night I attended a dinner in honor of the newly arrived Japanese fans, some thirty-five of them. Across the table from me sat three of what had to be the prettiest girls, flanked by equally handsome young men in horn-rimmed glasses and well-tailored suits. We talked politely of favorite Elvis songs – 'Wooden Heart', 'Hound Dog' and 'Way Down' – then discussed favorite movies. A quick consultation resulted in *Gone With the Wind*, then another voice a few seats away came up with *Out Of Africa*. I thought: east, west, our most pleasurable daydreams are of *Elsewhere*.

From the other end of the room, music started up. It was the Country Three-Plus-One Band, consisting of keyboard and bass with one man doubling on fiddle and guitar, plus, for this evening's entertainment, drums. The Japanese were listening to the real thing, in the real place, played in a style that Elvis grew up with. Their attention was rapt, their feet began tapping. Willie Wileman, a well-aged country musician and third cousin to Elvis, (the news flew around the room) sang 'Love Me Tender', accompanying himself on an acoustic guitar. The original song 'Auralee' dates back to the Civil War, and Willie, with his homespun inheritance and his blood connection, achieved a synchronicity of past and present that left no one in the room unmoved. *Way back then* had become *here and now*. It was even better than *Elsewhere*.

We went back to our meal, which was fried chicken, baked potatoes and a variety of vegetables. 'A typical meal of your South?' someone asked. 'Very typical,' I assured him. I now met Reiko Yokawa, disc jockey, music critic and lyricist. With her fluent English she was serving as interpreter for the group. She told me of the larger-than-life bronze statue of Elvis recently unveiled in Tokyo, and how fans from all over Japan had donated the money for it. I also learned of this group's interest in jazz. After paying their respects to Elvis at Graceland – through the years the Japanese have laid exquisite fans and kimonos on his grave – the group was going on to New Orleans.

When Buddy and Kay Bain performed I heard again, as in southern Holiness churches, that raw, pulsating throb of 'white soul', that joyous noise that sounded the heart-breaking blues notes as well. Then, aware of the visitors' travel plans, they sang about New Orleans in 'Jambalaya'. The Japanese knew all the words and joined in, and the room, every corner of it, became a sea of rhythmic thrumming, the clap upon clap detonating like staccato bursts of spontaneous combustion.

Later we all stood and sang, holding hands. At the end our joined hands reached skyward, and afterwards we were smiling and smiling at each other.

Then Reiko rose to speak, first in Japanese and then, for our benefit, in English. 'Take this opportunity of being in Tupelo,' she urged the group, 'to study its nature well. Its trees and flowers, its hills, lakes and streams, its earth and sky. For they all went into the making of Elvis.' I marvelled: how Japanese to know Elvis's background was really his foreground. How Zen-like, how like Gertrude Stein.

Afterwards we met the Australian contingent, just landed. It was led by the tallest of their number, a six-foot-four rocker with bushy sideburns, outback-weathered skin, his shirt open to the waist revealing a gold chain from which depended a shark's tooth. We, Japanese and Americans, our numbers swelled by the other Tupeloans, now reached out to yet another continent. The Australian rocker told me he was a mere lad when he first saw Elvis in *Jailhouse Rock*. It blew him away; he decided then and there to become a rocker: never changed his mind.

With new blood the party got its second wind. Groups collected, melted, regrouped. The noise level rose. I kept moving, making my way from clump to clump. A college girl from Tupelo said to me, 'The Australians love our Southern accents and we love theirs. We go up to each other and say, "I'll talk to you if you talk to me."'

Phyllis Harper, who had been with us the whole evening, came up to me looking thoughtful before going off to write her column. 'You know what?' she said in parting. 'I've just discovered something about myself. I love people. I must remember that.' I stood aside and let the animated crowd filter through my eyes and reached the only conclusion I could. How easily Elvis unites us all.

An hour away in Memphis, where I arrived the next day, its media, TV and print reporters greeted the 55,000 pilgrims not *quite* as graciously as it behooves the hosts of a city that gains millions of dollars yearly from these incursions. On TV a young reporter described the fans as 'middle-aged, overweight, with mortgaged homes' with a smirk that implied we could dismiss them. My first sight of a section of the crowd gathered in Memphis for Elvis Week revealed a different story. Strolling up and down Elvis Presley Boulevard, in an atmosphere made unique by the continual sound of Elvis music on a loudspeaker, I saw ages from eight to eighty, stout middle-aged couples more often than not accompanied by skinny teenagers. I didn't bother to ask them if their homes were mortgaged – isn't everyone's? I felt the restorative power of his music, which evaporated the hot weather and the soreness of my feet.

Most of the pilgrims were in groups, but a sizable amount of people (mostly men) were alone. They did not look lost, nor were they; they were here, at this time, remembering Elvis in their own chosen way. Another much larger group that needed sub-categories was the women: young and old, single and married, with and without husbands, grandmothers, mothers, daughters from all over the world.

The Candlelight Service was held the night before the anniversary of Elvis's death. It was organized by the Elvis Country Fan Club of Austin, Texas and had become an increasingly popular event. At 11 p.m. the gates of Graceland were to open, and visitors would light their candles from two torches that in turn had been lit from the eternal flame in the meditation garden where Elvis is buried. After a brief program, the Austin club would sing 'I Can't Help Falling in Love with You' and the visitors would join in the song as they walked towards Elvis's grave.

When I arrived around 10.30 the police on foot and on horse were out in force and the fans had begun to gather, and soon the crowd had grown to thousands. Wedged in on all sides, I noted uneasily that among the crowd were the very elderly and some in wheelchairs, as well as very young babies in the arms of their mothers. What would happen in the event of some accident blowing up into a full-scale riot? But gradually as the sweat rolled down me in rivulets I became aware that my close-quartered neighbors radiated heat but not anger. When the gates finally opened the bottlenecks created by only one entrance and exit made progress painfully slow. It was 3 a.m. before the last pilgrim got through, the crowd passing the time joking, exchanging good-humored comments on their plight and offering information about each other. It was as though they welcomed – or rather transcended – their physical discomfort for the opportunity it gave them to know their fellow beings of all nationalities.

As one of the speakers at the annual Memphis State University Memorial Service, I scrapped my planned speech and instead talked to the fans about themselves. I told them they could no longer be viewed as a sideshow or as examples of the culturally retarded. 'It is you who through the years since his death have kept Elvis alive so that millions more people every year are able to hear him and see him.'

Later I met a group of French fans who had also read my book and soon I was holding forth with them in French, reveling in my role of the moment as the world's-greatest-authority-on-Elvis. At that point I said to myself: *Right now I am at the epicenter of civilization as the whole world knows it.*

I became interested in what all of these Elvis fans, who had made him so much a part of their existence, did in their daily lives. With the help of some fans, especially Pat Geiger, mother of two and a recently retired executive assistant from North Springfield, Vermont, I compiled a brief on-the-spot list of jobs and vocations: bakery owner, a bakery cake decorator, elementary school teachers, junior high school teachers, director of a 2,000-member tenants' association, owner of a popular New York restaurant, Walden Books store manager, high-grade government employees from Washington (one at Housing and Urban Development, the other at Transportation), radio engineer, switchboard operator, manager of a florist's, several graphic artists, accountants, practical nurses, newspaper employees on production advertising and writing staffs, an aerobics instructor, an instructor in yoga, a lawyer. And two blackjack dealers from Vegas.

I stared at this list, so full of variety, and pondered long before it came to me what they all had in common: they were all reliable people. They had to be. Their jobs demanded that they showed up on a daily basis. One thing was sure: they were not Woodstock. They did not riot. They belonged to one of the largest peaceful international fellowships.

At the end of August I left Memphis and returned to Los Angeles. On TV I watched the thousands of people who came together in a vast stadium to see the Pope, and saw him. I thought of the thousands of people who went to football games and baseball and hockey games, and saw them; and of the thousands that went to the concerts of rock stars, and saw them.

Then I thought of the 55,000 people gathered in Memphis for a man whom they did not see, who had died ten years before, a man they held so firmly in their thoughts that he did, in essence, come back.

It was the same Pat Geiger, the retired businesswoman from Vermont who had helped me assemble the list of jobs held by the Elvis pilgrims, who worked almost single-handedly over the years to turn Elvis into a postage stamp. To this undertaking she brought her energy, her organizational ability, her likable outspoken personality, her sense of humor and one other trait – she was an inveterate letter writer. She wrote letters all the time and to all people or organizations on which she held opinions, whether positive or negative. Sometimes they answered her, sometimes they didn't. It made little difference; she was impelled to express herself in this way.

Pat got to work turning Elvis into a postage stamp as far back as '83, when she was in her sixties. A fellow fan told her that a person had to be dead for ten years to be eligible for stamphood. Her friend said, 'We've got time.' Pat had lived in Washington DC before moving to Vermont, and knew how slowly the mills can grind in a bureaucracy, so she sprang into action immediately and started writing letters requesting there be a US postage stamp in honor of Elvis. Pat wrote to the Postmaster General, who informed her that the Citizen Stamp Advisory Committee met twice a year to decide who shall become a stamp. She also learned that the proposed subject of the stamp stays on the Committee's List as long as interest remains, even if shown by only one person. Pat wrote to them twice every year. She wrote to congressmen and senators from every state in the Union. She became alert to any of their public pronouncements on Elvis. She also contacted fans and fan clubs urging them to write to the Advisory Board and sent petitions for them to sign.

In the end 50,000 letters had been received by the postal authorities requesting that Elvis become a stamp.

It is worth noting that in Elvis's death as in his life, the theme of twins stayed with it. For the first time in its history the Post Office left it up to the public to vote for which Elvis stamp, the Young Elvis or the Mature Elvis, they wanted. The cost of printing up the ballots was made up for by the extra postage people used to mail them.

On June 4, 1992, nine years after she had begun her campaign, Pat, now seventy-two, attended the ceremony to unveil the winning stamp in Graceland. The 'stamps' unveiled at Graceland were the large original paintings. After the announcement of the winner, the Young Elvis, an official said to Pat 'We know you favored the Mature Elvis stamp [she had voted for it thirty-five times], so we are offering the painting to you.' Graciously, Pat accepted. It hung on her wall in Vermont. Shortly afterwards the Elvis Presley Memorial Trauma Center asked if she were willing to loan it to them, she did so, first adding the canny proviso that if it was not treated with the respect it deserved she would reclaim it.

The Elvis stamp was first sold at the stroke of midnight, January 7/January 8, 1993 at the Graceland Branch of the US Post Office (yes, there is such a thing). The Elvis stamp would break many records. A stamp's profit is judged by the number purchased that are not used but saved, and more Elvis stamps were saved than any other before or since. The profit made on the saved stamps was $36 million. The stamp closest to Elvis's was that of Bugs Bunny, whose profit came to $7 million. The Elvis postage stamp would be the most successful issue in postal history, with a total issue of 500 million. Even better than bestowing immortality upon Elvis, it conferred upon him what no other accolade could: *respectability*. Now it was all right to wear an Elvis T-shirt. All right to love Elvis. Suddenly everybody did.

Epilogue

My mother died in March '96 aged ninety-nine, just two months before her hundredth birthday. It was timely. For several years she had been failing and required round-the-clock nursing.

Untimely was John Lorwin's death in February '99 aged forty-five. The son of my sister Betty, he was a lawyer and journalist who became a religious Jew. He had lived in Israel for fifteen years and was active in a peace organization made up of both Palestinians and Israelis. John died while hiking with friends in the desert near Jericho. Although they'd checked the weather report beforehand, they were caught in an unexpected flash flood. Three of them were able to cling to rocks and were saved, but three of them drowned, John among them. Betty flew to Israel for the funeral and was among over a hundred people at his graveside. A number of his Palestinian friends had illegally crossed the green line between Palestine and Israel to attend. Said Betty, 'He was with people he liked and doing something he liked. But I wish he'd been able to do it a little longer.'

For some years Betty, living in New York, was one of the leaders of both the Manhattan and the City Wide Task Force on the Housing Court setting up information centers in various boroughs as needed.

They serve mainly low-income tenants seeking information on their rights and court procedures and direct them to law officers that can give them assistance at no cost. Before that she worked as a reading tutor and in various youth programs. She now plays a role in the residents' association of her co-op in Brooklyn, where she lives near her daughter, playwright and producer Liza Lorwin, and her sixteen-year-old grandson Mojo.

Tracy's costume design work can be seen on both film and television. She has also co-written a film, *Coyote*, which is now in production. Her husband Jim has directed films including *Breathless*, *The Big Easy*, *Great Balls of Fire* and most recently a film on the rock star Meatloaf.

I am blessed with two grandchildren, Matthew, thirteen, and Ruby, eleven. When they come to see me we still play cards including Fish, BS and a heated game of War, each one still eating two glazed donuts, two slices of Domino deep-dish pizzas, a Coke and a dish of ice cream per session. They still like to see who can sail the most playing cards into a box placed in the middle of my living room.

From the time I began researching Elvis I found myself in a constant state of enlightenment. As each new fact dropped onto my lap I'd say to myself, 'I didn't know this before but I'll never not know it again.' Getting educated was the new thing happening to me. It was like being back in Dr Short's class at college, and learning about the Metaphysical Poets. I found getting educated more to my liking than getting experienced. I saw them as two different things. In a long-lived life, experience becomes pretty much the same thing occurring over and over again. Education is always new, always fresh. Elvis was giving me an education in things such as the history of the poor in the South; musical shape notes; the sol-fa method of teaching singing; double identity comic books; twinship; Holiness churches; and the folks from Above the Highway. With Elvis I was writing new sentences, not the old predictable ones.

It seems to me that the perception of innocence prepares us for the reception of education. So it is not surprising that I continue to find myself most at home in places that I do not belong, places that feel brand new yet intimate and filled with potential godshots.

Learning about my own country turned it into a new country,

making me keen to discover it further. Such was my goal when, for my next book, I chose the small upstart town of *Ferriday, Louisiana* on the banks of the Mississippi River. Though its population has never exceeded 5,000, it claims to have produced more famous people per square mile than any other town in USA. Among them evangelist Jimmy Swaggart, his cousin, rock star Jerry Lee Lewis, Howard K. Smith, one of the earliest TV anchors (he monitored the first TV Presidential debate between Kennedy and Nixon) and General Claire Lee Chennault, commander of the famed Flying Tigers in World War Two. By writing its biography I undertook to show why this might be so. Along the way home-boy Hiram Gregory, professor of anthropology, gave me the best answer yet as to why small Southern towns, both in fact and fiction, are so populated by eccentric, colorful, larger-than-life, downright theatrical people. 'Southerners are colorful, eccentric and so on, because their parents and grandparents were,' he said. 'It's their way of defending themselves in the family situation.'

I love where I am living now, near the LA County Museum, in what would have been called an urban village in the fifties. It is a good architectural mix of garden flats and twelve-story tower apartments spaced so that no view is blocked by another building. It is full of islands and roundabouts landscaped with drought-tolerant plants with a Mediterranean feel. There are bushes of flax and hybrid grasses from Australia and many flowering shrubs, and flowers bloom early in spring and late into autumn. Vividly colored small clumps of impatiens are carefully tended in doorways, and palm trees, jacarandas, eucalyptus, birch and other evergreen abound. Blazing sunlight shines through the large windows of my tower apartment, which is designed so that each one looks out onto what seems to be a different city. The Hollywood Hills fringe all horizons. The residents are a multi-cultural mix, representative of this most multi-cultural city of whites, blacks, Asians and Hispanics. Some five years ago the towers were given the Hollywood treatment and painted in sections of lemon, terracotta and teal blue, which the sun soon faded from garish to decorous.

I look out of my living room windows, which cover one whole wall. On autumn evenings I watch a burning sunset pulling out all its stops. I share in its exhilaration, and am content.

Index